ORGANIZATIONAL COMMUNICATION

ORGANIZATIONAL COMMUNICATION

Second Edition

R. WAYNE PACE
Brigham Young University

DON F. FAULES
University of Utah

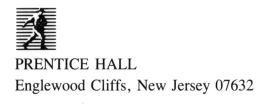

PRENTICE HALL
Englewood Cliffs, New Jersey 07632

Library of Congress Cataloging-in-Publication Data

Pace, R. Wayne.
  Organizational communication.—2nd ed. / R. Wayne Pace, Don F. Faules.
    p. cm.
  Rev. ed. of: Organizational communication, foundations for human resource
development. c1983.
  Includes bibliographies and indexes.
  ISBN 0-13-641614-4
  1. Communication in organizations. 2. Organizational behavior.
3. Personnel management. 4. Interpersonal relations. I. Faules,
Don F. II. Pace, R. Wayne. Organizational communication,
foundations for human resource development. III. Title.
HD30.3.P34 1989   88–19199
658.4′5—dc19   CIP

Cover design: Wanda Lubelska Design
Manufacturing buyer: Ed O'Dougherty

Printed in the United States of America
10 9 8 7 6 5 4 3 2 1

ISBN 0-13-641614-4

Prentice-Hall International (UK) Limited, *London*
Prentice-Hall of Australia Pty. Limited, *Sydney*
Prentice-Hall Canada Inc., *Toronto*
Prentice-Hall Hispanoamericana, S.A., *Mexico*
Prentice-Hall of India Private Limited, *New Delhi*
Prentice-Hall of Japan, Inc., *Tokyo*
Simon & Schuster Asia Pte. Ltd., *Singapore*
Editora Prentice-Hall do Brasil, Ltda., *Rio de Janeiro*

Acknowledgment is gratefully made for permission to use material from the following sources:

Pages 27–28: Excerpts from *The Process of Communication* by David K. Berlo, copyright © 1960 by
Holt, Rinehart & Winston, Inc. Reprinted by permission of the publisher.

Pages 48–49: From Michael Pacanowsky, "Communication in the Empowering Organization," Paper
presented at the University of Utah Summer Conference on Interpretive Approaches to the Study of
Organizational Communication, Alta, Utah, 1987. Used by permission of Michael Pacanowsky.

*These acknowledgments are continued on page 340, which constitutes an extension of the copyright
page.*

Contents

PART TWO   ORGANIZATION THEORIES

3 Classical Structural Theory   26

4 Transitional Theories   38

5 Contemporary Theories: Toward Subjectivism   54

PART THREE   ISSUES IN ORGANIZATIONAL COMMUNICATION

6 Communicative Efficiency: The Cost-Effectiveness of Organizational Communication   76

Preface

As W. Charles Redding has pointed out, "The study of organizational communication in the 1980s exhibits dramatic changes of focus, expansions of horizons, and inventions of new models. . . . However, the field has not yet cut itself off from its roots of the 1940s and 1950s."* In this book we respond to these dramatic changes of focus and expanded horizons while maintaining a foundation in the roots of the field of organizational communication. We hope to contribute to the identity of this changing field.

Since the first edition was published in 1983, it has contributed to an understanding of organizational communication and how its concepts and practices form a groundwork for a wide variety of extraordinary career opportunities. As you read this book, you will recognize two themes running throughout: (1) knowing about organizational communication can help you understand and function in organizations, and (2) organizational communication knowledge provides a firm foundation for working in a number of professional areas.

We have not made many distinctions between organizational communication and other approaches to organizations, such as organizational behavior or organizational psychology. We think our approach is more clearly about communication than psychology or behavior. However, just as some textbooks on organizational

*W. Charles Redding, "Stumbling Toward Identity: The Emergence of Organizational Communication as a Field of Study," in *Organizational Communication: Transitional Themes and New Directions,* Robert D. McPhee and Phillip K. Tompkins, eds. (Beverly Hills, Calif.: Sage, 1985), 52.

behavior and organizational psychology are used in courses on organizational communication, this book can readily be used in courses in other areas.

Changes from the first edition have been introduced to strengthen the content in areas where adopters and reviewers have noted shortcomings. New sections have also been added to give breadth and depth to the content and applications by including ideas and methods that encompass the most contemporary thinking on topics. Revisions for this edition include:

A typology for thinking about organizations, human beings, and the world, ranging from objective to subjective approaches.

Subjectivist considerations associated with each of the major issues in the field.

A restructuring of organization theories ranging from classical structural through transitional to contemporary theories, with a treatment of Karl Weick's theory of organizing and cultural theory.

A reexamination of cost-effectiveness, which forms a new chapter on organizational communication efficiency.

The addition of a chapter on media design and development.

Separate chapters on human resource and organization analysis.

A discussion of motivational and role, or positional, theories.

We now have a book that addresses key theories, issues, and applications in the field of organizational communication. It provides a treatment of both traditional topics and contemporary ones.

Our intent is to provide basic ideas and the type of framework that is worth supplementing and pursuing. The book is organized so that portions that emphasize theory or application can be used independently. We hope that the book offers both challenge and interest to the reader.

We feel good about the presentation and interpretation of ideas and the way in which the book has come together. Where there are inaccuracies, we feel chagrined and will repent.

We wish to acknowledge the support and contributions of family, friends, colleagues, faculty, and students who have thoughtfully read the book and offered suggestions.

We thank you who now read the book.

R. Wayne Pace
Provo, Utah

Don F. Faules
Salt Lake City, Utah

ORGANIZATIONAL COMMUNICATION

1

Concepts and Consequences

A book about organizational communication must account for at least two basic concepts—organization and communication. The current state of our knowledge about organizational communication has been developing for several decades, as both academicians and practitioners from quite different perspectives have analyzed and theorized about organizations and communication. As you shall see, the study of organizational communication is a study of the way people think about things as well as a study of the things themselves.

In our society, we value "good organization." Just about everyone has vowed at some time to "get it together" and "get organized." For example, organization is very prominent in the world of sports. The media seem delighted when they can point to a "no name team" that defeats its opponents by virtue of "organized team play." Although our culture tends to emphasize individualism, we also revere coordinated activity that produces excellence. In fact, we often hear people say "We have the team" or "We have the organization to carry that off." Besides being immersed in language that emphasizes "organizing," most of us belong to a variety of organizations. We try to belong to the best organizations, and people expect certain benefits from participating in organized behavior.

Because the concepts of organizing and organization are so pervasive in our everyday lives, it is easy to gloss over their complexity and significance. Making sense of organizational life is more than just arriving at definitions of such terms as organizing, organization, and organizational communication. These concepts can be and are used in very different ways with very different consequences.

We urge readers to maintain their commonsense notions of what these terms mean while we explore the forces behind the more specific concepts and definitions. The role that communication plays in the study of organization depends on how "organization" is conceptualized. In this chapter, we introduce alternative views on reality, human nature, and organization because these concepts guide our understanding of organizational communication and how it is practiced.

WHY DO PEOPLE STUDY ORGANIZATIONAL COMMUNICATION?

The traditional literature of the field stresses that communication and organizational success are related. To improve organizational communication is to improve the organization. This reasoning suggests the following:

1. There are universal elements that make an organization ideal.
2. These universal elements can be discovered and used to change an organization.
3. These elements and the way they are used "cause" or at least produce outcomes.
4. Organizations that function well have the right mix and use of these elements.
5. These elements are related to desired organizational outcomes.
6. Communication is one of the elements of organization.

This approach implies that ideas exist that can be generalized to produce desirable outcomes. The primary objective in studying communication is to improve the organization. Improving the organization is usually interpreted as "improving things to accomplish the objectives of management." In other words, people study organizational communication to become better managers. Some writers contend that management is communication (D'Aprix, 1982). Thus, most theories and prescriptions about organizations and organizational communication are written from a managerial perspective.

On the other hand, we often hear students say that they are interested in studying organizational communication because of their own difficult experiences in organizations. Much of their discontentment seems to stem from their feelings that the organizational system is depersonalized and discourages creativity and productivity. They express their feelings that organizations need to improve the quality of life in the workplace. They seem to be looking at the organization from a worker's perspective. They are interested in what the organization does for the people. Their reason for studying organizational communication is to discover ways to improve the quality of work life.

An organization may also be approached as an object of study in its own right. Some people consider the organization to be a fascinating and intriguing subject. Their main goals are to understand the organization through describing its organizational communication, to understand organizational life, and to discover how life is constituted communicatively. The emphasis is on how an organization is constructed and maintained through the communicative process. This approach focuses on what actually goes on in organizations and provides a level of explanation that rarely occurs in other approaches.

Organizations are also studied because people find them oppressive. A radical humanist may be interested in how humans create their own prisons within organizations. The radical structuralist, on the other hand, may be most concerned with organizations as dominating forces (Morgan, 1980, p. 609). These two lines of thinking produce critics who are interested in how organizational communication is used to control individuals who do not seem to be aware of the domination of the organization. The goal of the critic is to liberate individuals from oppression by providing an analysis and critique of what they see as an oppressive social order. They can, in that way, provide alternatives for changing the current organization.

Organizational communication is more than something people do. It is a discipline of study that can take a number of legitimate and useful directions. Although we recognize the value of the theorist, the practitioner, and the critic, in an introductory text all needs cannot be given equal time and space.

This text is directed at two types of readers: (1) Those who wish to better understand organizational behavior, and (2) those who wish to improve their performance as organizational participants. We see the study of organizational communication as a solid foundation for careers in management, human resource development, corporate communications, and other people-oriented assignments in organizations.

At the same time, we hope you find knowledge about organizations and organizing intriguing. Your understanding of organizational behavior and the role of communication in organizations will be enhanced by an understanding of three key concepts: reality, human nature, and organization.

ALTERNATIVE VIEWS OF REALITY

Our major concern in this section is the concept of *social reality* and how we make sense of the social world. We do not intend to solve the puzzle of what reality actually consists of or if things really exist outside of our minds. We feel confident that people experience the existence of physical things, but we are equally confident that people create the experiences they have with people and things.

What is important is that (1) different people behave in different ways toward what they consider to be objects worthy of scrutiny, and (2) those differences are based on how individuals think about those objects. A social object is simply one that has significance to a collectivity or calls for some type of action by people. In that sense, behaviors and things are social constructions, because they depend on people to make them significant.

If one views objects and behaviors as events constructed by people, one can also see human behavior as relying heavily upon social processes to hold the world together. Before we explore this theme in detail, let us provide a contrasting view that may be more familiar.

It is difficult to do justice to all facets of a debate that has spanned many years and disciplines, but the information in Figure 1.1 (Morgan & Smircich, 1980, pp. 491–500) allows for a general comparison and contrast of views of reality and the

	Reality as a Projection of Human Imagination	Reality as a Social Construction
CORE ONTOLOGICAL ASSUMPTIONS	The social world and what passes as "reality" is a projection of individual consciousness; it is an act of creative imagination and of dubious intersubjective status. This extreme position, commonly known as solipsism, asserts that there may be nothing outside oneself: one's mind is one's world. Certain transcendental approaches to phenomenology assert a reality in consciousness, the manifestation of a phenomenal world, but not necessarily accessible to understanding in the course of everyday affairs. Reality in this sense is masked by those human processes which judge and interpret the phenomenon in consciousness prior to a full understanding of the structure of meaning it expresses. Thus the nature of the phenomenal world may be accessible to the human being only through consciously phenomenological modes of insight.	The social world is a continuous process, created afresh in each encounter of everyday life as individuals impose themselves on their world to establish a realm of meaningful definition. They do so through the medium of language, labels, actions, and routines, which constitute symbolic modes of being in the world. Social reality is embedded in the nature and use of these modes of symbolic action. The realm of social affairs thus has no concrete status of any kind; it is a symbolic construction. Symbolic modes of being in the world, such as through the use of language, may result in the development of shared, but multiple realities, the status of which is fleeting, confined only to those moments in which they are actively constructed and sustained.
ASSUMPTIONS ABOUT HUMAN NATURE	**Humans as Transcendental Beings** Humans are viewed as intentional beings, directing their psychic energy and experience in ways that constitute the world in a meaningful, intentional form. There are realms of being, and realms of reality, constituted through different kinds of founding acts, stemming from a form of transcendental consciousness. Human beings shape the world within the realm of their own immediate experience.	**Humans Create Their Realities** Human beings create their realities in the most fundamental ways, in an attempt to make their world intelligible to themselves and to others. They are not simply actors interpreting their situations in meaningful ways, for there are no situations other than those which individuals bring into being through their own creative activity. Individuals may work together to create a shared reality, but that reality is still a subjective construction capable of disappearing the moment its members cease to sustain it as such. Reality appears as real to individuals because of human acts of conscious or unwitting collusion.
SOME EXAMPLES OF RESEARCH	Phenomenology	Ethnomethodology

FIGURE 1.1 Assumptions about Ontology and Human Nature (Source: From Gareth Morgan and Linda Smircich, "The Case for Qualitative Research," *Academy of Management Review*, 5 (October 1980), 494–495. Copyright © 1980 by the Academy of Management. Reprinted by permission of the publisher.)

← ————————————————————   ———————————————————— →

Reality as Symbolic Discourse

The social world is a pattern of symbolic relationships and meanings sustained through a process of human action and interaction. Although a certain degree of continuity is preserved through the operation of rule-like activities that define a particular social millieu, the pattern is always open to reaffirmation or change through the interpretations and actions of individual members. The fundamental character of the social world is embedded in the network of subjective meanings that sustain the rule-like actions that lend it enduring form. Reality rests not in the rule or in rule-following, but in the system of meaningful action that renders itself to an external observer as rule-like.

Reality as a Contextual Field of Information

The social world is a field of ever-changing form and activity based on the transmission of information. The form of activity that prevails at any one given time reflects a pattern of "difference" sustained by a particular kind of information exchange. Some forms of activity are more stable than others, reflecting an evolved pattern of learning based on principles of negative feedback. The nature of relationships within the field is probabilistic; a change in the appropriate pattern and balance within any sphere will reverberate throughout the whole, initiating patterns of adjustment and readjustment capable of changing the whole in fundamental ways. Relationships are relative rather than fixed and real.

Humans as Social Actors

Human beings are social actors interpreting their milieu and orienting their actions in ways that are meaningful to them. In this process they utilize language, labels, routines for impression management, and other modes of culturally specific action. In so doing they contribute to the enactment of a reality; human beings live in a world of symbolic significance, interpreting and enacting a meaningful relationship with that world. Humans are actors with the capacity to interpret, modify, and sometimes create the scripts that they play upon life's stage.

Humans as Information Processors

Human beings are engaged in a continual process of interaction and exchange with their context — receiving, interpreting, and acting on the information received, and in so doing creating a new pattern of information that effects changes in the field as a whole. Relationships between individual and context are constantly modified as a result of this exchange; the individual is but an element of a changing whole. The crucial relationship between individual and context is reflected in the pattern of learning and mutual adjustment that has evolved. Where this is well developed, the field of relationships is harmonious; where adjustment is low, the field is unstable and subject to unpredictable and discontinuous patterns of change.

Social Action Theory   **Cybernetics**

(continued)

FIGURE 1.1   *continued*

Reality as a Concrete Process

The social world is an evolving process, concrete in nature, but everchanging in detailed form. Everything interacts with everything else and it is extremely difficult to find determinate causal relationships between constituent processes. At best, the world expresses itself in terms of general and contingent relationships between its more stable and clear-cut elements. The situation is fluid and creates opportunities for those with appropriate ability to mold and exploit relationships in accordance with their interests. The world is in part what one makes of it: a struggle between various influences, each attempting to move toward achievement of desired ends.

Reality as a Concrete Structure

The social world is a hard, concrete, real thing "out there," which affects everyone in one way or another. It can be thought of as a structure composed of a network of determinate relationships between constituent parts. Reality is to be found in the concrete behavior and relationships between these parts. It is an objective phenomenon that lends itself to accurate observation and measurement. Any aspect of the world that does not manifest itself in some form of observable activity or behavior must be regarded as being of questionable status. Reality by definition is that which is external and real. The social world is as concrete and real as the natural world.

Humans as Adaptive Agents

Human beings exist in an interactive relationship with their world. They influence and are influenced by their context or environment. The process of exchange that operates here is essentially a competitive one, the individual seeking to interpret and exploit the environment to satisfy important needs, and hence survive. Relationships between individuals and environment express a pattern of activity necessary for survival and well-being of the individual.

Humans as Responding Mechanisms

Human beings are a product of the external forces in the environment to which they are exposed. Stimuli in their environment condition them to behave and respond to events in predictable and determinate ways. A network of causal relationships links all important aspects of behavior to context. Though human perception may influence this process to some degree, people always respond to situations in a lawful (i.e., rule-governed) manner.

Open Systems Theory

Behaviorism
Social Learning Theory

FIGURE 1.1 *continued*

accompanying beliefs about human nature. The range of views has been organized on a continuum from highly subjective views to highly objective views. The terms subjective and objective do not represent a value judgment concerning which view is best. The terms simply refer to alternative approaches.

One can understand the wide differences between the positions by analyzing the two extremes. An extreme objectivist looks at the social world in the same way as we think of the physical or natural world, as something concrete and separate from the person who is looking at and touching the world. The extreme subjectivist, on the other hand, maintains that nothing exists outside of the mind of the person doing the perceiving, and that reality is strictly a human process in which we create the physical objects in our minds and respond to them as if they existed as natural events.

We are less concerned with the merits of these two extreme positions than about *how we might behave if we held one or the other of the views,* especially in terms of how we might think about an organization. Because there are significant and specific differences between the objective and the subjective approaches, we will contrast them in more detail.

People who approach reality objectively see it as something concrete or physical with a structure that should be and can be discovered. Even if it is not discovered, the structure is still there and is independent of those who are trying to discover it. The world contains a certain order that is, in fact, waiting to be discovered. Most of what we call "science" is based on the objective approach. Scientists, the people who are trying to discover the nature of reality, use telescopes and microscopes to find out what makes things function. The functioning has an order, and a scientist is trying to discover that order—in the planets, in the patterns of animals, in the way in which cells multiply, and in the relationships among atoms.

A subjectivist looks at reality as a creative process in which the people create what is "out there." From a subjectivist's view, people *create* an order rather than *discover* the order of things. The world, and all the things in it, is basically unstructured, or at least it operates in ways that do not make sense in and of themselves.

Order is the way in which one thing follows from another in a particular sequence of events. In biology, for example, order is the subdivision of classes and subclasses in the classification systems for plants and animals. The question a subjectivist asks is, "Are plants and animals ordered naturally in the same way that biologists offer them?" Of course, a subjectivist's answer is that they are not; the biologist creates the order and imposes it on the plants and animals. Once you learn the biological classification system created by biologists, you may *think* the world is ordered in that fashion, but the reality is that scientists created the system and produced the order. The world of plants and animals is not ordered that way.

Organization/Organizing

How one orders people, things, and ideas in an organized fashion is affected by whether one begins from an objectivist's or a subjectivist's point of view. The objective approach suggests that an organization is a physical, concrete thing, that it is a structure with definite boundaries. The term "the organization" implies that something is tangible and actually holds people, relationships, and goals. Some people refer to this approach as the *container* view of organizations. The organization exists like a basket, and all the elements that make up the organization are placed in the container.

A subjective approach looks at an organization as activities that people do. Organization consists of the actions, interactions, and transactions in which people engage. Organization is created and maintained through the continually changing contacts people have with one another and does not exist separately from the people whose behavior constitutes the organization.

From the objective view, organization means structure; from the subjective view, organization means process. The degree of emphasis placed on behavior or on structure depends on which view you hold.

"Organization" is typically thought of as a noun, whereas "organizing" is recognized as a verb (Weick, 1979). Subjectivists regard organization as *organizing behavior*. Objectivists regard organization as structure, something stable. The use of the word "organizing" to refer to an organization may seem awkward regardless of which view you hold.

What do we mean by "organization"? The answer depends on the perspective taken, but, for our purposes, it is important to realize that neither perspective answers the question fully.

The devices used to describe organization provide insight into the challenge of capturing what organization is all about. A primary descriptive device is the *metaphor*. A metaphor compares one thing to another by talking about the first thing as if it were the second thing. For example, to say that "life is a game," is to use a metaphor comparing *life* with *game*. We could say "life is like a game," but the metaphor provides a stronger comparison. Metaphors not only help us see similarities and differences but also convey a feeling that literal descriptions fail to do. When someone says, "Pinning down a bureaucrat is the same as nailing jelly to a wall," a vivid image is conveyed. Metaphors provide the imagery for studying a subject.

The study of something, such as organization, can be based on exploring the features of the metaphors found in the particular subject under inquiry. Morgan and Smircich (1980) maintain that theorists choose metaphors that are based on assumptions about reality and human nature that commit themselves to particular kinds and forms of knowledge. Metaphors have a constraining and enabling influence on the theorists' thought processes.

The use of metaphor to study a subject requires that certain parts of the comparison be ignored while others are emphasized. For example, if you took the metaphor "life is a game" literally, it would be difficult to specify just what the rules are for the game of life. Morgan (1980) argues that a metaphor is based on partial truth, and the metaphor's most creative expression relies on "constructive falsehood," in which certain features are emphasized.

The major implications of this idea, according to Morgan, are that "no one metaphor can capture the total nature of organizational life," and that "different metaphors can constitute and capture the nature of organizational life in different ways, each generating powerful, distinctive, but essentially partial kinds of insight. . . . To acknowledge that organization theory is metaphorical is to acknowledge that it is an essentially subjective enterprise, concerned with the production of one-sided analyses of organizational life" (pp. 611–612).

Metaphors are used widely in the study and practice of organizational communication. For example, managers are fond of using sports metaphors to describe organizational behavior. They refer to "playing team ball," "knowing when to carry the ball and when to pass it," and "going for the home run." However, it is important that metaphors not be confused with what they are intended to describe. Sports metaphors may provide provocative description and some guidelines for expected behavior. But those with organizational experience realize that organizational life is much more complex than most sports games. Rules can vary depending on people, status, power, and external forces. In fact, several games with different rules may be operating at the same time, and sometimes unwritten rules dominate the play. Therefore, the differences as well as the similarities in metaphors make for creative and insightful comparisons. Metaphors help explain and illustrate complex concepts, but each metaphor explains in a certain way. We ought to be sensitive to how such devices can screen out thinking as well as enrich it. A way of seeing is also a way of not seeing. For example, a common traditional organizational metaphor, and one that reflects an objective approach, is that of the machine, as in "The organization is a well-oiled machine." Machines are concrete and their various parts can be observed in action. The metaphor simplifies matters by allowing us to see an organization as having interdependent and interchangeable parts that work in harmony. The systematic character of a machine is projected onto the organization. The underlying notion is that we can understand human organization from the same set of principles used to understand machines. However, significant differences must be taken into account when such comparisons are made. Human actors are less predictable, for example, then parts of machines. The differences between human beings suggest that they are not as interchangeable as parts of a machine. Parts of a machine also work in some predetermined fashion. They are programmed to do so. Parts do not care, but people do. Parts shape the machine only in a static sense. People create, maintain, change, and terminate organization through behaviors that are continually changing.

A prominent metaphor that demonstrates the subjective approach to organization is that of culture. The word "culture" is used in a variety of ways when referring to organization (Smircich, 1983, 1985; Pacanowsky & Trujillo, 1982; Putnam, 1983). When metaphor is used as a way of seeing and knowing the world, culture suggests that organizations exist only through people in interaction. Cultural analysis emphasizes symbolic behavior and the construction of reality through interaction. A major question provoked by the culture metaphor is "What are the words, ideas, and constructs that impel, legitimize, coordinate, and realize organized activity in specific settings?" (Smircich, 1985, p. 67). Although we find it hard to deny the potency of symbolic activity, it does not always represent actions taken. People do not always do what they say! In addition, external forces may be ignored when applying the culture metaphor.

We will elaborate on these and other metaphors in succeeding chapters. At this point, it is important to remember that one's conception of organization depends on one's assumptions about reality. The assumptions depend on whether one holds an objective or a subjective view of the world and people. Both approaches use metaphors that give us insight into some aspects of organization, but each falls short of a complete description of the complexity of organizational life. Because metaphors are incomplete, we need to be sensitive to what is unspoken when a particular metaphor is used. In addition to reflecting a view of reality, metaphors imply certain assumptions about humans. Remember that where and how human beings fit into organization theory depends on which approach you use. (See Morgan, 1986, for organizational metaphors.)

Images of Human Nature

Ideas about what humans are like and the nature of reality are interconnected (see Figure 1.1). Objective approaches place considerable emphasis on environment as a determining factor in explaining human behavior. People are shaped by their environments, and their success and survival depend on how well they adapt to this concrete reality. A significant part of the adaptive process is defining the environment properly and meeting *its* requirements.

Because the environment and the organization have structure, fitting the two so that maximum adaptation can take place is important. An organization's survival depends on its ability to adapt to and transact with the environment. Human beings are seen as information processors who respond to information found in the environment. The relationship between an individual and the person's context is determined by information exchange.

The subjective approach places humans in a more active and creative role. Humans are not products of an environment, but they create that environment. Their own creations may very well come back upon them ("What goes around comes around," so they say), but that is vastly different from saying that a concrete environment exists independently of people's actions. Human beings live in a symbolic world, and a symbolic environment is subject to change and multiple interpretations. Humans create, sustain, and terminate reality through the use of symbols. Humans do not just respond and adapt to what is out there. They create the environment and participate in the social process of creation. A large part of the human challenge is to recognize and adapt to the social process itself.

Alternative views of reality and human nature have an impact on what is considered important in the study of organizational behavior and communication. The next section discusses some of the general implications for the study of organizational behavior. The discussion of the implications for organizational communication is reserved for Chapter 2.

Implications for Organizational Behavior

STRUCTURE VERSUS BEHAVIOR

Given that objective approaches to reality promote the idea that the world consists of concrete, real things, it comes as no surprise that those approaches emphasize the importance of structure in guiding behavior. Although those who adhere to a structural approach would not maintain that structure alone is enough, they prefer the idea that structure, especially formal structure, represents the organization. McPhee (1985) cites elements of organization that are encompassed under the idea of structure:

> It would include things like official job titles, descriptions, and objectives for employees, along with their conditions of employment or employment contracts; the

official differentiation of divisions, departments, and work units; the book or books of standard operating procedures; the "corporate charter" and other documents establishing the legal basis of the organization, and so on. . . . I would include in structure the various systems for decision support, management information, work evaluation and compensation, and financial control. (p. 149)

Subjective approaches recognize structure, but the emphasis is placed on human behavior. Structure does not exist independently of the actions of people. People create structure, sustain it, and terminate it. There are those who maintain that structure is continuously created (see Column 2, Figure 1.1), which makes the concept even of routine activities problematic. A creative process is required in order for structure to be recognized as routine. Structure is not just there. It is enacted (Weick, 1969) and accomplished (Garfinkel, 1967) through the process of organizing (Weick, 1969, 1979).

The structural approach implies that if one understands the structure, one understands the organization. It is but a short step to the metaphor that it is possible to have a well-oiled machine if the right structure can be discovered. Furthermore, from this point of view, it seems reasonable to suggest that management consists of seeing that the right structure is executed in an appropriate fashion. Management is concerned with getting organizational participants to understand and adhere to the structure. Structure can be learned, and one can learn to perform a position and maintain the integrity of a structure.

The subjective view suggests that behavior and specific actions are the dominant forces in the organization. There is no structure until individuals work together to create it. Even then structure is a unique construction that may not last unless it is sustained through further interaction. Through symbolic means, people develop shared but multiple realities. Management, from this perspective, emphasizes the discovery of what those multiple realities are, what is shared, and what impact those discoveries might have on decision making in the organization. The subjective approach also suggests that managers could benefit from becoming sensitive to the reality-construction processes, because it is those processes that enable people to establish something that is called "routine."

PREDICTABILITY AND CONTROL

Objective approaches imply that humans are products of external forces that condition them to respond in predictable and determinate ways. This view also suggests that there is systematic order to human behavior. The tendency is to want to discover the forces at work so that organizational behavior can be predicted and controlled. Objective study focuses on the discovery of causal relationships (cause and effect). Once causal links are exposed, it is thought that order can be maintained and even altered by manipulating the elements of the organization.

Subjective approaches imply that order is created by the organizational participants. The subjectivists do not deny order but simply argue that there is no order until it is constructed by members of the organization.

Objectivists and subjectivists differ dramatically on how much order and control can be imposed on organizational behavior and the nature of the order and control that the organization has. For example, some maintain that organizational culture can and should be managed, while others contend that culture is an "emergent process" that cannot be controlled (Martin, 1985). While some highlight the control procedures that precede actions, others (Weick, 1977) emphasize the retrospective sense-making processes that follow actions. These ideas will receive more specific treatment in Chapter 5.

ROLE OF ENVIRONMENT

Objective approaches make it clear that environment is the driving force behind organizational behavior. Organizations are conditioned by the environment, and the survival of organizations depends on their ability to interpret the *real* environment and adapt to it. Much emphasis is placed on how well organizational structure and environmental structure fit together. Both structure and environment are considered to be things rather than creations. Theories of environmental determinism have had considerable influence on the study of organizational behavior (Lawrence & Lorsch, 1969; Burns & Stalker, 1961). Again, the organization must attend to the external environment and use its best adaptive strategies to achieve growth and survival.

The subjectivist looks at the importance of environment in a different way. A significant part of organizational behavior is how participants create the environment and how that creation affects their behavior (Weick, 1979). What counts is what is created, not what is "really" there, because what is there (if it is there at all) can only be understood through the symbolic processes and result in a subjective interpretation. Rather than ask questions about what kind of environment exists, the subjectivist asks questions about how participants make sense of whatever is called environment. These ideas will be developed in various portions of the text; a major implication to remember is that if environment is created, then it is possible to think of organizational change as a decision-making process.

SIMPLICITY VERSUS COMPLEXITY

Regardless of whether the perspective taken is objective or subjective, numerous metaphors are used to describe the organization. This suggests that organizations seem complex to almost everyone. Nevertheless, objective approaches tend to reduce organizations to interacting parts that respond and adapt to the environment, which implies more stability and routine than may be the case. Subjectivists contend that objectivists gloss over the importance of human creative processes and take them for granted. They argue that the constructive and reconstructive processes of reality are quite complex and changeable. Objectivists, they argue, tend to reduce human behavior to simple, basic terms.

It is appealing to think of humans as information processors, adaptive agents, or responding mechanisms. The terms provide convenient handles, and they seem to fit with our commonsense notions and observations. Nevertheless, subjectivists warn that such conceptions may offer only a grand delusion. When the richness and complexity of human behavior are stripped away, what remains is not human behavior and is not representative of organization. Rather than simplifying, it may be more helpful to analyze all the complexities, so that significant human processes can be taken into account.

The objectivist starts with a "real" world that is assumed to be complex and tries to reduce it to parts that are made understandable through the exploration of causal linkages. The subjectivist is interested in the complex notion of "world making" and the impact that process has on organization (Smircich, 1985). For the subjectivist, organizations are made understandable by discovering how organizational life is created by participants. We shall expand on the theme of simplicity/complexity in Chapter 2.

SUMMARY

In this chapter we have discussed key ideas that affect the way organizational behavior is conceptualized, studied, and practiced. Chapter 2 will focus on some of the impacts generated by the two major alternative views of reality and human nature.

REFERENCES

Burns, Tom, and G. M. Stalker, *The Management of Innovation*. London: Tavistock, 1961.

D'Aprix, Roger, *Communicating for Productivity*. New York: Harper & Row, Pub., 1982.

Garfinkel, Harold, *Studies in Ethnomethodology*. Englewood Cliffs, N.J.: Prentice-Hall, 1967.

Lawrence, Paul R., and Jay W. Lorsch, *Organization and Environment*. Homewood, Ill.: Richard D. Irwin, 1969.

McPhee, Robert D., "Formal Structures and Organizational Communication," in *Organizational Communication*, Robert D. McPhee and Phillip K. Tompkins, eds. Beverly Hills, Calif.: Sage, 1985.

Martin, Joanne, "Can Organizational Culture Be Managed?" in *Organizational Culture*, Peter J. Frost et al., eds. Beverly Hills, Calif.: Sage, 1985.

Morgan, Gareth, "Paradigms, Metaphors, and Puzzle Solving in Organization Theory," *Administrative Science Quarterly*, 25 (December 1980), 605–622.

Morgan, Gareth, *Images of Organization*. Beverly Hills, Calif.: Sage, 1986.

Morgan, Gareth, and Linda Smircich, "The Case for Qualitative Research," *Academy of Management Review*, 5 (October 1980), 491–500.

Pacanowsky, Michael E., and Nick O'Donnell-Trujillo, "Communication and Organizational Cultures," *Western Journal of Speech Communication*, 46 (Spring 1982), 115–130.

Putnam, Linda L., "The Interpretive Perspective: An Alternative to Functionalism," in *Communication and Organizations: An Interpretive Approach*, Linda L. Putnam and Michael E. Pacanowsky, eds. Beverly Hills, Calif.: Sage, 1983.

Smircich, Linda, "Concepts of Culture and Organizational Analysis," *Administrative Science Quarterly*, 28 (September 1983), 339–358.

Smircich, Linda, "Is the Concept of Culture a Paradigm for Understanding Organizations and Ourselves?" in *Organizational Culture*, Peter J. Frost et al., eds. Beverly Hills, Calif.: Sage, 1985.

Weick, Karl, *The Social Psychology of Organizing*. Reading, Mass.: Addison-Wesley, 1969.

Weick, Karl, "Enactment Processes in Organizations," in *New Directions in Organizational Behavior*, Barry M. Staw and Gerald R. Salancik, eds. Chicago, Ill.: St. Clair Press, 1977.

Weick, Karl, *The Social Psychology of Organizing*, 2nd ed. Reading, Mass.: Addison-Wesley, 1979.

2
Competing World Views

The phrase *world view* refers to one's assumptions about reality and human nature. In this chapter we will introduce some of the implications different world views have for the analysis and understanding of organizations. It seems clear that human organizations are highly complex, and even though we use metaphors to help us understand them, each metaphor falls short of guiding us toward full comprehension of how organizations work. It is also evident that the metaphor used depends on one's world view. The most provocative question is simply, "What impact do world views have and which one should be followed?"

IMPACT ON DEFINITIONS AND ANALYSIS

One's world view has an impact on how one defines the concept of organization. An objectivist, as we have pointed out, sees an organization as a concrete structure. An organization is a container that holds people and things; the people in the organization adhere to some common goals. If the organization is healthy, the interdependent parts work in a systematic way to produce desirable outcomes. Knowledge about organizations consists of recognizing what structures or designs produce what outcomes. The objectivist emphasizes structure, planning, control, and goals and places these major factors in a scheme of organizational adaptation. Environment determines the organizing principles. The objectivist seeks the "best form" of the organization, based on environmental conditions. This approach leads to looking for an optimum fit between organizational structure and some factor in the environment, such as technology, situational favorability, or uncertainty. Organizations are conceived as large information processors with input, throughput, and output. This structured system of behavior contains positions and roles that can be designed (prestructured) before the roles are filled by actors (Stogdill, 1966).

Objectivists treat the organization primarily as a unit. That is, to study the organization is to study the entire organization. The organization is an entity that acts or functions in particular ways. Questions may center on how organizations can best adapt to their environment to enhance growth and survival. Some theorists divide the organization into organization, environment, group-to-group, and individual-to-organization areas of study (Lawrence & Lorsch, 1969). However, all of these divisions are considered to be part of an entity called "the organization."

Subjectivists define organization as organizing behavior. Given this definition, knowledge of the organization must be obtained by looking at those specific behaviors and what they mean to the people doing them. Structure is important only to the extent that it is created and recreated by organizational participants. Although knowledge generated by the subjectivist may be used in a variety of ways, its main use is to understand organizational life as it is understood and constituted by organizational participants. A subjectivist's goal is not to gain control of the various forces (structure, planning, goals).

When the emphasis is placed on the interaction between the participants, as it is with a subjectivist's view, the concept of organization is not limited to large, complex industries or agencies. A family can be considered an organization just as General Motors can. The unit of analysis is the individual, not the entity called the organization. Organizations do not behave; only people behave (Weick, 1979). The subjectivist is concerned with the actions of the participants and the consequences of their actions and what they mean for the participants.

The objectivist typically views the organization as a large entity with a control structure comprised of procedures and policies. The system is ordered on the basis of logic in order to achieve a goal and contains different degrees of authority at various levels as well as particular kinds of activities performed by individuals (Tosi, 1975). In contrast, a subjectivist advocates a broader notion of organization. For example, the subjectivists Pacanowsky and Trujillo define an organization as the "interlocked actions of a collectivity" (1982, p. 122). A collectivity may be small or large; the critical aspect of the definition centers on "interlocked actions" and the meaning given to those actions.

THE NATURE OF ACTION

Human action is also viewed from different perspectives by the objectivist and the subjectivist. From the objectivist's view, action is purposive, intentional, goal-directed, and rational. People think things through; they act with intent, have goals in mind, and weigh the consequences carefully. The essence of this view is well represented in management textbooks. Readers are advised about planning, organizing, and executing their plans. (Mintzberg, 1980, p. 9). In addition, action is tightly constrained and controlled by the environment. Actions are environmentally determined, and the actor is constrained to behave in certain ways. For the subjectivist, action emerges from the social process of human interaction. The focus is on emergent behavior that depends on social construction that takes place during the process of interaction.

The contrast between these two notions of human action has an impact on the concepts of predictability and control. To believe as an objectivist is to believe that organizations can be managed and controlled by rational decisions that structure activities in accordance with environmental demands and individual capabilities. Plans can be laid out in advance and one should be able to predict outcomes.

Much of the literature on managerial styles of leadership is based on the idea that a manager's behavior produces certain kinds of responses from subordinates. Although this idea will be examined in greater detail later, both experience and the subjective view suggest that prescribed managerial behaviors can result in very different employee responses. It is comforting to think that managers might be able to enter a situation with some universal rules on how to manage. However, even the most routine situations can be problematical and unpredictable. In addition, managers seldom have time to contemplate their decisions with the thoroughness suggested by the objective, rational view.

Both views are "people-oriented," but they view people in different ways. Objectivists suggest that people are predictable, as long as the underlying forces of natural order can be specified. The main objective is to behave rationally and determine how people adapt to situations. Subjectivists emphasize that people create order and situations. Rather than trying to discover a natural order (which, to them, does not exist), it is more useful to become sensitive to how people create order, the meaning it has for them, and the consequences of their creations.

Objective approaches imply that order exists in a real world. That order can be discovered, and the world, as well as human behavior, can be predictable. For this perspective, models for human behavior emphasize order, simplicity, and sense based on how organizations *should* operate. The next short step, however, is the idea that once the order is discovered, the organizational participants can be regulated and controlled. Such thinking has stimulated numerous theories of motivation and the search for a way to motivate employees that can be generalized to all settings. From a subjectivist position, motivating others demands knowledge about the unique aspects of the participants and the world they have created. This requires knowing what that world and its symbols mean to them.

DEFINITION OF COMMUNICATION

Although we have alluded to the concept of communication, we have not yet provided a precise and contemporary definition of the term *communication*. Dance and Larson (1976) listed 126 different published definitions of communication, but it is neither practical nor feasible to review them here. The question we shall pursue for a moment, however, concerns how we should distinguish communication from other forms of behavior in an organization. The distinctions are both simple and complex. For example, is hammering a nail a form of communication? Is jogging communication? Is filing letters in a cabinet a type of communication? Is looking out the window on the twenty-fifth floor of an office building an example of communication? Is writing a memo a form of communication? The answers to these questions depend on the precision with which one thinks about the activities that constitute communication.

The simple answer is that none of the behaviors mentioned are actually communication. The complex answer is that, in a sense, all of them are part of the communication process. If we look at what happens when a person engages in communicating, we find that two general types of actions take place:

1. *Creating messages* or, more precisely, displays
2. *Interpreting messages* or displays

Figure 2.1 portrays these two processes by dividing the person with a jagged line.

Message-Display

To *display* means that you bring something to the attention of another or others. *The Random House Dictionary of the English Language* (1987) states that "to display is literally to spread something out so that it may be most completely and favorably seen." Thus to display is to put something in plain view and usually in a favorable position for particular observation. Hammering a nail or filing a letter or writing a memo, by themselves, may not constitute forms of communication. However, they would be considered communication behaviors *if* they made something else visible or put something into plain view or brought something to the attention of another person. For a display to be a form of communicative behavior, it must represent or stand for or symbolize something else. When you create a message-display, you engage in one aspect of communication—that aspect is calling attention to something. For example, when you get dressed in the morning, you create a display of yourself. You put yourself, or at least what you feel you think about yourself, in plain view. We think you are putting yourself in a favorable position for particular observation. Your clothing, jewelry, and facial covering (make-up or beard) represent yourself to others; they are your display.

There is an axiom of communication that says "A person can*not* not communicate" (Smith & Williamson, 1977, p. 61). Technically that means that a person cannot avoid being a message-display. What you show or put in plain view does represent you. You are a walking message-display. The same can be said of your office (Goldhaber, 1979). The office is a message-display. A campus, no matter how it looks, is a message-display for those who visit. Of course, a memo is also a message-display, since the memo represents the ideas being expressed. A speech is a message-display. A drawing, a newspaper, a flower arrangement, and a layout are all message-displays, provided they are designed to stand for something else, such as an idea or image or another object.

Message Interpretation

The second type of behavior that occurs when a person engages in communication is called interpreting message-displays (Redding, 1972). To *interpret* means to set forth, to bring out, or make sense of something. According to the *Random House Dictionary,* to interpret means to construe or understand something in a particular way. Communication can be distinguished from all other human and organizational behaviors because it involves the mental process of making sense out of people, objects, and events, which we called message-displays. The only message that really counts in communicating is the one that results from the interpretative processes (Redding & Sanborn, 1964). You may consciously or intentionally create a display of words, sounds, artifacts, and actions to portray a meaning you have, but the only meaning that has an effect on people is the meaning they assign. What you had in mind makes little difference; how the other person interprets what you did and said is what affects his or her feelings and actions.

INFORMATION AS MESSAGE-DISPLAYS

It is not uncommon for authors to define communication as the *transfer* (Luthans, 1973) or *exchange* (Katz & Kahn, 1966) of information. In this context, for example, *information* refers to the words (in written messages) and the sounds (in spoken messages) in our displays. Luthans (1973), however, included within his definition of information such things as sensory stimuli; languages of all types, including FORTRAN, statistics, and accounting; and nonverbal behavior. Ference (1970) referred to a "five-year forecast of industry sales" as information but defined information as "any input to a person in a communication system" (p. 83). Frequently throughout this book, reference will be made to information, in such contexts as "the flow of information" and "information processing." *Information* is a term used to designate what we have called message-displays and is frequently used to refer to profit-and-loss figures, performance evaluations, personal opinions expressed in letters and memos, technical reports, and operating data.

THE FALLACY OF MEANING TRANSFER

Although we seem to recognize that sending a person a letter, memo, or report, or even talking to him or her face to face, consists only of creating and delivering a display to the other person, we often fail to realize that the delivery of information is different from making sense out of the information. Frequently we behave as if the delivery of information or message-displays is actually the transfer of meaning from one person to another. We think that saying something—such as "pick up the binder and meet me at the administration building"—should mean exactly the same thing for both people involved. At least when you show up with a ball of string and I was expecting a ring binder, I am surprised that *you* made a mistake. Since I *told* you what to do, you should have done it. I said the words just right, and you should have gotten the meaning. In a statement like that, meaning sounds like something you throw at another person. It's their fault if they fumble it.

The realities of communication suggest that people interpret displays and create meanings. Meanings are *not* contained in the displays or events or words (Lee & Lee, 1957). The fallacy of meaning transfer is expressed in this great principle of communication: "Meanings are in people, not words." Postman and Weingartner (1969) recognized the operation of this fallacy in our schools when they observed that some teachers believe "that they are in the 'information dissemination' business. . . . The signs that their business is failing are abundant, but they keep at it all the more diligently'' (p. 13). The real business of people involved in communicating, including teachers, is helping people create meanings, helping people understand displays. When they assume that meanings are in the displays, they are perpetuating one of the great fallacies of communication.

What is the significance of understanding this meaning-transfer fallacy for a manager, section head, or supervisor? What should an organizational communicator do differently if he or she understands this fallacy? The answer is that the supervisor will *listen to the person, not just to his or her words.* The plaintive appeal to "Listen to what I mean, not what I say" is often heard after something has gone wrong. Remember, there are few, if any, instructions that cannot be misinterpreted by somebody. For example, the simple explanation of the flight attendant when handing out chewing gum that "It's for the ears" seemed clear until a passenger complained that gum was all right, but wouldn't something less sticky work better?

The major fallacies of communication are the assumptions that (1) meanings exist in information or message-displays, and (2) meanings can be transferred from one person to another. In reality, information and displays can only be presented or delivered to people; the recipients must make sense out of the displays. Thus, a person can*not* not display. Meanings are in people, not words. Listen to what a person means, not what he or she says.

Messages may be displayed in verbal (involving language) or nonverbal (nonlanguage) forms and by oral, written or pictorial means. Table 2.1 shows the most common categories of displays.

For a message-display of information to be meaningful, someone must interpret it as standing for something else—that is, the display serves a symbolic function. Any aspect of people and things may be given meaning by someone. Goldhaber (1979) suggests that meaning can be assigned to all of the following: the body and its appearance, especially the mouth and eyes, gestures, touching, posture, and general bodily shape; the volume, tone, rate, pauses, and nonfluencies of vocal expression; the environment, including spaces between people and the territorial cues they offer; time factors such as tardiness and promptness; building and room designs; clothing—dress for success; the display of material things such as artwork; parking spaces; and the number of staff members.

Both verbal and nonverbal message-displays are central to the functioning of an organizational communication system. In fact, the contact people have with one another and the interpretations they assign to the behavior, objects, and events, both present and absent from the immediate environment, constitute the crux of the organizational communication system.

TABLE 2.1 Examples of Types of Messages

	Verbal	Nonverbal
Oral	Interview	Speaking softly
Written	Report	Diagram or layout
Pictorial	Description of a scene	Sketch of a scene

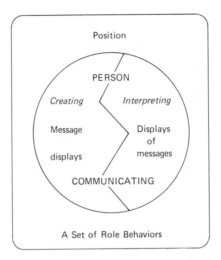

FIGURE 2.1   A Communication Unit

A COMMUNICATION UNIT

A system has been defined by de Sola Pool (1973) as "any continuing entity capable of two or more states" (p. 3). In a communication system the *states* are connections between people. In an organizational communication system the states are connections between *people in positions*. The basic unit of organizational communication is a person in a position. Figure 2.1 symbolizes that important relationship by portraying a person as the circle located inside the square position. As Bakke (1950) and Argyris (1957) explained, the person is socialized by the position, creating a circle that conforms more closely to the shape of the position; at the same time, the position is personalized, producing a figure that conforms more closely to the shape of the person.

A FUNCTIONAL DEFINITION
OF ORGANIZATIONAL COMMUNICATION

Organizational communication may be defined as the display and interpretation of messages among communication units who are part of a particular organization. An organization is comprised of communication units in hierarchical relations to each other and functioning in an environment. Figure 2.2 portrays the concept of an organizational communication system. The dotted lines represent the idea that relations are stipulated rather than natural; they also suggest that the structure of an organization is flexible and may change in response to internal, as well as external, environmental forces. Relations among positions, nevertheless, change officially only by declaration of organizational officials.

Organizational communication occurs whenever at least one person who occupies a position in an organization interprets some display. Because our focus is on communication among members of an organization, the analysis of organizational communication involves looking at many transactions occurring simultaneously. The system involves displaying and interpreting messages among dozens or even hundreds of individuals at the same time who have different types of relationships connecting them; whose thinking, decisions, and behaviors are governed by policies, regulations, and "rules"; who have different styles of communicating, managing, and leading; who are motivated by different contingencies; who are at different stages of development in various groups; who perceive different communication climates; who have different levels of satisfaction and information adequacy; who prefer and use different types, forms, and methods of communicating in different networks; who have varying levels of message fidelity; and who require the expenditure of different levels of materials and energy to communicate effectively. The interplay among all of those factors, and possibly many more, is what we call the *organizational communication system.*

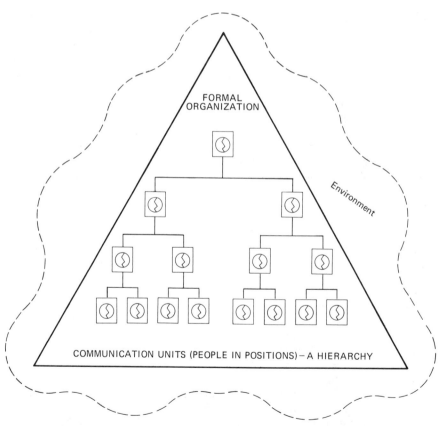

FIGURE 2.2 Organizational Communication System

A SUBJECTIVIST'S NOTATION

The central feature of organizational communication is the message-generating, interpreting, and handling activities of organizational members. What communication does in the organization and what it means depends on one's conception of organization.

If the organization is thought of as a preexisting structure or container, then communication may be conceived of as "a tangible substance that flows upward, downward, and laterally within the container" (Putnam, 1983, p. 39). In that view, communication functions to achieve the goals and objectives of the organizational system. More specific communication functions include work, maintenance, motivation, integration, and innovation messages (Farace, Monge, & Russell, 1977, pp. 56–57). Communication supports the organizational structure and its adaptation to the environment. If the organization is a large information processor, then the purpose of the communication process is to get the right information to the right people at the right times. From this perspective, organizational communication can be seen as "the processes for gathering, processing, storing, and disseminating the communication that enables organizations to function" (Farace, Monge, & Russell, 1977, p. 4).

When the organization is conceived of as people interacting and giving meaning to that interaction, communication becomes an organization-making function rather than just an organization-maintaining one. Communication does not just serve the organization; it *is* the organization. From this perspective, organizational communication "would center on the symbols that make organizational life possible. What are the words, ideas, and constructs that impel, legitimate, coordinate, and realize organized activity in specific settings?" (Smircich, 1985, p. 67). Communication, then, is central to organizational existence and does more than simply carry out organizational plans. In some schemes, communication is theorized to give insight into critical organizational behaviors (i.e., adaptation). For the subjectivist, communication is the critical behavior. To illustrate further, consider the role of communication in decision making. Most people would agree that communication is important to the decision-making process. However, some theorists go further and look at communication as the very fabric of the decision.

The issue of simplicity/complexity discussed in Chapter 1 is relevant here. The notions of organizational structure and functions help us to visualize an organization and the important role of communication. We do not deny the usefulness of such concepts; however, they take obvious features for granted. Understanding is gained through reducing the organization to such simple components, but understanding is also lost by not grasping its complexity. For instance, if we treat structure not as a tool for analysis but as a question of analysis, the complexity of something that was taken for granted becomes evident. What is structure? How is it created, executed, and changed? How is structure enacted or accomplished? These questions generate complexity consistent with subjective approaches.

Can organizational communication exist without people? If messages are treated as physical substances (an extreme objectivist position), communication can exist without people. Objectivists focus on getting information through the system, whereas the role of people is preeminent in a subjectivist's view of organizational communication. Messages are created, interpreted, and recreated in an ongoing process. Organizational communication does not exist until it is created and interpreted by people.

DIRECTION OF TEXT

The way we define organizational communication is affected by how we think the world operates and how we relate to events in the world. In Chapter 1 we reviewed two contradictory and competing views of the world: a subjectivist's and an objectivist's. These views are competitive and challenge one another.

The basic explanations about organizational communication in this book come from the traditional objective view. In fact, most of the research on and writing about organizational communication has been consistent with the traditional point of view. The information about issues in organizational communication is drawn from traditional ideas—the objective view.

However, because the analysis of organizational communication from a subjective point of view is somewhat new in the field, and because it contradicts, elaborates on, and often adds to what the traditional approach says about organizational communication, we would like to introduce you to some of the newer ideas. We have chosen to do this by means of comments about the traditional, usual way of talking about organizational communication.

Thus, throughout the text, we present the usual explanations about organizational communication, and then we add some comments from the subjective perspective that often challenges, criticizes, and gives an alternative way of thinking about the issues. We call this a "dialectical" approach to writing about organizational communication.

Since objective and subjective thinking about organizational communication are often on opposite sides of the issues, it is not possible to arrive at a single point of view. One may not be able to meld or bring about a convergence of the two views. We cannot smooth over the differences between objective and subjective approaches to organizational communication. But we can present both points of view so that you can ponder and evaluate them and see where they differ. Our intent is partly to provoke thought about organizational communication. We ask you not to be defensive about either point of view, but to seek to understand what organizational communication is about from both views. You may, as Lauffer (1985) points out, "protect [yourself] from the abuse of others who may be using them [ideas] incorrectly or selectively against your best interests" (p. 20). The theoretical structures presented here will be useful if a sense of perspective is maintained. Most of us go into situations with ideas and then modify them as the situation demands. This text is designed to provide some useful ideas.

SUMMARY

We have discussed the impact that world views have on the study and practice of organizational communication. These views (objective and subjective) influence how one conceptualizes organization, the nature of action, and the function of communication. We have defined organizational communication as the display and interpretation of messages among communication units and stressed that organizational communication occurs whenever at least one person who occupies a position interprets some display.

In Part Two, we will examine basic organization theories that have influenced the way organizational communication has been conceived and developed. We are less concerned with the chronology of theories than with the impact of the world views they represent.

REFERENCES

Argyris, Chris, *Personality and Organization.* New York: Harper & Row, Pub., 1957.

Bakke, E. Wight, *Bonds of Organization.* New York: Harper & Row, Pub., 1950.

Burrell, Gibson, and Gareth Morgan, *Sociological Paradigms and Organizational Analysis.* London: Heinemann, 1979.

Dance, Frank E. X., and Carl E. Larson, *The Functions of Human Communication: A Theoretical Approach.* New York: Holt, Rinehart, & Winston, 1976.

de Sola Pool, Ithiel, "Communication Systems," in *Handbook of Communication,* Ithiel de Sola Pool and Wilbur Schramm, eds. Skokie, Ill.: Rand McNally, 1973.

Farace, Richard V., Peter R. Monge, and Hamish M. Russell, *Communicating and Organizing.* Reading, Mass.: Addison-Wesley, 1977.

Ference, T. P., "Organizational Communication Systems and the Decision Process," *Management Science,* 17 (1970), 83–96.

Goldhaber, Gerald M., *Organizational Communication,* 2nd ed. Dubuque, Iowa: Wm. C. Brown, 1979.

Guba, Egon G., "The Context of Emergent Paradigm Research," in *Organizational Theory and Inquiry: The Paradigm Revolution,* Yvonna S. Lincoln, ed. Beverly Hills, Calif.: Sage, 1985.

Katz, Daniel, and Robert L. Kahn, *The Social Psychology of Organizations.* New York: John Wiley, 1966.

Kreps, Gary L., *Organizational Communication.* New York: Longman, 1986.

Lauffer, Armand, *Careers, Colleagues, and Conflicts.* Beverly Hills, Calif.: Sage, 1985.

Lawrence, Paul R., and Jay W. Lorsch, *Organization and Environment.* Homewood, Ill.: Richard D. Irwin, 1969.

Lee, Irving J., and Laura L. Lee, *Handling Barriers in Communication.* New York: Harper & Row, Pub., 1957.

Lincoln, Yvonna S., ed. *Organizational Theory and Inquiry: The Paradigm Revolution.* Beverly Hills, Calif.: Sage, 1985.

Luthans, Fred, *Organizational Behavior.* New York: McGraw-Hill, 1973.

Mintzberg, Henry, *The Nature of Managerial Work.* Englewood Cliffs, N.J.: Prentice-Hall, 1980.

Morgan, Gareth, *Beyond Method.* Beverly Hills, Calif.: Sage, 1983.

Pacanowsky, Michael E., and Nick O'Donnell-Trujillo, "Communication and Organizational Cultures," *Western Journal of Speech Communication,* 46 (Spring 1982), 115–130.

Postman, Neil, and Charles Weingartner, *Teaching as a Subversive Activity.* New York: Delacorte Press, 1969.

Putnam, Linda, "The Interpretive Perspective: An Alternative to Functionalism," in *Communication and Organizations: An Interpretive Approach,* Linda L. Putnam and Michael E. Pacanowsky, eds. Beverly Hills, Calif.: Sage, 1983.

Redding, W. Charles, and George A. Sanborn, *Business and Industrial Communication: A Source Book.* New York: Harper & Row, Pub., 1964.

Redding, W. Charles, *Communication within the Organization: An Interpretive Review of Theory and Research.* New York: Industrial Communication Council, 1972.

Smircich, Linda, "Is the Concept of Culture a Paradigm for Understanding Organizations and Ourselves?" in *Organizational Culture,* Peter J. Frost et al., eds. Beverly Hills, Calif.: Sage, 1985.

Smith, Dennis R., and L. Keith Williamson, *Interpersonal Communication: Roles, Rules, Strategies, and Games.* Dubuque, Iowa: Wm. C. Brown, 1977.

Stogdill, Ralph M., "Dimension of Organization Theory," in *Approaches to Organizational Design,* James D. Thomson, ed. Pittsburgh: University of Pittsburgh Press, 1966.

Thompson, James D., *Organization in Action.* New York: McGraw-Hill, 1967.

Tosi, Henry L., *Theories of Organization.* New York: John Wiley, 1975.

Weick, Karl, *The Social Psychology of Organizing,* 2nd ed., Reading, Mass.: Addison-Wesley, 1979.

3

Classical Structural Theory

The next three chapters focus on theories of organization and organizing. Pure objectivist theories are discussed in Chapter 3, some transitional theories are analyzed in Chapter 4, and theories that move toward a subjectivist view are treated in Chapter 5. Each chapter addresses the characteristics and main features of organizations from the perspective of the particular theory. A subjectivist's notation is appended to the chapters on classical structural theory and transitional behavioral and social systems theories. Contemporary theories are presented from the subjectivist's point of view.

The work of Blau and Scott (1962) serves as the foundation upon which we shall base the classical structural theory of organization. They distinguish between the general structure of *social organization* and the more specific structure called *formal organization,* about which we shall be concerned.

SOCIAL ORGANIZATION

The term *social organization* refers to the patterns of social interaction (the frequency and duration of contacts between persons; the tendency to initiate contacts; the direction of influence between persons; the degree of cooperation; feelings of attraction, respect, and hostility; and status differences) and the observed regularities in the social behavior of people that are due to their social circumstances rather than to their physiological or psychological characteristics as individuals.

To have pattern or regularity in social interaction implies that there are some linkages between people that transform them from a collection of individuals into a group or from an aggregate of groups into a larger social system. For example, a busload of people going to work at different locations in a city does not really constitute a social organization, but a busload of booster club members on their way to a football game does represent a social organization. The boosters are connected by some shared beliefs that result in a structure that is more than the sum of the individuals composing the group. The patterns of interaction among boosters may result in status differences. For example, highly integrated group members are different from isolates, leaders differ from followers, those who are highly respected are different from those who are not highly regarded. Social status differences develop a hierarchy in the social structure.

Relations also develop between groups, producing a different aspect of social status. The status of the group in the larger social system becomes part of the status of its members. For example, the status of the booster club tends to influence the status of those who belong to it; likewise, membership in an ethnic group, such as Native Americans, also affects one's status.

The networks of contacts and the shared beliefs of a group are usually referred to as its *structure* and its *culture*. Contacts serve to organize human conduct in an organization. As a person conforms to the expectations of group members, that conformity influences relations with others and in turn affects his or her social status; a person's status then begins to affect behavior so that it is consistent with social norms and improves the person's chances of achieving important goals. Socially organized interaction results.

Berlo (1960) suggests that communication is related to social organization in three ways:

First, social systems are produced through communication. Uniformities of behavior and pressures to conform to norms are produced through communication among group members.

Second, once a social system has developed, it determines the communication of its members. Social systems affect how, to, and from whom, and with what effects, communication occurs among members of the system. One's social status in the system, for example, increases the likelihood of talking to people of comparable status and decreases the probability of communicating with people of much higher or much lower status. In addition, the system determines the frequency of messages by restricting the kinds and numbers of people with whom occupants of a particular position can communicate. Finally, the system may affect how members treat their messages. A style develops that is characteristic of members of the social organization. A civic club, a government agency, or a large corporation develop ways of doing things, writing about activities, and talking about their work that are imposed on members of the system. People who communicate with one another over time tend to develop similar behavior patterns. As individuals are immersed in the system, their unique behaviors adapt to the demands of the system, resulting in behavior similar to those of other members of the system.

Third, knowledge about a social system can help us make accurate predictions about people without knowing much more than the roles they occupy in the system. A *role* refers to both a set of behaviors and a given position in a social system. We can, for example, talk about the role of *manager*. A manager is a role in a social system we call a *formal organization*. The term *manager* refers both to a set of behaviors that are performed in the company and to a position in the company. For every role there is a set of behaviors and a position. If we know what behaviors go with a role, we can make predictions about the person who occupies the position. There are, within a range, certain behaviors that go with the role of chief executive officer, supervisor, secretary, union steward, salesperson, clerk, accountant, public relations specialist, or training specialist. When we meet a person who occupies a given role-position, we can predict that he or she will do certain things because of the position. As Berlo summarizes, "Even if we do not know a person as an individual, even if we have had no prior communication with him to determine his attitudes, his knowledges, his communication skills, we still can make fairly accurate predictions from a knowledge of his position in one or more social systems" (p. 150).

FORMAL ORGANIZATION

In contrast to social organization that emerges whenever people associate with one another, there are organizations that are created deliberately for certain purposes. If the accomplishment of a particular objective requires some sort of collective effort, an organization is designed to coordinate the activities of many individuals and to furnish incentives for others to aid them. Businesses, for example, are formed to produce materials that can be sold, unions are organized to increase their bargaining power with employers, government agencies are created to regulate commerce. In these cases the goals to be achieved, the rules to be followed, and the status structure are consciously designed to anticipate and guide interaction and activities of members. The term *formal organization* is used to refer to these kinds of systems.

We shall look at some distinctive characteristics of formal organizations—popularly called *bureaucracies*—in an effort to understand important features of formal systems. The somewhat simplistic analysis that follows is intended to highlight and focus attention on aspects of formal organizations that may have implications for a preliminary understanding of organizational communication. To clarify the characteristics of a formal organization, we shall present ideas derived from the writings of Max Weber (1947), pronounced "Mox Veber," as analyzed and summarized by numerous scholars in the field. The enumeration of characteristics is consistent with those of other analysts, but this list is unique to our view.

To hold an appropriate perspective on Weber's analysis of bureaucratic or formal organizations, we need to realize that he developed his theory of organizations as an *ideal type*. That is, he did not describe organizations as they actually functioned nor did he provide a summary of the usual characteristics of bureaucracies; rather, he identified characteristics that are distinctive of the ideal formal organization. Weber attempted to portray a perfectly bureaucratized organization. He said, in effect, that bureaucracies are those organizations that exhibit the following combination of characteristics. For example, Weber's theory of bureaucracy suggests that efficiency is related to a hierarchical pattern of authority. This may or may not be true. Nevertheless, if a study of a number of organizations were to discover that hierarchical authority was *not* related to efficiency in those organizations, that finding would not be a basis for rejecting Weber's claims; it would only show that the organizations studied were not fully bureaucratized.

CHARACTERISTICS OF A WEBERIAN BUREAUCRACY

Most modern organizations, as well as some ancient ones, are organized consistent with Weber's theory of formal organizations. Although Weber was writing as early as 1910, his theory serves admirably well for comprehending key aspects of organizations from a classical structural point of view, and communicative interaction that occurs in that context, even today. Nevertheless, Weber's theory has been criticized and refined, leading to more sophisticated concepts of organizational functioning. Perrow's (1973) description of the rise and fall of bureaucratic theory suggests, however, the continuing interest in Weber's ideas:

> At first, with his celebration of the efficiency of bureaucracy, he was received with only reluctant respect, and even with hostility. All writers were against bureaucracy. But it turned out, surprisingly, that managers were not. When asked, they acknowledged that they preferred clear lines of communication, clear specifications of authority and responsibility, and clear knowledge of whom they were responsible to. . . . Gradually, studies began to show that bureaucratic organizations could change faster than nonbureaucratic ones, and that morale could be higher where there was clear evidence of bureaucracy. (p. 6)

What are the characteristics of an ideally bureaucratized organization? Analyses of Weber's work suggest the following ten features:

1. An organization consists of stipulated relationships among *positions*. The basic building blocks of any formal organization are positions. Organizational positions are almost always designated by titles, such as supervisor, machinist, lieutenant, sergeant, lecturer, senior analyst, trainer.
2. The broad purpose or plan of the organization is subdivided into tasks; organization tasks are distributed among the various positions as *official duties*. The definitions of duties and responsibilities are inherent in the position. Job descriptions are, of course, one method of meeting this characteristic. A clear division of labor among positions is implied by this feature, which makes possible a high degree of specialization and expertness among employees.
3. *Authority* to perform the duties is vested in the position. That is, the only time that a person is authorized to perform the duties of the position is when he or she legitimately occupies the position. Weber referred to this as *legal* authority. Authority is legitimized by a belief in the supremacy of the law. In such a system, obedience is owed to a set of principles, not to a person. This feature includes the requirement to follow directives originating from an office that is superior to one's own, regardless of who occupies the higher office. The government, a factory, the army, a welfare agency, churches, university, and a grocery store are examples of organizations based on legal authority.
4. The lines of authority and the positions are arranged in a *hierarchical order*. The hierarchy takes on the general shape of a pyramid, with each official being

responsible to his or her superior for subordinates' decisions, as well as for his or her own. The scope of authority of superiors over subordinates is clearly circumscribed. The concepts of *upward* and *downward* communication express this concept of authority, with information moving down from the position of broadest authority to the position of narrowest authority.

5. A formally established system of general but definite *rules and regulations* governs the actions and functions of positions in the organization. Much of the effort of administrators in the organization goes into applying the general regulations to particular cases. The hypothetical case of having the Internal Revenue Service determine your taxes is a good example. If you were to go to an IRS office to argue for a reduced tax load, the decision would most likely be made on the basis of a regulation specifying the rules for making such a decision. The official would then apply the regulation to your case and explain how much tax you owe. Regulations help ensure uniformity of operations and provide for continuity regardless of changes in personnel.

6. *Procedures* in the organization are formal and impersonal—that is, the rules and regulations are applicable to everyone who falls within the category. Officials are expected to assume an impersonal orientation in their contacts with clients and other officials. They are to disregard all personal considerations and to maintain emotional detachment. Impersonal procedures are designed to prevent the feelings of officials from distorting their rational judgment in carrying out their duties.

7. An attitude of and procedures for enforcing a system of *discipline* is part of the organization. For individuals to work efficiently, they must have the necessary skills and apply them rationally and energetically; however, if members of the organization were to make even rational decisions independently, their work would not be coordinated, making the efficiency of the organization suffer. Individuals who do not accept the authority of those above them, who fail to carry out the duties assigned to their positions, and who apply regulations with capriciousness are not pursuing organizational objectives consistent with the philosophy of efficiency. Thus, the organization needs a program of discipline to help ensure cooperation and efficiency.

8. Members of the organization are to maintain *separate private and organizational lives*. Families of organization members, for example, are not to make contact with employees during working hours. Some organizations take great pains to accommodate the personal lives of employees in order to allow them to devote their complete attention to their jobs. Many corporations buy the homes of employees, care for their families in country club surroundings, and discourage using the telephone for private calls to maintain the separation of private and organizational affairs.

9. Employees are selected for employment in the organization on the basis of *technical qualifications* rather than on political, family, or other connections. Officials are appointed to positions rather than elected by a group of constituents, which makes them dependent on superiors in the organization. The administration of civil service examinations by the U.S. government is one way of trying to select employees on the basis of technical competence. Recent decisions to require employers to select employees on the basis of bona fide occupational qualifications (BFOQs) are perfectly consistent with this characteristic of Weber's ideal bureaucracy.

10. Although employment in the bureaucracy is based on technical competence,

advancements are made according to seniority as well as achievement. After a trial period, officials gain tenure in positions and are protected against arbitrary dismissal. Employment in the organization constitutes a lifelong career, providing *security in the position.*

These characteristics lead toward rational decision making and administrative efficiency. Experts with much experience are best qualified to make technical decisions. Disciplined performance governed by abstract rules, regulations, or policies and coordinated by hierarchical authority fosters a rational and consistent pursuit of organizational goals.

POSITIONAL COMMUNICATION AND INFORMAL CONTACTS

The characteristics of a formal organization lead to a phenomenon that we call *positional communication* (Redfield, 1953). Relationships are established between positions, not people. The entire organization consists of a network of positions. Those who occupy the positions are required to communicate in ways consistent with the positions. Nevertheless, positional communication is upset in practice because not all activities and interactions conform strictly to the positional chart. The relationship between Position A and Position C does not exist separately from the relationship between Andrew and Zebe. The official organization chart can never completely determine the conduct and social relations of organization members. Yet, although it is impossible to completely insulate a position from the occupier's personality, organizational productivity depends most of the time on positional communication. This does not deny or discount the tremendous impact of informal relations on communication. In every formal organization there is likely to develop informal groups. However, since informal relations arise in response to the opportunities created by the environment, the formal organization constitutes the immediate environment of the groups within it and influences greatly the number and functioning of informal relations.

Although Weber's analysis of organization theory appears to describe many current operating organizations, a number of other philosophies and theories have contributed to an understanding of organizational functioning and, especially, organizational communication. Two lines of theory, in addition to communication theory, have provided useful insights: these are management theories and organization theories. Sometimes writers make little distinction between a theory of managing and a theory of organizing because they are often very much alike, but occasionally they differ. We shall briefly report on a classical theory of management that is compatible with Weber's formal theory of organization.

TAYLOR'S SCIENTIFIC MANAGEMENT

Weber's theory of bureaucracy focused primarily on organizing; it is considered to be the most important statement on formal organization, but it may be true that all theories of organization are basically theories of managing. Frederick W. Taylor (1856–1917) lived about the same time as Weber and also wrote about organizations; however, Taylor published *Principles of Scientific Management* whereas Weber's work was translated as *The Theory of Social and Economic Organization.* Both books dealt with issues of business enterprise from similar philosophies. Scott (1961) states that the classical doctrine of organizations and management can be traced directly back to Taylor's interest in functional supervision. Taken together, Weber and Taylor represent theories of organization and management that deal almost exclusively with the anatomy of formal organization and are referred to as classical structural theories. Taylor's approach to management is built around four key elements: division of labor, scalar and functional processes, structure, and span of control. Following Sofer's (1972) analysis closely, we shall briefly review the meaning of these four pillars.

Division of Labor

Division of labor refers to how the tasks, duties, and work of the organization are distributed. In bureaucratic terms the duties of the company are systematically assigned to positions in a descending order of specialization. Taylor suggested that workers should be relieved of the task of planning and of all clerical activities. If practicable, the work of every person in the organization should be confined to the execution of a single function, which is the notion of division of labor. Although not entirely serious, Parkinson (1957) formulated a number of principles that help explain how people in the organization manipulate this element. Parkinson studied the British Navy and concluded that "Work expands to fill the time available for its completion." He called the statement *Parkinson's Law.* His observations led him to realize that in organizations the task to be executed swells in importance and complexity in direct ratio to the amount of time to be spent on the task. Thus, he argued, the amount of work and the number of workers are not related. He illustrates how any small task can expand to fill the time available by describing a person who has all day to prepare a memo. An hour will be spent locating some paper, another in hunting for a pencil, a half an hour in search of the names and addresses, an hour and a quarter composing the memo, twenty minutes deciding whether to distribute it by hand or send it through the mails. The total effort will occupy a busy person for three minutes in total but will leave this person exhausted after a full day of doubt, anxiety, and toil.

Of course, managers, workers, and administrators begin to age and feel reduced energy with such exhausting days. According to Parkinson, the manager has three choices: resign, share the work with a colleague, or ask for assistance in the form of two subordinates. Only the third alternative is ever used. The corollary to Parkinson's Law is that "An official wants to multiply subordinates, not rivals." The inevitable consequence is called the *Rising Pyramid,* the second great pillar of classical management theory.

Scalar and Functional Processes

Scalar and functional processes deal with the vertical and horizontal growth of the organization. The *scalar process* refers to growth of the chain of command or the vertical dimension of the organization. By acquiring two assistants the manager has increased the size of the organization vertically, creating changes in the delegation of authority and responsibility, unity of direction, and obligations to report.

The division of work into more specialized duties and the restructuring of the more specific parts into compatible units are matters related to *functional processes* and the horizontal expansion of the organization. Both scalar and functional changes lead to the third pillar of classical management theory.

Structure

Structure has to do with logical relationships among functions in the organization. Classical theories concentrate on the two basic structures called *line* and *staff*. The *line structure* involves the authority channels of the organization as they relate to accomplishing the major goals of the organization. For example, in a valve manufacturing company, the line structure follows the order of positions responsible for getting the valves manufactured; the line authority consists of the president, the vice president of manufacturing, the managers, supervisors, and operatives who produce the valves. In the military the line authority involves those who have command functions, such as the company commander, the first sergeant, the squad leaders, and patrol leaders. The *staff structure* represents those positions that provide support for or help the line positions do their work better by offering advice, assistance, or service. Typical staff functions include purchasing and receiving, traffic control, business research, production planning, public relations, and training and development.

LINE

The primary value of differentiating between line and staff is in the area of decision making. The term *line* simply means that the final authority rests with positions in that structure. At the university, for example, the line structure for teaching and curricular decisions includes faculty members, department chairpersons, deans, and the academic vice president. The arrangement is hierarchical or pyramidal, since there are more faculty members than there are department chairs, more chairs than deans, and more deans than academic vice presidents. The library of a university is a staff function in support of teaching (and research, of course); however, the library has its own line structure, beginning with the director of the library and moving through functional heads such as circulation, acquisitions, and reference, down to specialty librarians in such areas as the social sciences, education, business, and physical sciences. Secretaries, clerks, and researchers represent staff positions.

STAFF

Staff personnel have traditionally provided advice and service in support of the line. The line has authority to command. The staff advises and persuades on behalf of its recommendations but has no authority to order the line manager to follow the suggestions. When a staff specialist's recommendations are accepted by his or her line superior, they are issued on the line manager's authority, not the staff specialist's. In this way the full authority of the line manager remains intact, and subordinates receive orders only from their line superior, thus maintaining a unity of command.

The role of staff as strictly advisory has changed radically over the years. Staff members are now often assigned limited line or command authority rather than general authority over an organizational unit. For example, the personnel department or the training and development department, even though a staff function, may prescribe the methods for on-the-job training of all new employees, regardless of their line assignment.

Tall and Flat Structures

Organization structures may take many forms, but at the extremes are two main types: the *tall* or *vertical* and the *flat* or *horizontal*. The tallness or flatness of an organization is determined almost solely by the differences in numbers of levels of authority and variations in the span of control at each level. Tall structures have many levels of authority, with managers exercising a narrow span of control. Tall organizations are often characterized by close supervision, team spirit, competition through personal relationships, gradual increases in responsibility, constant insecurity about status, emphasis on the techniques of management, and an abundance of rules and regulations. Flat organizations, on the other hand, seem to be characterized by and encourage individualistic and entrepreneurial activities. Flat structures have only a modest amount of direct supervision and fewer rules and regulations. Personnel assume wider responsibility at lower levels in flat structures, and the manager has less contact with them. The manager has to judge subordinates by less personal, objective standards of performance, and subordinates openly compete with one another in terms of their actual work rather than on the basis of their personal relations with the boss. Flat structures seem to be more appropriate for loosely supervised and technically simple, although individually more challenging, activities such as sales, service, political, and religious organizations. With its greater scope of individual freedom, flat structures more often tend to produce attitudes of enthusiasm and result in higher morale among employees.

Span of Control

Span of control refers to the number of subordinates a superior has under his or her supervision. Although it has frequently been stated that five or six subordinates is about all a manager can supervise, in practice the span of management varies widely. For example, in a retail chain that has only four levels of authority between the company president and first-line store supervisors, a manager may have twenty or thirty supervisors reporting to him or her. In contrast, in a manufacturing operation, with seven levels of authority, a manager may have only five to ten subordinates reporting to her or him. Some companies have as many as twelve levels of authority between the president and the first-line supervisors; in such situations the span of control may run below five.

SUMMARY

This chapter distinguished between two types of organizations: social and formal. Although the regularities in social behavior that produce social organizations make it possible to predict somewhat accurately how people will behave, formal organizations are specifically designed to produce efficiency and predictability in work settings. Ten characteristics of a formal, bureaucratic organization derived from the writings of Max Weber were discussed. Some principles of scientific management consistent with the ideas of Frederick Taylor were also identified. The works of Weber and Taylor represent the classical view of organization and management.

A SUBJECTIVIST'S NOTATION

Weber's ideal model represents the search for order, rationality, and regulation of human behavior. The language of classical structural theory is selective and misleading. Clark (1985) states, "Thoughtful planning, data-based decision making, forceful leadership, responsible action, accountability, responsiveness, efficiency, and cost-effectiveness sound so right and righteous that it is hard to entertain alternative perspectives to the images conveyed by these words" (p. 49). The words themselves tend to become guiding principles that are difficult to challenge. It is easy to assume that such principles operate in the organization or *should* be operative. Clark asks, "What, for example, are the antonyms of Weber's characteristics of bureaucratic administration? They are inefficient, unpredictable, irrational, incompetent, ignorant, and prejudicial!" (p. 49). These words and images can prevent us from looking at what actually occurs in the organization. What people do may encompass a wide range of behaviors and may be functional or dysfunctional depending on the situation.

Classical structural theory has a simplicity that is appealing. It suggests that once the right structure is discovered, behavior will be predictable, rational, and efficient. If everyone knows their roles, their responsibilities, and who they are responsible to, organizations can run smoothly. Structure determines behavior and produces predictability.

There are certain "sayings" that apply to these structural notions that are derived from the characteristics of a bureaucracy. Such adages include "the buck stops here" and "authority should be commensurate with responsibility." But what really happens in an organization? Clark (1985) describes counter-sayings, such as:

> *The buck never stops in an organization.* There is always either someone else to blame or some set of uncontrollable circumstances that no reasonable observer would pin on a single administrator—not even a chief executive officer. . . . *Authority and responsibility are almost never congruous in an organization.* While some persons are squandering authority by avoiding responsibility, others are accumulating responsibility in the hope of increasing their authority. Individual authority and responsibility in organizations are variables governed jointly by the day-to-day sense-making activities of organizational participant and designated organizational positions. (pp. 49–50)

One might contend that the first saying is what the organization should be like, and it would be if it met Weber's ideal type. However, organizations are created by people through negotiated meaning, and the ideal type is not likely to occur. More important, the term "ideal" is misleading. The idea that "the buck stops here" may not always be functional. It would be a painful world if "face saving" did not exist. Dispersal of blame in an organization is not always dysfunctional. There may be times when it is necessary to protect a person in order to protect a position. If authority and responsibility were always commensurate, it is likely that a great deal of work would never get done. One of the frustrations of coping with bureaucratic systems is presenting a problem to someone only to be told that "I am not responsible for that, it isn't my fault, and don't blame me!" Such people are content to shuffle papers and avoid blame rather than solve a problem.

The idea that relationships are established between positions instead of people places emphasis on structure rather than behavior. Positions become tangible objects that exist prior to and apart from human behavior. This concept ignores the subtleties of organizational behavior. An organizational map of positions might tell us what positions are supposed to exist and what communication should take place between what positions; however, positions do not exist until they have been acted out. In addition, communication establishes relationships, and positions do not communicate—people do. The behavior expected of a position or between positions can only be standardized in a general sense. How that behavior is carried out is unique, negotiated between the people involved. Positions exist only in the abstract until they are performed and validated by the participants. The roles in most organizations follow general guidelines, but a wide latitude of behavior exists in performing those roles. To think only of positions is to think in mechanical terms that mask the creative force of humans.

If the positional emphasis is to make sense, it should certainly do so when one examines sports games. The parameters are set by rules and the method of play is rather straightforward. Let's examine the double play in baseball. This play involves the positions of shortstop, second base, and first base. When an opponent is on first base and a ball is hit to the shortstop, the ball is thrown to second base and relayed to first base in order to put out two players. More is involved here than the positions; the positions only come to life when someone "plays" them. There is a second base in the abstract sense, but there is also Charlie, who plays second base. Yes, the shortstop does throw the ball to second base, but perhaps the real trick is throwing the ball to Charlie—who wants the ball in a certain place so that he can get off his best relay to first. To complicate matters, both the shortstop and second base have to account for an opposing player who is cruising toward Charlie at the speed of a runaway truck. The point is that the positions are not anything until they are played, and anyone who has ever watched a little-league game knows that there is considerable variance in how they are played. Relationships are established between positions only in a general and abstract sense. It is the unique behavior and relationships generated by people that dominate organizational life.

REFERENCES

Berlo, David K., *The Process of Communication.* New York: Holt, Rinehart & Winston, 1960.

Blau, Peter M., and W. Richard Scott, *Formal Organizations.* New York: Harper & Row, Pub., 1962.

Clark, David L., "Emerging Paradigms in Organizational Theory and Research," in *Organizational Theory and Inquiry: The Paradigm Revolution,* Yvonne S. Lincoln, ed. Beverly Hills, Calif.: Sage, 1985.

Parkinson, C. Northcote, *Parkinson's Law.* New York: Ballantine, 1957.

Perrow, Charles, "The Short and Glorious History of Organizational Theory," *Organizational Dynamics,* 2 (Summer 1973), 2–15.

Redfield, Charles E., *Communication in Management*. Chicago: The University of Chicago Press, 1953.

Scott, William G., "Organization Theory: An Overview and an Appraisal," *Journal of the Academy of Management*, 4 (April 1961), 7–26.

Sofer, Cyril, *Organizations in Theory and Practice*. New York: Basic Books, 1972.

Taylor, Frederick W., *Principles of Scientific Management*. New York: Harper & Row, Pub., 1911.

Weber, Max, *The Theory of Social and Economic Organization*, trans. A. M. Henderson and Talcott Parsons; Talcott Parsons, ed. Glencoe, Ill.: The Free Press and Falcon's Wing Press, 1947.

4
Transitional Theories

This chapter will explore the transition from classical structural theories of organization and management to the more contemporary behavioral and systems theories. Like eras in the history of people, aspects of earlier traditions form the foundation for future thinking about people and things. The older conceptions continue to exercise important influences on how we conceive of organizations, but refinements in our models begin to bring about curious and often practical changes in our formulations about organizations.

BEHAVIORAL THEORIES

Chester Barnard's Authority-Communication Theory

Perrow (1973) indicates that concerns had been expressed from the beginning about the implications of the classical theory of organization and the scientific doctrine of management. " 'Bureaucracy' has always been a dirty word, and the job design efforts of Frederick Taylor were even the subject of a congressional investigation" (p. 10). However, it was not until Barnard (1938) published *The Functions of the Executive* that a new line of thought emerged. He proposed that organizations are people systems, not mechanically engineered structures. A good, clear mechanical structure was not enough. Natural groups within the bureaucratic structure affected what happened, upward communication was important, authority came from below rather than from above, and leaders needed to function as a cohesive force.

Barnard's definition of formal organization—a system of consciously coordinated activities of two or more persons—highlighted the concepts of *system* and *persons*. People, not positions, make up a formal organization. His stress on the cooperative aspects of the organization reflected the importance placed on the human element. Barnard stated that the existence of an organization (as a cooperative system) depended on the ability of human beings to communicate and on their willingness to serve and work toward a common goal. Thus, he concluded that "The first function of the executive is to develop and maintain a system of communication."

Barnard also maintained that authority was a function of willingness to go along. He cited four conditions that must be met before a person will accept a message as authoritative:

1. The person can and does understand the message.
2. The person believes, at the time of the decision, that the message is not inconsistent with the purpose of the organization.
3. The person believes, at the time of the decision to go along, that the message is compatible with his or her personal interest as a whole.
4. The person is able mentally and physically to comply with the message.

This set of premises became known as the *acceptance theory of authority*— that is, authority originating at the top of an organization is, in effect, nominal authority. It becomes real only when it is accepted. However, Barnard recognized that many messages cannot be deliberately analyzed, judged, and accepted or rejected; rather, most types of directives, orders, and persuasive messages fall within a person's *zone of indifference.*

To visualize the idea of a zone of indifference, think of a horizontal line having a scale with zero percent as the center point and 100 at both ends. The wider the person's zone, the farther it extends in both directions towards the ends. A 100 percent willingness to go along shows the zone extending in both directions to the 100 percent marks. A complete rejection of the message (directive, order, request) shows a zone in which the marks are both touching zero.

100% ◄————————0————————► 100%

Willing   Rejection   Willing

Many messages in an organization are designed to widen the zone of indifference of employees. The width of a subordinate's zone tends to be different for each order; in one instance the subordinate may be warmly receptive and very willing to accept a request, for another the subordinate may be reluctant although not adamant about rejecting it, whereas in a third the subordinate may completely reject the request.

An instance of total authority communication rejection occurred during the Russo-Japanese War (1904–1905). The Russian ship *Potemkin,* according to the report, was conducting purposeless maneuvers in the Black Sea. The usual grudges held by sailors against officers were multiplied by a policy of harsh discipline. Knowing that the Russo-Japanese War was being badly mismanaged, agitators attempted to incite mutiny but made little progress on the *Potemkin*. However, one day the crew saw some maggoty meat hanging in the galley. In order to assure them that the meat was edible, the ship's doctor had to be called. At dinner the crew was served borscht made with the spoiling meat. As an act of rebellion the crew ate only bread and water, leaving the sickening soup untouched. This enraged the captain, who verbally attacked the crew in an effort to get them to eat. His effort failed, so the next officer in command stepped into the tense situation, called the armed guard, and ordered all sailors willing to eat to step forward. Of all the hundreds of crew members, all but thirty did. The officer ordered the stubborn crew members to be covered with a tarpaulin in preparation for having them shot. As the sailors huddled under the covering, the order to fire was given. The guards hesitated. At that moment other sailors rushed forward urging the guards to turn their rifles on the officers rather than their shipmates. While the senior officer shrieked commands and other officers stood aghast, the guards fired upon them. Most of the officers, including the captain, were shot and thrown overboard. Thus the formal authority was totally ineffective because it was rejected by both the crew and the armed guards (Moorehead, 1958).

Barnard equated authority and effective communication. The rejection of a communication was tantamount to rejection of the communicator's authority. By accepting a message or directive from another, a person grants authority to the formulator of the message and therefore adopts the position of a subordinate. Thus, Tannenbaum (1950) argued, the "sphere of authority possessed by a superior is defined for him by the sphere of acceptance" of his subordinates. The decision *not* to accept the authority and messages of a superior because the advantages may not be sufficient may result in some disadvantages, such as disciplinary action, monetary loss, or social disapproval. In some organizations the fear of such coercive acts may produce a willingness to accept a message even when the disadvantages alone do not.

Beyond a close relationship between authority and communication, Barnard viewed communication techniques (both written and oral) as essential to attaining the organization's goals and as the source of problems in the organization. "Communication techniques," he said, "shape the form and the internal economy of the organization. The absence of a suitable technique of communication would eliminate the possibility of adopting some purpose as a basis of organization" (p. 90). Thus it was largely Barnard who made communication a meaningful part of organization and management theory. He seemed thoroughly convinced that communication was the major shaping force of the organization.

Elton Mayo's Human Relations Theory

A year following Barnard's publication of *Functions,* Roethlisberger and Dickson (1939) issued their massive report on a large-scale investigation of productivity and social relations at the Hawthorne plant of the Western Electric Company. Referred to as *Management and the Worker,* it quickly became known as the *Hawthorne Studies.* The studies were conceived and directed by Elton Mayo with the assistance of Fritz Roethlisberger, both professors at Harvard University. Miller and Form (1951) refer to the Hawthorne Studies as the "first great scientific experiment in industry." A journal reviewer called it "the most outstanding study of industrial relations that has been published anywhere, anytime" (Miller & Form, p. 50). However, Whitehead, the statistician working on the studies, found "not a single correlation of enough statistical significance to be recognized by any competent statistician as having any meaning" (Miller & Form, p. 49).

What, then, was discovered that lead to such disparate, but at times laudatory, reactions to Mayo's work? The most pertinent results occurred during experiments on illumination. At first the researchers assumed that the brighter the lighting, the higher the worker output. Thus they decided to establish an experimental room with variable light conditions and a control room with constant light conditions. Two groups of workers were chosen to do their work in two different areas. Over a period of time illumination in the experimental room was increased to blinding intensity and then decreased to practically an absence of light. The results went like this: As the amount of illumination increased, so did worker efficiency in the experimental room; however, the efficiency of workers in the control room also increased. As lighting was diminished in the test room, efficiencies of both the test and the control groups increased slowly but steadily. When the illumination reached three foot-candles in the test room, operators protested, saying that they were hardly able to see what they were doing; at that point the production rate decreased. Up to that time the assemblers maintained their efficiency in spite of the handicap.

The results of the illumination experiments intrigued the researchers as well as management. So from 1927 to 1929, a superior team of researchers measured the effects of a wide variety of working conditions on employee production. The results were again consistent with the illumination experiments—regardless of the working conditions, production increased. The researchers came to the conclusion that these unusual and even more amazing results occurred because the six individuals in the experimental room became a team, with group relations being more important and powerful in determining morale and productivity than any of the working conditions—good or bad. The researchers concluded that the operators had no clear idea why they were able to produce more in the test room, but there was the feeling that "better output is in some way related to the distinctly pleasanter, freer, and happier working conditions" (Miller & Form, p. 48).

Two compelling conclusions have evolved out of the Hawthorne Studies, often referred to jointly as the *Hawthorne Effect:* (1) The very act of paying attention to people may change their attitudes and behavior, and (2) High morale and productivity are promoted if employees have opportunities for interaction with each other. Mayo, later in life (1945), wrote what has become a summation of the interests communication specialists bring to the analysis of organizations:

> I believe that social study should begin with careful observation of what may be described as communication: that is, the capacity of an individual to communicate his feelings and ideas to another, the capacity of groups to communicate effectively and intimately with each other. That is, beyond all reasonable doubt, the outstanding defect that civilization is facing today. (p. 21)

Taken together, the work of Barnard and Mayo represents a behavioral approach to organizations. Mayo is often attributed with initiating the *human relations movement.* In fact, Perrow (1973), building on the insights of Barnard and Mayo, asserted that the human relations movement came into its own following World War II. Sofer (1973) pointed out that Mayo and his colleagues created a scientific demonstration showing that "a group had a life of its own, complete with customs, norms, and effective social controls on its members" (p. 80). Guilbot (1968) observed that "after the Hawthorne studies it had to be granted that an informal structure of social relations did exist behind the formal organizational structure and that numerous phenomena could not be explained on any other grounds" (pp. 232–233). One great contribution of the early behavioral theorists was the reorientation of thinking about organizations and management from that of purely structure and task to considerations of people and morale.

One pointed criticism of the human relations movement is its overwhelming preoccupation with people and their relationships and its disregard of the total resources of an organization and its members. A concern about responding to both personal and organizational needs has been a significant consequence of the groundwork laid by early behavioral theorists. An important distinction is made currently between developing good human relations and developing the human resources of an organization. Organizational communication seeks to provide the background for developing the quality of human resources in an organization, rather than just developing the quality of human relations, as important as they may appear.

Bakke and Argyris' Fusion Theory

Sensing the enormity of the problem associated with satisfying both the divergent interests of individuals and the essential demands of the bureaucratic structure, Bakke (1950) proposed a *fusion process.* He reasoned that the organization, to some degree, molds the individual, while at the same time the individual also influences the organization. The result is an organization that is *personalized* by the individual employee and individuals who are *socialized* by the organization. Hence every employee takes on characteristics of the organization, and every position appears to be uniquely like the individuals who occupy them. After fusion (a.f.), every employee looks more like the organization, and every position in the organization is modified to the special interests of the individual.

Argyris (1957), a colleague of Bakke's at Yale University, expanded and refined Bakke's work. He argued that there is a basic incongruity of incompatibility between the needs of mature employees and the requirements of the formal organization. The organization has goals to accomplish that clash with the goals of individual employees. Employees experience frustration as a consequence of the incongruence. Some may leave; some may adapt; and some may stay, lower their work standards, and become apathetic and uninterested. Through this conflict others learn not to expect satisfaction from the job. Many people have learned from personal experience that adjusting to the demands of a formal organization is not easy and should not be expected to occur automatically.

Likert's Linking Pin Theory

Rensis Likert of the University of Michigan is credited with developing what is popularly known as the *linking pin model* of organization structure. The linking pin concept is one of overlapping groups. Each supervisor is a member of two

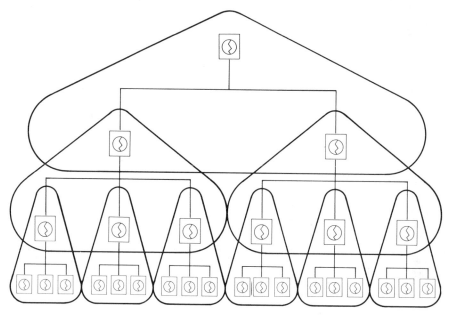

FIGURE 4.1   Linking Pin Model of Organization

groups: the leader of a lower unit and member of an upper unit. The supervisor functions as a linking pin, tying the work group to another group at the next level. The linking pin structure provides a group-to-group, in contrast to a person-to-person, relationship. Rather than fostering a downward orientation, a linking pin organization encourages an upward orientation. Communication, supervisory influence, and goal attainment are all directed upward in the organization. As Figure 4.1 implies, group processes play an important role in making the linking pin organization function efficiently. All groups must be equally effective, since the organization can be no stronger than its weakest group.

Luthans (1973) argued that the linking pin concept tends to emphasize and facilitate what is supposed to occur in the bureaucratic, classical structure. The superior-subordinate, hierarchical pattern, however, often results in a downward focus, while inhibiting upward and lateral communication. The slowness of group action, which is part of the linking pin organization, must be balanced with the positive advantages of participation—contributions to planning, more open communication, and member commitments—that accrue from the linking pin structure.

SYSTEMS THEORIES

Scott (1961) argues that "the only meaningful way to study organization . . . is as a system" (p. 15). He suggests that the basic parts of an organizational system are the individual and the personality that he or she brings to the system; the formal structure, which we have discussed at length earlier; the informal pattern of interactions; status and role patterns that create expectations; and the physical environment of work (Figure 4.2). These parts are woven into a configuration called an *organizational system*. All of the parts are interrelated and interact with each other. Each part is linked to all of the other parts. Although there are other theories about how the parts are connected, the primary linking process is communication.

The systems concept focuses on the arrangement of parts, relationships between parts, and the dynamics of the relationships that lead to unity or wholeness. The concept of *system* is so encompassing it defies easy definition. A simple definition would screen out the complexity and sophistication of the concept, and yet extensive explanation leads to intricacies that are not readily comprehensible. Although a detailed explanation of the contribution and influence of systems theory to organizational study is beyond the scope of this book, certain items warrant attention. Even at the most general level, systems concepts enable one to conceive of an organization as a whole that is greater than the sum of its parts by virtue of its dynamics. These dynamics take into account structure, relationships, and idiosyncratic behaviors.

General systems theorists (Bertalanffy, 1968; Boulding, 1965; Rapoport, 1968) have identified some principles that apply to all types of systems. That is, machines, organisms, and organizations all have similar processes and can be described with common tenets. We agree with Fisher (1978) that "system theory is a loosely organized and highly abstract set of principles, which serve to direct our thinking but which are subject to numerous interpretations" (p. 196). In the following discussion, we have adapted Fisher's explanation of the tenets of systems theory (pp. 196–204).

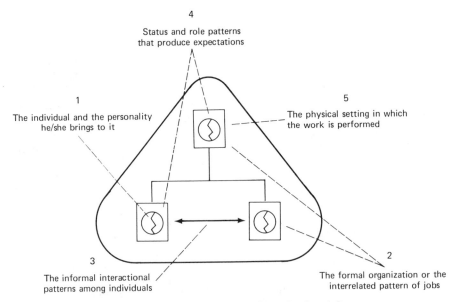

FIGURE 4.2 The Parts of an Organizational System

Any discussion of systems involves the notion of interdependence. Simply stated, interdependence suggests that a mutual dependence exists among components or units of a system. A change in one component brings about change in every other component. Understanding the concept of interdependence is an integral part of defining systems and systems theory.

1. *Nonsummativity.* Nonsummativity suggests that a system is not just a sum of its parts. When the components are related to each other in mutual dependence (interdependent), the system takes on an identity separate from the individual components. For example, what two people might build together through interaction is quite different from what might result by taking each individual's behavior and adding them together. The nonsummativity of components of a system is more important, systemically, than the individual units themselves.

2. *Elements of Structure, Function, and Evolution.* Structure refers to relationships between components of a system. Superior/subordinate relationships, for example, may be distinguished on the basis of status, a structural element. Structure reflects order. A bureaucracy, for example, is a highly structured system that reflects a high degree of order.

The actions one performs in conjunction with others are considered to be part of the functional element in a social system. Functions, or actions and behaviors, constitute the primary means by which people are identified in a social system. The person's actions are the events in a social system.

The evolution of a system, or the changes and nonchanges in a system over time, affects both the structural and functional elements, and the complexity of a system is related to the extent to which both functional and structural elements vary.

3. *Openness.* Organizations are social systems. Their boundaries are permeable, which allows them to interact with their environments, thereby importing energy and information. Open systems are characterized by *equifinality,* which means that "The same final state may be reached from different conditions and in different ways" (Bertalanffy, 1968, p. 40); it also means that organizations that start with the same initial conditions may reach different end states.

4. *Hierarchy.* A system may be a suprasystem to other systems within it as well as a subsystem to a larger system. The flow of information across the boundaries of a system can affect the structural-functional behaviors of the system. Systemic analysis of communication involves subsystems, systems, and suprasystems, and each represents a different level of analysis. Weick (1969, p. 45) suggests that "If there are different levels of analysis (e.g., individual, group, organization, society), the only way we can learn much about any of these levels is if we know how they are tied together, that is, how one level interacts with another level." These tenets will be explored further in the section that examines contemporary theory.

Katz and Kahn's Social Systems Theory

Classical and behavioral theories often refer to communication primarily in terms of forms of communication activity, rather than as a linking process. Communication as a linking process takes on special meaning if we accept Katz and Kahn's (1966) telling point that social structures differ from mechanical and biological structures. Physical and biological entities such as automobiles and animals have anatomical structures that can be identified even when they are not functioning. When a biological organism ceases to function, the physical body can still be examined in a postmortem analysis.

When a social system ceases to function, it no longer has an identifiable structure. The reason is that social systems are structures of events or happenings rather than physical parts and have no structure apart from their functioning. The communication network of an organization, for example, has little resemblance to the circulatory or nervous system of biological organisms, although we tend to compare the two quite often. Because the analogies seem impelling, we are frequently deterred from grasping the essential differences between social systems and biological systems.

Social systems consist, on the whole, of people. They are imperfect, but the constancy of relationships can be very high. In fact, organizations can have a very high turnover but still exist and function effectively. The *relationships among the people,* not the people themselves, allow an organization to persist far longer than the biological people who fill positions in the organization. Formal organizations have procedures by which the parts (people) can be readily replaced so they can continue to function into an unspecified future. Biological organisms have forces that wear out their parts which often cannot be replaced.

Katz and Kahn explain that most of our interactions with others are communicative acts (verbal and nonverbal, spoken and silent). "Communication—the exchange of information and the transmission of meaning—is the very essence of a social system or an organization" (p. 223). They assert that it is possible to subsume under the concept of communication such forms of social interaction as "exertion of influence, cooperation, social contagion or imitation, and leadership" (p. 224). As you shall see, we take a perspective consistent with this view and consider communication as the primary linking process in organizations with a number of corollary processes emerging out of the communicating that occurs in organizations. We refer to those special forms of communication as organizational communication skills and activities.

Systems theory recognizes that an organized state requires the introduction of constraints and restrictions to reduce random communication to channels that are appropriate for accomplishment of organizational goals. Organizational development, for example, may require the creation of new communication channels. Katz and Kahn claim that the "very nature of a social system . . . implies a selectivity of channels and communicative acts—a mandate to avoid some and to utilize others" (p. 226).

In summary, Scott (1961) points out that "organizations are comprised of parts which communicate with each other, receive messages from the outside world, and store information. Taken together, these communication functions of the parts comprise a configuration representing the total system" (p. 18). It might be said that, from a systems point of view, communication is the organization. Hawes (1974), in fact, has expressed this very point: "A social collectivity is patterned communicative behavior; communicative behavior does not occur *within* a network of relationships but is that network" (p. 500). For our purposes in an introductory book on organizational communication, we can assume the existence of organizations and proceed to explain and hopefully understand something about their functioning, the manner in which the people interrelate, and some of the impelling issues that affect the way in which the people and the organization develop. We shall treat some of these basic issues in the next part of this book.

Ad-hocracy and the Buck Rogers Theory

Some of our most improbable visions of space exploration have come from the fantasies of the creators of the fictional and famous figure Buck Rogers. Taking the lead from Buck, futuristic authors such as Alvin Toffler (1970) have written about *future shock* and the inevitable consequences of rapid change on all aspects of our lives. Formal organizations have been touched in these analyses. Toffler dedicates an entire chapter to "Organizations: The Coming Ad-hocracy." Bennis (1966) predicts "The Coming Death of Bureaucracy." Luthans (1973) observes that "many practicing managers are becoming disenchanted with traditional ways of organizing" (p. 168). The predictions indicate that we are moving into a postbureaucratic era of organizational theory based on the futuristic concept of rapidly changing organizational structures. Toffler describes it this way: "What we see here is nothing less than the creation of a disposable division—the organizational equivalent of paper dresses or throw-away tissues" (p. 133).

According to Bennis (1966), the social structure of the *new* bureaucracy will be, in a word, *temporary*. The organization will consist largely of *task forces* that are created in response to a particular problem. The manager, in an organization of continuously changing structure, becomes a coordinator, a connector, a linker of various project groups. Skills in human interaction and communication will be of great value, since some of the major tasks will be relaying information and mediating understanding and differences between groups. Bennis argues that people will "have to learn to develop quick and intense relationships on the job, and learn to bear the loss of more enduring work relationships" (p. 35).

Toffler summarizes the characteristics of the new bureaucracy, called an *ad-hocracy,* as fast-moving, rich with information, highly active, constantly changing, filled with transient units and extremely mobile individuals. In the ad-hocracy, it is the work itself, the problem to be solved, the task to be done that attracts the commitment of employees, rather than the organization. Even professional loyalties become short term, because specialists derive their rewards from the intrinsic satisfaction of doing a difficult task well. They are loyal to their standards, not their superiors; to their problems, not their jobs. The ad-hocrats employ their skills and talents in solving problems within the temporary groups and environment of the organization, but only as long as the problems interest them.

Toffler notes that the titles of positions in some ad-hocracies are prefaced by the term *associate*. The term suggests an equality typical of the new organization— that is, *associate* connotes one who works with, rather than is subordinate to, others in the organization. Its use reflects a shift from vertical hierarchies to more lateral communication patterns. In a consulting and training company, we adopted the title *Organizational Associates* to convey the meaning that colleagues are coequals in the attack on organizational problems. The professional staff of associates is highly task oriented, deriving satisfaction from the anticipation of dealing with problems wherever they occur.

Toffler offers some words of caution that may lead us to the next part of this book. He guardedly observes that the "Ad-hocracy increases the adaptability of organizations; but it strains the adaptability of people" (p. 150). Each change of relationship in the organization brings with it some costs in personal adjustment, meaningful relations, and satisfaction. Social tension, psychological strain, and individual coping are all aggravated by the rapid change, temporary work circumstances, and lack of organizational commitment. The constant changes in organizational relationships place a heavy adaptive burden on people. Scrambling, we are propelled by our work into the Buck Rogers organization of the future.

For some the future may be arriving too soon. For most of us the future is now. For example, in 1965 Stewart provided guidelines for "Making Project Management Work." Project organization is the nearest equivalent we currently have to ad-hocracy. Even today the literature on organization theory is replete with descriptions of *matrix* organizational patterns, *intermix* project organization, *aggregate* project organization, *individual and staff* project organization, and *free-form* organization. A common contemporary Buck Rogers theory of organization is the matrix organization. It is a project organization superimposed on the more traditional functional organization. The functional department heads have line authority over projects by collaboration between the appropriate functional and project managers. Many conclude, consistent with Toffler's speculations, that matrix organization has reduced corporate loyalty and identification with the organization. Nevertheless, Luthans (1973) pointed out "that many modern organizations which are facing tremendous structural and technical complexity have no choice but to move to such an arrangement" (p. 177).

Naisbitt and Aburdene (1985) contend that the corporation must be reinvented to meet the demands of the new information society. They point out that companies such as Scandinavian Airlines Systems, W. L. Gore & Associates, Inc., and New Hope Communication have radically restructured their organization charts. These innovative companies represent current efforts to create the corporation of tomorrow.

Gore, Inc., stresses self-management and an open organization. According to Pacanowsky (1987), Gore's structure

> *looks like* a lattice, a regular cross-hatching of lines, representing an unrestricted flow of communication with no overlay of lines of authority. As Bill Gore defines it, a lattice organization means "one-on-one communication" with whomever you need to talk to in order to get a job done, no fixed or assigned authority but leadership that evolves over time and that fluctuates with the specific problems at hand that most need attention, and tasks and functions that are organized through personally made commitments—not through job descriptions and organization charts. (p. 4)

Pacanowsky suggests that Gore, Inc., sustains an "empowering culture" by following six rules:

1. Distribute power and opportunity widely.
2. Maintain a full, open, and decentralized communication system.
3. Use integrative problem-solving methods.
4. Practice challenge in an environment of trust.
5. Reward and recognize people to encourage high-performance ethics and self-responsibility.

6. Become wise by living through and learning from organizational ambiguity, inconsistency, contradiction, and paradox.

Matrix, lattice, project, and ad-hocratic organizations are the communication organizations of the present and future. The study of communication is, in such circumstances, the study of organization. Management in matrix and lattice configurations is simply the practice of organizational communication. Present organization practices confirm early theoretical predictions; the first function of an executive is, indeed, to create and maintain a system of communication. The communication system is the organization. Organizational communication is the Buck Rogers theory of organization.

SUMMARY

In this chapter, we analyzed behavioral and systems theories of organization. Behavioral theories included Barnard's authority-communication theory, which made the first function of an executive that of developing and maintaining a system of communication; Mayo's human relations theory, which made informal group relations more important and powerful in determining morale and productivity than working conditions; Bakke and Argyris' fusion theory, which proposed an incompatibility between employee needs and organization needs which is minimized by personalizing the organization and socializing the individual and results in the fusion of employee and organization; and Likert's linking pin theory, which conceives of the organization as a number of interconnected groups in which each supervisor is a leader of a lower unit and a member of a higher unit and serves as the linking pin connecting the groups. Katz and Kahn's social systems theory, which focuses on relationships among people and conceives of an organization as parts that communicate with each other, receive messages, and store information, and Toffler's and Bennis' futuristic ad-hocracy, which functions with temporary relationships, disposable divisions, associates, and matrix patterns, were offered as current views of organizations. The lattice scheme of organization has been presented as an example of open communication, shared responsibility, and commitment.

A SUBJECTIVIST'S NOTATION

The behavioral theorists altered classical theories by moving from considerations of pure structure and task to those of people and morale. However, the alterations still only represent variations on underlying themes of objectivist (bureaucratic) views. To elaborate, we will look at the notions of structure, goals, communication, and organization.

Although the work cited in this chapter stresses the importance of informal organization, it does not challenge the legitimacy and predominance of formal organization. A common suggestion is that the informal and formal should be negotiated, or fused together. But it is clear that the resulting structure is still conceived by those in charge. The informal organization is viewed as something that requires attention so that it does not disturb the real work of the organization.

The literature suggests that looking at goals means examining the organization's goals. It is implied that these goals are universal, agreed upon, and understood by everyone. Just as in the classical theories, the behavioral theorists cling to a rational (objectivist) model of organization. Pfeffer (1982) states that "the critical distinguishing feature of organization theories taking the rational perspective is the element of conscious, foresightful action reasonably autonomously constructed to achieve some goal or value" (p. 7). Experience in the organizational setting teaches us that there are multiple goals arising from various factions. These are negotiated with more formally stated goals, and the result may or may not resemble the original concept of a hierarchical organization or structure. The rational (objective) perspective also suggests that organizations and people know what their goals are before they are carried out; therefore, reaching those goals is just a matter of reconciling differences between the individual and the organization. It is more complex than that. Many times organizations do not know what their goals are until they have been achieved. We will develop this idea more fully in the discussion of organizational processes.

The role of communication becomes more visible and central in the behavioral theories, but the function of communication is much the same as in the bureaucratic model. Communication is deemed essential to attaining the organization's goals, and these goals are managerial goals. Communication effectiveness is thought of in managerial terms. Mayo's human relations theory is concerned with the link between communication and productivity. Barnard touts communication technique as a way to exercise authority. In the Likert scheme communication may be directed upward, but its major purpose is to inform the hierarchy so that adjustments can be made. The primary function of communication in these theories is regulation and control.

Although the behavioral models are more people oriented than their predecessors, there is still a clear-cut distinction between something called an organization and the behavior of the people in it. The implied definition still emphasizes organization as a concrete, "real" entity, which can have a formal structure or an informal st ucture. Which is the "real" organization? The fusion process cited earlier moves back to the formal structure. Behavioral theorists view people and their behavior as an important influence in the organization, but structure is still the dominant force.

Looking at the organization as a social system not only gives a more comprehensive picture but squares with the commonsense notion that an organization is composed of structural and personal dimensions and the interaction of those dimensions. Although this concept moves beyond classical models of organization, it still obscures the human element in organization. The system is often conceived of as having a life of its own, which is generated and guided by underlying principles that are applicable across biological and social structures. This concept promotes a mechanistic view of human behavior and communication. The unique social construction and the interpretation of interaction between individuals is accorded little influence in such schemes.

Silverman (1971, pp. 39–40) states:

> The Systems approach stresses the way in which the action of the parts is structured by the system's need for stability and goal-consensus, and emphasizes the processes of

integration and adaptation. The alternative approach argues . . . that organisations are merely the ever-changing product of the self-interested actions of their members. . . . "Society makes Man" (Systems), "Man makes Society" (Action).

He goes on to suggest that the real debate is about the relative merits of analyzing organizations "from the transcendental view of the problems of the system as a whole, with human action being regarded as a reflection of system needs, or from the view of interaction that arises as actors attach meanings to their own actions and to the actions of others" (p. 41). The subjectivist position stresses that individuals and their interactions construct the system, and, although the system may constrain individuals, it does so by meanings that are human products.

When organizations are thought of in terms of interdependent parts that function to sustain the system, there is a tendency to downplay the significance of socially constructed meaning. The system can take on a machine-like image in which the organization is seen as a large information processor whose parts are not only interdependent but interchangeable. Relationships between people are only important in such a formulation because the relationships allow the system to function and sustain itself. One is led to believe that if the people were removed, the organization would still exist by virtue of established relationships, or if people were shifted about, the same relationships would remain. Organization is thought of as very ordered and concrete. Can relationships exist without people? Does "relationship between roles" refer to the prescribed behavior, or the actual behavior and interpretation of that behavior? The subjectivist position maintains that the life given to an organization is just that—given by interacting participants who focus on the meaning of that interaction.

General systems theory emphasizes the similarity of processes that occur with a machine, organism, or organization. If the metaphors of machine and organism are taken too literally, one is likely to forget that organizations have no physical parts and have no structures apart from their functioning. People's actions are significant to what an organization is. The search for similarity of processes can create a false order in which humans are seen as highly predictable and merely reactive.

The open systems approach to organization focuses on the environment in which the system is located. Organizations operate across boundaries and transact with other social systems to ensure their survival. Organizations are systems that are part of other systems, such as institutions and societies. The challenge is to identify those aspects of the environment that the system (organization) must adapt to in order to sustain itself at an optimum level. The factors in the environment are said to provide the basis for organizational structure (Woodward, 1965; Emery & Trist, 1965; Burns & Stalker, 1961; Lawrence & Lorsch, 1967). The approach suggests that organizational adaptation is a rather simple and concrete process. However, Silverman (1971, pp. 36–37) challenges these notions by asking

why, if organisations "must" adapt to their environment, they do so, if at all, at such varying rates? The answer that is normally given is that one of the components of the system, . . . is the predispositions of the members. . . . Their predispositions derive from the cultural system of the society and are another input into the organisation which must be taken into account. . . . It may also be argued, however, that the environment, as perceived by the observer, never exerts this sort of influence on patterns of interaction within organisations. The explanation of why people act as they do may lie not in a combination of "objective" and "subjective" factors, but in a network of meanings which constitute a "world-taken-for-granted."

It may be helpful at this point to review Figure 1.1 in Chapter 1. The systems perspective can be located toward the objective end of the continuum.

Communication from a systems perspective places attention on the acquisition, processing, and dissemination of information. This concept is indeed important, but it is necessary to remember that information and situations are created, and responses are dependent on the meanings held by organizational participants. The following chapter will extend those ideas.

REFERENCES

Argyris, Chris, *Personality and Organization.* New York: Harper & Row, Pub., 1957.

Bakke, E. Wight, *Bonds of Organization.* New York: Harper & Row, Pub., 1950.

Barnard, Chester I., *The Functions of the Executive.* Cambridge, Mass.: Harvard University Press, 1938.

Bennis, Warren G., "The Coming Death of Bureaucracy," *Think Magazine* (November–December 1966), 30–35.

Bertalanffy, Ludwig Von, *General System Theory: Foundations, Development, Applications.* New York: George Braziller, Inc., 1968.

Boulding, Kenneth E., "General Systems Theory—The Skeleton of Science," *Management Science,* 2 (1965), 197–208.

Burns, T., and G. M. Stalker, *The Management of Innovation.* London: Tavistock, 1961.

Emery, F. E., and E. L. Trist, "The Causal Texture of Organizational Environments," *Human Relations,* 18 (1965), 21–32.

Fisher, B. Aubrey, *Perspectives on Human Communication.* New York: Macmillan, 1978.

Guilbot, O. Benoit, "The Sociology of Work," *International Encyclopedia of the Social Sciences,* Vol. 7, 232–233. New York: Macmillan, 1968.

Hawes, Leonard C., "Social Collectivities as Communication: Perspective on Organizational Behavior," *Quarterly Journal of Speech,* 60 (December 1974), 500.

Katz, Daniel, and Robert L. Kahn, *The Social Psychology of Organizations.* New York: John Wiley, 1966.

Lawrence, Paul R., and Jay W. Lorsch, *Organization and Environment.* Cambridge, Mass.: Harvard University Press, 1967.

Likert, Rensis, *New Patterns of Management.* New York: McGraw-Hill, 1961.

Luthans, Fred, *Organizational Behavior.* New York: McGraw-Hill, 1973.

Mayo, Elton, *The Social Problems of an Industrial Civilization.* Cambridge, Mass.: Harvard University Press, 1945.

Miller, Delbert C., and William H. Form, *Industrial Sociology.* New York: Harper & Row, Pub., 1951.

Moorehead, Alan, "The Russian Revolution, Part II: Relentless Rise of the Conspiracy," *Life,* 44 (January 20, 1958), 60–70, 75–82.

Naisbitt, John, and Patricia Aburdene, *Re-inventing the Corporation.* New York: Warner Books, 1985.

Pacanowsky, Michael, "Communication in the Empowering Organization," Paper presented at the University of Utah Summer Conference on Interpretive Approaches to the Study of Organizational Communication, Alta, Utah, 1987.

Perrow, Charles, "The Short and Glorious History of Organizational Theory," *Organizational Dynamics,* 2 (Summer 1973), 2–15.

Pfeffer, Jeffrey, *Organizations and Organization Theory.* Boston: Pitman, 1982.

Rapoport, Anatol, "Foreword" in *Modern Systems Research for the Behavioral Scientist,* Walter Buckley, ed. Chicago: Aldine, 1968.

Roethlisberger, Fritz J., and William J. Dickson, *Management and the Worker.* Cambridge, Mass.: Harvard University Press, 1939.

Scott, William G., "Organization Theory: An Overview and Appraisal," *Journal of the Academy of Management* (April 1961), 15, 18.

Silverman, David, *The Theory of Organisations.* New York: Basic Books, 1971.

Sofer, Cyril, *Organization in Theory and Practice.* New York: Basic Books, 1973.

Stewart, John M., "Making Project Management Work," *Business Horizons* (Fall 1965), 57–59.

Tannenbaum, Robert, "Managerial Decision Making," *The Journal of Business,* 23 (1950), 22–39.

Toffler, Alvin, *Future Shock.* New York: Random House, 1970.

Weick, Karl E., *The Social Psychology of Organizing.* Reading, Mass.: Addison-Wesley, 1969.

Woodward, Joan, *Industrial Organization: Theory and Practice.* London: Oxford University Press, 1965.

5

Contemporary Theories

Toward Subjectivism

The behavioral and social systems theories discussed in Chapter 4 were categorized as transitional theories because they represent a more subjective position on the continuum (Figure 1.1). As the interpretations move along that continuum they stress a more central role for the symbolic behavior and creative capacities of humans. We are not suggesting that the more subjective theories are the "right" ones, but that various positions on the continuum are receiving increasing attention today. Some theorists contend that this is not just a slight modification of old theories but a paradigm (world view) revolution (Lincoln, 1985).

Whether we should assimilate and adopt contemporary subjective theories may be arguable, but there is little question that they represent changes in fundamental ways of thinking that challenge the dominant scientific/objective view of the world. In this chapter, we will discuss two theories that contrast with the objective view of organization. They do not, of course, represent all contemporary thinking about organizations, but they are the theories that have had a major impact on the field. (Clark, 1985; Geertz, 1973; Schwartz & Ogilvy, 1979). As a preface to a detailed analysis of the two major perspectives, we will briefly summarize dimensions of the corresponding world view so that you might see how it applies to organizational theory. What does the organization look like from this changing perspective?

1. Organizations are viewed as being more complex, and attempts to reduce them to simple elements and processes are questioned. The organization tends to develop a complex culture that has unique characteristics.

2. The idea of an order of natural and social laws is replaced by notions of multiple sets of order and interaction between the orders. Organizations are composed of several sets of order, with dynamics of interaction that are mutual and occurring at the same time.

3. Organization is viewed less in machine terms and more in terms of the holograph metaphor to get at the complex dynamics of the organization. Lincoln (1985) states:

> The power of this metaphor [holograph] is that every piece contains complete information about the whole. This is a particularly powerful concept when considering, for instance, genetic materials, in which a single cell is said to contain information about the entire organism, or in organizations, in which information about some subunit might provide information regarding the whole operation. (34–35)

4. The organization and its future state is seen as less predictable and controllable than suggested by earlier theoretical models.

5. Organizational behavior is better reflected by a complex causal model than one that emphasizes simple cause-and-effect relationships. Notions of mutual causality are more useful in representing the dynamics of growth, change, and evolution.

6. Students of organization are showing increasing willingness to consider various ways of viewing organizational behavior, and the laws-and-instances explanation is giving ground to one that emphasizes cases-and-interpretation. The search for foundational knowledge that can be generalized as truth is giving way to the idea that a particular perspective produces its own brand of knowledge and truth. The search for some grand, comprehensive theory that might deal with the complexity of organization is viewed with increasing skepticism.

In the following sections we will describe two contemporary theories that reflect shifts in thinking that have been taking place in organizational theory.

WEICK'S THEORY OF ORGANIZING

The work of Karl Weick is provocative and influential. Some of the spirit of this work is captured by Lundberg (1982) when he explains:

> To the Alice in each of us, Karl Weick is the white rabbit. The allusion, of course, is to Lewis Carroll's magical tale. Recall the proper English girl, Alice, in her garden, a somewhat formal garden with distinct boundaries. Along comes the white rabbit who catches Alice's attention and prompts her to follow him through the garden boundary, whereupon she fell into a new world. Professor Weick's book does draw our attention, and, if we allow ourselves, will enable us to breach conventional conceptual practices and intellectual domains. Like Alice we may explore and achieve new experiences with the paradoxical wonders of what we thought were familiar territories. (113–114)

In the following sections we will examine Weick's model by extending the key ideas presented in the previous chapters. The model is heavily invested in systems theory, but that is only one theoretical strand in the overall model. Kreps

(1986) explains the model on the basis of "sociocultural evolutionary" theory, information theory, and systems theory. While the model represents a systems theory, the treatment is distinctly different in that human processes receive much more prominence. Our purpose is to illustrate the subjective aspects of the theory and discuss some of the implications for organizational communication.

Conception of Organization

Weick (1979) states that "the word *organization* is a noun, and it is also a myth. If you look for an organization you won't find it. What you will find is that there are events, linked together, that transpire within concrete walls and these sequences, their pathways, and their timing are the forms we erroneously make into substances when we talk about an organization" (p. 88). The focus is clearly on *organizing* rather than *organization*. The process of organizing creates what is called an organization. Emphasis is placed on activity and process. Does an organization have structure? Yes, it does, but "The structure that determines how an organization acts and how it appears is the structure that is established by regular patterns of interlocked behaviors" (Weick, 1979, p. 90). The organization is a system that adapts and sustains itself by reducing the uncertainty that it faces. It is a system of "interlocked behaviors," and that is the key to its functioning. Behaviors are interlocked when the behaviors of one person are contingent on the behaviors of others.

Critical Features of Organizing

Theories discussed in the previous chapters view structure, behavior, and environment as key organizational factors. That is also true of the Weick scheme, but the factors themselves are seen from a different perspective. Structure, in earlier theories, was viewed as hierarchy, policies, and organizational design, whereas Weick sees structure as activity and, more specifically, as communication activity. The organizational structure is defined by interlocked behaviors.

The role of people and their behavior is noted in discussions of behavioral and systems theories. However, those approaches look at how people and their behavior serve the organization. In such theories, communication is typically thought to reflect important underlying characteristics of the organization. A distinction is made between behavior and structure. The Weick formulation suggests that structure is identified by its organizing behaviors. Communication does not reflect important processes; it is the important process. Process creates structure. Weick's conception is that a system is clearly human in nature. Humans do not simply serve an organization; they are the organization.

Human beings face a complex and often uncertain environment, which Weick maintains is the reason for organizing. In Chapter 4 we cited a number of theorists who give priority to the role of environment. They have been referred to as *environmental determinists* because they view the environment as determining everything from organizational design to specific organizational behaviors. Again, the notion is that once the environment has been properly identified, a fit can be made between the organization and the environment to ensure continuity and optimum functioning of the organization. A transaction takes place between organization and environment. The term *environment* might refer to market conditions, competition, laws and regulations, and technology.

Weick does not draw a sharp boundary between organization and environment. He takes a more subjective view and argues that people are actively involved in creating the world about them. Organization members do not simply react; they create. They "enact" their environment through interaction and the creation of meaning. The environment in large part is socially constructed, so organizational members are looking at a creation rather than an objective reality. Any event that occurs is a creation—through the interpretation of those who decide what happened and the significance it might have. We will elaborate this idea in the section "Implications for Organizational Communication." The main point for now is that "rather than talking about adapting to an external environment, it may be more correct to argue that organizing consists of adapting to an enacted environment, an environment which is constituted by the actions of interdependent human actors" (Weick, 1969, p. 27).

What is involved in organizing? Weick (1979) defines organizing "as a consensually validated grammar for reducing equivocality by means of sensible interlocked behaviors" (p. 3). *Consensual validation* means that organizational reality arises out of experiences that are shared and validated by others. These experiences are shared with others through *symbol systems. Grammar* refers to the rules, conventions, and practices of the organization. These conventions help people get things done and provide the basis for interpreting what has been done. *Equivocality* refers to the level of uncertainty or ambiguity that organizational members face. Organizing helps reduce the uncertainty about the information that confronts organizational members when they are trying to make decisions that enable the organization to survive and succeed. The phrase *sensible interlocked behaviors* in Weick's definition represents a key idea embedded in the subjectivist point of view. Interlocked behaviors are communication behaviors in which meaning becomes a socially negotiated process. What is sensible or "real" is dependent upon the consensual validation (agreement and corroboration) between organizational members. Organizational reality is a social construction that takes place through interaction.

Organizations come into being because organizing activity is necessary to combat the ambiguity and uncertainty that humans face. Organizations must manage this equivocality, and they do so by giving meaning to events. Weick is quite specific about the behaviors of organizing. The critical unit of analysis is the *double interact,* in which A communicates to B, B responds to A, and A makes some adjustment or gives some response to B. This kind of specific communication activity forms the basis of organizing. These interlocked communication behaviors enable the organization to process information. Organizations also cope with the equivocality of information by the use of rules. The less equivocal the message input into the system, the more likely it will be that preset rules will be used. The more equivocal the message input into the system, the more likely it will be that communication cycles (double interacts) will be used to deal with the uncertainty. The more uncertainty an organization faces, the greater the requirement for the use of communication cycles.

The Process of Organizing

There are three major phases in the process of organizing. Weick (1979) specifies these phases as "enactment (bracketing some portion of the stream of experience for further attention), selection (imposing some finite set of interpretations on the bracketed portion), and retention (storage of interpreted segments for future application)'' (p. 45). Rules and communication cycles are applied in each phase when organizational members process information.

The *enactment phase* simply means that organizational members recreate their environment by assigning and negotiating a particular meaning for an event. In the *selection phase,* rules and communication cycles are used to determine sufficient reduction of equivocality. The *retention phase* allows the organization to store information about the way the organization has responded to various situations. Successful strategies become rules that can be applied in the future. The various phases have an impact on each other. For example, retention knowledge may guide the organization in its enactment and selection processes.

Thus far we have looked at the notions of organization, organizing, and organizing phases developed by Weick. In the following sections we will consider the more general aspects of his work and its implications from a subjectivist stance.

The Nature of Organizations/Humans

It is appropriate to align organizations and humans because the organization is a human system—a system constructed by humans. In the system conceived by Weick, things are in a constant state of change (evolution). Events in human systems are seldom, if ever, of a singular cause-effect nature but are more clearly represented by dynamic interaction and multideterminism. Change rather than stability is the norm, and evolutionary change is an inherent function of any organization that tries to maintain itself. The processes of organizing constitute the lifeblood of the organization in this adaptive process. The tenets of systems theory discussed in the Chapter 4 are applicable to Weick's theory. The concept of openness is especially relevant. Weick goes beyond the typical systems theorist by suggesting that organizations not only interact with their environments, but they enact them. The creative/adaptive processes in rules and communication cycles exhibit the concept of equifinality. The negotiation of meaning greatly influences the end state of an organization.

We will not detail the relevance of each tenet, but the concept of *interdependence* merits some attention. As you recall, the idea suggests that there is mutual dependence among components or units in an organization. A change in one component brings about change in every other component. This concept further suggests that the systemic character of an organization is a carefully ordered one in which units are tightly bound together. Such systems are said to be *tightly coupled.* Couplings refer to processes that affect the joint behavior of organizational components. Weick (1976) posits the notion of *loosely coupled systems.* An event that takes place in a system might affect other components of that system, but not right away. The event could be absorbed by one component and be passed on to others at a later date. An analogy sometimes used to illustrate loose coupling is that of a set of dominoes. If the dominoes are placed standing on end at regular intervals and in a straight line, a push (an event) at the head of the line will bring all of the dominoes down. This version illustrates a tightly coupled system. If the dominoes are spaced at irregular intervals, a push on one will make it fall as well as maybe one or two others. One domino may teeter and fall a bit later than the others—an event analogous to a loosely coupled system. Such systems not only exist, but they are often highly desirable. Loosely coupled systems have both functional and dysfunctional aspects. For example, components of an organization may persist because the organization is less inclined to respond to each change in the environment; but the system may not be selective about what is preserved. When facing a new situation, one component of a system can adapt with relative ease without affecting the rest of the system; of course, this means less uniformity and standardization in the system, which may be a shortcoming. If part of the system fails, that failure may be confined to that part of the system; on the negative side, however, help to that part of the system might be delayed because of its independent nature.

Weick's view of the organization raises questions about the existence and even the desirability of a rational, goal-directed, and tightly ordered system. According to earlier theories, in a rational organization a problem could be seen and defined, possible solutions could be carefully generated, and the best solution could be selected. The underlying assumption was that thought precedes action. Weick (1977a) asserts, however, that "organizations talk to themselves in order to clarify their surroundings and learn more about them. . . . Organizations examine retrospectively the very displays that initially they created as pretexts for sense making. Organizations talk in order to discover what they are saying, act in order to discover what they are doing" (p. 282). This idea suggests that action preceding thought may be the rule rather than the exception. This retrospective sense-making process is a departure from classical models. Goals may be formulated and accounted for after action has been taken. For example, Weick (1985) advises administrators to "be willing to leap before you look. If you look before you leap, you may not see anything. Action generates outcomes that ultimately provide the raw material for seeing something" (p. 133). Weick (1985) notes that in contemporary discussions of organization, "rationality is viewed (1) as a set of prescriptions that change as the issue changes, (2) as a facade created to attract resources and legitimacy, and (3) as a postaction process used retrospectively to invent reasons for the action" (p. 110).

How much order is there in an organization? The language of organizational theories includes efficiency, predictability, proactive planning, data-based decision making—all terms that imply a high degree of order that is predetermined. Weick (1977b) suggests that "the effective organization is (1) garrulous, (2) clumsy, (3) superstitious, (4) hypocritical, (5) monstrous, (6) octopoid, (7) wandering, and (8) grouchy" (pp. 193–194). This language portrays a very different image of the organization. Weick reminds us that the stream of experience can be chopped up and labeled in arbitrary but reasonable ways. We cannot elaborate on each label here, but let's examine the notion of garrulousness. This term means that organizations talk a great deal and that talk defines and constrains effectiveness. "What organizations say and do provides displays that they can examine reflectively to understand what is occurring" (Weick, 1977a, p. 195). "What is occurring" serves as the data for decision making and is produced by the quality and quantity of talk. Viewed in this way, the garrulous label not only makes sense but also allows us to see different dimensions of the organization. The labels suggest that organizations are human and, as such, their behaviors are subjective in nature. Creations may come about through searching, trial-and-error, and what might be labeled irrational behaviors under other schemes.

Weick (1983, p. 28) presents an analogy that illustrates the value of behaviors that may not fit with traditional theories. Imagine a clear glass jug that contains flies and bees. When the jug is placed in a window and a shaft of sunlight hits it, the flies and bees behave differently. The bees cluster (respond in an orderly way) toward the sunlight even as the heat rises. The flies zing about and bounce off the walls of the jug, but they eventually escape the deadly heat by passing through the jug's mouth. The bees are not so fortunate; they fail to engage in what might be called a variety of searching or random behaviors, which are clearly functional in this case. An organization's capacity for variety, what may be called random behavior, may be very important to survival. This is not to say that order is absent. "Organizations may be anarchies, but they are organized anarchies. Organizations may be loosely coupled, but they are loosely coupled systems. Organizations may resort to garbage can decision making, but garbage cans have borders that impose some structure" (Weick, 1985, p. 109).

Implications for Organizational Communication

To study organization is to study organizing behavior, and the heart of that behavior is communication. Organizations talk in order to know; talk constitutes their intelligence and adaptive capacity. To discover what organizations are thinking, it is critical to examine the interlocked behaviors (double interacts) of the members. What people say and validate with each other produces an environment that organizes their activities—especially their thinking.

Talk is the raw data of sense making and decision making. Individuals actively construct their worlds. The question is not "Have we discovered the correct underlying order?" but "What order have we created and what impact does it have?" Smircich (1983) applies the "enacted environment" concept to management by explaining that "managers must look to their actions and inactions, not to the environment, for explanations of their situation. The environment often serves as a convenient scapegoat for placing blame and denying responsibility" (p. 230).

According to Weick (1977a), people make sense out of experience with the aid of *punctuation* and *connection*. "Punctuation means chopping the stream of experience into sensible, nameable, and named units, and the activity of connection involves imposing relationships, typically causal relationships, among the punctuated elements" (p. 280). Because of the arbitrary nature of this labeling process, it is important to know what the raw data are and how the data are generated. Then it is possible to know how organizations interpret that data and on what basis.

Weick (1985) gives a number of implications for administrative practice. One that is particularly relevant to organizational communication is:

> To manage meaning is to view your organization as a set of procedures for arguing and interpreting. In any organizational assessment, ask questions such as these: How do we declare winners of the argument? When do we interpret? What interpretations do we tend to favor (blind spots?)? Whose interpretations seem to stick? (p. 133)

He focuses, then, on communication and the role that it plays in structuring a world that prompts one decision over another.

To consider a created world is also to consider the language of that world. The language that sounds so right—"efficient," "cost-effective"—may screen out thinking about how the labels were attached. Perhaps an octopoid organization with gangly tentacles has more to recommend it than a systemic one with an orderly algorithm. In addition, workable disorder casts doubt on the notion of an ideal organization that contains the right mix of the right elements.

Weick's theory of organizing challenges taken-for-granted ways of thinking and allows us to see the significance of a subjective view of the world. We appreciate Weick's (1977) statement that

> talk about "a reality" is simply one way that people try to make sense out of the stream of experience that flows by them. To say that there is a reality, an environment, and then to search for and discover underlying patterns in those superimposed structures is one way to make sense of that stream. But the tenuousness of this process, nevertheless, as well as the actor's central role in its execution, are captured only if we remain attentive to reality as metaphor. (p. 278)

This alternative view gives us insight into human behavior and communication. In the next part of the chapter we will discuss another prominent subjective world view.

A CULTURAL THEORY OF ORGANIZATION

The "buzz word" for organizational study and consulting in the 1960s and throughout much of the 1970s was *systems*. The rational, objective view of the world was, and still is, in vogue. However, the term *culture* may certainly be said to have achieved the status of a buzz word in the late 1970s and into the 1980s. Buzz words are "in" words that are usually used in a variety of ways not only because they represent current ideas, but also because they indicate that the user is "with" the state of the art. Such terms are attention grabbing but often misleading. When Hi Fi (high fidelity) sound was new, one restaurant advertised a Hi Fi Sandwich. Explain that one! In the following sections we will discuss why the concept of culture has achieved serious consideration, explore concepts of organizational culture, examine organizational culture issues, and, finally, point out some implications for organizational communication.

Culture and the Shift Toward Subjectivism

In the past twenty years there has been growing concern about the role of human action and symbolic behavior in organizational study. Theorists (Weick, 1969; Silverman, 1970, among a number of others) have raised significant questions about a rational model of organizational behavior. Symbolic behavior is deemed to be significant; yet it is unaccounted for in a rational model that emphasizes structure and environmental adaptation. Because symbolic processes often contradict the premises of objectivity, they cannot be simply tacked on to rational models. Traditional rational models cannot bear the weight of subjective views because they represent a different world view (paradigm). This recognition has enhanced the appeal of subjective approaches.

Although students of organizational behavior tend to expect too much out of theories, it is true that rational theories of human behavior have been a disappointment in terms of predicting behavior. Principles derived from such theories are more articles of faith than a set of reliable prescriptions. Explanations that follow an objective view of the world tend to account for the bare bones of the organization but exclude the soul. People need to get a "feel" for the organization in order to know how to react to any information about it. An organization is not just any object of study; it is a human enterprise. The reaction to past models of organizational behavior, then, has prompted a shift toward subjectivism and the cultural concept.

The market appeal of the term "culture" among academics and practitioners should not be discounted. To explain this statement we must explore some of the language associated with objective and subjective views. Those views that tend toward the objective view of reality and human nature have been labeled as the *functionalist* perspective (Parsons, 1964). Structural, behavioral, and social systems theories represent this perspective. They are concerned with the mechanisms that secure stability of the organization. Organizational analysis focuses on the efficiency of the processes and structures that maintain the system. Some of the metaphors associated with the functionalist perspective include machines, organisms, and systems.

Subjective views of reality and human nature are called the *interpretive* perspective (Morgan, 1980). This perspective maintains that the social world does not exist in a concrete sense, but that it is constructed by the interactions and consensual validation of individuals. Analysis from this perspective centers on how organizational reality is created and the understanding of symbolic discourse that makes up organizational life. Relevant subjective schools of thought for the interpretive perspective include hermeneutics, ethnomethodology, phenomenology, and symbolic interactionism. Some of the metaphors generated by the interpretive perspective include *accomplishment* (Garfinkel, 1967); *enacted sense making* (Weick, 1977a); *language game* (Wittgenstein, 1968); *text* (Ricoeur, 1971); and *culture* (Pondy & Mitroff, 1979; Turner, 1971). Much of the language of subjectivism does not help us have an image of the organization. The metaphors are abstract and removed from experience. But the term "culture," not only captures the imagination but also helps most people make comparisons between the symbolic aspects of a culture and those of a particular organization.

When people talk about an organization as "another world," "a different country," or a "self-contained society," they are on the doorstep of the notion of constructed reality. Of course, a term's appeal can also be its undoing, especially if it is used in so many ways that it becomes meaningless and confusing. Our main point here is that the term "culture" serves as a stimulator of thought and as an anchor, much as the term "system" did for the objective theories.

Finally, we believe that the economic challenges of the 1970s and the 1980s precipitated a close look at the idea of culture. Stiff competition from such rivals as Japan brought about much self-examination. What do they do that the United States doesn't do? How do their workers live and what do they believe? How do they achieve their level of quality? The competition might be viewed as culture vs. culture. In 1982, when unemployment was 9.5 percent, the prime rate was over 16 percent, and trade deficits soared, the business world was ready to give serious consideration to ideas that might help them compete in the world market.

At that time several books appeared with popular views of culture. *Corporate Culture* (Deal & Kennedy, 1982) discussed how the stuff of culture—values, symbols, rites, and rituals—might have impact on a company's overall performance. Also in 1982, Peters and Waterman presented *In Search of Excellence,* in which they examined the traits of organizations that had achieved excellence. They identified primary themes that were applicable to the organizations studied. These themes could be construed as cultural in that they represent the values of those organizations.

In addition to global competition, corporations face the prospect of change due to the value shifts of members and clients. Naisbitt and Aburdene (1985) asserted that "the corporation is an analogue for the rest of society. We are re-inventing education, health care, politics, and virtually all our social structures. But the corporation is often the quickest and most responsive to change. . . . Customers, unlike other constituents, vote every day, and that hastens corporate evolution" (p. 1). If an organization has a culture and its survival depends on its ability to change, then the question of how to change culture is critical. The notion of cultural change has also given impetus to the study of organizational symbolism and its meaning. Thus far, we have used the term "culture" in a variety of ways. In the next section we will explore those usages.

Concepts of Organizational Culture

The term "culture" has been assigned a variety of meanings. Generally speaking, when people interact over time, they form a culture. Each culture develops written and unwritten expectations of behavior (rules and norms) that influence the members of that culture. But people are not only influenced by the culture; they create the culture. Each organization has one or more cultures that contain expected behaviors—written or unwritten. Implicit in the concept of culture is an appreciation of the way organizations are molded by unique sets of values, rituals, and personalities. Louis (1985) suggests that a group's culture can be characterized as "a set of understandings or meanings shared by a group of people. The meanings are largely tacit among members, are clearly relevant to the particular group, and are distinctive to the group" (p. 74). Culture, then, involves interaction over time, behavioral expectations, shaping and being shaped, unique characteristics that set one culture apart from another, and a set of meanings/logics that enable group action.

The idea that an organization is "like a culture" captures the interest of both functionalist (objective) and interpretive (subjective) perspectives, but in different ways and for different reasons. Although our task in this chapter is to examine some subjective theories, a brief contrast between perspectives will highlight the subjectivist position. First, there is the matter of *cultural content.* Both perspectives recognize that one culture may be distinguished from another by its values, rites and rituals, practices, vocabulary, metaphors, and stories. The functionalist sees these as elements (variables) that make up an organizational culture. Such elements may be manipulated and controlled so that they affect organizational outcomes. For example, Deal and Kennedy (1982) describe key attributes of organizational culture and then suggest that if these elements are developed, they will lead to business success. Embodied in this approach are the notions of predictability, control, and cause-and-effect linkages, which are found on the objective side of the continuum (Figure 1.1).

The interpretivist focuses on the process of communication and the sense making of organizational members. How do members construct their organizational reality? What do events mean to them? The stories and rituals are displayers and indicators of organizational sense making (Pacanowsky & O'Donnell-Trujillo, 1982, pp. 124–125). It is the sense making itself that is most critical to the interpretivist. While a functionalist might try to determine what stories are in the system and what impact they might have on organizational outcomes, an interpretivist would be more interested in how stories are told, who tells them, and what meaning they hold for organizational members.

How is organizational culture defined? One way is to think of the organization as being made of "things," or cultural artifacts, stories, and rituals. If these artifacts are viewed as concrete entities with "real" existence, the perspective is functionalist, and organizational culture is perceived as artifact. If organizational culture is thought of as sense making, then it is identified through sense-making processes, and symbolic behavior becomes a focal point. It becomes necessary to listen to what people say in order to see how their experience takes on meaning.

The interpretative (subjective) point of view sees organizational culture as processes of sense making that construct organizational reality and thereby give meaning to the membership. The concept of sense making is as important to the interpretive view of culture as enacted sense making is to Weick's (1977a) theory of organizing. The displayers and indicators of organizational culture are not "givens" that just exist. They must be constructed, and the meanings given to them must be generated and regenerated in interaction. The displayers and indicators (stories, rites, rituals) are thought of as action rather than things. Pacanowsky and O'Donnell-Trujillo (1982) maintain that "as members constitute their relevant constructs, practices, rituals, and so forth, these constructs, practices, and rituals are mini-accomplishments embedded in the larger ongoing accomplishment of organizational culture" (p. 126). The key term is *accomplishment* in that it indicates action, and ongoing action at that. The displayers and indicators of culture can also be placed under the broad rubric of *organizational symbolism* (Dandridge, Mitroff, & Joyce, 1980). What is significant to the sense-making concept of culture is the meaning of symbolism to organizational members as they shape organizational reality and as they are shaped by their own constructions.

As one proceeds along the subjective-objective continuum, symbolic displayers and indicators are understood in different ways. The complexity of the sense-making process makes it difficult to present a comparison that captures the nuances involved. Perhaps Geertz (1973) says it best when he contends that "man is an animal suspended in webs of significance he himself has spun. . . . Culture [is] those webs, and the analysis of it [is] therefore not an experimental science in search of law but an interpretive one in search of meaning" (p. 5). Such an analogy reminds us that much as the spider spins a web, humans spin a reality that has impact on them. Just as in the case of the spider, the web that is spun by humans enables their movement and vision; but it also constrains their movement and vision. If webs of significance are thought of as stories, rituals, rites, metaphors, organizational practices, and values, then the prominence of symbolic behavior in culture is clear. There are several drawbacks to these comparisons. From a subjective stance the culture is more than the web; it is also the spinning itself. In addition, humans do not spin alone. Webs of significance must be negotiated between members of the organization. When a spider traverses the web, the process is less complex than when humans share the meaning of webs of significance. Human webs are more fragile and elusive than the tangible web of the spider. They may seem routine, but each new web is negotiated between organizational participants even though members may be unaware of the exchanges that have taken place. The web provides a structure, a context, a network of meaning that has been spun through interaction. It is within this context that people interpret and make sense of events. Organizational culture is identified by discovering the web and its spinning.

Pacanowsky and O'Donnell-Trujillo's (1982) interpretation of Geertz's web analogy recognizes the dual nature of organizational culture. They assert that ''if these two components of culture are to be studied—culture as structure and culture as process—then . . . researchers must not be content simply with accounts, but must also be present during occasions of naturally occurring discourse'' (p. 123). These features of organizational culture are recognized and explained in a different way by Smircich. She contends that culture is not only something an organization *has* (artifacts, structure), but also something that an organization *is* (process, sense making). The research agenda from this perspective ''is to explore the phenomenon of organization as subjective experience and to investigate the patterns that make organized action possible'' (Smircich, 1983, p. 348). An interpretive (subjective) approach emphasizes communication patterns within the organization and what those patterns mean to the participant.

Thus far we have discussed how organizational culture might be defined. There are other conceptual issues that should be noted. Louis (1985) presents a conceptual framework organized into natural, purposeful, and reflective levels of analysis. At the natural level, the concerns are origins (Where does culture come from?); outcomes (What does culture lead to?); and manifestations/artifacts (What does culture look like?). The purposeful level of analysis concerns issues of management. What can be done with, to, or about the culture? The reflective level looks at the nature and characteristics of culture. What constitutes the essence of a culture and makes it distinctive? Although any one study may involve several levels of analysis, an interpretive approach would most likely correspond to the reflective level.

In this section we have talked about the nature of culture, the objective and subjective views of culture, and different levels of cultural analysis. These themes raise certain issues that need to be addressed. However, before we embark on that discussion, some focus can be achieved by highlighting a subjective perspective of organizational culture.

ORGANIZATIONAL CULTURE AS SENSE MAKING

Commenting on various usages of and the popularity of the notion of culture, Smircich (1985) contends that ''we turned to the idea of culture for a fresh slant on organizational life, for something different. But for the most part, we're not getting it'' (p. 59). She stresses that if culture is to be more than just another element (variable) applied to traditional (objective) ways of thinking, it is necessary to concentrate on "meaning" and cultural analysis of organizational life. Cultural analysis of organizational life, from a subjective perspective, focuses on symbols and people in interaction. Organizational life is symbolic construction.

The sense-making (subjective) stance sees culture as a symbolically created context that allows people to make sense of events. They *make* culture and sense through interaction. Organizational life (reality) is put together communicatively. The primary question for the organizational participant is "What do I need to know and say to function in this setting?" The knowing and saying are the sense-making processes that make up the organizational culture. When investigators tap into the "saying" of organizational members, they are examining both sense making and culture.

Organization is symbolic behavior, and its very existence depends upon the shared meanings and interpretations that come about through human interaction. Organization "depends upon the existence of common modes of interpretation and shared understanding of experience which allow day to day activities to become routinized or taken-for-granted. When groups encounter novel situations, new interpretations must be constructed to sustain organized activity" (Smircich, 1981, p. 1). Looking at sense making is looking at the taken-for-granted behavior of the people who have constructed the organization. Symbols and symbolic behavior make organizational life possible. Think of the web analogy cited earlier and how the web both enables and constrains the movement of the spider. Symbolic behavior both enables and constrains the movement and vision of an organization. To understand symbolic behavior is to understand how a particular organization shapes its actions or inactions. More specifically, "what are the words, ideas, and constructs that impel, legitimate, coordinate, and realize organized activity in specific settings? How do they accomplish the task? Whose interests are they serving?" (Smircich, 1985, p. 67). The critical features of culture as sense making focus on shared meaning, symbolic behavior, interaction, and taken-for-granted behavior.

The principle underlying Weick's (1977a) concept of enacted sense making are also applicable here. Humans have a great deal to do with making their world, and the created world comes back to guide their activities. One interpretive critique of management theory points out that "givens" are actually problematic creations. Smircich (1983) looks at the work of Bittner (1965) and Burrell and Morgan (1979) to argue that traditional (functionalist, objective) research has an inherent language problem. While

> such terms as "structure," "resources" and even "organization" are typifications that organizational actors invoke to make sense of their everyday experience . . . social scientists [should] address themselves to the ways organizational members use such terms as "structure," "hierarchy," and "resources," as concepts for constructing an organizational world. In other words these constructs should become the topic of analysis rather than tools for analysis. (pp. 223–224)

To get a feel for the "culture-as-sense-making" perspective, substitute displayers and indicators of organizational culture (stories, rites, values) for the preceding organizational terms. The key idea is not that an organization has such displayers, but how organizational members may have created them, how they use them to construct a context that has impact on their interpretation of events, and how they sustain or alter them through communication. The emphasis on a subjectively constructed world is not new (Berger & Luckmann, 1966; Geertz, 1973, 1983; Hallowell, 1955; Schutz, 1967). What is more contemporary is the incorporation and application of the ideas to organizational communication. Because of the variety of meanings attached to culture and because some of those meanings challenge traditional beliefs, certain issues arise.

Organizational Culture Issues

We have explored what organizational culture is and how it might be described. However, it is evident that different definitions of culture lead to different cultural theories. Such definitions are influenced by different objective and subjective views. In addition to what it is and how it should be studied, the concept of organizational culture raises a number of other issues. What is the appropriate level of cultural analysis? What is the purpose of cultural analysis? Can culture be managed? What are the ethical implications of such study? How can such cultural analyses be evaluated? What is the value of cultural analysis?

LEVEL OF ANALYSIS

Organizational culture can be studied at different levels, including macroanalytic and microanalytic perspectives. For example, the organization itself can be viewed as being embedded in the larger cultural context of society (Smith & Simmons, 1983); the organization might be seen as participating in a distinctive culture developed within a particular industry (Putnam, 1985); the organization can be studied as a single, unified cultural entity (Meyer, 1982a,b); and a fourth analytic level views organizations as being composed of a number of subcultural groups (Watson, 1982; Riley, 1983; and Schall, 1983). All of these levels represent legitimate areas of study. However, it is important to identify the boundaries of study and the significance of those boundaries. For example, Van Maanen and Barley (1985) state that "unitary organizational cultures evolve when all members of an organization face roughly the same problems, when everyone communicates with almost everyone else, and when each member adopts a common set of understandings for enacting proper and consensually approved behavior" (p. 37). Thus, an organization can be viewed as a homogenous, unitary collective; however, the discovery of cultural action in organizational life is more likely to take place at the group level of analysis. This discovery depends upon finding elements or actions that make one group different from another. Subcultures are more likely to exhibit those actions.

WHAT IS THE PURPOSE OF CULTURAL ANALYSIS?

The answer to this question usually promotes conflict because the traditional literature is so heavily invested in the managerial perspective. This managerial bias assumes that good knowledge is knowledge that helps one manage in the most efficient way. The traditional (functionalist) approach centers on the management of organizations. It emphasizes predictability, control, and an objective world view. Although a number of purposes of cultural analysis could be examined, we will discuss two general ones that contrast the schools of thought. The first looks at cultural analysis as a tool for managing organizational effectiveness. The second considers cultural analysis as a means of understanding. The managerial perspective sees culture as a given—a tool that can be used to analyze a situation in order to improve the situation. It is almost as if an understanding has already been achieved and that the things that make up culture can be used. For example, Deal and Kennedy (1982) explore four key attributes of organizational culture and then emphasize that "strong" organizational cultures lead to bottom-line concerns—profit and continuity. Popular managerial (and simplistic) perspectives treat culture as the magic element (variable) that can be manipulated to lead to high profits and national visibility. When applied as a formula, the notion of culture has not reached expectations (Rhodes, 1986). Even in a more sophisticated treatment (Pfeffer, 1981), the focus is on the management of symbolism for the purpose of meeting the goals of those in charge. If humans are thought of as adaptive agents who respond to forces in their environment, then a manager who controls the symbolic environment would be able to regulate behavior. Of course, the nature of humans and ideas about control are very much at issue. We do not use the term "managerial bias" in a pejorative sense, but rather to indicate the purpose and interest of a particular group. When cultural analysis is approached as a means of understanding, the purposes are more inclusive and complex.

Organizational culture does not belong to management; it belongs to all members of the organization. Cultural analysis does not stress what *should* happen from management's perspective but what *does* happen. Organizational culture can exist in any organization and organization can refer to a variety of groups. Size is not the issue; organizing activity is. Culture is not a tool of analysis, but an object of analysis. It is not a given that should be taken for granted. It must be discovered through the eyes of the people that create it. Culture is not a concrete thing, but the emergent behaviors that create and sustain the patterns that can be called culture.

Theorists treat the notion of "understanding" in a variety of ways. Pacanowsky and O'Donnell-Trujillo (1982) state: "we are interested in understanding how that organizational life is accomplished communicatively" (p. 122). The purpose of an analysis is to discover how culture is enacted or performed through communication (Pacanowsky & O'Donnell-Trujillo, 1983). If one understands the idea of performance in an organization and what it means, a big step has been taken toward understanding the culture. Smircich (1983), referring to interpretive research and consulting, concludes that "the ultimate purpose is to lead to a more informed, more self-conscious organization" (p. 239). Theorists who stress cultural analysis as a means of understanding are careful to avoid the functionalist notions of prediction and control. They focus on taken-for-granted behaviors and concepts because so little is known about how organizations create their realities and the impact of those creations.

Understanding and self-awareness are not sterile concepts. Understanding, or knowledge, has a number of potential and significant uses. It allows an organization to examine its underlying logic so that it might critique and change itself. Just as consciousness-raising groups remind their members of certain inequities, an organization that engages in the reflective process can do the same. A critique of an organization should not be limited to its profit-making ability. The type of knowledge produced by cultural analysis can serve several functions. For the student of organizational behavior, "organizational culture research has theory-generative, theory-contextualizing, and even theory-testing possibilities [for the participant]. . . . Each organizational culture study can provide any member (manager, worker, volunteer) with an overall picture of the organization" (Pacanowsky & O'Donnell-Trujillo, 1982, p. 129). This knowledge not only helps people see the underlying logic of what they do; self-examination and awareness of the sense-making process can trigger change.

CAN CULTURE BE MANAGED?

Different schools of thought conflict on this issue.

Culture pragmatists generally see culture as a key to commitment, productivity, and profitability. They argue that culture can be—indeed, should be and has been—managed. . . . Cultural purists . . . find it ridiculous to talk of managing culture. Culture cannot be managed; it emerges. Leaders don't create cultures; members of the culture do. Culture is an expression of people's deepest needs, a means of endowing their experiences with meaning. (Martin, 1985, p. 95)

The answer to the question of whether culture can be managed depends on one's definition of culture. The more complex the definition, the more difficult the management issue becomes. It is easier to deal with cultural artifacts than with deeply rooted sense-making processes. When large-scale cultural changes are considered, both objectivists and subjectivists agree that such changes are difficult and quite costly. Even the most popular versions of organizational culture (Deal & Kennedy, 1982) recognize the high costs.

Uttal (1983), writing in *Fortune,* suggests that "for all the hype, corporate culture is real and powerful. It's also hard to change, and you won't find much support for doing so inside or outside your company. If you run up against the culture when trying to redirect strategy, attempt to dodge; if you must meddle with culture directly, tread carefully and with modest expectations" (p. 72). Although such a statement shows skepticism of cultural change, the key word is *expectations.* Massive cultural overhauls are extremely difficult. That does not mean that managers cannot have impact on significant aspects of a culture. Martin (1985) maintains that when theorists consider the question of managing culture, they prefer to rephrase it to "Are there conditions under which culture can be managed?" She concludes that although different authors hold divergent views about what culture is, these same authors agree about the kinds of conditions that expedite or block the management of culture. The answer to the question of managing culture, then, depends on one's definition of culture, the nature of the process or change, and the conditions underlying the change or management process.

WHAT ARE THE ETHICAL IMPLICATIONS?

If culture is an "expression of people's deepest needs, a means of endowing their experiences with meaning" as suggested earlier, then once the culture is exposed, whose interests should be served by that knowledge? If cultural analysis gets at the very core of meaning for humans in the workplace, how is that knowledge to be used? Can all voices of the organization be heard? There are many concerns about the interests that dominate workplace decision making (Habermas, 1972, 1975)—certainly more than we can discuss here. We leave that important task to the critic. Nevertheless, it is important to state the issues, even in capsule form. Deetz (1985) asks, "Do we as a society like or want to be what current organizational practices recommend for us? Is there any way we or anyone else can have a say in the matter? In what ways is wider representation possible? To me, these are the critical ethical questions" (p. 266). He suggests that those who do cultural analysis should go beyond the goal of understanding, because "merely understanding the means by which consensual realities are formed and perpetrated says little about whether such a consensus adequately represents different competing interests" (p. 268). It is important to examine the conditions of consensus, power distributions, and the interests represented.

HOW SHOULD CULTURAL ANALYSIS BE EVALUATED?

The question of what counts as good cultural analysis may receive a variety of answers. The concept of organizational culture not only has given rise to conflicting definitions, but also has prompted a variety of research methods, goals, and outcomes. The standards for cultural analysis are still being developed. Strine and Pacanowsky (1985) take a cue from Weick (1983) by selecting "good" examples of interpretive research and discussing what makes them good. They do not develop a set of guidelines for evaluating research, but provide a framework within which evaluation can take place. This framework is concerned with the intended audience of the analysis and how an author functions as a source of authority. Cultural analyses may be presented from the authority of an analytic scientist, conceptual theorist, conceptual humanist, or particular humanist. All of the authorized positions require different evaluative guidelines. Each is responsive to a particular audience and nuance of organizational life. This approach illustrates the complex and ongoing nature of creating evaluative criteria for cultural analysis. General guidelines derived from studies of routines and practices in the organizational setting help in assessing cultural studies. The following evaluative questions are derived from statements made by Bantz (1983) concerning criteria for evaluating research that emphasizes the subjective constructions and interpretations of organizational participants.

1. Does the study provide descriptions and interpretations of organizational messages, meanings, and expectations?
2. Are the organization's messages, meanings, and expectations presented as understood by the members of the organization?
3. Is the organization, as presented, recognizable to members of the organization (not identical or accepted, but recognizable)?
4. Do the findings of the study make the organization accessible to nonmembers?
5. Is the final product skillful in its use of argument and language?

Although evaluating cultural analysis is likely to provoke disagreement among theorists, these are some features that appear necessary for "good" studies. Such studies are descriptive—so much so that one can "feel" the organization. Geertz (1973) uses the term "thick description" to refer to the type of narrative that helps one see and feel the subtleties of organizational life. A presentation of this sort works the same way as a good novel or movie. It helps one image and get "caught up'' in the story. If the purpose is to understand, emphasis is placed on description and interpretation. It is more important to understand what a culture is, and what it makes possible, than to label it good or bad. Judgments will no doubt be made, but studies that concentrate on description and interpretation are more likely to give a complete and full account of organizational life. Good studies reveal how organizational members make sense of and construct their world. They give the reader a good idea of what it would be like to be a part of such an organization. The reader knows what he or she would have to know to function in the organization and what it would take to fit in or advance in the organization.

Finally, the significance of the use of argument and language cannot be overestimated. Pacanowsky and O'Donnell-Trujillo (1982) contend that ''an account of organizational culture begs not for an assessment of its reliability and validity, but for an assessment of its plausibility and its insight'' (p. 123). Plausibility and insight are determined by argument and language. The quality of the writing is critical to the evaluation of cultural analysis. Some would go so far as to say that the truth of the interpretive study lies in its writing (Pacanowsky, 1981).

What is the value of cultural analysis? What does it tell us? There is usually less conflict about such questions when culture is treated as just another element (variable) in the traditional view of organizations. In that case culture is considered to be a potent variable that has impact on organizational performance. But what does a subjective approach tell us? We would contend that an organization that has a better understanding of itself is in a better position to critique and change itself. In a pragmatic sense, to understand the sense-making processes in an organization is also to understand the basis for decision making and managing. Managers have been criticized for not being people oriented and for lacking sensitivity in the management process. What should they be sensitive to? D'Aprix (1982) suggests that a manager must learn the ''appropriate touches'' with his or her people. An understanding of the sense-making process and how members construct a particular reality gives insight into sensitivity and the appropriate touches.

Because cultural analysis focuses on taken-for-granted behavior and excludes preconceived scientific constructs, it is sometimes accused of not saying much. However, an interesting contradiction arises. This type of research often presents a threat to organizations. Conventional research tends to present findings in a very global, generalized way without specific reference to individuals; cultural analysis can get very specific and tell a great deal about individuals. Specific language is linked to specific individuals and parts of the organization. Conventional research allows the organization to know ahead of time just what will be studied and how. Outcomes may be more a matter of demonstration than discovery. This is not true for cultural analysis, which examines emergent behavior and networks of meaning. Researchers arrive at significant questions; they do not start with them. Just where the inquiry may lead cannot be specified at the outset. Skrtic (1985) states that ''Administrators of organizations who would rather not have their problems understood so clearly would do well to choose conventional over qualitative research into their operations'' (p. 215). Viewed in this way, cultural analysis may tell too much!

In addition to contributing to pragmatic concerns, cultural analysis adds another dimension to our understanding of organizational life. Understanding can be looked at in a technical (cognitive) sense, but there is also a *feeling* (affective) sense that deserves consideration. Smircich (1985) suggests that ''organizations are representations of our humanity, like music or art; they can be known through acts of appreciation. . . . Organizations are symbolically constituted worlds, like novels or poems; they can be known through acts of critical reading and interpretation. . . . Organizations are symbolic forms, like religion and folklore; they are displays of the meaning of life'' (p. 66). Our breadth of understanding should have room for more than the technical issues. An understanding that contains feeling not only tells us more about organizational life, but it can tell us something about ourselves. The organization is a fascinating object of study because it is a human object that represents part of all of us. How capable an individual is in "reading" and appreciating an organization demands more than technical knowledge.

Implications for Organizational Communication

The role of communication in organizational culture can be seen differently depending on how culture is conceptualized. If culture is thought of as a collection of symbolic artifacts that are communicated to organizational members for organizational control, then communication can be conceived of as a vehicle that enables that outcome. If culture is construed as sense making, the process of communication itself becomes the focal point of interest because that is what sense making is. Both stances have value, but we will stress the implications of the subjective view because it adds a different dimension to traditional study.

The study of organizational communication from a cultural perspective involves more than examining only the official exchanges between selected people with status. Everyday talk reveals organizational sense making and networks of shared meanings that may exist. Taken-for-granted behaviors that allow routine and organizing to exist are embedded in communication.

The way messages are interpreted depends on the symbolically created context in which they occur. Predicting the reactions to messages has little chance of accuracy without a knowledge of the organizational context. One cannot be sensitive to a different culture without being sensitive to its language. The same holds true for organizational culture. It is necessary to know and be able to interpret how an organization uses language.

Those who engage in organizational change must inevitably identify and deal with organizational culture. From a sense-making perspective this means knowing how an organization communicates. To know a culture is to understand what it makes possible for its members. Looked at in traditional terms, a particular organization might appear to be irrational and disorganized, but the organization may have created a culture that works for it. Even communication that seems random, contradictory, and obtuse may serve important functions for the members of an organization.

SUMMARY

In this chapter our goal was to illustrate the impact of subjectivism on organizational communication. We selected two prominent contemporary organizational theories that represent subjective thinking, we explained why each theory has achieved recognition, and described the prominence of communication concepts in each. In addition, we explored the issues raised by the theories. Finally, we discussed the implications each theory has for organizational communication.

In Part Three we will discuss issues in organizational communication that arise from a functionalist perspective. If we were to derive the issues from a subjectivist position, they would no doubt be cast in a different way. We believe that the subjectivist view does inform, and for that reason we have added a subjectivist notation for each issue. Even a note stressing that a point of concern may be a nonissue provides contrast and a note of caution. When ideas stand in opposition, they are more likely to receive greater scrutiny.

REFERENCES

Bantz, Charles R., "Naturalistic Research Traditions," in *Communication and Organizations: An Interpretive Approach,* Linda Putnam and Michael E. Pacanowsky, eds. Beverly Hills, Calif.: Sage, 1983.

Berger, P. L., and T. Luckmann, *The Social Construction of Reality.* Garden City, N.Y.: Doubleday, 1966.

Bittner, E., "The Concept of Organization," *Social Research,* 32 (1965), 239–255.

Burrell, G., and Gareth Morgan, *Sociological Paradigms and Organizational Analysis.* London: Heinemann, 1979.

Clark, David L., "Emerging Paradigms In Organizational Theory and Research," in *Organizational Theory and Inquiry: The Paradigm Revolution,* Yvonna S. Lincoln, ed. Beverly Hills, Calif.: Sage, 1985.

D'Aprix, Roger, *Communicating for Productivity.* New York: Harper & Row, Pub., 1982.

Dandridge, Thomas, Ian Mitroff, and William Joyce, "Organization Symbolism: A Topic to Expand Organizational Analysis," *Academy of Management Review,* 5 (1980), 77–82.

Deal, Terrence E., and Allan A. Kennedy, *Corporate Culture: The Rites and Rituals of Corporate Life.* Reading, Mass.: Addison-Wesley, 1982.

Deetz, Stanley, "Ethical Considerations in Cultural Research in Organizations" in *Organizational Culture,* Peter J. Frost et al., eds. Beverly Hills, Calif.: Sage, 1985.

Garfinkel, Harold, *Studies In Ethnomethodology.* Englewood Cliffs, N.J.: Prentice-Hall, 1967.

Geertz, C., *The Interpretation of Cultures.* New York: Basic Books, 1973.

Geertz, C., *Local Knowledge: Further Essays in Interpretive Anthropology.* New York: Basic Books, 1983.

Habermas, J., *Knowledge and Human Interests,* J. Shapiro, trans. Boston: Beacon, 1972.

Habermas, J., *Legitimation Crisis,* T. McCarthy, trans. Boston: Beacon, 1975.

Hallowell, A. I., *Culture and Experience.* Philadelphia: University of Pennsylvania Press, 1955.

Kreps, Gary L., *Organizational Communication: Theory and Practice.* New York: Longman, 1986.

Lincoln, Yvonna S., *Organizational Theory and Inquiry: The Paradigm Revolution.* Beverly Hills, Calif.: Sage, 1985.

Louis, Meryl Reis, "An Investigator's Guide to Workplace Culture," in *Organizational Culture,* Peter J. Frost et al., eds. Beverly Hills, Calif.: Sage, 1985.

Lundberg, Craig, "Open Letter to Karl Weick," *Journal of Applied Behavioral Science,* 18 (1982), 113–117.

Martin, Joanne, "Can Organizational Culture Be Managed?" in *Organizational Culture,* Peter J. Frost et al., eds. Beverly Hills, Calif.: Sage, 1985.

Meyer, Alan D., "Adapting to Environmental Jolts," *Administrative Science Quarterly*, 27 (1982a), 515–537.

Meyer, Alan D., "How Ideologies Supplant Formal Structures and Shape Responses to Environments," *Journal of Management Studies*, 19 (1982b), 45–61.

Morgan, Gareth, "Paradigms, Metaphors, and Puzzle Solving in Organization Theory," *Administrative Science Quarterly*, 25 (1980), 605–622.

Naisbitt, John, and Patricia Aburdene, *Re-inventing the Corporation*. New York: Warner Books, 1985.

Pacanowsky, Michael E., "Writing: Science, Fiction, and the Interpretive Approach," Paper presented at the SCA/ICA Joint Sponsored Summer Conference on Interpretive Approaches to the Study of Organizational Communication, Alta, Utah, July 26, 1981.

Pacanowsky, Michael E., and Nick O'Donnell-Trujillo, "Communication and Organizational Cultures," *Western Journal of Speech Communication*, 46 (Spring 1982), 115–130.

Pacanowsky, Michael E., and Nick O'Donnell-Trujillo, "Organizational Communication as Cultural Performance," *Communication Monographs*, 50 (June 1983), 126–147.

Parsons, Talcott, *Structure and Process in Modern Societies*. Glencoe, Ill.: Free Press, 1964.

Peters, T. J., and R. H. Waterman, *In Search of Excellence*. New York: Harper & Row, Pub., 1982.

Pfeffer, Jeffrey, "Management as Symbolic Action: The Creation and Maintenance of Organizational Paradigms," in *Research in Organizational Behavior*, Vol. 3, 1–52, Larry L. Cummings and Barry M. Staw, eds. Greenwich, Conn.: JAI Press, 1981.

Pondy, Louis R., and Ian I. Mitroff, "Beyond Open System Models of Organization," in *Research in Organizational Behavior*, Vol. 1, 3–39, Larry L. Cummings and Barry M. Staw, eds. Greenwich, Conn.: JAI Press, 1979.

Putnam, Linda L., "Bargaining as Organizational Communication," in *Organizational Communication: Traditional Themes and New Directions*, Robert D. McPhee and Philip K. Tompkins, eds. Beverly Hills, Calif.: Sage, 1985.

Rhodes, Lucien, "That's Easy for You to Say," *INC.* (June 1986), 63–66.

Ricoeur, Paul, "The Model of the Text: Meaningful Action Considered as a Text," *Social Research*, 38 (1971), 529–562.

Riley, Patricia, "A Structurationist Account of Political Culture," *Administrative Science Quarterly*, 28 (1983), 414–437.

Schall, Maryan S., "A Communication Rules Approach to Organizational Culture," *Administrative Science Quarterly*, 28 (1983), 557–581.

Schutz, A., *The Problem of Social Reality*. The Hague: Martinus Nijhoff, 1967.

Schwartz, P., and J. Ogilvy, *The Emergent Paradigm: Changing Patterns of Thought and Belief*. Menlo Park, Calif.: SRI International, 1979.

Silverman, David, *The Theory of Organisations*. New York: Basic Books, 1970.

Skrtic, Thomas M., "Doing Naturalistic Research into Educational Organizations," in *Organizational Theory and Inquiry: The Paradigm Revolution*, Yvonna S. Lincoln, ed. Beverly Hills, Calif.: Sage, 1985.

Smircich, Linda, "Studying Organizations as Cultures," Paper in preparation for *Research Strategies: Links Between Theory and Method*, Gareth Morgan, ed., March 1981.

Smircich, Linda, "Implications For Management Theory," in *Communication and Organizations: An Interpretive Approach*, Linda L. Putnam and Michael E. Pacanowsky, eds. Beverly Hills, Calif.: Sage, 1983.

Smircich, Linda, "Is the Concept of Culture a Paradigm for Understanding Organizations and Ourselves?" in *Organizational Culture*, Peter J. Frost et al., eds. Beverly Hills, Calif: Sage, 1985.

Smith, Kenwynk, and Valerie M. Simmons, "A Rumpelstiltskin Organization: Metaphors on Metaphors in Field Research,'' *Administrative Science Quarterly*, 28 (1983), 377–392.

Strine, Mary S., and Michael E. Pacanowsky, ''How to Read Interpretive Accounts of Organizational Life: Narrative Bases of Textual Authority,'' *The Southern Speech Communication Journal*, 50 (Spring 1985), 283–297.

Turner, Barry A., *Exploring the Industrial Subculture*. London: Macmillan, 1971.

Uttal, Bro, ''The Corporate Culture Vulture,'' *Fortune*, October 17, 1983, 67–72.

Van Maanen, John, and Stephen R. Barley, ''Cultural Organization: Fragments of a Theory,'' in *Organizational Culture*, Peter J. Frost et al., eds. Beverly Hills, Calif.: Sage, 1985.

in *Organizational Culture*, Peter J. Frost et al., eds. Beverly Hills, Calif.: Sage, 1985.

Watson, Tony J., ''Group Ideologies and Organizational Change,'' *Journal of Management Studies*, 19 (1982), 259–275.

Weick, Karl E., *The Social Psychology of Organizing*. Reading, Mass.: Addison-Wesley, 1969.

Weick, Karl E., ''Educational Organizations as Loosely Coupled Systems,'' *Administrative Science Quarterly*, 21 (1976), 1–19.

Weick, Karl E., ''Enactment Processes in Organizations,'' in *New Directions in Organizational Behavior*, Barry M. Staw and Gerald R. Salancik, eds. Chicago: St. Clair Press, 1977a.

Weick, Karl E., ''Re-Punctuating the Problem,'' in *New Perspectives on Organizational Effectiveness*, Paul S. Goodman and Johannes M. Pennings, eds. San Francisco: Jossey-Bass, Inc., 1977b.

Weick, Karl E., *The Social Psychology of Organizing*, 2nd ed. Reading, Mass.: Addison-Wesley, 1979.

Weick, Karl E., ''Organizational Communication: Toward a Research Agenda,'' in *Communication and Organizations: An Interpretive Approach*, Linda L. Putnam and Michael E. Pacanowsky, eds. Beverly Hills, Calif.: Sage, 1983.

Weick, Karl E., ''Sources of Order in Underorganized Systems: Themes in Recent Organizational Theory,'' in *Organizational Theory and Inquiry: The Paradigm Revolution*, Yvonna S. Lincoln, ed. Beverly Hills, Calif.: Sage, 1985.

Wittgenstein, Ludwig, *Philosophical Investigations*. G. E. M. Anscombe, trans. Oxford: Blackwell, 1968.

6

Communicative Efficiency

The Cost-Effectiveness of Organizational Communication

The study of organizational communication involves a number of concerns about communication that relate to how organizations function. These concerns may affect what happens in an organization and how effectively the organization operates. In this part of the book, we shall review arguments, evidence, research, and explanations on these issues. Although we may not resolve how each issue affects organizations, you may gain a great deal of insight into the manner in which issues can be addressed. We would like the reader to look at these issues in the organizations in which they hold membership. Think about, for example, the flow of information, the climate, costs, networks, and the fidelity of messages. Consider how they affect what happens in the organization. Reflect on leadership styles, motivation, relationships, and group processes and conflict. These are the issues that may need to be resolved in order for organizations to function smoothly.

We focus on "people" issues and emphasize symbolic behavior. However, we must acknowledge that the technology of a system has profound effects on aspects of organizational structure and process. We recommend Culnan and Markus (1987) for an analysis of the evidence and arguments about the impact of electronic media on organizational communication. These researchers focus on the electronic communication technology used to support communication within organizations. They discuss the features of voice messaging, electronic mail, various conferencing systems, and integrated systems. You can obtain a specific and pragmatic discussion of how organizations use the newer media from Zygmont (1988), who discusses video conferencing and the technologies that unite widely dispersed organizational operations. The discussion of point-to-point digital videoconferencing and its interactive nature demonstrates the dramatic changes that technology can bring to the organization.

An understanding of what makes communication and people effective in organizations is critical. We must remember, however, as Thayer pointed out, that "there is always some kind of investment or expenditure whenever communication occurs" (1968, p. 154). Organizational communication has its costs. Vardaman, Halterman, and Vardaman (1970) analyzed the costs associated with written communication in an organization and concluded that "if an organization can markedly improve the handling of its written communications, it can go a long way in cutting unnecessary administrative operational costs, as well as significantly decreasing the costs of the documents themselves" (p. 1). The first step in managing communication costs, of course, is to recognize the places where costs occur.

One of the purposes of this chapter is to describe some general perspectives and useful ideas concerning the costs associated with organizational communication. In some areas, such as dictation (Rogers, 1979) and publications (Griese, 1978), specific costs have been calculated; however, for most kinds of communication, we have little information about actual costs. Nevertheless, an understanding of the potential costs of communicating and the enormous expenditures that may engulf us when we communicate may help organizations contain costs and make communicating more *efficient*.

DEFINITION OF EFFICIENCY

The cost of something is the price one pays to accomplish, acquire, or maintain it. The cost of communicating is what a person invests or expends to communicate. Expenditures may take various forms, including actual money and mental energy. In general we think of costs as the loss experienced in producing something. Thus, in communicating, the costs are represented by what losses are experienced.

Most of us are aware, nevertheless, that we are not likely to get what we want out of communicating unless we are willing to invest something in the process. What we hope for, most of the time, is to accomplish our communicative objectives with minimum costs. Farace, Taylor, and Stewart (1978) point out that the overall effectiveness (achieving an objective) of organizational communication is limited by the resources that can be devoted to communicating and, conversely, that the degree of effectiveness depends upon the number of resources expended on communicating. Thus, they conclude, "the critical decision topic for managers is the selection of those effectiveness criteria which need to be maximized in order to achieve the greatest overall efficiency of communication in the organization" (p. 274).

The *efficiency of a communication act* is the ratio between how well it accomplishes a desired result and what expenditures are required to carry out the act. In other words, an efficient communication act is one that experiences little loss (as represented by expenditures of time, energy, and resources), yet produces a highly desirable result. We can portray relationships among effectiveness, cost, and efficiency by the following equation:

$$\text{Efficiency} = \frac{\text{Effectiveness}}{\text{Costs}} = \frac{\text{Desirable consequences}}{\text{Expenditures of time, energy, resources}}$$

We can evaluate an organizational communication act or system in terms of the cost required to achieve a particular level of effectiveness and arrive at an index of efficiency. The index of efficiency is the foremost consideration in any analysis of the status and quality of an act or system of communication.

Efficiency can be thought of in another way. Consider this. As every act of communication requires the expenditure of time, energy, and resources, what we should be concerned with is the *return we get on the investment of time, energy, and resource.* We may be foolhardy and fail to invest adequately in communicating just when the return may be the greatest. The return on investment is probably one of the most frequently overlooked considerations in organizational communication. We often think about how effective our communicating can become or how much we can save by not communicating, but the real issue is what kind of return we can get on an investment in communication.

RETURN ON INVESTMENT

Return on investment (ROI) is a measure of the relative success of a company or an action by looking at the ratio of return to the amount invested. This ratio is usually the key measure in rating overall performance. ROI theory does not look at results or profits or effectiveness as an absolute indicator of success, but as a return on what has been invested. The goal of most activities is to optimize returns (profits or effectiveness) from the resources invested in the business.

You can no doubt think of many examples where thinking about the return on investment has helped people make decisions about how much to invest. Take, for example, the preparation of a newsletter or bulletin for mailing to prospective customers. How many bulletins should you prepare? The answer may be found in the idea of ROI. If you printed 1,000 copies and contacted 10 people who were interested in your product, then increased the print run to 10,000 copies and located 200 people, which distribution provided the highest return on the investment?

Communicating interpersonally functions on the same ROI principles. If it takes a great deal of energy to maintain a pleasant acquaintanceship with one person but only a small investment of energy to have a friend who provides you with considerable pleasure, which of the two friends are you more likely to try to cultivate?

When a man and a woman consider sharing their lives, would it not make sense to consider what kind of communicative inputs are necessary to achieve their mutual goals? If you really want to have a successful relationship, you will need to make an investment. You will be inclined to invest more when you calculate that the return will be higher.

Increased return on investment can be caused by changing different ratios. For example, in business, an improvement in rate of return can come from a higher percentage of profit to sales, or by getting more product out of a given plant, or by reducing the cost of sales for a given product.

An increased return on investment can come from changes in the ratios in communication, also. For example, you can get a higher return by maintaining the same effectiveness but lowering the investment, or by investing more and increasing the quality of the outcome.

An advantage of using return on investment as a way of thinking about organizational communication is that it focuses on a central concern: to achieve objectives with the least investment. ROI deemphasizes mere increases in costs such as effort and resources and focuses instead on the combination of factors that make for successful communication.

Let us look individually at each of the elements that go into the index of efficiency. We will consider the costs that are associated with communicating.

TYPES OF COSTS

One way of looking at costs is in terms of direct or financial loss, psychological expenditures, and loss in job performance (Vardaman et al., 1970). On the other hand, costs can be examined in terms of whether they relate to the individual involved, the message itself, the channels involved, the media used, or the total system (Thayer, 1968). For purposes of this analysis we shall lean heavily upon the first system but modify the categories to accommodate as wide a spectrum of communication forms and formats as possible, not just written communication. Thus we can think of three types of costs: physical resource expenditures, human resource expenditures, and production losses. We shall discuss each of these major types of costs in more detail.

Expenditures of Physical Resources

When we expend or lose physical resources, we usually see a fairly direct monetary loss, although some types of direct costs may be more difficult to measure. Thinking about the phrasing of a message takes time, which represents direct labor costs, but determining when you started to think about the message and when you stopped and whether the time was spent exclusively on thinking about the message may be more difficult to specify than the expenditure of other types of resources. Nevertheless, an inventory of different types of physical resource expenditures may be useful. Let us look at four categories of physical resources: buildings, equipment, supplies, and labor.

BUILDINGS

Although the entire physical plant of an organization contributes to communication, some places are more communication-prone then others. Offices, for example, serve a primary communication function. The locations of some offices cost more because they are closer or farther away from central business operations. The furnishings of some offices are more expensive than others. The sizes of some offices are larger than others. In general the cost of an office varies with the position in the organization. Positions of higher status tend to have more expensive offices associated with them. Some offices cost more because they require more security. Secretarial spaces, exit and entrance doors, alarm systems, and corridors are often provided to enhance the security and protect the communication process and communicators from invasion or interruptions. Rooms where confidential conversations occur may cost considerably more than those where nonconfidential communication occurs. Some portion of all buildings—including offices, work rooms, and storage areas—is devoted to communication activities and represents a cost of communicating.

COMMUNICATION EQUIPMENT

A great deal of equipment in an organization has been designed and is used exclusively for communicating. Typewriters, dictating and transcribing machines, copiers, telephones, tape and video recorders, computers, calculators, and printing machinery are examples of *communication technology*. Filing cabinets, tapes, discs, desks, and storage shelves are all types of equipment used to maintain and keep messages. Television sets and teletype machines, monitors, and consoles are other types of equipment used to display messages. One of the major direct costs of contemporary organizations is the investment in communication equipment.

SUPPLIES

Even with the vast array of communication equipment available, often little can be done without the accompanying supplies. Paper, ink, fluids, punch cards, spirit masters, mag cards, pens, pencils, note pads, staples, paper clips, rubber bands, postage, and telephone services are usually referred to as *supplies and expenses*. Although some supplies may be exceptional, nearly everything listed is part of the expense of communicating.

LABOR

We usually think of communication labor costs as those involved in thinking up a message, putting the message into some proper form, distributing the message to appropriate members of the organization, and receiving, processing, and responding to messages. These costs are usually associated with the originators of messages and the receiver-interpreters of messages.

Originator Costs. Originators tend to engage in four types of activities that are associated with costs: thinking, composing, transcribing, and presenting.

Thinking. Some time is spent in just thinking about messages prior to composing them. Frequently the amount of time spent mentally reviewing ideas and alternatives is greater than the amount of time taken to write out the message.

Composing. Putting the message into some form—a speech outline, an essay, or report—also takes a great deal of time. I compose all papers, manuscripts, reports, and other written materials at a typewriter. Some people write longhand, whereas others speak into a dictating machine. Rogers (1979) contends that a manager can save a considerable amount of time and money by using machine dictation rather than writing longhand or dictating to a secretary. She claims that paperwork production costs can be reduced 50 to 75 percent. She cites the figures in Table 6.1 to support her analysis. The average speed for writing in longhand is

TABLE 6.1   Costs of Composing

A Manager's Annual Salary of	Makes Every Hour Worth	And Results in a Yearly Cost of
$20,000	$10.25	$2,501
$25,000	$12.81	$3,126
$30,000	$15.37	$3,750
$35,000	$17.92	$4,372
$40,000	$20.48	$4,997
$50,000	$25.60	$6,246

Source: From Florence Rogers, "Dictation: Key to Office Effectiveness," *The Personnel Administrator* (September 1979), 25–28, 34.

about fifteen words per minute. The average speed for dictating to a secretary is about thirty words per minute. The average speed for composing using dictation equipment is about sixty words per minute. Thus a manager making $40,000 a year who spends ten hours a week handwriting paperwork costs the organization about $9,994 each year. The same manager using dictation equipment could process paperwork four times faster, making the annual cost to the organization $2,498. Thus a single manager using dictating equipment could save the organization $7,496 in a year. There is little doubt that the costs of composing messages are a real, direct expenditure in time and salaries to an organization.

Transcribing.   Transcribing refers to the process of making a copy of materials in a medium other than that in which it was originally composed. To transcribe may involve making a recording of a program, making a written or typewritten copy of orally dictated materials, or translating notes from a lecture into a manuscript. This process of reproducing a message from one form or medium into another involves considerable expense for most organizations. Rogers (1979) also calculated the cost of transcribing materials in an organization. She reported the figures and analysis in Table 6.2. The average speed at which a secretary can transcribe from handwritten copy is about fifteen words per minute. The average speed at which one can transcribe from shorthand notes is about forty-five words per minute, but the average speed at which transcriptions can be made from recorded dictation is seventy-five words per minute. These figures show that a $15,000-a-year secretary who spends ten hours per week transcribing handwritten drafts costs the organization $3,840 per year. The same secretary can handle the same amount of textual materials from dictation equipment nearly five times as fast, making the annual cost about $768. Thus an annual savings of $3,072 would occur just in transcribing. As you can tell, there are real monetary costs involved in communicating, but there are ways of reducing costs when we are aware and working on the problem.

TABLE 6.2   Costs of Transcribing

A Transcriber's Annual Salary of	Makes Every Hour Worth	And Results in a Yearly Cost of
$10,000	$5.12	$1,250
$15,000	$7.68	$1,873

Source: From Florence Rogers, "Dictation: Key to Office Effectiveness," *The Personnel Administrator* (September 1979), 25–28, 34.

Presenting.   Several different kinds of expenditures are considered under the category of presenting messages. The time involved in conducting meetings, giving speeches, appearing on television programs, and engaging in conversations all constitute direct costs. In addition, the costs of producing written materials are part of the presentational costs of communicating. Griese (1978) reported data on the costs of producing company magazines, magapapers, newspapers, and newsletters. See Table 6.3. The figures are based purely on costs of production and exclude mailing expenses and salaries of editorial staffs. Griese cautions us that these figures may not be representative of all company publications in the categories cited, but they do suggest that communicating does constitute a major cost to organizations.

Receiver-Interpreter Costs. Receiver-interpreters accrue similar communicating costs to those of originators of messages. We shall briefly examine four costs: receiving the message, understanding it, thinking about it, acting upon the message.

Receiving.   The reception of a message refers to getting it physically. For a written message, reception may begin with the internal mail service and its delivery expenses, the process of sorting within a department, and opening and distributing the letters, circulars, invoices, announcements, notices, and other items to actual receivers for their handling. The reception of an oral message follows a similar pattern, including making contact with a secretary or administrative assistant, scheduling a time, waiting for the appointed time, and being escorted into the contact's office. Salespeople know the expense of "getting received" for oral communication as vividly as any group.

Goldhaber, Dennis, Richetto, and Wiio (1979) reviewed some research completed in Europe on the effects of office relocations on communication costs. Most of the costs studied concerned reception of messages: "Thorngren showed in Sweden and Goddard in England (1977) that after relocation, most workers retained 30 percent of their old communication contacts" (p. 56). Pye (1976) concluded that after an office had been relocated, "a civil servant's telephone costs would increase by about 50 pounds per year" (about $125), suggesting that economic benefits derived from the relocations did *not* offset the increased costs of maintaining contacts in the old locations.

The cost-benefit ratio (efficiency) of receiving messages may be affected by the use of newer means of transmitting and displaying images, such as video-phones and microcomputer-video interactive systems (Floyd, 1980). The FYI file section of

TABLE 6.3   Costs of Producing Written Materials

Type of Publication	Mean Cost per Thousand
All magazines	$568.06
Award-winning magazines	$413.04
Magapapers	$344.01
Newspapers	$290.23
Newsletters	$166.19

the *Training and Development Journal* listed five ways in which "video helps managers become communicators" by helping them:

Receive timely and tangible data;

Communicate specific recommendations, policies, and procedures to selected employees;

Acquire new management skills;

Eliminate redundant training and briefing tasks;

Evaluate their presentational effectiveness.

The main point being made is that video systems, whether coupled with computers or telephones, are a timely investment that can make the reception of information and contacts more cost-effective. As managers often say, "The name of the game is return on investment." The truly effective manager is *not* one who simply saves money but is one who spends money wisely. The costs involved in receiving messages can be enormous. New ways for making the reception of information more efficient are being considered every day.

Understanding. The costs involved in comprehending the meaning of a message are also important. The actual amount of time that it takes to understand a message may vary from person to person and vary with the content and style of the message itself. The more detailed and complex the message, the greater the likelihood that the costs of understanding it will be higher. On the other hand, there are also costs associated with not understanding or with misunderstanding a message. When a message is misunderstood, additional information may be required, more time may be devoted to preparing other messages, still more time may be needed to follow up and correct the misunderstanding. Every act beyond the misunderstanding may add to the cost of communicating.

Thinking. Some time is usually desirable for pondering the consequences of each message. This time is also a cost, although it may very well be the most efficient way to spend time. Mentally rehearsing and reviewing what might be said later or how an appropriate response may be made can reduce the time and effort put into the next cycle of originator costs. Both slow and hasty responses may increase the labor and supplies costs of communication, but they also affect the next category of costs—the human factors.

In summary, expenditures of physical resources include such items as buildings, offices, meeting rooms, and work and storage areas; communication equipment such as typewriters, dictating and transcribing machines, copiers, telephones, video systems, computers, printing machinery, filing cabinets and storage cabinets, and teletype and television units; supplies that allow messages to be prepared and sent, including paper and ink, fluids, cards, pens, pencils, postage, and telephone services; and labor associated with both the originator and the receiver-interpreter of messages. Originator labor costs may be assigned to thinking, composing, transcribing, and presenting; receiver-interpreter costs are associated with physically getting a message, understanding or misunderstanding it, and thinking about the consequences of responding to it. Even though we have analyzed the expenditure of physical resources according to several categories and separately for originators and receiver-interpreters, Thayer (1968) rightly observed that the "efficiency of any message is . . . encounters-specific; it depends upon the participants, the situation, the timing, etc.—upon all of the conditions of any specific communication encounter" (p. 159).

Direct expenditures of physical resources such as office space and labor are important aspects of the costs of communication in an organization; however, the negative impact on interpersonal relationships and losses of human resource potential may be even greater communication costs than the losses associated with physical resources.

Expenditures of Human Resource Potential

Communication can have a positive and impelling effect on human beings in an organization. Communication can also produce powerful negative consequences. Costs are represented by losses and expenditures of resources. The losses and expenditures of human resources occur most often as negative consequences on people in the organization. Let us look at six major losses and expenditures related to human resources.

1. *Loss of interest and motivation.* Poor communication has its quickest and most deadly cost in losses of interest and motivation among organization members. Employees fail to direct their energies toward accomplishing organization goals. They perform at minimal levels and are distracted easily. Much of what they do is only indirectly related to getting the work done, with considerable emphasis on social interaction.

2. *Loss of trust and support.* As interest and motivation disappear and disinterest and reduced levels of activity become apparent, efforts to reestablish the former levels of interest are met with distrust and nonsupport. Modest resistance becomes apparent. Dislike and indications of withdrawal from making contacts with those who are distrusted become obvious.

3. *Interpersonal conflict.* Major signs of deteriorating interpersonal relationships create tension between people in the organization. Minor disagreements surface with angry outbursts occurring frequently. Individuals seem cross and exhibit uneven dispositions, flaring up at unpredictable times. Moderate degrees of absenteeism are noticeable. Some people refuse to engage in conversations with colleagues. On the other hand, verbal aggression substitutes for problem solving.

4. *Indiscriminate opposition.* Organization members become preoccupied with their own goals and categorically oppose suggestions without much reason. If an idea appears likely to be beneficial for them, they will support it; on the contrary, if a proposal appears to infringe on some prerogative of theirs or appears likely to not advance their cause noticeably, organization members oppose it. The merits of an idea are seldom considered.

5. *Rigidity.* Opposition leads to rigid and inflexible ways of doing things. Legalistic procedures, literal interpretations of rules and regulations, and impulsive and

uncaring decisions result. Illnesses occur more frequently, and disappointments, defeat, and unhappy feelings dominate relationships.

6. *Emotional stress.* Eventually organization members begin to experience emotional stress. Minor problems and small disappointments around the office throw people into a dither—states of disorientation. Self-doubt surges. The harder people work, the less productive they are. At the end of a day the stress makes employees physically exhausted, although they have done very little physical work. Too much stress begins to take its toll on physical health. Ailments such as high blood pressure, heart disease, peptic ulcers, and some forms of arthritis strike. Stress is expensive. Good productive people have mental breakdowns and make mistakes that ultimately cost organizations millions of dollars in direct expenses.

The costs of expenditures of human resource potential are difficult to assess, but estimates of losses caused by stress-produced illness are staggering. The costs of reduced production and performance in an organization are very real.

Production Losses

Expenditures of human resource potential are nearly always reflected in losses in production and performance on the job. Conflict, opposition, distrust, rigidity, and emotional stress lead to reduced productivity. Six production losses seem apparent.

1. *Distortion of goals and objectives of the organization.* One of the major production losses that results from poor communication is the distortion of the goals of the company. Through anxiety, distrust, lack of support, rigidity, and other human resource issues, employees evolve patterns of work that facilitate the successful accomplishment of only the things they want to do. Emphasis is given to tasks that may be only partially related to the main goals of the organization. At a college, for example, teaching may be a key goal. However, faculty members may gradually make community service or consulting more important activities, resulting in a distortion of the actual goals of the school.

2. *Misuse of resources.* Another consequence of poor communication is the misuse of both physical and human resources. Money may be budgeted for purchases that are only marginally effective, and employees may be assigned tasks that do not take full advantage of their abilities. Because of mistrust a highly competent employee may be given routine duties to perform, which never allows the employee an opportunity to make significant decisions and progress in the organization.

3. *Inefficiency in performance of duties.* Because of communication problems, employees may perform their jobs with some degree of inefficiency. Through anger an employee may decide to use more paper than is necessary, to take more time than need be, or to route information along more complex channels. In each case poor communication contributes to a less efficient use of resources and contributes to inefficiency in the organization.

4. *Inept performance.* Poor communication can lead directly to doing a job badly, even to doing it wrong. Unskillful, incompetent, inept completion of a task probably contributes to waste and loss in the use of physical and human resources as often as any other cause. Although inefficiency can often be tolerated, incompe-

tence leads more quickly to intolerable conditions than does any other form of performance. In fact, incompetence is usually grounds for dismissal. Nevertheless, much inept performance could be eliminated or at least minimized through effective communication.

5. *Lack of coordination.* Inefficiency and ineptness may be reflected in lack of coordination, or lack of coordination may result in inefficiency and incompetence. Nevertheless, the act of bringing together the elements of a situation to create a harmonious set of relationships and produce action that accomplishes a goal is so intimately connected with the quality of communication that the lack of communication or a reduction in the quality of communication that results in lack of coordination is a serious organizational loss in and of itself.

6. *Delays and work stoppages.* Although the distortion of goals, misuse of resources, inefficiency in performance, inept work, and lack of coordination all have serious effects on production and result in losses, complete work stoppages or major delays are probably the ultimate consequences of poor communication and result in the greatest amount of direct production loss. Strikes may occur over a multitude of issues, but at the heart of most differences is some degree of poor communication. The ability to resolve disagreements is also a function of the quality of communication. Merrihue (1960) has described step-by-step procedures for communicating during a strike. He points out, however, that the most effective approach was "talk based on mutual respect from careful and continuous communication within the company" (p. 276).

There can be little doubt that the consequences of poor communication are costly—costly in terms of production losses and detrimental effects on human beings.

EFFECTIVENESS

The second element in the index of efficiency is *effectiveness*. In organizational communication, we deal with two kinds of effectiveness: organizational effectiveness and communication effectiveness.

Organizational Effectiveness

Steers (1977) develops the position that "effectiveness is perhaps best understood in terms of the attainment of optimized goals; that is, organizational effectiveness can be viewed as the extent to which an organization can acquire and utilize its available resources to attain feasible operative and operational goals" (p. 135). Sanford, Hunt, and Bracey (1976) argue that "organizations are effective to the degree that they achieve their goals, provide satisfaction for their members, and grow and develop in their ability to continue to do both of these things" (p. 35).

All of these authors take a fairly strong functional, or objective, view of organizational effectiveness; they assume that organizations have clear goals, whether they are operative or operational, that can be achieved. Weick (1985) takes this assumption of rationality to task when he argues that "organizations use rationality as a facade when they talk about goals, planning, intentions, and analysis, not because these practices necessarily work, but because people who supply resources believe that such practices work and indicate sound management'' (p. 110).

Organizational effectiveness may still be judged by whether goals are achieved, but how goals are identified and accomplished may be affected by one's view of effectiveness. Weick (1985) suggests that the process through which goals are identified may be different from what we usually assume. Organizational members demonstrate their rationality (that is, the idea that they move from determined goals to their accomplishment) through *retrospective justification*. That is, actions occur first, followed by the invention of reasons why the actions occurred. Finally, the whole sequence is inserted, after the fact, into the organization's history. "The action is reframed as a response to a threat, a solution to a problem that becomes clear only after the action was finished, a response to something that no one realized was a stimulus until the outcome became evident" (Weick, 1985, p. 111).

Effectiveness, in the sense of retrospective justification, would probably be measured by how well the reasons justified the actions rather than how well the actions suited the goals. Weick explains the weakness in judging effectiveness from retrospective justification as "failing to realize that such designs are retrospective intentions that were not present while the action unfolded. The steps actually responsible for effectiveness seldom can be discovered after the event has occurred." (pp. 113–114).

The problem of recognizing organizational effectiveness is highlighted through this description of an organization as an "unconventional soccer match."

> The field for the game is round; there are several goals scattered haphazardly around the circular field; people can enter and leave the game whenever they want; they can say "that's my goal" whenever they want to, as many times as they want to, and for as many goals as they want to; the entire game takes place on a sloped field, and the game is played as if it makes sense. (Weick, 1985, p. 106)

How would you determine when the organization is effective? The answer, most likely, lies in the pockets of agreement that small groups of organization members have about the game and what the rules are for play. Obviously, there may be less agreement than first meets the eye, but we shall assume that organizational effectiveness will be judged by how well members, groups of members, and the entire collection of groups seem to be moving toward the accomplishment of general goals.

Steers (1977) is direct in his observation about the role of communication in organizational effectiveness:

> In any organizational endeavor, the role of communication is of central importance. This is particularly true in regard to the issue of organizational effectiveness. Communication patterns and processes represent the necessary vehicle by which employee activities are coordinated and directed toward the goals and objectives of an organization. (p. 147)

We accept this statement as a fairly accurate one, given our understanding of the critical importance of communicative processes in organizations. How one determines when communication is effective is also a compelling question. Let us look at communication effectiveness.

Communication Effectiveness

Although the literature on organization theory often states that the effectiveness of organizational communication is a key determinant of organization effectiveness, the literature is often quite silent about the conditions that make for communication effectiveness. One author who has written on this aspect of efficiency is Thayer (1968, pp. 137–152). The following description of some criteria to evaluate the effectiveness of both communication and organizational communication is based on his theories.

Building on the definition and conceptualization of communication expressed earlier, you will recall that communication involves two basic categories of activities:

1. Displays, which are often thought of as the products or behaviors of the originator of a message. We think of these displays as the performance of a message as well as the elements in the environment or the context in which the message is initiated.
2. Interpretations, which consist of the mental processes people go through in order to make sense out of the displays to which they are exposed. Thayer (1968) called this a person's "take-into-account-ability" (p. 28).

Given these definitions of communication, what conditions need to be met for communication to be considered effective? Let us identify several criteria:

1. We might think of effectiveness as the *accurate* display of a message. That is, when a communicator initiates a display that fits the idea precisely, then the process of communication can be considered effective. Unfortunately, if the display is not also artistic, compelling, and useful, it may stand as a monument to ineffectiveness. Thus, we may be able to judge the accuracy, artistry, compellingness, and usefulness of a message-display, but not its effectiveness—because effectiveness is more a function of the receiver-interpreter of a message than it is a function of the creator of a display. Nevertheless, the accurate, artistic, compelling, and useful display of a message are key criteria for evaluating the effectiveness of at least one aspect of the process of communication.

2. Regardless of the quality of the display, little about communication effectiveness makes sense unless the message-display is taken into account by an interpreter. In fact, it is possible to argue that the effectiveness of any communicative transaction is wholly a function of the interpreter's ability to comprehend and make sense of a message-display. This criterion is often referred to as the *fidelity* of a message transaction. The interpreter must be able to construct the meaning, or sense—or the display itself—so that it is similar to what the initiator, or originator, of the display intended. Regretfully, effectiveness is more often judged by what the parties to the transaction actually do than by the quality of the display or the fidelity of the interpretation.

3. The true effectiveness of a message, it could be argued, depends on the degree to which the parties involved in communicating act upon the messages. The criterion used here is, "Did the other party act consistent with what the message requested or implied?" It may be, however, that the message-display asked for or implied

actions different from what the originator intended. Would communication be effective if the other person acted consistent with the message but inconsistent with what the originator intended?

Even more confounding is the question of choice in communication. Suppose the interpreter did comprehend the message-display in the manner intended by the initiator but just did not agree with it and, subsequently, did not act as requested? What if the interpreter of the message, on the other hand, did comprehend the display as intended, did agree with the message, and would have acted as intended, but other circumstances beyond the control of the interpreter interfered with his or her ability to act? Would communication be judged ineffective?

The most complicated aspect of the effectiveness of communication may be depicted by this kind of instance: As the message-display is constructed, the initiator has an inaccurate idea of what he or she wants the interpreter to do. The interpreter then understands the message differently from what the initiator intended and actually behaves consistent with what the initiator should have wanted, which was different from what the initiator asked for. Was communication effective?

We could take a pragmatic approach and say that effectiveness is anything that works. However, it may be more useful to consider the creation of a display, the interpretation of a display, and acting upon one's interpretation as three different operations that should be evaluated separately.

4. Looking at a communicative transaction as a nonintentional act, effectiveness may be viewed as how satisfied any individual is with how he or she acquires and uses the information he or she needs as well as the manner in which his or her intentions have been achieved by others.

Thayer raises an interesting question in this context with an insightful example:

> Suppose, for example, a manager asks for certain data to be supplied to him. The receiver of the request complies. So that encounter was effective, in that sense. But suppose also that the data he requested either was not the best data he could have obtained for his purposes, or was of a magnitude or complexity far beyond his ability to assimilate. Given these consequences for his own input side, was the encounter effective or not? (p. 141)

What if the consequences of effective communication in one instance turn out to be detrimental to one or more of the parties involved? Should the more complex process be judged ineffective?

5. Effectiveness at the organizational level—the one that most concerns us—depends on the effectiveness of communication at the other levels (intrapersonal, interpersonal, technological) as well as criteria that applies to the overall system. The puzzling element here is that effectiveness at one level may be detrimental, or at least ineffective, at another level. Thus we are impelled to think of organizational effectiveness as a balance across levels. Thayer refers to organizational communication effectiveness as "some satisfactory suboptimization of effectiveness at the various levels at which it could be assessed—i.e., some satisfactory degree of effectiveness on balance" (p. 143).

Finally, and in summary, we suggest three cautions about communication effectiveness, all of which argue that effectiveness is limited, in the end, by all the circumstances within which people try to communicate.

1. "We cannot communicate to another beyond his [or her] abilities to comprehend nor beyond the consequences he [or she] sees for himself [or herself] if he [or she] (a) comprehends and behaves accordingly, (b) comprehends but doesn't (or can't) behave accordingly, [and/or] (c) misunderstands and therefore doesn't initiate the behavior intended by the originator" (Thayer, p. 150).

2. "One's effectiveness as a communicator depends first upon the implicit facilitators and inhibitors (the circumstances) which establish consequences as possible, inevitable, or impossible" (Thayer, p. 151).

3. A person's effectiveness depends, then, upon his or her ability to recognize what is possible to accomplish communicatively and upon his or her tactical competence to succeed in those circumstances in which achievement is possible (Thayer, p. 151).

4. Finally, effectiveness depends on one's techniques of communication, although techniques can be effective only to the extent that the circumstances have been accurately recognized (Thayer, pp. 151–152).

Keeping this introduction to the idea of communication effectiveness in mind, let us now consider how effectiveness is translated into organizational activities.

ORGANIZATIONAL COMMUNICATION POLICIES

Most organizations have a manual of policies that cover a wide variety of activities, including the duties, responsibilities, and authority of employees; human resource planning; employee records; compensation; benefits; safety; equipment maintenance; training; marketing selection and expansion; and growth plans. The policies provide general but definite guidelines for all employees in carrying out their assignments. Policies give direction to and provide standards for making decisions. Policies standardize ways of thinking about and doing things. They provide for uniform treatment of problems and people.

Policies are also statements by which the effectiveness of communication in the organization can be judged. Deviations from policy may lead to less efficient communication; they may cost more and be less effective. Farace, Taylor, and Stewart (1978) point out that the overall effectiveness of organizational communication is limited by the resources that can be devoted to communicating; the degree of effectiveness depends upon the amount of resources expended on communicating. Thus, they conclude, "the critical decision topic for managers is the selection of those effectiveness criteria which need to be maximized in order to achieve the greatest overall efficiency of communication in the organization" (p. 274). Melcher and Beller (1967) describe criteria for the selection of channels and methods of communicating when a choice between formal and informal channels or some combination would allow an administrator to be more effective or when a choice between oral, written, or some combination of those methods might increase an administrator's effectiveness. A comprehensive organizational communication policy should probably include statements on all areas of effectiveness.

Although communication is one of the most pervasive activities occurring in most organizations, a policy statement on organizational communication is usually the most frequently missing section in the policy manual. The purpose of this chapter is to outline the general features of some communication policies for use in organizations. To accomplish this purpose, the concept of policies is defined, some basic requirements for stating policies are reviewed, and a list of communication activities and how policies might be phrased to cover them as well as an example of an organizational communication policy are presented.

DEFINITION OF POLICY

A *policy* is a general statement that is designed to guide a person's thinking about decision making in an organization. A policy specifies a definite course of action to be followed under certain circumstances. Often policies are merely implied rather than stated directly. For example, incoming correspondence may be placed in a manila folder and filed in a drawer for several days, after which it is sorted and distributed to appropriate individuals for reading and replies. A new employee may observe this practice and ask why correspondence is handled in that manner. The secretary who does the filing may not be entirely clear on the reasons for such a procedure, but the explanation will surely be grounded in the expression, "It's policy."

What the secretary means is that there is some understanding that correspondence will be placed in a manila folder and filed in a drawer for two to four days, depending on how full the folder gets, after which the mail is separated according to employee and placed in the employees' mailboxes. In reality an employee, long parted from the organization, may have been rushed one day and simply used the manila folder device as a means to reduce work overload. Over time the practice was followed rather strictly, allowing it to be interpreted as a policy. Thus what began as a temporary activity in a limited area developed into an organization-wide course of action to be adhered to rigorously and, at times, needlessly.

Policies, in any case, consist of general statements, or *understandings* when not stated, that tell what kinds of actions should be taken in a given circumstance. For example, a policy statement of PACECO, Inc., on the issue of discrimination in employment, might be stated as follows: "PACECO shall provide employment, training, compensation, promotion, and other conditions of employment without regard to race, color, religion, national origin, sex, or age, except where age or sex are essential, bona fide occupational qualifications." This policy statement clearly asserts that PACECO, Inc., employees are to take actions that provide employment without discrimination.

IMPORTANT FEATURES OF POLICIES

Effective policies are guided by five basic requirements:

1. *Policies should reflect the goals of the organization*. Policies should translate the plans and objectives of the organization into statements that guide the thinking of managers and operators. Policies should emerge out of the basic philosophy and

overall directions of the organization. Thus by studying the policies of the organization, you ought to have a fairly clear idea of what the organization is about and what it values.

2. *Policies should be internally consistent.* This guideline asks that policies be developed logically and appropriately from one another. Policies should neither contradict one another nor countermand policies of higher and lower orders within the organization. This means that policies in one part of the organization must be phrased so that they do not conflict with policies in another part.

3. *Policies should allow for discretionary decision making.* Policies represent general statements that *guide the thinking* of members of the organization. Policies should avoid dictating specifically how a person is to behave. Rules and procedures, on the other hand, are designed to channel action, and they allow for little or no discretion. Policies are often implemented by means of a set of rules and procedures directing employees to act in specific ways. Policies have a degree of ambiguity and uncertainty associated with them. Policies must be interpreted.

4. *Policies should be written down.* Writing a policy down, of course, does not make it a clear and concise statement, but a policy that cannot be written down is usually, at minimum, ambiguous and, at most, fuzzy, inconsistent, and potentially irrelevant. The issuance of a written policy does not ensure that it will be understood, either. If the policy is written, however, it can be reviewed and updated. Even at that, a great deal of interpersonal communication is usually necessary to make the application of policies consistent and fair.

5. *Policies should be communicated to members of the organization.* Although policies may reflect the goals of the organization, may be stated carefully so as to be fully consistent with one another, may allow for the proper discretionary decision making, and may be written down, they will be ineffective unless they are adequately distributed to members of the organization. Since policies are written with some ambiguity involved, they must be interpreted for those who are to apply the policies. Continued application of a policy to specific situations, unfortunately, tends to gradually evolve into a procedure that eventually becomes a regulation that is often applied as a rule, with no discretion. The process of communicating policies is a continuing activity. Policies ought to be discussed on a regular basis to make certain that they are being applied with discretion as guides to thinking rather than as rules for action.

Communication policies represent a set of objectives that the organization wishes to achieve with regard to communication. As with policies guiding manufacturing, sales, and finance, communication policies express the philosophy of the organization so as to achieve some consistency in attitude and practice throughout the organization. In an organization where there are no formal communication policies, each individual manager, supervisor, section head, and employee may have his or her own communication policies that may conflict with those of other members of the organization with whom he or she interacts. Sigband (1969) observed that

> when firms have no philosophy of communications we almost invariably have as a result:
>
> 1. Little or no discussion on controversial issues (labor problems, salaries, promotion, layoffs, etc.),

2. Different ways of handling similar issues throughout the organization,
3. Continued discussion on superficial and surface topics to the exclusion of items of real importance to individuals in and outside the firm. (p. 63)

Seybold (1966) reported an analysis of the formal written communication policy statements of eighty large companies, which revealed a wide range of philosophies regarding why managers or supervisors should communicate with employees. Some policies, for example, indicated that managers should keep employees informed because the *employees want information;* others stated that *employees have a right to know things;* others expressed the philosophy that managers should communicate with employees in order to give the *employees a feeling of participating in decisions.*

Burhans (1971) observed that even though organizations may differ in their formally stated policies, communication difficulties in an organization may arise frequently because *employees* of a firm or work group may have preferences for certain communication policies and practices that differ from that of their supervisors, without the supervisors being aware that the differences exist. Burhans developed a *Communication Policy Preference Scale* of thirty-five items that appeared to be sensitive to both the communication preferences of employees and their supervisors' misassumptions about those preferences. The items represented a fairly full range of answers to five basic questions:

1. Why communicate?
2. What should be communicated?
3. When should it be communicated?
4. Who should communicate to whom?
5. How should an organization's management communicate with its employees?

Within certain limitations those five questions (Why, What, When, Who, and How) establish a framework for thinking about the content of a communication policy. Sigband (1969), however, suggested that an adequate communication philosophy might include the following points:

1. Employees should be informed about ongoing activities of the company.
2. Employees should be informed about company goals, objectives, plans, and directions.
3. Employees should be informed about negative, sensitive, and controversial issues.
4. Employees should be encouraged to participate in a steady flow of two-way communications.
5. Employees should meet periodically with their supervisors for discussions of job performance and appraisal.
6. Meetings should be held to explore important areas and to encourage free expression.
7. Employees should have important events and situations communicated to them as quickly as possible.

Sigband concluded that "when a philosophy such as this is established, a policy will evolve. This then permits *all* managers *in all* of the company's plants to recognize their boundaries. They know what, when, and how completely they may communicate with their subordinates'' (p. 65).

Sigband offers two key reservations concerning implementing a communication policy. He suggests that there are constraints, boundaries, and limits. Judgment must be used. A corporate philosophy of communication, he asserts, is not ''a license to communicate everything to everyone'' (p. 65). On the other hand, an effective philosophy of communication, he argues, commits the organization to a long-range plan of informing others, opening channels of communication, and developing a freer flow of ideas.

SUMMARY

The costs of communicating in an organization are related to the price a person or organization pays to communicate. The costs of communicating affect the efficiency (cost-effectiveness) with which communication takes place and with which the organization functions. We have reviewed three basic types of costs associated with communication: expenditures of physical resources, expenditures of human resources, and losses in production. If we realize that there is always some investment or expenditure when communication occurs, we shall be more sensitive to ways of reducing the costs, thus improving the efficiency of communication in organizations.

A SUBJECTIVIST'S NOTATION

To understand organizational life involves determining how symbols (words, ideas, constructs) provide the underlying logic of organized activity and assessing *whose interests are being served by this activity*. Discussions of communication efficiency usually have three critical shortcomings. First, communication efficiency is determined strictly from a managerial perspective. Second, when efficiency is discussed, attention is diverted from the heart of communication (negotiated meaning) and placed on the forms and artifacts of communication. Finally, there is a tendency to focus on only one function of communication and downplay or ignore the others. We will discuss each of these shortcomings.

Notions of efficient and effective communication typically represent managerial criteria, whereas other organization members may have their own ideas about what constitutes effective communication. Descriptions of some organizational cultures (e.g., advanced technology) reveal that traditional communication promoted by management may actually inhibit progress (Kidder, 1981). It is not that efficiency is an unworthy concept; it just gives a limited picture. A knowledge of the total organizational culture may demonstrate that formulas concerning efficiency do not fit the particular organization. There is value in understanding all facets of an organization so that all voices can be heard.

Communication efficiency can be elaborated best when communication is conceived of as memos, newsletters, and those tangible costs that can be tagged with a price. But that is not the critical aspect of organizational communication. The meaning generated, altered, and sustained in a created context is the most significant aspect of communication. Even memos and newsletters have to be acted out and assigned meaning before they are anything more than pieces of paper. People make sense of things through interaction, which is so pervasive it cannot be singled out for measurement. An evolutionary process, such as interaction, does not lend itself to measurement by mechanical concepts. Communication is not like fuel, which can be fed into a machine to see how long it will run.

An organization's communication may have impact on its overall performance. Symbolic factors, for example, may have a major effect on attitudes and behaviors that translate into profit, but that is only one function served by communication. People talk to get things done, but talking also does much more than that. People enact their environments in order to cope and make sense. An analysis of an organizational culture uncovers the expression of people's needs and how they have endowed their experiences with meaning. Needs are investments too. A person's needs have an impact on organizational efficiency and affect the bottom line. That is *not* the point, however. The bottom line for organization members is different and deserves consideration (Scott & Hart, 1979).

When discussions turn to efficiency and policy, there is a tendency to become "memo and manual" oriented and ignore what actually happens in organizations. The *communication in use* is a far cry from the communication suggested in policy manuals. When are policy manuals used? In the typical organization, policy manuals are used when there is some crisis or event that is out of the ordinary. Even then, policies may be interpreted to fit what the practice has been rather than what it should have been. Organizations are best understood by examining their everyday behavior.

REFERENCES

Burhans, David T., Jr., "The Development and Field Testing of Two Internal Communication Measuring Instruments," unpublished paper, California State College, Los Angeles, December 1971.

Culnan, Mary J., and M. Lynne Markus, "Information Technologies," in *Handbook of Organizational Communication*. Frederic M. Jablin et al., eds. Beverly Hills, Calif.: Sage, 1987.

Farace, Richard V., James A. Taylor, and John P. Stewart, "Criteria for Evaluation of Organizational Effectiveness: Review and Synthesis," in *Communication Yearbook 2*, Brent D. Ruben, ed., 271–292. New Brunswick, N.J.: Transaction Books, 1978.

Floyd, Steve, "Designing Interactive Video Programs," *Training and Development Journal* (December 1980), 73–77.

Goldhaber, Gerald M., Harry S. Dennis III, Gary M. Richetto, and Osmo A. Wiio, *Information Strategies*. Englewood Cliffs, N.J.: Prentice-Hall, 1979.

Griese, Noel L., "Cost per Thousand; Yardstick for Measuring Publication Effectiveness," *Journal of Organizational Communication* (1978), 26–29.

Kidder, T., *The Soul of a New Machine*. Boston: Little, Brown, 1981.

Melcher, A. J., and R. Beller, "Toward a Theory of Organizational Communication," *Academy of Management Journal*, 10 (March 1967), 29–52.

Merrihue, Willard V., *Managing by Communication*. New York: McGraw-Hill, 1960.

Pye, R., "Effect of Telecommunications on the Location of Office Employment," *OMEGA*, 4 (3), 1976.

Rogers, Florence, "Dictation: Key to Office Effectiveness," *The Personnel Administrator* (September 1979), 25–28, 34.

Sanford, Audrey C., Gary T. Hunt, and Hyler J. Bracey, *Communication Behavior in Organizations*. Columbus, Ohio: Chas. E. Merrill, 1976.

Scott, William G., and David K. Hart, *Organizational America*. Boston: Houghton Mifflin, 1979.

Seybold, Geneva, *Employee Communication: Policy and Tools*. New York: National Industrial Conference Board, Inc., 1966.

Sigband, Norman B., "Needed: Corporate Policies on Communications," *S.A.M. Advanced Management Journal* (April 1969), 61–67.

Steers, Richard M., *Organizational Effectiveness: A Behavioral View*. Santa Monica, Calif.: Goodyear Publishing Co., 1977.

Thayer, Lee, *Communication and Communication Systems*. Homewood, Ill.: Richard D. Irwin, 1968.

Vardaman, George T., Carroll C. Halterman, and Patricia Black Vardaman, *Cutting Communications Costs and Increasing Impacts*. New York: John Wiley, 1970.

Weick, Karl E., "Sources of Order in Underorganized Systems: Themes in Recent Organizational Theory," in *Organizational Theory and Inquiry*, Yvonna S. Lincoln, ed. Beverly Hills, Calif.: Sage, 1985.

Zygmont, Jeffrey, "Face to Face," *SKY*, February 1988, 10–16.

7

The Directions of Information Flow

What Is Communicated, to Whom, and How in Organizational Communication

The direction of something is the line along which it proceeds with regard to a terminating point. In organizational communication we talk about information that proceeds formally from a person of higher authority to one of lower authority—downward communication; information that proceeds from a position of lower authority to one of higher authority—upward communication; information that moves along people and positions of approximately the same level of authority—horizontal communication; or information that moves among people and positions that are neither superior nor subordinate to one another and that are in different functional departments—cross-channel communication. We also refer to information that flows informally along the "grapevine." We shall examine each of these types of directional communication more closely. Figure 7.1 portrays the four formal directions of information flow in an organization. We shall discuss those first.

DOWNWARD COMMUNICATION

Downward communication in an organization means that information flows from positions of higher authority to those of lower authority. We usually think of information moving from management to employees; however, in organizations most of the links are in the management group (Davis, 1967). Figure 7.2 shows how

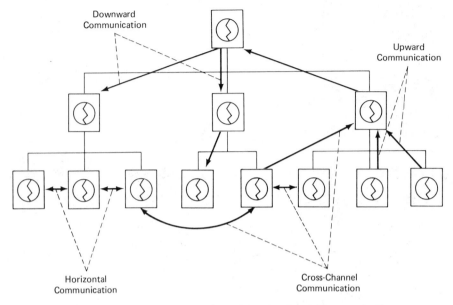

FIGURE 7.1 Four Directions of Organizational Communication

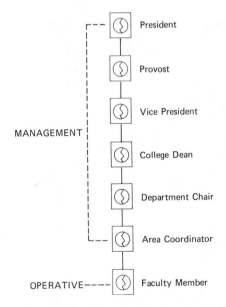

FIGURE 7.2 Organization Chart Showing Six Levels of Management and One Level of Operative

the communication structure of a university has six management levels and only one operative level.

You can see how the emphasis in organizational communication can often move toward managerial communication in which the primary concerns are with downward communication, getting information through the management group and *to* the operative group. There are two important concerns that we shall discuss: (1) what kinds of information are disseminated from management levels to employees and (2) how the information is provided.

Kinds of Information Communicated down the Line

Five types of information are usually communicated from superiors to subordinates (Katz & Kahn, 1966): (1) information about how to do a job, (2) information about the rationale for doing jobs, (3) information about organizational policies and practices, (4) information about an employee's performance, and (5) information to develop a sense of mission.

How to Do a Job. This type of information concerns what employees are expected to do and how they are to do it. Job instructions in the form of orders, directives, explanations, operations manuals, and job descriptions are some of the more common ways of providing this kind of information.

Rationale for Doing Jobs. This type of information is designed to let employees know how their jobs are related to other tasks and positions in the organization and why they are doing a particular job. In a broader sense this type of information helps employees to recognize how their jobs aid the organization in accomplishing its objectives.

Organizational Policies and Practices. In addition to information about specific job duties and how they fit into the total organization, employees are informed about hours of work, salaries, retirement programs, health benefits, vacation and sick leave, incentive programs, and penalties and punishments. Faculty members, for example, are obligated to attend general university faculty meetings, commencement exercises, and, occasionally, special convocations and forums. The university also has policies governing grading practices, office hours, research activities, and consulting that must be communicated to employees.

Employee Performance. Information about how well things are going is important to the efficient and effective functioning of a system. Information for employees about how well they are doing in their jobs is also extremely important in maintaining a successfully operating organization. Employees frequently complain, however, that they do not know how their supervisors view their performances. Performance appraisal interviews, management-by-objectives, merit reviews, wage and salary administration, performance evaluation or rating programs are all ways of assessing the adequacy of employee job performance. However, the single most difficult task for most supervisors is communicating information about how their subordinates are doing. Informing hard-working employees that their job performance has inadequacies strikes fear in the hearts of even the most fearless supervisors. Negative information tends to reduce motivation and may potentially affect performance negatively, resulting in less effective work than before the appraisal. On the other hand, the performance of some workers is pretty much determined by the system, making individual evaluations of performance meaningless. Assembly-line workers, for example, are often unable to do their jobs more efficiently than the entire line permits.

Mission of the Organization.   Loyalty to the organization, its products, services, and contributions to society is an important ingredient in organizational strength. One company reported coming to the conclusion that the good it was doing for employees and the country would not be understood unless

> (1) its deeds would, in fact, measure up to sound economic analysis; (2) . . . it could somehow help its employees understand the rudiments of business economics; and (3) . . . its employees had some sound basis for evaluating the fairness of the count-less decisions the company had to make if it was to continue to operate in the balanced best interests of its employees, its customers, its share owners, its suppliers and distribution associates, and the rest of the public. (Merrihue, 1960, pp. 46–47)

Identification with the mission of the organization is the consequence of communicating information about the broad goals and objectives of the organization and the contributions the organization is making not only to employees but also to society in general.

Employees at all levels in the organization feel a need to be informed. Top management lives in an information world. The quality and quantity of information must be high in order to make meaningful and accurate decisions. Top management must have information from all units in the organization, and it must get information out to all units. The flow of information from top management down to operatives is a continuous and difficult activity. The selection of ways to provide information involves not only the expenditure of direct monetary resources but also psychic and emotional resources.

How Information Is Provided Down the Line.   The methods by which information is communicated down the line may be grouped into four classes: (1) oral, (2) written, (3) pictorial, (4) oral-written-pictorial combinations. Before listing a variety of oral, written, and pictorial methods of downward communication, two issues deserve consideration: (1) what methods seem to be viewed by managers as most effective in getting the word out and (2) what methods seem to be used most frequently.

Level (1972) surveyed supervisors and asked them to rate the effectiveness of different combinations of methods for different types of communication situations (Table 7.1). The four methods were (1) written only, (2) oral only, (3) written followed by oral, and (4) oral followed by written. The oral-followed-by-written method was rated *most effective* in six of the ten situations and was never rated as inappropriate for any situation. Situations requiring immediate action but with some follow-up later, those of a general nature with documentation desired, and those involving positive interpersonal relations seemed best handled by the oral-followed-by-written method.

The oral-only method was ranked most effective in situations involving repri-

TABLE 7.1   Most Effective versus Least Effective Methods for Communicating with Employees in Ten Different Situations

Situation	Most Effective	Least Effective
1. Communicating information requiring immediate employee action	Oral followed by written	Written only
2. Communicating information requiring future employee action	Written only	Oral only
3. Communicating information of a general nature	Written only	Oral only
4. Communicating a company directive or order	Oral followed by written	Oral only
5. Communicating information on an important company policy change	Oral followed by written	Oral only
6. Communicating with your immediate supervisor about work progress	Oral followed by written	Oral only
7. Promoting a safety campaign	Oral followed by written	Oral only
8. Commending an employee for noteworthy work	Oral followed by written	Written only
9. Reprimanding an employee for work deficiency	Oral only	Written only
10. Settling a dispute among employees about a work problem	Oral only	Written only

Source: From Dale A. Level, Jr., "Communication Effectiveness: Method and Situation," *The Journal of Business Communication,* 10 (Fall 1972), 19–25. Reprinted by permission of Dale A. Level, Jr., and the American Business Communication Association, publisher of *The Journal of Business Communication.*

mands and settling disputes but least effective in six other situations, although four of the six situations were also ranked most effective for the combination oral-followed-by-written method. This implies that the oral method is desirable but not by itself.

The written-only method was ranked most effective when information for future action was needed, when the information was general, and when no personal contact was necessary. The written-followed-by-oral method was not ranked most effective or least effective for any situation.

Dahle (1954) studied the actual effectiveness of five methods of transmitting information from management to employees (downward) in business and industrial settings. The results of his study are summarized in Table 7.2 and indicate that using oral and written methods to present information was most effective.

In contrast to the research on effectiveness of different methods of transmitting information to employees, studies of the frequency with which certain methods are used suggest an upside-down relationship. Peters' (1949, p. 42) early report indicated that "posters and bulletin boards" were used by 96 percent of the companies in his survey, whereas only 32 percent used small group meetings. Level and Dahle both discovered that oral and oral accompanied or followed by written methods were most effective. Bulletin boards and written only were both less effective. Although contemporary organizations are usually more sensitive to these issues, there is a strong tendency to use methods that are less costly on the surface and that appear to provide some degree of effectiveness.

TABLE 7.2   Relative Effectiveness of Five Methods of Transmitting Information from Management to Employees in Business and Industrial Settings

Rank Order*	
1	Presenting information in both oral and written forms (*oral and written*)
2	Presenting information to a group orally, using no written materials or visual aids (*oral only*)
3	Presenting information to each member of the group in written form, with no supplementary oral or visual explanation (*written only*)
4	Posting the information on a bulletin board (*bulletin board only*)
5	Making no presentation of the information in either oral or written form (*grapevine only*)

Source: From Thomas L. Dahle, "An Objective and Comparative Study of Five Methods of Transmitting Information from Management to Business and Industrial Employees," *Speech Monographs,* 21 (March 1954), 21–28. Reprinted by permission of the publisher.

*1 = Most effective, 5 = least effective

Criteria for Selecting Methods

Six criteria are often used for selecting methods of communicating information to employees (Level & Galle, 1980), although a comprehensive theory has not been fully stated (Melcher & Beller, 1967).

1. *Availability.* Those methods that are currently available in the organization will tend to be used. After an inventory of available methods, the organization can decide what methods could be added for a more effective program overall.

2. *Cost.* The method judged to be least costly will tend to be selected for routine and nonurgent information dissemination. When nonroutine and urgent dissemination is necessary or desirable, more costly but faster methods will probably be used.

3. *Impact.* The method that seems to provide the greatest impact or impression will frequently be chosen over a method that lacks flair or is fairly standard.

4. *Relevance.* The method that seems most relevant to the purpose to be achieved will be chosen more often. A short, informative purpose may be accomplished with a conversation followed by a memo. If the communication of complex details is the purpose, a written technical report may be the method chosen.

5. *Response.* The method selected will be influenced by whether a specific response to the information is desired or necessary. In a training setting it may be desirable to use a method that allows and encourages trainees to react and ask questions. In such a case a face-to-face meeting would probably be the method chosen.

6. *Skills.* The methods that seem to fit the abilities of the sender to actually use *and* the abilities of the receiver to comprehend will tend to be used over those that seem beyond the skills of the communicator or that seem beyond the capabilities of the employee to understand. A glossy brochure will probably not be used if the communicator does not feel capable of producing it; if the employees' level of education is limited, a complex manual of instructions would probably not be a good method to use.

A SHORT INVENTORY OF COMMUNICATION METHODS

Methods of communicating in organizations are described in detail in other books and articles (Brown & Reid, 1979; Hunt, 1980; Level & Galle, 1980; Peters, 1949; Reuss & Silvis, 1981; Rosenblatt, Cheatham, & Watt, 1977; Sigband & Bateman, 1981). We shall simply provide an inventory of methods that may trigger some alternative ideas when considering what communication methods to use.

ORAL METHODS

Employee meetings
    Large group, mass, or informational
    Small discussion groups or task
    Social meetings
Collective bargaining
Grievance interviews
Labor-management committees (outside of collective bargaining)
Public address systems
Counseling interviews
Company chaplains
Radio programs
Phonograph recordings
The grapevine
Telephone
Intercom system
Paging system
Closed-circuit television
Speeches and oral reports
Conferences
Teleconferences
Briefings
Lectures and training workshops
Videotape presentations
Daily interpersonal contacts
Recognition and special award activities
Supervisor's home visits
Family night
Luncheons with selected employees
Unstructured visits to the shop and office
Audio tape recordings

WRITTEN METHODS

Letters
Memos and reports
Facsimile reproductions
Teletype
Telegrams
Electronic longhand
Newspapers
Magazines
Handbooks
Manuals
Bulletins
Inserts and enclosures
House organ
Daily news digest
Individualized benefits reports
Annual financial report
Magapapers
Progress reports
Directory of employees
Anniversary books
Booklets
Job descriptions
Policy manuals
Announcement flyers
Postcards to employees
Paycheck stub messages
Research and development brochures
Industry books
Tour booklets

PICTORIAL METHODS

Ad reprints
Calendars
Sample product kits
Billboards
Corporate art exhibits
Films

Slide presentations

Puzzles and quizzes

Picture books

Photographs

Exhibits and displays

Graphics

Logo and trademarks

Charts and graphs

Posters

Cartoons and comic strips

Visits to the plant

The design, development, creation, display, and use of various methods has become highly specialized. At many universities and colleges, programs in design, advertising, marketing, journalism, public relations, film, video, and instructional media are dedicated to making the methods of communication more exciting and effective. The ability to recognize and select appropriate methods for enhancing human resource development is important for individuals in organizational communication interested in careers in HRD. Individually and in combination, these methods help get information down the line.

UPWARD COMMUNICATION

Upward communication in an organization means that information flows from lower levels (subordinates) to higher levels (supervisors). All employees in an organization, except possibly those at the top level, may communicate upward—that is, any subordinate may have good reason to either request information from or give information to someone with more authority than he or she has. A request or comment directed toward an individual with broader, higher, or more extensive authority is the essence of upward communication.

Values of Upward Communication

Upward communication is important for a number of reasons. We shall list a few functions, values, and arguments for up-the-line communication.

1. The upward flow of information supplies valuable information for decision making by those who direct the organization and supervise the activities of others (Sharma, 1979).
2. Upward communication lets supervisors know when their subordinates are ready for information from them and how well subordinates accept what they have been told (Planty & Machaver, 1952).
3. Upward communication allows, even encourages, gripes and grievances to

surface and lets supervisors know what is bothering those who are closer to the actual operations (Conboy, 1976).

4. Upward communication cultivates appreciation and loyalty to the organization by giving employees an opportunity to ask questions and contribute ideas and suggestions about the operation of the organization (Planty & Machaver, 1952).
5. Upward communication permits supervisors to determine whether subordinates got the meaning that was intended from the downward flow of information (Planty & Machaver, 1952).
6. Upward communication helps employees cope with their work problems and strengthen their involvement in their jobs and with the organization (Harriman, 1974).

What Should Be Communicated up the Line?

Most analyses and research on upward communication suggest that supervisors and managers ought to get information from subordinates that

1. Tells what the subordinates are doing—their work, achievements, progress, and plans for the future.
2. Describes unsolved work problems on which subordinates may need or would like some type of assistance.
3. Offers suggestions or ideas for improvements within their unit or the organization as a whole.
4. Reveals how subordinates think and feel about their jobs, their coworkers, and the organization.

Figure 7.3 summarizes some of the information that supervisors and managers ought to learn about subordinates through upward communication.

What Employees Feel about Their Jobs

1. How satisfied are employees with their pay in relation to other jobs in the organization, similar jobs in the industry and community?
2. Are working hours and shift rotations felt to be reasonable?
3. Is the work load fairly distributed?
4. Are the tools, equipment, and office furniture of good quality and adequate?
5. Are the formal standards for personal appearance well known and accepted?
6. Do subordinates believe that supervisors observe the rules and regulations that they are expected to follow?
7. Do subordinates feel that all possible candidates for promotion from within are given full and honest consideration?
8. Do employees feel that people are laid off or discharged unreasonably?

FIGURE 7.3 What Supervisors Should Learn Through Upward Communication (Source: Reprinted, by permission of the publisher, from "Upward Communications: A Project in Executive Development" (pages 304–318) by Earl Planty and William Machaver, *Personnel*, January 1952 © 1952 American Management Association, New York. All rights reserved.

10. Do employees feel that supervisors are interested in helping with personal or family problems that may affect attitudes at work?

What Employees Feel About Coworkers

1. Do employees feel that their coworkers, supervisors, subordinates, department, and company are efficient?
2. Do employees feel that supervisors have favorites?
3. Do employees feel that they are adequately supervised?
4. Do subordinates feel that they are being trained and developed to advance in the organization?
5. Do employees feel that supervisors and managers resist new ideas of subordinates without evaluating their worth?
6. Are grievances handled promptly and fairly?
7. Do employees feel that supervisors and managers understand their needs and desires?
8. How do subordinates get along with their coworkers?

What Employees Feel About the Organization

1. Do the organization's actions live up to its promises and expressed policies as an employer?
2. Is the organization financially strong?
3. Are organization managers able to maintain its competitive position?
4. What is the organization's reputation in the community?
5. What do employees' families think of the employees' jobs and opportunities in the organization?
6. Do employees feel they know far enough in advance about serious changes so they can adjust to them?
7. Do employees feel that equal pay is given for equal work?
8. Do employees know and accept personnel practices regarding illness, leave of absence, vacation leave, and so forth?
9. Do employees believe that the health, insurance, and retirement programs are fair and adequate?
10. Do employees feel that the recreational and educational or training facilities are adequate and available?
11. Do employees understand the annual report?
12. Do employees consider lunch and snack food prices to be fair and the food to be of high quality?

FIGURE 7.3 *continued*

Why Is It Difficult to Get Information up the Line?

Merrihue (1960) observed that "it would have been wiser to have first bulldozed and paved an uphill street from employees to top management, but that is a much more complex and time-consuming task and most of us are not quite sure that we, as yet, know how to do it" (p. 195). Harriman (1974) reported that "we surveyed hundreds of companies in the United States and Canada. . . . We encountered no experts, studies or programs on upward communications" (pp. 148–149). They may be right. Upward communication may be too complex and too time-consuming and have too few organization managers who know how to get information up the line.

The difficulty of getting information up the line was alluded to by Davis (1967) when he noted that a manager's

status and prestige at the plant are different from the workers'. He probably talks differently and dresses differently. He can freely call a worker to his desk or walk to his work station, but the worker is not equally free to call in his manager. The worker usually lacks ability to express himself as clearly as the manager, who is better trained and has more practice in communication skills. Neither can the worker have a specialist prepare his communication, but this service is usually available to the manager. Just as the worker lacks technical assistance, he also usually lacks the use of certain media, such as plant magazines, public-address systems, and meetings. The worker is further impeded because he is talking to a man with whose work and responsibilities he is not familiar. (p. 344)

Sharma (1979) lists four reasons why upward communication seems so difficult:

1. *The tendency for employees to conceal their thoughts.* Studies have shown, for example, that employees feel that they will get into trouble if they speak up to their supervisors and that the best way to move up in the organization is to agree with their superiors.
2. *The feeling that supervisors and managers are not interested in employee problems.* Employees report quite frequently that their managers are not concerned about their problems. Managers may not respond to employee problems and may even stifle some upward communication because it might make them look bad to their superiors.
3. *A lack of rewards for employee upward communication.* Frequently supervisors and managers fail to provide either intangible or tangible rewards for maintaining open upward communication channels.
4. *The feeling that supervisors and managers are inaccessible and unresponsive to what employees say.* Either supervisors are too busy to listen or the subordinates cannot find them. If the supervisor is located, he or she is unresponsive to what the subordinate says.

The combination of these four feelings and beliefs creates a powerful deterrent to the expression of ideas, opinions, and information by subordinates, especially if the process and procedures by which upward communication is to occur are unwieldly and cumbersome.

How Can Information Get up the Line?

Jackson (1959) noted that the forces that direct communication in an organization are, on the whole, motivational. Employees tend to communicate in order to accomplish some goal, to satisfy some personal need, or to try to improve their immediate circumstances. He suggests that any program of organizational communication must be based on a climate of trust. When trust exists, employees are more likely to communicate ideas and feelings more freely, and supervisors are more likely to interpret what employees mean more accurately.

The importance of creating and maintaining a climate of trust cannot be stated too frequently. Upward communication just will not occur when supervisors feel that they must guard against employees talking to the manager above them. Rogers and Agarwala-Rogers (1976) describe an effort by a large Eastern bank to stimulate upward communication with a "sound-off" program. Employees were encouraged to take their complaints and suggestions to the personnel department or to managers above their supervisors if they did not receive satisfaction from their immediate supervisors. It was discovered that supervisors felt that any contact between their subordinates and the supervisors' bosses was threatening and improper. Employees did not think it was improper, but they did feel that it was dangerous. As one employee said, "You bypass the supervisor once and go to Personnel, the first thing they do is get the supervisor on the phone and tell him everything. Next, you're in trouble" (p. 98). Wendlinger (1973) discovered a similar situation in a large West Coast bank. He reported "that there was no way to confidently express an opinion or solve a problem when normal channels had broken down. Some employees feared the possibility of reprisals as a result of bypassing their supervisors with such ideas or proposals, and others were concerned that management—seemingly remote in a rapidly growing organization—was not really interested in their attitudes and opinions" (p. 17).

To facilitate upward communication Wendlinger's organization created an "Open Line" program in which employees were able to submit problems, complaints, or opinions to top management with their identities being kept completely confidential, known only to the Open Line coordinator, with a guaranteed candid written reply from management which was sent to the employee's home. The success of the program was attributed to two factors: the employee's identity was protected, and the answers were honest. The coordinator of Open Line was given one mission: to make the job itself unnecessary, which means arriving at a time when free and open communication precludes the need for Open Line, where mutual trust and understanding make upward communication an easy job.

Principles of Upward Communication

Planty and Machaver (1952) identified seven principles to guide programs of upward communication. The principles seem as applicable today as when they were formulated.

1. *An effective upward communication program must be planned.* Although confidentiality and candor undergird all effective communication programs, supervisors and managers must stimulate, encourage, and find ways to promote upward communication.

2. *An effective upward communication program operates continuously.* Subordinates must initiate information to and request information from higher levels regardless of how things are going. Supervisors and managers must be receptive to information from subordinates and be willing to respond to what they receive when the organization is functioning smoothly as well as when things seem to be going badly.

3. *An effective upward communication program uses the routine channels.* Without denying any employee the opportunity of making contact with and being heard

by managers at any level, information should flow upward through the organization following the usual, routine steps. Problems and requests for information should move upward through the organization until they reach the person who can take action; if that person can provide the information or resolve the problem, there should be little need to go beyond that point.

4. *An effective upward communication program stresses sensitivity and receptivity in entertaining ideas from lower levels.* Differences in interpretations and perceptions of events should be expected. A person's position in the organization encourages him or her to see things differently and to assign different meanings to them. Differences in values and priorities lead to differences in inferences and conclusions. Listening in order to understand what a person means is basic to effective upward communication.

5. *An effective upward communication program involves objective listening.* Supervisors and managers must devote the time to listening to subordinates in an objective way. Reactions that distract from the seriousness of information and irritating listening habits show that upward communication is not really desired. Hearing a subordinate out, putting him or her at ease, and reducing tensions reveals a receptive intent and a willingness to hear contrary opinions, implied criticisms, and alternative points of view.

6. *An effective upward communication program involves taking action to respond to problems.* Active listening may get new ideas into the open, but a failure to take action only creates resentment and undermines the good faith in upward communication. When changes in policies or actions should be made, just listening without adjustments denies the idea of effective upward communication. If action cannot be taken, the subordinate should be informed and reasons given for why changes cannot be made.

7. *An effective upward communication program uses a variety of media and methods to promote the flow of information.* The most effective method of upward communication is daily face-to-face contacts and conversations among supervisors and subordinates. Beyond continuing interpersonal interaction within the organization and outside the workplace, the following may serve as a checklist of upward communication methods:

Suggestion systems ("Speak Up," "Sound Off," "Open Line")

Grievance procedures

Attitude and information surveys

Counseling interviews

Rumor clinics

Question boxes

Employee round tables

Manager's luncheons

Performance appraisals

Dial-the-Boss telephone system

Employee letters

Organization development activities

Human resource development and training

Reports and memos

Union publications

Grapevine

In summary, this section has reviewed the values of upward communication in an organization, discussed what kinds of information should be communicated up the line, analyzed why it is difficult to get information from lower levels to higher levels in an organization, described the climate that seems most conducive to getting information to flow upward, and listed seven principles of an effective program of upward communication. For additional specific analysis of upward influence and message processes see Schilit and Locke (1982), Stohl and Redding (1987).

Two directions of information flow have been considered—downward and upward. Together they constitute what is often called *vertical communication.* Information is also shared among organization members who occupy positions of approximately the same level of authority; we refer to it as *horizontal communication.*

HORIZONTAL COMMUNICATION

Horizontal communication consists of sharing information among peers within the same work unit. A work unit is comprised of individuals who are located at the same authority level in the organization and have the same superior. Thus at a university, a work unit may be a department. A department of communication, a department of organizational behavior, and a department of instructional science all include faculty members who are supervised by a chairperson. Communication among faculty members in one of the departments is what we call horizontal communication. Communication between faculty members in one department and faculty members in another department is what we shall call *cross-channel communication*—that is, information is shared across functional boundaries, or work units, and among people who are neither subordinate nor superior to one another.

Purposes of Horizontal Communication

Research and experience suggest that horizontal communication occurs for at least six reasons:

1. *To coordinate work assignments.* Members of a training and development department have a major training activity to organize and deliver. They need to meet to coordinate who will do what.

2. *To share information on plans and activities.* When ideas from several minds promise to be better than ideas from just one person, horizontal communication becomes critical. In creating the design of a training program or a public relations campaign, members of a department may need to share information on their plans and what they will be doing.

3. *To solve problems*. Recently three student interns were given assignments in the same general location. They met and engaged in horizontal communication in order to reduce the number of unnecessary trips and share rides. They were able to reduce costs and to work together to arrive at their organization assignments with fewer problems.

4. *To secure common understanding*. When changes are proposed in the requirements for an academic major, faculty must work together in order to produce a common understanding about what changes should be made. Meetings and conversations among faculty members at the same organizational level and within the same department are especially important in achieving understanding.

5. *To conciliate, negotiate, and arbitrate differences*. Individuals frequently develop preferences and priorities that eventually lead to disagreements. When this occurs, horizontal communication among members of the work unit is essential to conciliating differences. In fact, some differences may need to be negotiated or arbitrated. It is only through horizontal communication that priorities can be accommodated and conflicts resolved.

6. *To develop interpersonal support*. Because we spend a great deal of time interacting with others on the job, we all derive some degree of interpersonal support from our colleagues. Much of our horizontal communication is for the purpose of strengthening interpersonal ties and relationships. Coworkers often have lunch together and meet at breaks to strengthen interpersonal relationships. Horizontal communication plays an important part in producing rapport among employees and encouraging a cohesive work unit. Employees at the same level who interact frequently seem to have less trouble understanding one another. Interaction among colleagues provides emotional and psychological support.

Methods of Horizontal Communication

The most common forms of horizontal communication involve some type of interpersonal contact. Even written forms of horizontal communication tend to be more casual. Thus horizontal communication occurs most often in these ways:

1. *Committee meetings*. Most coordination, sharing of information, conciliating, and problem solving takes place in meetings.

2. *Informal interaction during breaks*. Members of work units may often work individually and in somewhat isolated settings, but during breaks and at lunch time they have an opportunity to engage in horizontal communication. Faculty, for example, regularly talk in the hallway between their offices when they do not have appointments or classes.

3. *Telephone conversations*. A great deal of information is shared among employees over the telephone. Work activities are coordinated as well as some differences negotiated by means of telephone conversations. In fact, the telephone probably speeds up and increases the number of contacts with other members of the organization, especially when they are located at the end of another hallway or on the other side of the building.

4. *Memos and notes*. Handwritten or typed notes and memos are some of the most common ways of keeping in touch with coworkers. Although a subordinate may feel inhibited in sending his or her supervisor a handwritten note about a work problem, it would not be uncommon or unexpected to leave a note for a colleague.

5. *Social activities.* Bowling teams and groupings at picnics are often made up of individuals who are at the same level in the organization. Much horizontal communication occurs when coworkers gather for social activities.

6. *Quality circles.* A quality circle is a voluntary group of workers who have shared areas of responsibility. It is primarily a normal work group who produce a part of a product or service. Members of the circle meet together each week to discuss, analyze, and suggest ideas for improving their work. They are trained in the use of specific problem-solving procedures and specific techniques, such as cause-and-effect diagrams, pareto diagrams, histograms, checklists, and graphs. Circle leaders are trained in leadership skills, adult learning methods, and motivation and communication techniques. Circle meetings are held on organization time and on organization premises. Quality circles are generally given full responsibility for identifying and solving problems (Yager, 1980).

Barriers to Horizontal Communication

Barriers to horizontal communication have much in common with those affecting upward and downward communication. Lack of trust among coworkers, intense concerns about upward mobility, and competition for resources can affect the way in which employees at the same level in the organization communicate with one another.

CROSS-CHANNEL COMMUNICATION

In most organizations a need exists for employees to share information across functional boundaries with individuals who occupy positions that are neither subordinate nor superior to their own. For example, departments such as engineering, research, accounting, and personnel gather data, issue reports, prepare plans, coordinate activities, and advise managers about the work of individuals in all parts of an organization. They cross functional lines and communicate with people who supervise and are supervised but who are neither superior nor subordinate to them. They lack line authority to direct those with whom they communicate and must rely primarily on selling their ideas. Nevertheless, they have considerable mobility within the organization; they can visit other areas or leave their offices just to engage in informal conversation (Davis, 1967).

Staff specialists are usually the most active in cross-channel communication because their responsibilities usually influence what occurs in several authority chains of command or positional networks. The training and development unit, for example, may have contacts with production, sales, industrial relations, purchasing, research, and engineering as well as with customers, for customer training. Staff specialists frequently have closer contact with top management, which permits them to short-circuit the authoritative system. Davis (1967) rightly observes that "the results are both good and bad. Communication upward and downward tends to be improved, but lower management often waits in insecurity with the fear that it is being bypassed or criticized without an opportunity to answer" (p. 346).

Because of the potentially large number of cross-channel contacts by staff specialists and others who need to make contacts in other chains-of-command, it is important to have an organization policy to guide cross-channel communication.

Fayol (1916/1940) demonstrated that cross-channel communication was appropriate, and even necessary at times, especially for employees who were lower in a channel. As shown in Figure 7.4, Employee P may save time and conserve resources by communicating directly with Employee Y. Because of the potential for undermining the authority channels and for losing control over the flow of information, two conditions must be met as part of using Fayol's Bridge:

1. Each employee who wishes to communicate across channels must secure permission in advance from his or her direct supervisor (in Figure 7.4, P would secure permission from Supervisor H). In some cases the permission may be granted in the form of a general policy statement indicating the circumstances that justify cross-channel communication.
2. Each employee who engages in cross-channel communication must inform his or her supervisor what happened as a result of the meeting.

The importance of cross-channel communication in organizations prompted Davis (1967) to suggest that the application of three principles would strengthen the communication role of staff specialists:

1. Staff specialists must be trained in communication skills.
2. Staff specialists need to recognize the importance of their communication role.
3. Management should recognize the role of staff specialists and make greater use of it in organizational communication.

Both horizontal and cross-channel communication involve lateral relationships that are essential to effective organizational communication. In this section we have focused primarily on *positional communication,* which involves the flow of information between people in positions in an organization. Employees

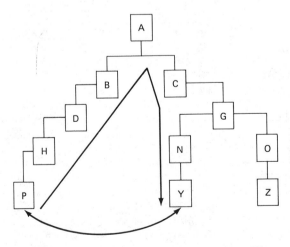

FIGURE 7.4   Fayol's Bridge for Employee P

often communicate from their positions. Frequently, however, organization members communicate with others without regard to their positions. This results in one or more *personal communication networks*. Positional communication is usually referred to as *formal communication;* personal communication is usually called *informal communication.* We shall briefly analyze the idea of personal or informal communication in an organization.

INFORMAL, PERSONAL, OR GRAPEVINE COMMUNICATION

When employees communicate with one another without regard to position in the organization, the factors directing the flow of information are more personal. The direction of information flow is less stable. Information flows upward, downward, horizontally, and across channels with little, if any, regard for designated positional relationships. Since this informal, personal information emerges from interaction between people, it appears to flow in unpredictable directions, and its network is referred to as a *grapevine.* The metaphor seems apt; a grapevine seems to grow and send out shoots in all directions, capturing and hiding the fruit under a cover of heavy leaves, almost defying detection. Information that flows along the grapevine network appears to be fickle and furtive as well. In terms of communication the grapevine has been described as "a person-to-person method of relaying secret reports which cannot be obtained through regular channels" (Stein, 1967, p. 616). Informal communication does tend to consist of "secret" reports about people and events that do not flow through official, formal channels. Information obtained through the grapevine concerns "what someone said or heard" rather than what was announced by authorities. At least the sources seem to be "secret" even if the information itself is not.

Characteristics of the Grapevine

Although research on characteristics of the grapevine is not extensive, enough has been completed over the years to suggest the following characteristics (Davis & O'Connor, 1977):

1. The grapevine functions largely through word-of-mouth interaction.
2. The grapevine is generally free of organizational and positional restraints.
3. The grapevine moves information rapidly.
4. The grapevine network is described as a *cluster chain* because each relayor tends to tell a cluster of people rather than just one other person.
5. Participants in a grapevine network tend to take one of three roles: liaisons, isolates, or dead-enders (those who usually do not pass the information on).
6. The grapevine tends to be more a product of the situation than of the people in the organization.
7. The sooner a person knows about an event after it happens, the more likely he or she is to tell others.
8. If information being told to a person concerns something in which he or she is interested, he or she is more likely to tell the information to others.

9. The predominant flow of information on the grapevine tends to occur within functional groups rather than between them.
10. Generally, from 75 to 90 percent of the details of the message being transmitted by the grapevine are accurate; however, as Davis (1967) notes, "People tend to think the grapevine is less accurate than it really is because its errors are more dramatic and consequently more impressed on memory than its day-to-day routine accuracy. Moreover, the inaccurate parts are often more important" (p. 244).
11. Grapevine information is usually somewhat incomplete, lending itself to misinterpretation even when the details are accurate.
12. The grapevine tends to exert some influence in the organization, whether for good or evil; thus an understanding of the grapevine and how it can contribute positively to the organization is important.

How to Work with the Grapevine

The number and detrimental effects of messages passed along the grapevine can be controlled by keeping the formal channels of communication open, allowing for candid, accurate, and sensitive upward, downward, horizontal, and cross-channel communication. Effective supervisor-subordinate relationships seem crucial to controlling grapevine information. Supervisors and managers should let employees know that they understand and accept information on the grapevine, especially since it reveals something about employee feelings, even if the information is incomplete and untrue.

SUMMARY

In summary, information flows in four formal directions in organizations: downward, upward, horizontally, and through cross-channels. The formal directions involve positional communication. However, organization members often communicate with one another without regard to their positions, resulting in a personal communication network. The personal communication system is often referred to as the grapevine and transmits informal or "secret" messages or information that does not flow through formal channels. Because the information on the grapevine is usually quite accurate but often incomplete, it may exert a powerful influence on those who are part of the system. Thus it is important for supervisors and managers to understand and help the grapevine benefit the organization.

A SUBJECTIVIST'S NOTATION

An interpretive perspective shifts the emphasis in management from regulating and controlling to interpreting and understanding. The interpretive practitioner focuses on making organizational realities clear so that members can examine their constructions to see what impact they are having on organizational action. Smircich (1983) asserts that "The adoption of the interpretive perspective leads managers to clarify the various realities in a setting and to remove distortion in their understanding of what is going on, in order to contribute to the more informed practice of organization'' (p. 225). This perspective is different from traditional management theory because it emphasizes what *is* going on among employees rather than what *should* go on from a managerial stance. Traditional managers are interested in the direction of flow because they think in terms of order and control. From this view, the information that counts is the information that management wants its members to have.

What are the consequences of thinking in terms of directions of flow of information? The most obvious shortcoming is that *meaning*, the very heart of communication, is placed in a secondary role. In other words, this view tends to equate information and communication. As you recall from earlier discussions, communication relies heavily on interpretation. The concepts of direction and flow suggest that communication is a type of substance that moves about in an orderly fashion within well-prescribed boundaries. Putnam (1983) points out that "By treating messages as physical substances, functionalists locate the *essence of communication* in transmission and channel effects" (p. 39). Communication is a process of shared and negotiated meanings; it is not a tangible substance that can be moved along selected channels at will.

Another consequence of emphasizing the directions of flow is that managers start thinking of communication as a highly predictable and mechanical process. We have already provided a caution against this type of thinking in earlier chapters, but once the idea of the direction of flow becomes a focal point, it tends to shape thinking toward an objective and concrete point of view. Reddy (1979) observes that people talk about communication as though it involved an actual pipeline. He suggests that a preponderance (70 percent) of the expressions used in talking or writing about communication emphasize what he has labeled the *conduit metaphor*. This idea suggests that meanings are *in* messages and are transferred by communication. After examining twenty-one management textbooks, issues of *supervisory management*, and the comments of managers, Axley (1983) concluded that conduit metaphorical expressions are predominant.

What is the impact of the conduit metaphor? Of course, words do not *mean*, only people mean, and meanings cannot be transferred like physical objects. Among the communication postulates advanced by Redding (1972) are the notions that (1) Anything is a potential message, and (2) The message received is the only one that counts. Communication is not a transferable commodity. When it is conceived as such, the complexity of the process is lost. Axley (1983) contends that "the conduit metaphor ultimately engenders and promotes the viewpoint that *communication is easy* and requires very little effort to be done successfully" (p. 17). Because of the multiple meanings assigned to messages and the negotiation of those messages through interaction, the process of communication requires far more involvement than the term *information flow* suggests. Another consequence of this emphasis is that management information is viewed as *the* information. If organizational reality is to be understood, there must be an effort to examine the information that *drives* the organization. This kind of information may or may not be managerial in nature. What is called informal communication may be just as crucial—and sometimes more so—as formal communication in the achievement of a task.

Rather than accepting the blinders of the terms *direction* and *flow*, it would be more productive to look for *clusters of meaning* and their effect on organizational action. What information is in the system; what information is used or sought; who uses it; and what functions are served by the information?

REFERENCES

Axley, Stephen R., "Conduit: A Performative Metaphor for Communicating in Organizations," Paper presented at the University of Utah Summer Conference on Interpretive Approaches to the Study of Organizations, Alta, Utah, 1983.

Brown, Harry M., and Karen K. Reid, *Business Writing and Communication*. New York: Longman, 1979.

Conboy, William A., *Working Together . . . Communication in a Healthy Organization*. Columbus, Ohio: Chas. E. Merrill, 1976.

Dahle, Thomas L., "An Objective and Comparative Study of Five Methods of Transmitting Information from Management to Business and Industrial Employees," *Speech Monographs*, 21 (March 1954), 21–28.

Davis, Keith, *Human Relations at Work: The Dynamics of Organizational Behavior*. New York: McGraw-Hill, 1967.

Davis, William L., and J. Regis O'Connor, "Serial Transmission of Information: A Study of the Grapevine," *Journal of Applied Communication Research*, 5 (1977), 61–72.

Fayol, Henri, *General and Industrial Management*, Constance Storrs, trans. New York: Pitman Publishing Corporation, 1940. (Originally published in 1916).

Harriman, Bruce, "Up and Down the Communications Ladder," *Harvard Business Review* (September–October 1974), 143–151.

Hunt, Gary T., *Communication Skills in the Organization*. Englewood Cliffs, N.J.: Prentice-Hall, 1980.

Jackson, Jay M., "The Organization and Its Communications Problem," *Advanced Management* (February 1959), 17–20.

Katz, Daniel, and Robert Kahn, *The Social Psychology of Organizations*. New York: John Wiley, 1966.

Level, Dale A., Jr., "Communication Effectiveness: Method and Situation," *The Journal of Business Communication*, 10 (Fall 1972), 19–25.

Level, Dale A., Jr., and William P. Galle, Jr., *Business Communications: Theory and Practice*. Dallas: Business Publications, Inc., 1980.

Melcher, Arlyn J., and Ronald Beller, "Toward a Theory of Organization Communication: Considerations in Channel Selection," *Academy of Management Journal*, 10 (March 1967), 39–52.

Merrihue, Willard V., *Managing by Communication*. New York: McGraw-Hill, 1960.

Peters, Raymond W., *Communication within Industry*. New York: Harper & Brothers, 1949.

Planty, Earl, and William Machaver, "Upward Communications: A Project in Executive Development," *Personnel*, 28 (January 1952), 304–318.

Putnam, Linda L., "The Interpretive Perspective: An Alternative to Functionalism," in *Communication and Organizations: An Interpretive Approach*, Linda L. Putnam and Michael Pacanowsky, eds. Beverly Hills, Calif.: Sage, 1983.

Redding, W. Charles, *Communication within the Organization*. New York: Industrial Communication Council, 1972.

Reddy, M., "The Conduit Metaphor—A Case of Frame Conflict in Our Language About Language," in *Metaphor and Thought*, A. Ortony, ed. Cambridge: Cambridge University Press, 1979.

Reuss, Carol, and Donn Silvis, eds., *Inside Organization Communication*. New York: Longman, 1981.

Rogers, Everett M., and Rekha Agarwala-Rogers, *Communication in Organizations*. New York: The Free Press, 1976.

Rosenblatt, S. Bernard, T. Richard Cheatham, and James T. Watt, *Communication in Business*. Englewood Cliffs, N.J.: Prentice-Hall, 1977.

Schilit, W. K., and E. A. Locke, "A Study of Upward Influence in Organizations," *Administrative Science Quarterly*, 26 (1982), 304–316.

Sharma, Jitendra M., "Organizational Communications: A Linking Process," *The Personnel Administrator*, 24 (July 1979), 35–43.

Sigband, Norman B., and David N. Bateman, *Communicating in Business*. Glenview, Ill.: Scott, Foresman, 1981.

Smircich, Linda, "Implications for Management Theory," in *Communication and Organizations: An Interpretive Approach*, Linda L. Putnam and Michael E. Pacanowsky, eds. Beverly Hills, Calif.: Sage, 1983.

Stein, Jess, ed., *The Random House Dictionary of the English Language*. New York: Random House, 1967.

Stohl, Cynthia, and W. Charles Redding, "Messages and Message Exchange Processes," in *Handbook of Organizational Communication*, Fredric M. Jablin et al., eds., 451–502. Beverly Hills, Calif.: Sage, 1987.

Wendlinger, Robert M., "Improving Upward Communication," *Journal of Business Communication*, 11 (Summer 1973), 17–23.

Yager, Ed., "Quality Circle: A Tool for the '80s," *Training and Development Journal* (August 1980), 60–62.

8

Climate, Satisfaction, and Information Adequacy

Have you ever had the experience of working on a job, having your supervisor come by and watch what you're doing for a few moments, and then kind of shrug and say, "Huh"? You ask, "Is there something wrong?" The reply you hear is, "Oh, nooo." Your supervisor walks away. Later you're taking a break, and two guys working in your area saunter up to the drink dispenser where you are standing. They just look at you and lean against the wall with their backs to you. You decide to stop at the personnel office and check on your overtime. Although you've been in the personnel office many times, the clerk asks your name and where you work. The clerk thumbs through the file drawer, looks at you, and shakes his head in a puzzled way. He says, "What did you say your name is?" You reply, "Never mind!" and frown deeply as you slam the door on your way out. Under your breath you mutter, "What is the matter with this place?" You look up at the sky expecting to see dark clouds signaling a thunderstorm. The sun is bright, and the sky is a beautiful blue. You wonder. Your mind storms. "It's the climate," you say. "We have a terrible climate in this organization!"

DEFINITION OF CLIMATE

Just as the weather creates a physical climate for a region, the way in which people communicate creates a psychological climate for an organization. A climate is the generally prevailing weather conditions of an area. The physical climate is a composite of temperature, air pressure, humidity, precipitation, sunshine, cloudiness, and winds throughout the year that is averaged over a series of years. The *communication climate* is a composite of human behaviors, perceptions of events, responses of employees to one another, expectations, interpersonal conflicts, and opportunities for growth in the organization throughout the year that is averaged over a series of years. You may experience a pattern of weather conditions that give you an inaccurate impression of the physical climate of a region; in the same way you may receive an inaccurate impression of the communication climate of an organization based on a short visit or some unusual interpersonal interactions. Sometimes, however, the weather on a particular day gives you a good picture of the physical climate just as a few interpersonal contacts can give you a clear picture of the communication climate.

IMPORTANCE OF CLIMATE

Is the physical climate of an area important? Is the communication climate of an organization important? Blumenstock (1970) explains that the physical climate "affects our way of life": the clothing we wear, the food we raise, the houses we construct, the transportation we use, the kinds of plants and animals in the area. In a similar fashion the communication climate of an organization affects the way we live: to whom we talk, whom we like, how we feel, how hard we work, how innovative we are, what we want to accomplish, and how we seem to fit into the organization. Redding (1972) states that *"the 'climate' of the organization is more crucial than are communication skills or techniques (taken by themselves) in creating an effective organization"* (p. 111).

The distinction between the overall climate of an organization and the communication climate of an organization is not easy to make, but the difference is important enough to try.

ORGANIZATIONAL CLIMATE

A definition by Goldhaber, Dennis, Richetto, and Wiio (1979) describes the idea of organizational climate; they suggest that organizational climate consists of the perceptions of organization members about (1) how they can act or behave, and (2) what seems responsible for the way others act or behave. This suggests that organization members sense or feel or perceive that certain aspects of the organization influence how they can behave in the organization. Organization members also explain why other members of the organization act the way they do in terms of the forces that influence their behavior. The literature on organizational climate (James & Jones, 1974; Taylor & Bowers, 1972; Waters, Roach, & Batlis, 1974) suggests that six aspects of organizational life have a strong effect on perceptions that lead to conclusions about the overall organizational climate.

1. *The importance of human beings in the organization.* The more organization members feel that they can act the way they do because human beings are considered important in the organization, the more highly they tend to rate the overall

organization climate. If they believe that human beings are considered to be unimportant in the organization, then the overall organization climate will be considered less desirable. The logic of the overall organization climate is about the same for the five other aspects of the organization.

2. *The flow of information in the organization.* The more organization members feel that they can act the way they do and others can act the way they do because the flow of information is adequate, the more highly they tend to rate the overall organization climate. If the flow of information is inadequate, the organization climate tends to be rated lower.

3. *Practices related to motivating employees.* If organization members view motivational practices in a positive way and feel that they behave and others behave in response to the motivational practices, they tend to rate the organization climate more highly. If the motivational practices (such as incentives, compensation, work conditions, benefits) are viewed as negative, then the organization climate will be rated lower.

4. *Decision-making practices.* The more that organization members feel that their actions and the actions of others are caused by positive decision-making practices, the more positively the overall organization climate is rated. If decision-making practices are viewed negatively and seem to be the cause of their behavior, organization members tend to rate the organization climate lower.

5. *Technology and work resources.* If organization members consider the materials, procedures, and equipment to be up-to-date and well maintained, allowing them to perform their work well, they tend to consider the organization climate to be higher than if they feel that the equipment and materials are holding them back from performing their jobs effectively.

6. *Upward influence.* The organization climate tends to be rated more highly if organization members feel that they have some influence on what happens in their departments, and the organization climate tends to be rated lower if organization members feel they are unable to influence those who supervise them.

The overall climate of an organization consists of perceptions by organization members of six dimensions of organizational life, which includes information flow and some practices involving communication; however, some perceptions directly involve the climate in which communicating occurs. This is called the *organizational communication climate*.

COMMUNICATION CLIMATE

The climate of communication in an organization is a composite of evaluations and reactions to certain activities that take place in an organization. The organizational communication climate involves three interacting parts, as shown in Figure 8.1.

Thus the climate in which communication occurs is a consequence or result of how organization members perceive (hold attitudes and expectations about or are satisfied with) such organizational features as its policies, information flow, work to be done, pay and benefits, promotions, coworkers, and supervisors in terms of how these features demonstrate to the organization members that the organization trusts them and allows them the freedom to take risks; supports them and gives them

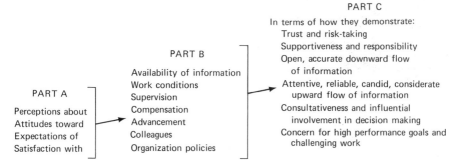

FIGURE 8.1   The Interacting Parts of Organizational Communication Climate

responsibility in doing their jobs; is openly providing accurate and adequate information about the organization; attentively listens and gets reliable and candid information from subordinates; actively consults organization members so that they see that their involvement is influential in decisions in the organization; and has a concern about high standards and challenging work (Goldhaber, 1979; Goldhaber et al., 1979; Jablin, 1980; Sanford, Hunt, & Bracey, 1976; Timm, 1980).

The existence of a phenomenon such as an organizational communication climate is often criticized until some way of measuring it has been developed. Dennis (1974) reported creating a questionnaire that measured five important components of communication climate. Peterson and Pace (1976) developed the *OA Communication Climate Inventory* (CCI) designed to measure the six dimensions of climate mentioned here, which were derived from the analysis of managerial climate completed by Redding (1972). Bednar (1977), Baugh (1978), and Applbaum and Anatol (1979) have used the instrument in research. Tests of the CCI's internal reliability show coefficients ranging from .80 to .97, which are generally considered very satisfactory. Factor analysis of the CCI indicates the emergence of one main factor. Applbaum and Anatol (1979) reported that the CCI "may be a valid index of overall organizational communication climate" (p. 10).

We now need to identify relationships between the communication climate in organizations and other organizational variables such as structure, regulations, morale, and interpersonal relationships. In that way we can recognize those dimensions of communication that ought to be scrutinized in order to improve the overall organization climate and ultimately the effectiveness and efficiency of the organization. We shall discuss some ways to identify problem areas and make improvements in the organizational communication system in later chapters.

Organizational and communication climate are important, as we mentioned earlier. It is so important, in fact, that some organizations base their recruiting and investment appeals on having high ratings of climate. The Kollmorgen ad (see Figure 8.2) illustrates the high regard held for a great organization climate.

Another construct or idea that has surfaced from research on organizational issues, particularly those surrounding the idea of productivity and employee satisfaction, is that of communication satisfaction. Downs (1977) reported that communication satisfaction has several identifiable dimensions itself and that instruments can measure it.

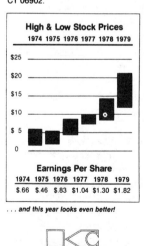

FIGURE 8.2 The Kollmorgen Ad (Source: From *Time* (September 22, 1980), 79. Reprinted by permission.)

COMMUNICATION SATISFACTION

According to Redding (1972), the term *communication satisfaction* has been used to refer to "the over-all degree of satisfaction an employee *perceives* in his total communication environment" (p. 429). The construct of *satisfaction* enriches the idea of communication climate. Climate includes the organization member's satisfaction with the availability of information. Satisfaction, in this sense, refers to how well the available information fulfills the organization member's requirements or demands for information, from whom it comes, the ways in which it is disseminated, how it is received and processed, and what kinds of responses one receives. Satisfaction is concerned with differences between what a person would like in terms of communication in an organization and what a person has in that regard. The organizational communication climate should clearly be affected by perceptions of how well the communicative activities of an organization satisfy a person's demands.

Satisfaction with communication is a function of what one gets compared with what one wants. Satisfaction should *not* be tied to any conception of message (displaying or interpreting) effectiveness. If the communication experience meets a requirement, it is likely to be regarded as satisfying, although it may not be particularly effective as far as standards of creating, displaying, and interpreting messages are concerned. You may feel a need for certain kinds of information or for having information presented to you in a particular way. When information is communicated in ways consistent with what you feel you would like, then you should experience satisfaction with communication.

The items that contribute most to satisfaction with communication in an organization are not fully identified, but the work of Wiio (1978), Downs and Hazen (1977), and Beckstrom (1980) suggest some dimensions. From Wiio's and Downs and Hazen's research Beckstrom constructed a questionnaire designed to measure ten factors of organizational communication satisfaction which were generally held in common by the earlier researchers. A factor analysis of responses revealed eight factors accounting for 55.1 percent of the variance. The factors that comprise satisfaction with organizational communication appear to be a combination of the following:

1. *Satisfaction with the person's job.* This included items about pay, benefits, promotion, and the work itself. Apparently satisfaction with aspects of the job contributes to satisfaction with communication.

2. *Satisfaction with the adequacy of information.* This factor included items about the degree of satisfaction with information about policies, new techniques, administrative and staff changes, future plans, and personal performance. Satisfaction with information received about the organization seems important to a concept of organizational communication satisfaction.

3. *Satisfaction with a person's ability to suggest improvements.* This factor included items such as places where communication ought to be improved, notification of changes for purposes of improvement, and the specific strategies used in making changes. Satisfaction with the kinds of changes being made, how the changes are to be made, and being informed about the changes appears to have relevance to satisfaction with organizational communication.

4. *Satisfaction with the efficiency of various channels of communicating.* This factor included items about the ways in which information is disseminated through an organization, including house organs, bulletins, memos, and other written materials. Communication satisfaction appears to be related to a person's view of how efficiently the media of an organization are used to disseminate information.

5. *Satisfaction with the quality of media.* Items related to this factor involved concerns about how well written materials were phrased, the value of the information when received, the balance and availability of information, and the promptness of the arrival of information. This suggests that concerns about the appearance, appropriateness, and availability of information have an effect upon a person's satisfaction with communication in an organization.

6. *Satisfaction with the way in which coworkers communicate.* This factor included items about horizontal and informal communication and about the degree of satisfaction derived from discussing problems and getting information from coworkers. This factor implies that satisfaction with communication in an organization is related in part to satisfactory relationships with peers.

7. *Satisfaction with communication involving the organization as an entity.* This factor included items involving relationships with the organization, support from the organization, and information from the organization. It appears that satisfaction with communication in the organization is affected by aspects of the organization often associated with communication climate, such as trust, support, and high performance goals.

In discussing communication satisfaction research, Downs (1977) observed that subjects tended to see a relationship between communication and satisfaction in the organization, with comments about communication climate and relationships with supervisors being most prominent. Such relationships suggest that supervisory styles have a powerful influence in both perceptions of climate and perceptions of satisfaction.

Closely related to the idea of communication satisfaction is the issue of *actual level of information* that any given member of the organization has about organization affairs. Redding (1972) referred to this as *information adequacy.* Beyond having adequate information about the organization, the question arises concerning whether having information is related in any way to goals of the organization—such as productivity, satisfaction, and employee development.

INFORMATION ADEQUACY

Information adequacy represents the actual amount of information accurately understood by a given group of organization members, plus their perceptions of whether they feel adequately informed (Redding, 1972). A cloud hanging over this issue concerns *what organization members ought to be told.* Usually decisions about what employees should know are made by top management of the organization. However, when lower-level employees report that the information they receive is inadequate, those decisions are made by the employees themselves. In any case information adequacy depends on some definition of what information ought to be known.

In a research program on measuring the effectiveness of employee communications being conducted at Southern Illinois University, Bateman and Miller (1979) reported developing the following list of topics on which employees might like to be informed:

fringe benefits
division products
employee hobbies
news about company
cartoons and jokes
how division products are used
employee recreational news
charity funds and drives
departmental features
savings bond programs
business trends affecting company
all products
executive promotions
employee safety
news about retirees
how company products are used
compensation
new or improved products
sales progress
free enterprise system
recipes and cooking hints

They also developed a checklist of subjects that employees might like to discuss with their supervisors; the list included

machine or job-related problems
time off
state of the division
potential layoffs
performance evaluation
procedures
fringe benefits
the company in general
overtime
tools and equipment
incoming orders

vacation time

plant or office procedures

how well the employee is doing

pay and pay increases

For purposes of their study Bateman and Miller chose six areas over which to develop a multiple-choice, objective examination to measure information adequacy. The areas were

wages and benefits

corporate diversity

business issues and problems

overseas business

acquisitions and growth

safety

Whether these are the best areas and the kinds of information that an employee ought to know has not been answered by any research reported at this time. The issue seems to be a substantial one for organizations, because, as Walton (1962) observed: "If each employee really mastered *all* the communications humming about him, he would have precious little time for anything else but that" (p. 22). Nevertheless, the general rule seems to be one of general and widespread ineffectiveness of downward communication, at least as far as information adequacy is measured by actual informational tests (Redding, 1972).

SUMMARY

In this chapter we have discussed the idea of organizational communication climate, organizational communication satisfaction, and information adequacy. We pointed out that the climate of an organization consists of how members of the organization can act and what they feel is responsible for the way others act. The climate in an organization, we also suggested, may be more important in creating an effective organization than are communication skills or techniques. The communication climate of an organization consists of the perceptions by organization members of characteristics of the organization in terms of how they demonstrate such behaviors as trust, supportiveness, and consultativeness. Organizational communication satisfaction refers to how well the available information fulfills the requirements of organization members for information and how it is handled. Information adequacy refers to what organization members ought to be told and whether the available information meets the need.

A SUBJECTIVIST'S NOTATION

Organizational climate is determined by looking at how people communicate with one another. An organizational world constructed by an organization's members contains values, norms, attitudes, and practices. The subjective processes and interactions that create, recreate, alter, or sustain these factors should be the focus of study rather than each individual's response or a total of all of the responses in an organization. From a subjective perspective, it is the *interaction* that is crucial to climate.

Climate is not an individual property but an attitude that organization members generate, share, and sustain. Imagine a group of workers talking during lunch break. A new worker says, "My supervisor is really on the ball!" Other workers respond, "Must be someone that I don't know. Most of these guys only talk to chew you out." "Yeah, that's my experience." "Me too, in fact, the guys in those positions don't even know what our jobs require." Now suppose that each time the new worker says something positive about a supervisor, fellow workers either say something contradictory or simply don't say anything. It is likely that the new worker will resort to silence until the prevailing view can be sustained in some way. This sort of interaction tells the researcher or manager about climate. It is important to note that what is not said is quite significant in assessing climate. Poole and McPhee (1983) describe several subjective approaches to the notion of climate. An interpretive emphasis conceives of climate as a collective attitude that is "continually produced and reproduced by members' interaction" (p. 213). Poole and McPhee reinforce the interaction idea by pointing out that "it is not enough to characterize this climate as simply a set of expectations and beliefs. We must also discover how these beliefs, attitudes, and values are created and maintained, what the climate means to members, and how it influences organizational life" (pp. 213–214).

What should the observer look for in the interaction? The climate of an organization is revealed through both the content of the messages and the symbolic forms used. Collective attitudes are revealed in vocabulary, metaphors, stories, and accounts. Anyone who has worked in an organization that was on its "last legs" understands the language of pessimism, lost hope, and survival. In such a situation, no one has to distribute a climate inventory to determine climate. Everyday exchanges give insight into how climate is produced and sustained. Schrank (1978) describes informal talk as "schmoozing" and suggests that "though the work itself is important to the workplace community, what is most neglected by those concerned with its problems is the nature of the human relationships. The rituals such as greetings on arrival, coffee breaks, lunchtime, smoke breaks, teasing, in-jokes, and endless talk about almost everything are the important ways in which the community maintains itself" (p. 78).

Climate has some far-reaching implications, and the study of climate involves more than determining whether Company X is a pleasant place to work. Meyer (1981) reports a study that demonstrates how symbolic forms (stories, and metaphors) upheld ideologies, substituted for organizational directives, and helped guide reactions during a time of crisis. The employees of one hospital took pride in their self-reliance and efficiency. They characterized themselves as a "lean and hungry organization." Members of another hospital system referred to themselves as a chaotic group, but one that valued innovation, pluralism, and professional autonomy. When the hospitals were faced with a doctors' strike, they responded very differently. Meyer concluded that "Memorial did not foresee the jolt and reverted to its original state when the tremors ceased; Community anticipated the jolt, learned during the adjustment process, and underwent subsequent organizational changes. Although the two hospitals experienced equivalent decline in occupancy, their responses were more consistent with their ideologies than with the objective realities imposed by the strike'' (p. 16). When organizational members interact and use symbolic forms, those forms provide rationale for organizational action. They also indicate what is expected from an organizational climate.

REFERENCES

Applbaum, Ronald I., and Karl W. E. Anatol, ''An Examination of the Relationship between Job Satisfaction, Organizational Norms, and Communication Climate among Employees in an Organization,'' Paper presented at meetings of the Communication Association of the Pacific, Honolulu, 1979.

Bateman, David N., and Jeffrey L. Miller, ''Measuring the Effectiveness of Employee Communications,'' Paper presented at the annual meeting of the American Business Communication Association, December 1979.

Baugh, Steven, ''Communication Climate in a School District,'' unpublished doctoral dissertation, Brigham Young University, 1978.

Beckstrom, Mark R., ''Measuring Communication Satisfaction in an Organization: The Design of a Measurement Instrument, Testing Its Reliability and Validity,'' unpublished master's thesis, Brigham Young University, 1980.

Bednar, David A., ''The Measurement of Communication Climate in Organizations: The Reliability of a New Inventory,'' unpublished master's thesis, Brigham Young University, 1977.

Blumenstock, David I., ''Climate,'' *The World Book Encyclopedia,* Vol. IV, 520–524. Chicago: Field Enterprises Corporation, 1970.

Dennis, Harry S., ''The Construction of a Managerial Communication Climate Inventory for Use in Complex Organizations,'' Paper presented at the annual meeting of the International Communication Association, New Orleans, 1974.

Downs, Cal W., ''The Relationship between Communication and Job Satisfaction,'' in *Readings in Interpersonal and Organizational Communication,* R. C. Huseman, C. M. Logue, and D. L. Freshley, eds., 363–376. Boston: Holbrook Press, Inc., 1977.

Downs, Cal W., and Michael D. Hazen, ''A Factor Analytic Study of Communication Satisfaction,'' *The Journal of Business Communication,* 14, No. 3 (1977), 63–73.

Goldhaber, Gerald M., *Organizational Communication,* 2nd ed., Dubuque, Iowa: Wm. C. Brown, 1979.

Goldhaber, Gerald M., Harry S. Dennis, III, Gary M. Richetto, and Osmo A. Wiio, *Information Strategies: New Pathways to Corporate Power.* Englewood Cliffs, N.J.: Prentice-Hall, 1979.

Jablin, Frederic M., ''Organizational Communication Theory and Research: An Overview of Communication Climate and Network Research,'' *Communication Yearbook 4.* New Brunswick, N.J.: Transaction Books, 1980.

James, L. R., and A. P. Jones, ''Organizational Climate: A Review of Theory and Research,'' *Psychological Bulletin,* 81 (1974), 1096–1112.

Meyer, Alan D., ''How Beliefs, Stories and Metaphors Uphold Ideologies that Supplant Structures and Guide Reactions,'' Paper presented at the SCA/ICA Jointly Sponsored Summer Conference on Interpretive Approaches to the Study of Organizational Communication, Alta, Utah, July 26, 1981.

Peterson, Brent D., and R. Wayne Pace, ''Communication Climate and Organizational Satisfaction,'' unpublished paper, Brigham Young University, 1976.

Poole, Marshall Scott, and Robert D. McPhee, ''A Structurational Analysis of Organizational Climate,'' in *Communication and Organization: An Interpretive Approach,* Linda L. Putnam and Michael E. Pacanowsky, eds. Beverly Hills, Calif.: Sage, 1983.

Redding, W. Charles, *Communication within the Organization: An Interpretive Review of Theory and Research.* New York: Industrial Communication Council, Inc., 1972.

Sanford, Aubrey C., Gary T. Hunt, and Hyler J. Bracey, *Communication Behavior in Organizations.* Columbus, Ohio: Chas. E. Merrill, 1976.

Schrank, Robert, *Ten Thousand Working Days.* Cambridge, Mass.: MIT Press, 1978.

Taylor, J. C., and D. G. Bowers, *Survey of Organizations.* Ann Arbor: Institute for Social Research, University of Michigan, 1972.

Timm, Paul R., *Managerial Communication: A Finger on the Pulse.* Englewood Cliffs, N.J.: Prentice-Hall, 1980.

Walton, Eugene, ''Project: Office Communications,'' *Administrative Management,* 23 (August 1962), 22–24.

Waters, L. K., D. Roach, and N. Batlis, ''Organizational Climate Dimensions and Job-Related Attitudes,'' *Personnel Psychology,* 27 (1974), 465–476.

Wiio, Osmo A., *Contingencies of Organizational Communication.* Helsinki: Institute for Human Communication, 1978.

9
Networks, Patterns, and Roles

The Flow of Information in Organizations

The accomplishment of most organizational tasks is related to how well information is communicated to people in all parts of the organization. The process of making information available to organization members and securing information from them is referred to as the *flow of information*.

DEFINITION OF FLOW

To describe something as a *flow,* it must move or proceed continuously. Water in a stream flows because it issues from some source and proceeds along its course. Any continuous movement may be called a flow. Thus we think of information flowing throughout an organization because, at least perceptually, it issues from some source and appears to move somewhat continuously from person to person. Technically, information *does not* literally flow. In fact, information itself does not move. What does seem to happen is the display of a message, the interpretation of the display, and the creation of another display. The creation, display, and interpretation of messages is the process by which information is distributed throughout organizations.

The concept of *process* implies that events and relationships are moving and changing continuously, that events and relationships are dynamic. A dynamic relationship or event is one involving energy and action. Thus what we call the flow of information in an organization is actually a dynamic process in which messages are constantly and continuously being created, displayed, and interpreted. The process is ongoing and constantly changing—that is, organizational communication is not something that happens and stops. Communication takes place all the time.

Organizational communication may be thought of as a "happening"—an experience that started before you entered the process and continues after you make an exit. To begin communicating means that you are aware that the experience is happening. As an event, communication always has something that precedes it and something that follows it. You step into the process not knowing very precisely what came before or what will take place after and being somewhat vague about what is actually taking place at the moment.

Guetzkow (1965) has appropriately pointed out that the flow of information in an organization may occur in one of three ways: simultaneously, serially, or in some combination of the two. We shall examine the meanings of these ways of disseminating information in organizations.

SIMULTANEOUS MESSAGE DISSEMINATION

A great deal of organizational communication is person to person, or dyadic, involving only a source and an interpreter as the final destination. However, it is also fairly common for a manager to want information to get out to more than one person, such as when changes in a work schedule need to be made or when a group needs to be briefed on a new procedure. Frequently messages—called memos or memorandums—are sent to many individuals in an organization. On occasion, such as a university-wide faculty meeting, the top executive or president wishes to send a message to all members of the organization. Many organizations publish a house organ—a magazine or a newsletter that is mailed to all members of the organization. When all members of a particular unit—a department, college, or division—are to receive information at about the same time, we call the process *simultaneous message dissemination* (Figure 9.1).

When the same message needs to arrive at different locations at the same time, plans should be made to use a simultaneous message dissemination strategy or technique. The selection of a dissemination technique on the basis of timing (simultaneous arrival) necessitates thinking about dissemination methods a little bit differently than we usually do. For example, one of the main concerns is whether the message can be distributed at the same time. You might think of a written memo as

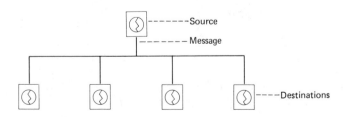

FIGURE 9.1 Simultaneous Message Dissemination

a sure-fire way of sending a message to all members of an organization at the same time. However, the mail service might delay receipt of the memo for some individuals, and some individuals may not pick up their mail for several days. On the other hand, a meeting might be a way of getting information to everyone in the organization at the same time, but, as you can appreciate, the schedule of some individuals may not permit them to attend a meeting, especially if they must travel to attend. The memo is a written medium whereas a meeting is an oral, face-to-face medium. Either or both methods may facilitate the simultaneous dissemination of information to a particular group of organization members; either or both may be ineffective.

With the development of telecommunication media, the task of disseminating information to everyone on a simultaneous basis has been simplified for some organizations. At a given time widely located employees may all tune in to a designated channel on their television monitors and simultaneously see and hear the chief executive officer provide information. Occasionally a large proportion of the population of the United States is able to listen and visually respond to a message from the President by seeking access to a television set. Television allows a single speaker to make contact with all members of an organization on an individual basis, without the necessity of them coming together or having a printed document delivered to them. With the development of more sophisticated cable and telephone systems coupled with video images, it may be possible for entire organizations to have visual and vocal contact with one another while remaining at their individual places of work. Simultaneous message dissemination may be more common, more effective, and more efficient than other ways of facilitating the flow of information in an organization.

SERIAL MESSAGE DISSEMINATION

Haney (1962) has explained that a considerable amount of information is disseminated in chain-of-command organizations—business, industry, hospitals, military, government agencies—by means of serial communication. Rogers and Shoemaker (1971) noted that researchers on the diffusion of innovations—new farm practices, new medicines—"found that ideas usually spread from a source to an audience of receivers via a series of sequential transmissions" (p. 13). When information is disseminated by means of a series of one-to-one-to-one contacts in which the originator of a message displays the message for a second person who in turn interprets and reproduces the message for a third person, the process is called *serial message dissemination* (Figure 9.2). Strictly speaking, the flow of information in an organization occurs in this serial, successive, reproductive sequence. Haney (1962) notes that "serial transmission is clearly an essential, inevitable form of communication in organizations" (p. 150).

The serial dissemination of information involves the extension of the dyad so that a message is relayed from Person A to Person B to Person C to Person D to Person E in a series of two-person transactions in which each individual beyond the originator first interprets and then displays a message for the next person in the sequence.

As you can determine by examining Figure 9.2, serial message dissemination

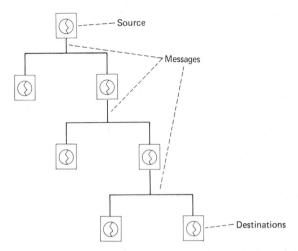

FIGURE 9.2   Serial Message Dissemination

represents a pattern of "who talks to whom." It has, as one of its most significant features, a pattern of dissemination. When messages are disseminated in a serial fashion, information spreads on an irregular time schedule, thereby arriving at different destinations at different times. Individuals tend to be aware of information at different times. Because of differences in awareness of information, problems in coordination may develop. Time lags in the dissemination of information may make it difficult to make decisions because people are just not informed. When large numbers of people are to be informed, serial processes may require a longer period of time to get the information to them. Of course, as we shall discuss later, the fidelity, or accuracy, of the information may suffer as a result of the frequent interpretations and reproductions involved in the serial dissemination of messages.

Of great significance to organizational communication is the fact that hierarchically structured organizations—bureaucracies, for example—make most of their decisions on the basis of information and other decisions resulting from this serial communication process. Messages are received at each level in the organization, interpreted, and integrated into a body of information to be transmitted to the next level. Information tends to be tailored to fit the needs of the person or group to whom it is being sent. Ference (1970) explains that "the tailoring may require only a shift in emphasis and an underplaying of undesirable matters" (p. 84), not the transmission of false information. He also suggests that the integration of information at each level and position in the organization in preparation for sending it to the next position may include "interpretation, reconciling conflicting reports, discarding information, and applying weights to information from different sources" (pp. 85–86).

Because the serial dissemination and gathering of information are inevitably related to the functioning of hierarchically structured, bureaucratic organizations, it is especially urgent that we understand some of the usual, even natural, consequences of the serial reproduction of information on the content of organizational communication messages. Since organizational structures and the serial dissemination of messages are intimately related, we shall now discuss the effects of various patterns of communication flow on key organization features.

PATTERNS OF INFORMATION FLOW

Although formal organizations rely heavily on general serial processes for gathering and disseminating information, specific patterns of information flow evolve out of regular interpersonal contacts and routine ways of sending and receiving messages. Katz and Kahn (1966) point out that a pattern or organized state of affairs requires that communication among the members of the system be restricted. The very nature of an organization implies limitations on who can talk to whom. Burgess (1969) observed that the peculiar characteristic of communication within organizations is that "message flows become so regularized that we actually may speak of communication networks or structures" (p. 138). He also noted that formal organizations exert control over the communication structure by such means as the designation of authority and work relations, assignment of offices, and special communication functions.

The experimental analysis of communication patterns suggests that certain arrangements of "who talks to whom" have fairly prominent consequences on organizational functioning. We shall compare two contrasting patterns—the wheel and the circle—to illustrate the effects of restricted information flow on organizations (Figure 9.3). The wheel is a pattern in which all information is directed toward the individual occupying the central position. The person in the central position receives contacts and information provided by other organization members and solves problems with the advice and consent of the other members. The circle allows all members to communicate with one another only through some sort of relayor system. No one member has direct contact with all other members, nor does any one member have direct access to all the necessary information to solve problems. Several different combinations of contacts are possible: A may communicate with B and E but not C and D; B may communicate with A and C but not D and E; C may communicate with B and D but not A and E; D may communicate with C and E

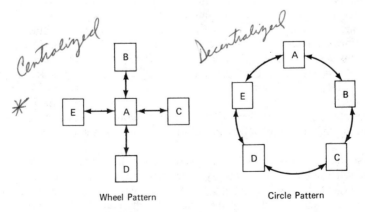

Wheel Pattern   Circle Pattern

FIGURE 9.3 Two Basic Communication Patterns

TABLE 9.1   Effects of Two Patterns on Ten Organizational Communication Processes

Organizational Communication Variable	Wheel Pattern	Circle Pattern
Accessibility of members to one another	Low	High
Control of message flow	High	Low
Morale or satisfaction	Very low	High
Emergence of leader	High	Very low
Accuracy of solutions	Good	Poor
Speed of performance	Fast	Slow
Number of messages sent	Low	High
Emergence of stable organization	Fast	Very slow
Adaptability to job changes	Slow	Fast
Propensity to overload	High	Low

but not A and B; and E may communicate with D and A but not B and C. For D to communicate with A, information must be relayed through E or C and B.

Results of research on the wheel and circle patterns suggest that they produce quite different consequences (Bavelas, 1950; Bavelas & Barrett, 1951; Burgess, 1969; Leavitt, 1951; Shaw, 1956, 1958). Table 9.1 summarizes the effects of the wheel and the circle patterns on ten organizational communication variables.

The circle pattern, involving combinations of relayors, tends to be superior to the wheel pattern, involving highly centralized communication flow, in overall accessibility of members to one another, morale or satisfaction with the process, number of messages sent, and adaptability to changes in tasks; on the other hand, the wheel pattern allows for more control over message flow, experiences rapid leader emergence and a stable organization, demonstrates high accuracy in solving problems, is fast in solving problems, but seems prone to message and work overload.

Burgess (1969) observed that in order to solve problems in experiments, group members had to "learn how to properly and efficiently manipulate the experimental apparatus; and to efficiently transfer messages to the position or positions with which they are linked" (p. 150). This implies that certain complex role behaviors may need to be learned in order to make the communication patterns function in any optimal way. Some recent research on communication networks in large organizations suggests that a distribution of network roles is important to the efficient functioning of an organization. We shall summarize some of the concepts on network roles in order to highlight these new developments.

COMMUNICATION NETWORK ROLES

An organization consists of people in positions. As individuals in those positions begin to communicate with one another, regularities in contacts and "who talks to whom" develop. The location of any given individual in the patterns and networks that emerge impose a role upon that person. Some individuals occupy more central positions, such as Person A in the wheel pattern, that require them to receive and process more information than do other members of the network. Individuals who occupy central positions need to have skills for handling information since they will have to receive, integrate, and see that the appropriate information gets disseminated to the right people in a timely, accurate, and complete manner. Network analysis has revealed the characteristics of a number of communication network roles (Figure 9.4). We shall identify and briefly describe seven roles (Danowski, 1976; Farace, 1980; Farace, Monge, & Russell, 1977; Farace, Taylor, & Stewart, 1978; Richards, 1974; Roberts & O'Reilly, 1978; Rogers & Agarwala-Rogers, 1976).

Clique Member

A *clique* is a group of individuals who have at least half of their contacts with each other. Farace et al. (1977) indicate that a clique is identified when "more than half of their communication is with each other, when each member is linked to all other members, and when no single link nor member can be eliminated and have the group break apart" (p. 186). You might wonder whether members of a clique are or need to be in close physical proximity to one another, such as occupying adjoining offices or working in the same department. Research on small group ecology (Sommer, 1969) suggests that individuals were more likely to "interact with people whom they could see" (p. 61). The environment also has an impact on the development of contacts. Smith (1973) summarized research on constraints of the environment on behavior in organizations and concluded that the environment "may prevent certain patterns of communication. If it permits them, this still does not ensure that those patterns will arise, but the prevented patterns are definitely ruled out" (p. 55). Thus it seems consistent with experience to have Rogers and Agarwala-Rogers (1976) conclude that "most clique members are relatively close to each other in the formal hierarchy of the organization, suggesting the similarity of the formal and informal communication systems" (p. 130).

One requirement of clique membership is that individuals must be able to make contact with one another, even by indirect means. Baird (1977) analyzed the impact of a person's attitudes on the choice of media used in making contacts. He postulated that we might be more attracted to some people than to others and observed that "in communicating with those we like, we usually use the most immediate channel available: face-to-face, even though it may necessitate traveling relatively long distances; telephone calls become too expensive. On the other hand face-to-face contact with those we dislike usually is avoided; we resort to written communication or to sending messages through intermediaries" (p. 260). His concept of *immediate* was derived from Mehrabian (1971) and refers to situations involving "an increase in the sensory stimulation between two persons" (p. 3). Thus face-to-face contact is the most immediate, whereas letters and relayors are less immediate.

It is likely that cliques will consist of individuals whose environmental circumstances (offices, work assignments) permit contact, who like one another, and who find contacts of high immediacy satisfying. These three conditions do suggest that cliques may frequently consist of individuals who have both formal, positional reasons for making contacts as well as informal, interpersonal reasons.

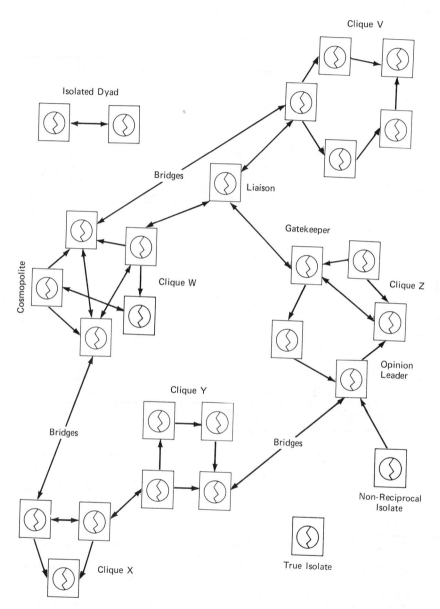

Clique V

Isolated Dyad

Bridges

Liaison

Gatekeeper

Cosmopolite

Clique W

Clique Z

Opinion Leader

Clique Y

Bridges

Bridges

Non-Reciprocal Isolate

True Isolate

Clique X

FIGURE 9.4 Hypothetical Network Diagram Showing Communication Network Roles

Isolate

The first task of network analysis is to identify those who are members of cliques and those who are not. Since clique members are individuals who have more than half of their contacts with other members of the clique, *isolates* are those who have less frequent contact or no contact at all with other group members. The concept of isolate is relative and must be defined for each analysis of communication networks. Networks are usually defined in terms of the content of messages. Thus it is possible for an organization member to be an isolate in a network whose messages concern governmental relations with the organization but to be a central clique member when messages concern the internal administration of a division of the organization. Some organization members are isolates when it comes to the personal lives of other employees but are clearly clique members when messages concern changes in organization policies and procedures.

Goldhaber (1979) has summarized the characteristics of isolates. He suggests that isolates differ from clique members by being

1. Less secure in their self-concepts;
2. Less motivated by achievement;
3. Less willing to interact with others;
4. Younger and less experienced with the system;
5. Less often in positions of power in the organization;
6. More inclined to withhold information than facilitate its flow;
7. Relatively more dissatisfied with the system; and
8. Concerned that the communication system is closed to them.

Bridge

A *bridge* is a member of a clique who has a predominant number of intragroup contacts and who also has contact with a member of another clique. A bridge serves as a direct contact between two groups of employees. Farace et al. (1977) estimate that the distortion of messages will increase when contacts between and linkages among cliques are handled primarily by bridges. As a relayor of messages and a central figure in the communication system of a clique, a bridge is susceptible to all of the conditions that produce information forfeiture, message decay, and distortion.

Liaison

The relayor relationship discussed in an earlier chapter is illustrated most clearly by the liaison communication network role. A *liaison* is a person who links or connects two or more cliques but who is *not* a member of any of the groups connected. Liaisons have been the subject of research longer than any other role because they were recognized early as critical to the functioning of an organization or social system (Coleman, 1964; Davis, 1953; Jacobsen & Seashore, 1951; Schwartz, 1977; Schwartz & Jacobsen, 1977; Weiss & Jacobsen, 1955). Liaisons tie units of the organization together and represent people through whom much of the information of the organization is funneled. Ross and Harary (1955) noted that "if a liaison person is a bottleneck, the organization suffers badly, while if he is efficient, he tends to expedite the flow of the entire organization" (p. 1).

Most of the evidence suggests that liaisons are important roles for the effective functioning of an organization. They can facilitate the flow of information or block it. Rogers and Agarwala-Rogers (1976) suggest that "liaison roles may have to be formally created in an organization if they do not exist informally" (p. 138).

The major differences between liaisons and nonliaison members of an organizational communication system have been summarized by Farace et al. (1977). Figure 9.5 shows the major differences between liaisons and nonliaisons in terms of their actual communication behaviors, how they perceive themselves, and how others perceive them.

The distinctiveness of the liaison role stems not so much from any special personal characteristic as from the unique relayor function they hold in the communication network (Rogers & Agarwala-Rogers, 1976).

Gatekeeper

Gatekeeping, report Katz and Lazarsfeld (1955), means "controlling a strategic portion of a channel . . . so as to have the power of decision over whether whatever is flowing through the channel will enter the group or not" (p. 119). In an

Objective Characteristics of Liaisons

1. Liaisons have higher agreement (between themselves and others with whom they talk) about the identity of their contacts than do nonliaisons.
2. Liaisons are more likely to serve as first sources of information than are others in the organization.
3. Liaisons have higher formal status in the organization than do nonliaisons.
4. Liaisons have been organizational members for longer periods of time than have nonliaisons.
5. The levels of formal education and the ages of liaisons are similar to those of nonliaisons.

Liaisons Perceive Themselves as

6. having greater numbers of communication contacts in the organization;
7. having greater amounts of information with respect to the content dimensions upon which their role is defined;
8. participating in a communication system that is more "open"—information is seen as more timely, more believable, and more useful;
9. having greater influence in the organization.

Liaisons Are Perceived by Others as

10. having greater numbers of communication contacts in the organization;
11. having a wider range throughout the organizational structure;
12. having more information on the content dimensions on which the network is defined;
13. having more control over the flow of information in the organization;
14. having more influence over the "power structure" of the organization;
15. more competent at their organizational activities.

FIGURE 9.5 Characteristics of Liaisons (Source: From *Communicating and Organizing* by Richard V. Farace, Peter R. Monge, and Hamish M. Russell, Copyright © 1977 by Richard V. Farace, Peter R. Monge, and Hamish M. Russell. Reprinted by permission of Random House, Inc.)

organizational communication network a *gatekeeper* is a person who is strategically located in the network so as to exercise control over what messages will be disseminated through the system. The gatekeeper is most noticeable in serial communication networks, since information and messages can be controlled at just about every link. Every relayor in a serial chain can be a gatekeeper. Thus our discussion of the functions of a relayor—linking, storing, stretching, and controlling—represents a description of the activities of a gatekeeper.

In a university, the chair of a department is a fairly clear example of a gatekeeper at work. Faculty are asked to funnel their requests through the chair. The dean, the superior of a chair, in turn funnels information for the faculty back through the chair. The chair controls what information the faculty will receive about the budget, directives and requests from the dean, and information about hiring, firing, and retiring. Figure 9.6 portrays a typical gatekeeper which many of you will recognize. In order for a faculty member to have access to the chair, he or she must negotiate past the gatekeeper—the department secretary. The secretary provides the chair with information about people who want appointments and provides selected information to assist the chair in deciding how the appointment will proceed. One positive consequence of having an efficient secretary-gatekeeper is the reduction in communication load. The secretary-gatekeeper may screen out or handle a great many contacts that may considerably relieve the load on an administrator. A secretary-gatekeeper may also keep a manager from knowing important information and reduce the manager's effectiveness. One interesting research question concerns what guidelines a gatekeeper, such as a secretary, uses in deciding what information should get into the system or to the manager.

Opinion Leader

In contrast to official leaders who exercise authority in organizations by virtue of the positions they hold, there are individuals without a formal position within all social systems who guide opinions and influence people in their decisions. These individuals, called *opinion leaders,* are sought out for their opinions and influence. They are the people who keep up on things and whom others trust to let them know what is really going on. Katz and Lazarsfeld (1955) describe the opinion leader as an "almost invisible, certainly inconspicuous, form of leadership at the person-to-person level of ordinary, intimate, informal, everyday contact" (p. 138).

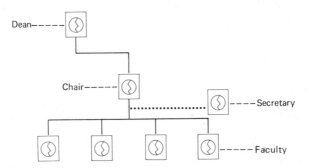

FIGURE 9.6 Example of a Gatekeeper Role

The characteristics of opinion leaders identified in studies of communities, as opposed to businesses and agencies, were summarized by Pace (1969) and indicate the following:

1. Opinion leadership is more common during the middle years of life rather than during either youth or seniority, although a few senior opinion leaders have been recognized as the most powerful in public affairs.
2. Women have rarely been mentioned as opinion leaders.
3. Opinion leaders are usually long-term, permanent residents in the community and belong to a number of community organizations.
4. Opinion leaders in the United States are usually white, native-born and Protestants, although members of racial and ethnic minority groups assume opinion leadership within their respective minority populations.
5. No social stratum appears to have a monopoly on opinion leadership, with individuals in all walks of life exercising personal influence on other members of the community.

Formal organizations, as well as communities, have opinion leaders who influence what people believe and do. They serve a key communication function by influencing opinion formation and attitude change. They are asked for their opinions, and members of the organization listen to them (Peterson, 1973).

Cosmopolite

A cosmopolitan person is one who belongs to all the world or one who is free from local, provincial, or national ideas, prejudices, or attachments. A *cosmopolite* is an individual who has contact with the outside world, with individuals beyond the organization. Cosmopolites link organization members with people and events beyond the confines of the organization structure. Organization members who travel a lot, are active in professional associations, and read regional, national, and international publications tend to be more cosmopolitan. They have more frequent contact with sources outside the organization and serve as conduits or channels for new ideas to enter the organization.

SUMMARY

We have discussed seven communication network roles:

Clique Member
Isolate
Bridge
Liaison
Gatekeeper
Opinion Leader
Cosmopolite

Each role plays a special part in communication networks. The clique member is the heart of the system and serves as the final destination for most messages. The isolate challenges the system and creates a degree of uncertainty in the effectiveness of the message dissemination program. The bridge is a central information-processor who provides direct connections between different cliques. The liaison integrates and interconnects cliques. The opinion leader facilitates the formation and change of attitudes and aids in informal decision making. The gatekeeper controls the movement of messages and contacts in order to minimize overload and increase effectiveness. The cosmopolite connects the organization with people and ideas in the larger environment.

A SUBJECTIVIST'S NOTATION

The flow of information is not an orderly or predictable process, but more than that; what information means depends on context. To find meaning, it is necessary to look at the interrelationships that create the structure and pattern. These interrelationships are complex and illusive. Setting aside patterns or networks of communication for examination is a highly arbitrary and artificial undertaking. An interpretive analysis reveals that an organization is made up of interactive influences, mutual constraints, multiple orders, and simultaneous interests. The complexities are obscured if one thinks in terms of a simplistic order and patterns of communication.

Schwartz and Ogilvy (1979) use the metaphor of the holograph and maintain that "everything is interconnected like a vast network of interference patterns" (p. 14). Examining information in one part of an organization can reveal information about the whole organization. The interpretive position emphasizes the meaning attributed to communication exchanges and the meaning derived from the context of these exchanges. If you were to go to several organizations, ask managers how they disseminate information, then ask organizational members how they obtain information, the answers would reveal a discrepancy between the managerial view and actual practice. If you observe information-gathering behaviors, you will see further discrepancies. All of this suggests that the organizational culture provides a context by which information is generated and processed.

The classical studies that examine the impact of communication patterns such as the wheel and circle were designed in order to control and order communication. However, these theoretical patterns do not represent actual communication in organizations. The studies controlled who could speak to whom. In more realistic settings, people may have access to others and be able to communicate with them, but that does not mean that they will. Individuals in actual settings may be placed in structured situations, but they alter those structures through emergent negotiated behaviors. The resulting structure or pattern is determined by actual communication.

Network analysis may obscure patterns of interchange and the meanings attached to those exchanges. Richards (1985) describes a study in which medical practitioners were asked from whom they sought advice and information and to whom they gave advice and information. Only one physician in twenty who was listed by a recipient as a source of information said he was a source for that recipient. Richards explains: ''An interpretivist researcher would want to talk with the physicians and uncover how they interpreted both the question about giving or seeking information and the process of giving or seeking information. In this case, the interpretivist would discover that 'giving advice or information' is not the inverse of 'seeking advice or information.' How could this be? It seems that many physicians go to conferences at which other physicians known as experts in their field give presentations. Many of those in the audience feel they are receiving advice or information from the speakers, but the speakers do not count the members of the audience as 'coming to them for advice or information.' Much advice and information is obtained informally, perhaps over a game of golf. . . . Those who receive information may know they are doing so, while those giving information may feel they are simply having a friendly conversation'' (pp. 125–126). This research indicates the complexity of networks. The significance of a network lies in its meaning for the participants.

Information flow may be governed by cultural factors. One of our graduate students traced messages in a retail organization to determine information flow. The managers were interested in getting information through the system in a reasonable amount of time. The student traced several messages in the organization and discovered that they stopped at a certain point. A manager suggested that the messages were not potent enough to travel through the entire organization; thus, he further suggested a message about himself that was sure to raise some eyebrows. This rather ''juicy'' message was sent through the system. Again, the message stopped at the same point. Through a number of interviews, the investigator discovered that ''stories'' existed in one organizational unit concerning someone who had been fired for passing along information; those stories tended to regulate the flow of information.

REFERENCES

Baird, John E., Jr., *The Dynamics of Organizational Communication.* New York: Harper & Row, Pub., 1977.

Bavelas, Alex, ''Communication Patterns in Task-Oriented Groups,'' *Journal of the Acoustical Society of America,* 22 (1950), 725–730.

Bavelas, Alex, and Dermot Barrett, ''An Experimental Approach to Organizational Communication,'' *Personnel,* 27 (March 1951), 38–50.

Burgess, R. L., ''Communication Networks and Behavioral Consequences,'' *Human Relations,* 22 (1969), 137–160.

Coleman, J. S., ''Relational Analysis: The Study of Social Organizations with Survey Methods,'' *Complex Organizations: A Sociological Reader,* A. A. Etzioni, ed., 441–453. New York: Holt, Rinehart & Winston, 1964.

Danowski, James A., ''Communication Network Analysis and Social Change,'' in *Communication for Group Transformation in Development,* Goodwin C. Chu, Syed A. Rahim, and D. Lawrence Kincaid, eds., 277–306. Honolulu: East-West Communication Institute, Communication Monograph, No. 2, September 1976.

Davis, Keith A., ''A Method of Studying Communication Patterns in Organizations,'' *Personnel Psychology,* 6 (1953), 301–312.

Farace, Richard V., ''Organizational Communication,'' in *Human Communication: Principles, Contexts, and Skills,* Cassandra L. Book, ed., 166–193. New York: St. Martin's Press, 1980.

Farace, Richard V., Peter R. Monge, and Hamish M. Russell, *Communicating and Organizing*. Reading, Mass.: Addison-Wesley, 1977.

Farace, Richard V., James A. Taylor, and John P. Stewart, "Criteria for Evaluation of Organizational Communication Effectiveness: Review and Synthesis," in *Communication Yearbook 2*, Brent D. Ruben, ed., 271–292. New Brunswick, N.J.: Transaction Books-International Communication Association, 1978.

Ference, T. P., "Organizational Communication Systems and The Decision Process," *Management Science*, 17 (1970), 83–96.

Goldhaber, Gerald M., *Organizational Communication*. Dubuque. Iowa: Wm. C. Brown, 1979.

Guetzkow, Harold, "Communications in Organizations," in *Handbook of Organizations*, James G. March, ed., 537. Skokie, Ill.: Rand McNally, 1965.

Haney, William V., "Serial Communication of Information in Organizations," in *Concepts and Issues in Administrative Behavior*, Sidney Mailick and Edward H. Van Ness, eds., 150–165. Englewood Cliffs, N.J.: Prentice-Hall, 1962.

Jacobsen, Eugene, and Stanley Seashore, "Communication Practices in Complex Organizations," *Journal of Social Issues*, 7 (1951), 28–40.

Katz, Daniel, and Robert Kahn, *The Social Psychology of Organizations*. New York: John Wiley, 1966.

Katz, Elihu, and Paul F. Lazarsfeld, *Personal Influence*. New York: The Free Press, 1955.

Leavitt, Harold J., "Some Effects of Certain Communication Patterns on Group Performance," *Journal of Abnormal and Social Psychology*, 46 (1951), 38–50.

Mehrabian, Albert, *Silent Messages*. Belmont, Calif.: Wadsworth, 1971.

Pace, Ronald F., "A Study of Opinion Leaders in Summit County and Their Attitudes toward Federal Aid Programs Affecting Local Education and Highway Systems," unpublished master's thesis, Institute of Government Service, Brigham Young University, May 1969.

Peterson, Brent D., "Differences between Managers and Subordinates in Their Perception of Opinion Leaders," *Journal of Business Communication*, 10 (1973), 27–37.

Richards, William D., "Network Analysis in Large Complex Systems: Techniques and Methods—Tools," Paper presented at the Annual Meeting of the International Communication Association, New Orleans, 1974.

Richards, William D., "Data, Models, and Assumptions in Network Analysis," in *Organizational Communication: Traditional Themes and New Directions*, Robert D. McPhee and Phillip K. Tompkins, eds. Beverly Hills, Calif.: Sage, 1985.

Roberts, Karlene, and Charles A. O'Reilly III, "Organizations as Communication Structures," *Human Communication Research*, 4 (Summer 1978), 283–293.

Rogers, Everett M., and Rekha Agarwala-Rogers, *Communication in Organizations*. New York: The Free Press, 1976.

Rogers, Everett M., with F. Floyd Shoemaker, *Communication of Innovations: A Cross-Cultural Approach*. New York: The Free Press, 1971.

Ross, I. C., and F. Harary, "Identification of the Liaison Persons of an Organization Using the Structure Matrix," *Management Science*, 1 (April–May 1955), 251–258.

Schwartz, Donald F., "Liaison Roles in the Communication of a Formal Organization," in *Communication in Organizations*, Lyman W. Porter and Karlene H. Roberts, eds., 255–271. Middlesex, England: Penguin Books, Ltd., 1977.

Schwartz, Donald F., and Eugene Jacobsen, "Organizational Communication Network Analysis—The Liaison Communication Role," *Organizational Behavior and Human Performance*, 18 (1977), 158–174.

Schwartz, P., and J. Ogilvy, *The Emergent Paradigm: Changing Patterns of Thought and Belief*. Menlo Park, Calif.: SRI International, 1979.

Shaw, M. E., "Random Versus Systematic Distribution of Information in Communication Nets," *Journal of Personality,* 25 (1956), 59–69.

Shaw, M. E., "Some Effects of Irrelevant Information upon Problem Solving by Small Groups," *Journal of Social Psychology,* 47 (1958), 33–37.

Smith, Peter B., *Groups within Organizations.* London: Harper & Row, Pub., 1973.

Sommer, Robert, *Personal Space.* Englewood Cliffs, N.J.: Prentice-Hall, 1969.

Weiss, R. S., and Eugene Jacobsen, "A Method for the Analysis of the Structure of Complex Organizations," *American Sociological Review,* 20 (1955), 661–668.

10

Message Fidelity and Distortion

The Effects of Communication Systems on Message Content

"Why can't people get things straight?" How frequently has this question been asked silently or out loud in an organization? Probably as often as employees get together to discuss problems with the boss, or bosses talk about misunderstandings with employees. Routine person-to-person communication is subject to a multitude of pitfalls and processes that have detrimental effects on understanding. Many of the problems stem from the way in which human beings process information. Other sources of misunderstanding are a function of the system by which messages are distributed throughout an organization. Organizational communication is subject to not only the maladies of interpersonal interaction but also to the anomalies of relaying messages through human links in a communication system.

DEFINITION OF FIDELITY AND DISTORTION

Communication fidelity refers to the ability of a person to reproduce or recreate a message accurately. In human communication the term _fidelity_ is used to describe the degree of correspondence between an initiated message and an individual's reproduction of that message. As we mentioned in Chapter 2, a message has at least two dimensions: a display and an interpretation. A display consists of verbal or language symbols, nonverbal behavior (including vocal and physical actions), appearances, and spatial relations. In communicating, a person simply creates and presents a display of sounds, movements, and emblems that can be taken to symbolize or represent something else. The display dimension of a message is a pattern of symbols that can be perceived by someone. Individuals have the capacity to interpret aspects of a display. An interpretation is the act and process of assigning meaning to and making sense out of a display.

The measurement of message fidelity or its opposite, message distortion, is complicated by the two dimensions of display and interpretation. If fidelity is the degree of correspondence between an initiated message and a reproduced message, then we must be prepared to measure the correspondence between an initiated display and some form of reproduced display, plus the correspondence between some form of intended meaning or interpretation and the reproduced or imputed interpretation or meaning associated with the display. A lack of fidelity is usually demonstrated by some type of distortion resulting from changes between the initial display and the reproduced message-display or some differences between an intended meaning and the meaning imputed to the display as part of the reproduction.

Serial reproduction studies illustrate most clearly how distortion is identified by comparing the correspondence between message-displays. A message, usually verbal but often pictorial, is prepared in advance so as to be consistent in length, content, and style. The message is presented to a person who listens to it and, after a specified period of time, reproduces the message. The reproduction may be accomplished by writing, by orally repeating the message, or by recording the message on audio or video tapes. The fidelity of the message-display is determined by comparing the original message with the reproduced message. Verbal messages can be compared directly by (1) counting the number of words that are exactly the same in both messages and/or by (2) counting the number of predetermined themes occurring in both displays.

The correspondence between the intended meaning of a message-source and an imputed meaning of the reproducer of the messages is more difficult to compare than are message-displays. However, differences in meanings and distortions in the meanings of messages may be the most critical aspect of organizational communication. Authorities on communication have forcefully argued that the only message upon which a person can act is the message (interpretation or meaning) that the person creates, regardless of the display (Redding, 1972). Two people may read the same memo and impute quite different meanings to it. The only meaning that counts is the one created by the receiver of the message. Since it is not possible to measure meanings directly, research on communication fidelity has used attitude instruments and associative group analysis (Szalay, Windle, & Lysne, 1970) procedures to get as close as possible to meanings.

In the real organization world the measure of message fidelity may be more related to how a person completes his or her work than it is to how precisely the message-display or the meaning of the message is reproduced. A popular laboratory exercise on message reproduction involves having one person give another person instructions on how to reproduce a drawing. Haney (1964) reported research using figures that appeared to be drawings of domino blocks. The criteria for accuracy were the orientation of the rectangles to one another and the arrangement of the circles within the rectangles. To be considered accurate, the reproduced drawings had to meet both criteria. Brissey (1964) devised a procedure for measuring fidelity by having subjects complete a task described by a message rather than by analyzing the reproduced message directly. Subjects were given instructions concerning how to complete a prearranged display on a pegboard. Fidelity was measured by the extent to which pegs were placed in the correct holes. Any holes not filled and all pegs outside the design were considered to be inaccuracies. He reasoned that as the adequacy of the message decreased, a receiver's uncertainty about where to place pegs correctly in the display would increase. Higher message fidelity would result in fewer errors. Alkire, Collum, Kaswan, and Love (1968) had subjects select the correct design from among several, based on instructions received from another person. The person giving the instructions had a copy of the design and created his or her own initial descriptions. Such a procedure seems to simulate actual organizational communication situations, since the initiator of the message had to create the original message.

In this chapter we are concerned with what happens to the content of a message as it flows throughout an organization. Personal experience and communication research have confirmed the idea that information and the meaning of messages change from what was intended as they are passed from individual to individual in an organization. The processes of upward, downward, horizontal, and cross-channel communication all occur by contacts that are simultaneous (one person contacting other members of the organization directly) or serial (one person serving as a relayor between two other members of the organization). Messages that are distributed by simultaneous contacts are susceptible to changes and distortions associated with interpersonal communication. We shall review some personal communication factors that affect the interpretation of messages. The serial reproduction of a message is compounded by systematic errors or biases that stem from the information-processing activities of human links in communication systems. Distortions in messages are accelerated when a series of human relayors interpret and display their versions of what was meant. Thus we shall also look at how messages are affected by the serial process of information distribution.

PERSONAL FACTORS THAT DISTORT MESSAGES

We shall discuss a number of principles that reflect personal factors that contribute to the distortion of messages. These factors issue naturally from our concept of communication as the act and process of assigning meaning to displays. A display is anything that activates one of our senses—seeing, hearing, tasting, smelling, feeling. At any moment we are bombarded by a limitless variety of displays originating from inside ourselves as well as from outside. Hence the first factor that contributes to the distortion of messages is related to our perception of displays.

Principle 1: People Perceive Things Selectively

Our sensory receptors—eyes, ears, fingers, noses, tongues—are physically limited so that they can respond to only a few of the stimuli impinging upon them. Each of us responds to those sensations that get past our natural barriers or limitations, that seem most pertinent to our situation, and that are consistent with our own personal preferences and perspectives. The fidelity, or accuracy, of information is limited by the selective perceptions we make.

Selectivity means that a person is able to focus on some sensations while excluding others. In fact, in order to focus on one aspect of a situation you must ignore other aspects of it. Look out the window and concentrate on an activity across the street. Can you also look at what is happening on the table in front of you? Visually you can look through the bugs on a windshield, or you can focus on the bugs and actually be unable to see the hood of the car. The same process occurs with our minds. Try this experiment: Think very hard about a problem you are having. Mentally analyze the problem. Do you block out what other people in the room are doing and saying? If you concentrate on what is happening inside you, you will ignore what is happening outside you. If you are worried about what your supervisor will think about the report you have just finished, you may very well not hear some of the things he or she says.

Principle 2: People See Things Consistent with What They Believe

Our perceptions are affected by the way we talk about people, things, and events. What we believe changes our perceptions. If we expect to see a friend react in a negative way to a suggestion, we shall no doubt perceive him or her to react negatively. This is sometimes called the *Pygmalion Effect.* If we believe that people are very smart and intelligent, we will tend to see their behavior as consistent with our belief. On the other hand, if other people see that we expect great things from them, they will try to behave consistently with our expectations.

Such characteristics as friendliness, attractiveness, loyalty, and supportiveness are judgments that we project on other people. I may see you as trusting whereas the person working right next to me may see you as untrusting. Part of the judgment of trust may be related to selectively focusing on some reactions while selectively ignoring other reactions; it may also be a function of a preconception or belief that you are untrusting, which may encourage someone to selectively perceive certain acts that he or she feels are untrusting. Beauty is in the eye of the beholder. Trust, supportiveness, warmth, and kindness are also perceptions.

Believe and ye shall see. A person will probably expect quite different patterns of behavior from another individual if he or she believes that the person is

Able to cope	vs.	Unable to deal with events
Friendly and well-intentioned	vs.	Unfriendly and evil-intentioned
Worthy and important	vs.	Worthless and unimportant
Trustworthy and dependable	vs.	Untrustworthy and unpredictable
Helpful and enhancing	vs.	Frustrating and impeding

Principle 3: Language Itself Is Inaccurate

Our perceptions of people, things, and events never correspond exactly to reality because we selectively see them and because we tend to see what we believe about people, things, and events. In communicating we use language to represent our perceptions. Our talking involves language that is supposed to portray or describe that about which we are talking. It is through language that we make our private perceptions somewhat public so that others may get some idea of what we mean. Language does not diminish the importance of nonlanguage. Nonverbal signals clue others in to what we mean. In fact, we shall talk more about them later.

Nevertheless, we must not lose sight of the basic principle that language symbols do not accurately represent what a person means. Why is that?

First, words are not the things they represent. The word *tree* is not the object *tree*. The word *manager* is not the person *manager*. Words can only refer to or represent events, happenings, activities, and people.

Second, in order for language to refer to a constantly changing world, we develop generalizations about a group of activities and relationships and apply words and terms to describe the characteristics they have in common. We call these generalizations *abstractions*. The larger the number of activities, relationships, or people referred to by a word, the more abstract the word is. The fewer activities to which a word refers, the more specific it is. Technical language tends to be less abstract and more specific. The term *phoneme* is more specific than the term *symbol;* the term *symbol,* however, is more specific than the term *display.* Even our most specific language is still abstract. We actually have a somewhat limited number of words to refer to an almost unlimited number of atoms, movements, feelings, reactions, stars, planets, and even universes. Because of the constantly changing multitude of things and events in the world, our language just cannot be too accurate in what it represents.

Third, when we use language to talk about differences, one of our basic tendencies is to allow only two alternatives—good or bad, for example.

The way we use language in our everyday work tends to be fairly bipolar, or at least to give the impression that our choices fall into either-or categories. Language itself encourages this tendency. To see for yourself how strong this tendency is, try this exercise:

On the right side of this page, list the *opposites* of the following words.

calm   _____

exciting   _____

intelligent   _____

fast   _____

kind   _____

Now in the space between the two lists, write in one or more words that refer to or describe the in-between positions. For example, if a person was neither calm nor agitated, what word would describe him or her? Most people are neither intelligent nor stupid. What word describes them?

Truly accurate language represents people and things as they actually exist. With so many gradations in feelings, reactions, and existences, there is little wonder that our language is limited in its ability to represent the world and the things that happen in it (Haney, 1967).

Principle 4: The Meaning of a Message Occurs at Both Content and Relational Levels

A message consists of both verbal or language (oral and written) and nonverbal or nonlanguage (aural and pictorial) symbols. What a person says and how a person behaves combine to make a message-display. Each message can be analyzed at a *content* or denotative level and at a *relational* or interpretive level (Watzlawick, Beavin, & Jackson, 1967).

The content, or denotative, level of meaning concerns the ideas, things, people, events, and happenings to which the message literally refers. You are functioning at the content level when you respond to the information of the message—that is, when you respond to the ideas, attitudes, opinions, and facts referred to by the message, you are dealing with the message at the content level.

The relational, or interpretive, level of meaning concerns how the message is to be taken, for example, lightly or seriously. When you say, "Smile when you say that," you are dealing at the relational level because your comment tells the other person how to interpret the message and what kind of relationship you are to have. The relational level indicates how the information and the relationship is to be understood. Your attitudes toward other people are expressions at the relational level.

Lack of fidelity, distortions, and misunderstandings often result from our failure to recognize relational information and distinguish it from content, or denotative, information.

Principle 5: Distortions are Encouraged by Inconsistencies between Verbal and Nonverbal Aspects of a Message

A basic axiom of communication theory is that *a person cannot not behave.* Thus as Redding and Sanborn (1964) have concluded, "Communication is always going on, then, whether one desires it or not—so long as there is someone to interpret what we say, or fail to say, or do, or fail to do" (p. 31). It has been estimated that in a conversation involving two people, verbal aspects of a message account for less than 35 percent of the social meaning whereas nonverbal aspects of a message account for 65 percent of the social meaning (Knapp, 1972). On the other hand, Mehrabian (1971) states that "a person's nonverbal behavior has more bearing than his words on communicating feelings or attitudes to others" (p. 44). He estimates that 7 percent of the total feeling is derived from verbal aspects, 38 percent from vocal aspects, and 55 percent from facial aspects, resulting in 93 percent of the feeling communicated being based on nonverbal features.

Since the dominant source of meaning and feeling derived from a message comes from the nonverbal dimensions, it is not surprising to discover that inconsistencies between nonverbal behaviors and the verbal aspects of a message reduce its fidelity. When some inconsistency occurs between words and actions, we tend to believe what we infer from the nonverbal behaviors. Our messages may be misunderstood, be distorted, or lack fidelity if our nonverbal behaviors fail to support what we say. Knapp (1972) has identified six ways in which nonverbal behaviors support our verbal comments:

1. *Nonverbal behaviors may repeat what is expressed verbally.* Since nonverbal behaviors, like gestures, usually precede what is said, it might be more accurate to say that verbal statements repeat nonverbal behaviors. In any case when you agree with a person, notice that you tend to nod your head in agreement just prior to saying, "I think maybe you are right." The verbal and nonverbal behaviors tend to repeat or confirm each other.

2. *Nonverbal behaviors may contradict what is expressed verbally.* You may have experienced a nonverbal behavior contradicting a verbal statement when being told, "I'd really like to go with you," but said in a tone of voice that you knew meant something else. You might have rushed through the house slamming doors and dropping your coat, only to remark to someone, "I don't care. I'm not in a hurry." A more common experience is when a close friend stands looking longingly at a new suit of clothes, but comments, "Oh, It's nothing; I'm not interested." Nonverbal behaviors may very well clearly contradict verbal statements made in organizations.

3. *Nonverbal behaviors may substitute for what could be expressed verbally.* When you go back to your apartment or room, don't say anything. Just open the door and leap into the air, smile, and clench your fists. Your roommate or spouse may not need verbal confirmation of the nonverbal display. With a little practice you may be able to identify a great many substitute nonverbal displays.

4. *Nonverbal behaviors may modify or elaborate on verbal messages.* You may indicate a change in attitude through nonverbal behaviors before the verbal expression of such a change occurs. You might, for example, say that you aren't all that sure about going to a movie tonight and let your nonverbal behaviors elaborate the statement into a definite "no." A supervisor may tell a subordinate that things seem a little slow, but the squint of the supervisor's eye and the turned-down mouth more clearly fill out the verbal message so that the subordinate understands that things are at a standstill.

5. *Nonverbal behaviors may emphasize parts of a verbal message.* If you have ever greeted someone you haven't seen for a long time, you may recall the special emphasis given to the greeting: "Oh, hi." As you uttered those very short verbal expressions, you may have hugged the other person, shook his or her hand firmly and warmly, and smiled broadly. A supervisor may speak to a subordinate about finishing a piece of work with some clearly nonverbal emphases, such as raising eyebrows, speaking more slowly, and gesturing firmly.

6. *Nonverbal behaviors may regulate the flow of messages between people.* If you are having a conversation with someone and you have another appointment, you may try to signal nonverbally by moving your eyes or shifting from leg to leg or smiling tensely that the other person should stop speaking and terminate the conversation. If you want the other person to continue talking, you may nod your head and say, "Uh huh," or look at the other intently and attentively. In these ways you control who talks, how long, how often, and about what.

Misunderstandings, distortions, and nonfidelity in communication may result from our failures to recognize or respond to the nonverbal cues that accompany what people say verbally. Since a great deal of the meaning involved in a communicative exchange comes from nonverbal behaviors, lack of fidelity and distortion may frequently be traced to failures to recognize and understand nonverbal signals.

Principle 6: Message Ambiguity Often Leads to Distortions

Ambiguity may be defined as some degree of uncertainty associated with information or actions. If a statement you make seems ambiguous to me, that means that I am uncertain how to take what you say. There are three types of ambiguity that may occur in communication: ambiguity of meaning, ambiguity of intent, and ambiguity of effect (Thayer, 1968).

Ambiguity of meaning concerns the uncertainty of predicting what the originator of a message means. To the extent that you cannot readily and efficiently determine what a person meant when he or she said or wrote a message, the message will have a degree of ambiguity for you. The greater the ambiguity of meaning, the greater the difficulty you will have in comprehending the message.

Ambiguity of intent concerns the uncertainty of predicting why the originator of a message said or wrote this particular message to you at this particular time in this particular way and under these particular conditions. To the extent that you cannot figure out why the person is communicating with you, the message will be ambiguous to you. For example, suppose you go home and find a note pinned to your bedroom curtain with this message on it: "The president of the university called and wants to talk to you tomorrow morning." Why would the president want to talk to you? What does he or she want? The degree to which you are unable to answer such questions indicates how ambiguous the intent of the message is to you.

Ambiguity of effect concerns the uncertainty of predicting what the consequences of responding to a message might be. You may accurately interpret the meaning of the note about the president's request for a meeting—the president wants you to arrive at his or her office in the morning; you may even predict his or her intent fairly accurately—to talk to you about your standing in the university; however, what will be the effect or consequence of understanding the message, arriving at the president's office, and engaging in a conversation about your standing in the university? Of course, nothing may come of it; on the other hand, what might be some possible consequences? The extent to which some of these questions have unclear answers is the extent to which the message involves ambiguity of effect.

A person may fail to comprehend a message or distort its meaning because of an inability to determine what the originator of the message means, why the message was sent, or what the consequences are of comprehending the message in a particular way.

Principle 7: Memory Propensities Toward Sharpening and Leveling Details Encourage Distortion to Occur

Some evidence suggests that people may have some patterns associated with their memory systems that lead to distortions in verbal communication. Holzman and Gardner (1960) developed a schematizing test that differentiated between *levelers* and *sharpeners*. Individuals who are levelers had fewer correct memories of an incident or story and tended to show more loss and modification of the overall structure of the story than did those who were sharpeners. Gardner and Lohrenz (1960) demonstrated that the serial reproduction of a story underwent different fates when transmitted through separate chains of levelers and sharpeners. Levelers lost more themes, lost more of the overall story, and showed increasingly more fragmented messages than did sharpeners. A person may be structured toward leveling information or toward sharpening information. A propensity toward stripping away the details in a verbal message is called *skeletonizing* (Paul, 1959), and a propensity toward the invention of details is called *importing*. Each of us may have a memory propensity that leads toward leveling, stripping away, or skeletonizing details in messages or a memory propensity that leads toward sharpening, inventing, or importing details into messages. In either case a memory propensity may contribute to distortions and lack of fidelity in communication.

Principle 8: Motivational Factors May Encourage Message Distortions

Three basic motivational factors tend to produce changes in messages that result in lack of fidelity: attitudes toward the message content; desires, self-interest, and motives of communicators; and attitudes of intended receivers.

1. *Attitudes toward the message content.* A study by Johnson and Wood (1944) demonstrated that subjects who held positive attitudes toward a racial minority tended to "abstract" the positive information about them from a passage containing both positive and negative information; on the other hand, a subject who had negative attitudes tended to abstract negative information from the same passage. The tendency for communicators to distort information in a message according to their attitudes seems to be well supported by other research (Alper & Korchin, 1952; Bouillut & Moscovici, 1967; Higham, 1951; Manis, Cornell & Moore, 1974).

2. *Desires, self-interest, and motives of communicators.* Jackson (1959) suggested that people in organizations communicate or fail to communicate with others in order to accomplish some goal, satisfy a personal need, or improve their immediate situation. Downs (1967) identified four major biases that produce distortions in the communication of officials in bureaucracies: (1) They tend to distort information by exaggerating data that reflect favorably on themselves and to minimize data that reveal their shortcomings. (2) They tend to prefer policies that advance their own interests and the programs they advocate and to reject those that injure or fail to advance their interests. (3) They tend to comply with directives from superiors that favor their own interests and drag their feet or ignore those that do not. (4) They tend to take on additional work if it is directly beneficial to their own goals and avoid work that weakens their ability to achieve their own goals.

Haney (1962) described three motives that encourage distortions to develop in messages: (1) The desire to convey simple messages. The communication of complex information is difficult and psychologically taxing on the individual; thus organization members tend to simplify messages before or as they pass the information along. (2) The desire to convey a "sensible" message. When a person receives a message that doesn't seem to make sense, the desire is to make sense out of it before passing it along. Most of us tend to avoid sending along messages that seem illogical, incomplete, or incoherent. (3) The desire to make message sending as pleasant (or at least as painless) as possible for the sender. Organization members tend to avoid conveying messages that are painful for them. Instead they make changes that soften the message and make it less painful.

3. *Attitudes of intended receivers.* There is evidence to support the idea that the initiator of a message will tend to distort it in the direction of the announced attitude of whoever is to receive the message. This may be a subcategory of motivational factors, since expressing ideas contrary to those held by an intended receiver may be viewed as potentially painful.

So far we have discussed eight principles that represent personal factors that contribute to the distortion of messages in communication. In summary, the principles appear as follows:

1. People perceive things selectively.
2. People see things consistent with what they believe.
3. Language itself is inaccurate.
4. The meaning of a message occurs at both content and relational levels.
5. Distortions are encouraged by inconsistencies between verbal and nonverbal aspects of a message.
6. Message ambiguity often leads to distortions.
7. Memory propensities toward sharpening and leveling details encourage distortions to occur.
8. Motivational factors may encourage message distortions.

We shall now review some of the organizational factors that contribute to the distortion of messages.

ORGANIZATIONAL FACTORS THAT DISTORT MESSAGES

Characteristics of organizations themselves tend to encourage distortions to occur in messages. We shall briefly review a number of organizational factors that contribute to message distortion in organizational communication.

1. *Occupying a position in an organization influences the way a person communicates.* By becoming a functioning member of an organization who occupies a position with duties and authority assigned to it, an individual acquires a point of view, a value system, and develops expectations and limitations that are different from a person who holds a different position or is a member of a different organization entirely. A supervisor, for example, is compelled at times to look at the functioning of the organization differently from subordinates. The supervisor must react to production problems somewhat differently from the way a particular subordinate might react to them. In fact, a supervisor must think about the organization in a different way. The person within the organization sees its operations differently from an outsider. Each position in an organization demands that the person who occupies it must perceive and communicate about things from the perspective of the position. Occupying a position tends to contribute to distortions in organizational communication messages (Katz & Kahn, 1966).

2. *Hierarchical—superior-subordinate—relationships influence the way in which a person communicates.* The arrangement of positions in hierarchical fashion suggests to those who occupy the positions that one set of individuals is "superior" and another set is "subordinate." The fundamental difference is one of perceived status. People and positions located higher in the hierarchy have greater control over the lives of those who are located lower in the organization. Lower-downs find it desirable to be cautious in communicating with higher-ups. Information may be distorted because a subordinate is careful to talk about things that his or her superior is interested in hearing and to avoid topics and ways of saying things that are

sensitive to the boss. The superior, on the other hand, would not wish to discuss things that tend to undermine his or her position in the organization by reflecting negatively on his or her competence and decision-making abilities. Even between friends, hierarchical relationships affect what can be discussed and the way in which things can be discussed (Strauss & Sayles, 1960).

3. *Restrictions in who may communicate with whom and who may make decisions influence the way in which a person communicates.* Coordination of activities and the flow of information in an organization require some centralization of decision making. To avoid having members of the organization going in too many different directions, making contradictory decisions, and having imbalances in work loads, an organization is structured so that certain decisions are made by a limited number of individuals. We have referred to them in different ways—as liaisons, gatekeepers, people in authority, decision makers, or superiors—but in nearly all cases those individuals get information from a variety of others within and without the organization. When central decision makers receive too much information too fast or have too many decisions to make too quickly, distortions are likely to occur as a result of *overload.*

When too many messages or contacts enter a system or the messages or contacts come too fast to be handled properly, one or more of the individuals or units in the organization will experience overload. Networks, organizations, and individuals create ways of adjusting to and avoiding messages when an overload appears to be developing. To maintain an uninterrupted sequence in processing information, individuals may do some of the following:

1. Ignore some messages.
2. Delay responding to unimportant messages.
3. Answer or respond to only parts of some messages.
4. Respond inaccurately to certain messages.
5. Take less time with each message.
6. React to messages at only superficial levels.
7. Block messages before they can enter the system.
8. Shift the burden of responding to some messages to others.
9. Create a new position or unit to handle specialized kinds of messages.
10. Reduce standards to allow for more errors in responding to messages.

Each of these adjustments encourages distortion to develop in messages.

4. *Impersonalization of organizational relationships influences the way in which a person communicates.* One fundamental characteristic of formal organizations is that relationships are to be formal and impersonal. The impersonalization of relationships leads to the suppression of emotional messages. In order to hide or disown emotional expressions, individuals develop ways of keeping others from expressing their emotions. Eventually organization members avoid or refuse to consider ideas that might allow or encourage the release of feelings. The consequence, in the long run at least, is a lessened awareness of the impact of a person's feelings on others and an inability to predict accurately the emotional reactions of others. Ultimately the organization is comprised of individuals who cannot communicate their feelings and who substitute rules for solving problems.

5. *The system of rules, policies, and regulations governing thoughts and actions influences the way in which a person communicates.* As a philosophy of impersonal relationships encourages the development of a system of rules that substitutes for authentic problem solving, so the characteristic of having general but definite policies for guiding decisions leads to impersonal relationships. A rigid application of rules and policies to behavior and decisions leads to an inability to make compromises and fosters impersonality and lack of emotional communication. Rules encourage the evolution of rigid, routine, and traditional patterns of communicating. Institutionalization of behavior is the consequence, with remote and distant, rather than face-to-face, interpersonal communication. Positional relationships are reinforced, and interpersonal relationships are discouraged. Information and messages may be distorted to accommodate the rules and maintain impersonality.

6. *Task specialization narrows a person's perceptions and influences the way in which a person communicates.* Although specialization has contributed immensely to national productivity by increasing efficiency, it is also the source of many communication problems. Individuals identify with their own areas of expertise, learn entire vocabularies unknown to other employees, and often fail to integrate their efforts with other departments. The result is often a bottleneck in the flow of information or a great deal of "buck passing" from one person to another because the client's problem is not in the employee's area of specialization. To some extent specialization fosters conflicts through competition for resources to accomplish narrow objectives. Although competition may help keep employees functioning with alertness, it may lead very quickly to destructive relationships and dysfunctional communication. Specialization may be the source of much of the message distortion that occurs in organizations. Task specialization leads to what some call *trained incapacity, or a limited ability to perform general organizational functions.* Accompanying an incapacity to do varied tasks is the inability to perceive the total picture and act for the good of colleagues and the organization. Such limited perspectives reduce a person's ability to comprehend other's problems, resulting in lower levels of empathy. Without empathy, understanding may be diminished and distortion increased.

We have identified six general organizational characteristics that encourage the distortion of messages in communication. Since organizational communication is affected by personal and organizational factors, it is a small wonder that communication proceeds as well as it does. Some of the reasons why organizational communication has as much fidelity and facilitates the work of organizations as it seems to have done lies in what Downs (1967) calls "antidistortion factors in the communication system" (p. 118).

ANTIDISTORTION FACTORS

Messages in every organization are subject to a degree of distortion, but formal organizations also have forces that limit the amount of distortion that occurs in communication. Although the antidistortion forces may reduce the level of distortion below that implied by the lengthy list of personal and organizational factors contributing to distortion, they do not entirely eliminate distortion. Downs (1967) lists four general ways in which organization members attempt to increase the fidelity of information communicated in an organization.

1. Establish more than one channel of communication. When an employee (manager or operative) believes that information he or she is receiving may be distorted, one way to counter the distortion is to verify the information through multiple sources of messages. This can be done in several ways:

a. Use sources of information outside the organization, including publications, friends in other organizations, clients of the organization, suppliers of the organization, social acquaintances, political contacts, and the grapevine.

b. Create overlapping areas of responsibility among employees so that an element of competition is introduced into the communication process. Each person learns that any distortions in his or her reports may be revealed by the reports of other employees. For example, a manager who receives three conflicting reports and is unable to determine which has the greatest fidelity may be led to search for accuracies and distortions with greater care.

2. Develop procedures for counterbalancing distortions. If we assume that those who work in organizations realize that personal and organizational factors produce distortions, then those who receive information can routinely adjust reports to counteract the distortions contained in them. To the extent that a manager, for example, has accurately identified the distortions, he or she can adjust the information more closely to the original design. When counterbalancing procedures are used throughout the organization, as they tend to be, much of the cumulative effect of personal and organizational distortion factors tends to be reduced. The main distorting effect will be the inaccurate estimate of the source and degree of distortion in the information.

If a person does not know what kinds of distortions are included in a report, he or she will have difficulty making adjustments. The only alternative is to discount or possibly not use the information in making decisions. There is a tendency, of course, for managers, as well as other employees, to adjust potential distortions in a direction that tends to benefit them most rather than in terms of objective estimates of real fidelity. Superiors and subordinates tend to resolve those kinds of questions in their own favor, of course. The weakness of using counterbalancing procedures is that organization decision makers may distort decisions in the very process of attempting to reduce distortions.

3. Eliminate the intermediary between the decision maker and those who provide information. This can be done by maintaining a basically flat organization structure or by using various bypassing strategies.

By reducing the number of links in the communication network, the number of relayors through which information may be filtered and distorted is reduced. Flat organizations require a wide span of control. Subordinates have a larger degree of discretion because supervisors spend less time with each subordinate. The number of messages passed between levels in the organization is lower than in tall structures, since supervisors need to approve fewer actions. The tendency in flat structures is toward less vertical communication distortion.

All organizations have ways in which employees can circumvent the usual chain of command and communicate directly with officers or managers two or more levels higher in the organization. Although bypassing may have some detrimental consequences for other aspects of the organization, it does help reduce distortion that occurs when messages must pass through a large number of relayors at different levels in the organization. The major types of bypassing seem to be the following.

a. *The straight scoop.* Higher-level managers make direct contact with individuals below them in the hierarchy in order to get the "straight scoop" from the "horse's mouth."

b. *The check-out.* A manager seeks to test ideas before putting them on record through official channels; thus the manager checks out a proposal informally before announcing it formally by making contact with employees at other levels in the organization.

c. *The end run.* A supervisor has a manager who distorts information passed up the line, so the supervisor makes an end run around the manager to a higher-level official.

d. *The speed-up.* A supervisor wants to get information to a higher-level executive for some urgent purpose; hence the supervisor speeds up the information-flow process by contacting the higher-up executive directly.

e. *The co-option.* A manager wants to provide lower-level supervisors with an opportunity to be involved in the decision-making process, so he or she conducts oral briefings or has meetings involving individuals of different levels in the organization or of entire units. By involving supervisors of lower levels with their immediate supervisors, the middle-line supervisor is effectively bypassed.

4. *Develop distortion-proof messages.* One way to reduce distortion is to create message systems that cannot be altered in meaning during transmission, except through direct falsification. To be distortion-proof, a message must be able to be transmitted without condensation or expansion (skeletonizing or importing) between the source and the terminating point. Obviously only a very small proportion of all messages directed to any individual in an organization can be distortion-proof. Nevertheless, carefully prepared codes and easily quantifiable information may represent messages that are less subject to distortion through selective omission of qualifiers, shifts in emphasis, ambiguous terminology, and other perceptual and language factors that affect many messages.

So far we have discussed personal tendencies and organizational characteristics that permit, facilitate, and encourage messages to be distorted. We have also noted some antidistortion forces that limit the amount of distortion that actually occurs in organizations. As a final section in this chapter, we would like to identify six kinds of modifications that occur in messages that lead to distortions and that reduce the fidelity. These modifications are based on a review of the work of Bartlett (1932), Paul (1959), Allport and Postman (1947), and others, but follow the outline of Lee and Lee (1957).

MODIFICATIONS IN MESSAGES THAT LEAD TO DISTORTIONS

Six kinds of modifications take place during the reproduction of messages in organizations:

1. *Omissions.* Details that are not mentioned at all in later transmissions but that were included in the original message and seemed to be overlooked by the relayor.
2. *Losses.* Details that are mentioned by an early relayor but that are dropped in part or completely later in the chain.
3. *Changes.* Details that are moved to a different location in the message, roles made to appear different, events reported in different order, and ideas that have different interpretations.
4. *Additions.* Details that are not mentioned in the original message but that appear as new information in later reproductions.
5. *Elaborations.* Details that are part of the original message but that are highlighted and amplified.
6. *Adjustments toward definiteness*. Details that are included in the original message as qualified statements but are later made to appear more definite by dropping phrases such as, "I think," "It may have been," or "It looked like."

THE EFFECT OF DISTORTIONS

There has been little effort devoted to evaluating the effect of distortions on organization members and processes; nevertheless, everyday organizational living suggests that constantly distorted messages have a detrimental effect on people and results in some, if not all, of the following consequences:

1. Reduced morale
2. Lowered motivation
3. Diminished status
4. Alienation
5. Anxiety
6. Monotony
7. Rejection of authority
8. Confusion

SUMMARY

In this chapter we defined message fidelity and distortion in terms of the correspondence of a reproduced message with that of an original message. It was suggested that messages have two dimensions: a display of verbal symbols and nonverbal behaviors and an interpretation or intended and imputed meaning. Eight principles relating to perception, language, nonverbal behaviors, ambiguity, memory, and motivation were discussed as factors that contribute to the distortion of messages.

Six characteristics of formal organization were discussed in terms of how they influence the distortion of messages. Four general antidistortion forces that function in organizations were also discussed. Finally, six types of modifications that lead to distortions were identified and characterized, and eight effects that distorted messages have on people in an organization were listed.

A SUBJECTIVIST'S NOTATION

One must not forget where the *essence* of communication resides. Meaning does not reside in the message itself or in perceptual filters that may impede message reception; rather, meaning lies in the interaction between people and their interpretations of what is going on. The *event* is of particular importance in the organization. The assigning of meaning to an event, real or imagined, produces a shared social reality or underlying logic for organizational members. People need to make sense and achieve order. They do so by *punctuating* events and thereby assigning meaning to them.

Weick (1977) details the activities involved in this process. "Punctuation means chopping the stream of experience into sensible, nameable, and named units, and the activity of connection involves imposing relationships, typically causal relationships, among the punctuated elements" (p. 280). Some authors emphasize how people can see different relationships among prepunctuated behaviors. Watzlawick (1977) describes a punctuation problem that occurred during World War II when U.S. soldiers were stationed in Great Britain. Both U.S. soldiers and British women accused each other of being sexually aggressive. He reports:

> In both cultures, courtship behavior from the first eye contact to the ultimate consummation went through approximately thirty steps, but the sequence of those steps was different. Kissing, for instance, comes relatively early in the North American pattern (occupying, let us say, step 5) and relatively late in the English pattern (at step 25, let us assume), where it is considered highly erotic behavior. So when the U.S. soldier somehow felt that the time was right for a harmless kiss, not only did the British girl feel cheated out of twenty steps of what for her would have been proper behavior on his part, she also felt she had to make a quick decision: break off the relationship and run, or get ready for intercourse. If she chose the latter, the soldier was confronted with behavior that according to his cultural rules could only be called shameless at this early stage of the relationship. (pp. 63–64)

This cross-cultural example shows how people can punctuate a sequence of events quite differently as well as the ramifications of such differences.

Weick (1977) notes that punctuation does involve imposing relationships among events in a sequence, but his main interest is on how those events become singled out and named. He stresses that the labels assigned to events are rather arbitrary. When organizational members chop up their experiences and label them in order to make sense, that process constitutes their reality and directs their organizational activity. The issue, then, is not how to keep messages intact, but to become aware of how messages may shape behaviors and exclude alternative ways of thinking.

REFERENCES

Alkire, A., M. Collum, J. Kaswan, and L. Love, "Information Exchange and Accuracy of Verbal Behavior under Social Power Conditions," *Journal of Personality and Social Psychology,* 9 (1968), 301–308.

Allport, G. W., and L. J. Postman, *The Psychology of Rumor.* New York: Holt, Rinehart & Winston, 1947.

Alper, T. G., and S. J. Korchin, "Memory for Socially Relevant Material," *Journal of Abnormal and Social Psychology,* 47 (1952), 25–37.

Bartlett, F. C., *Remembering.* London: Cambridge University Press, 1932.

Bouillut, J., and S. Moscovici, "Transformation des messages transmis en fonction de l'interest des sujets et de l'image du destinataire," *Bulletin du C.E.R.P.,* 16 (1967), 305–322.

Brissey, F. L., "An Experimental Technique for the Study of Human Communication," Technical Report, Communication Research Laboratory, University of Montana, 1964.

Downs, Anthony, *Inside Bureaucracy.* Boston: Little, Brown, 1967.

Gardner, R. W., and L. J. Lohrenz, "Leveling-Sharpening and Serial Reproduction of a Story," *Bulletin of the Menninger Clinic,* 24 (November 1960), 295–304.

Haney, William V., "Serial Communication of Information in Organizations," in *Concepts and Issues in Administrative Behavior,* Sidney Mailick and Edward H. Van Ness, eds., 150–165. Englewood Cliffs, N.J.: Prentice-Hall, 1962.

Haney, William V., "A Comparative Study of Unilateral and Bilateral Communication," *Academy of Management Journal,* 7 (June 1964), 128–136.

Haney, William V., *Communication and Organizational Behavior.* Homewood, Ill.: Richard D. Irwin, 1967.

Higham, T. M., "The Experimental Study of the Transmission of Rumor," *British Journal of Psychology,* 42 (1951), 42–55.

Holzman, P. S., and R. W. Gardner, "Leveling-Sharpening and Memory Organization," *Journal of Abnormal and Social Psychology,* 61 (1960), 176–180.

Jackson, Jay M., "The Organization and Its Communications Problem," *Advanced Management,* February 1959, 17–20.

Johnson, W., and C. B. Wood, "John Told Him What Joe Told Him: A Study of the Process of Abstracting," *Etc.,* 2 (1944), 10–28.

Katz, Daniel, and Robert L. Kahn, *The Social Psychology of Organizations.* New York: John Wiley, 1966.

Knapp, Mark L., *Nonverbal Communication in Human Interaction.* New York: Holt, Rinehart & Winston, 1972.

Lee, I. J., and L. L. Lee, *Handling Barriers in Communication.* New York: Harper & Row, Pub., 1957.

Manis, M., S. C. Cornell, and J. C. Moore, "Transmission of Attitude-Relevant Information through a Communication Chain," *Journal of Personality and Social Psychology,* 30 (1974), 81–94.

Mehrabian, Albert, *Silent Messages.* Belmont, Calif.: Wadsworth, 1971.

Paul, T. H., "Studies in Remembering: The Reproduction of Connected and Extended Verbal Materials," *Psychological Bulletin,* 1 (1959), Monograph 2.

Redding, W. Charles, *Communication within the Organization.* New York: Industrial Communication Council, Inc., 1972.

Redding, W. Charles, and George A. Sanborn, *Business and Industrial Communication: A Source Book.* New York: Harper & Row, Pub., 1964.

Strauss, George, and Leonard R. Sayles, *Personnel: The Human Problem of Management.* Englewood Cliffs, N.J.: Prentice-Hall, 1960.

Szalay, L. G., C. Windle, and D. A. Lysne, "Attitude Measurement by Free Verbal Associations," *Journal of Social Psychology*, 82 (1970), 46.

Thayer, Lee, *Communication and Communication Systems*. Homewood, Ill.: Richard D. Irwin, 1968.

Watzlawick, Paul, Janet Helmich Beavin, and Don D. Jackson, *Pragmatics of Human Communication*. New York: W. W. Norton & Co., Inc., 1967.

Watzlawick, Paul, *How Real Is Real?* New York: Vintage Books, 1977.

Weick, Karl E., "Enactment Processes in Organizations," in *New Directions in Organizational Behavior*, Barry M. Staw and Gerald R. Salancik, eds. Chicago: St. Clair Press, 1977.

11

Managerial and Leadership Styles

A managerial or leadership style is the consistent patterns of behavior perceived by others when a person is attempting to influence them. As a general rule a person's managerial or leadership style develops over a long period of time and represents what many people think of as a leadership personality. Subordinates or followers expect, and feel, that they get certain types of behaviors from each leader. The behaviors are related to the content of the job or task, to personal relationships, or to some combination of both. Thus we talk about leaders whose styles lean toward getting the task done or lean toward maintaining personal relationships. Most managerial and leadership theories advanced over the past several decades have recognized the importance of these two aspects of style (Hersey & Blanchard, 1974).

The managerial or leadership styles occurring in an organization may be the result of many factors, including some that are beyond a single manager's control, such as economic conditions in the organization or in the country. Managerial style is, however, quite directly related to three elements over which a manager has some control: (1) a manager's assumptions about people and what motivates them; (2) a manager's perceptions of what he or she can do to influence others; and (3) a manager's views of the resources over which he or she has control. Thus a manager might assume that people are basically interested in their own affairs, that they work harder if one keeps a close eye on them, that the manager has the ability and time to watch their work, and that the manager has little control over the financial resources to reward them, but that the manager can submit reports to the boss about people who do not work as hard as he or she thinks they should. As a manager with those assumptions, perceptions, and controls, what might we expect to find you doing during the day? What type of leadership style might you reflect to the employees whom you supervise? How would that affect the work of the employees? The answers to these questions have their foundations in the theories of managerial and leadership styles that follow.

MANAGING AND LEADING: A CONCEPT

Contemporary organizational communication theorists tend to accept the definition of leadership offered by Tannenbaum, Weschler, and Massarik (1961), who describe leadership as *interpersonal influence, exercised in a situation and directed, through the communication process, toward the attainment of a specified goal or goals.* The essence of leadership and managing, in this view, is interpersonal influence. The manager attempts to affect the subordinate through communication. Leadership is more or less effective depending on how successful the communicative acts are in influencing the follower. Thus when a supervisor's objective is to influence someone, or when a change in a subordinate's behavior rewards the supervisor or at least reinforces or supports the supervisor's communicative attempts to influence, the supervisor is engaging in leadership (Bass, 1960).

Any member of an organization—not just a manager or supervisor—may engage in some leadership. Small leadership attempts take place all of the time. Everyone tries to influence someone else from time to time; nevertheless, a supervisor or manager engages in leadership constantly. A major portion of a manager's job is to provide leadership, to be the person who communicates in order to influence. Leadership consists of sending and receiving influential messages between the leader and those being led. Whether a supervisor produces a change in a subordinate depends on some decision on the part of the subordinate; a supervisor cannot produce a change in a subordinate without that subordinate doing something. Positive action taken by the subordinate (successful leadership) reinforces or rewards the supervisor's leadership attempt and encourages the supervisor to try other leadership attempts. Inactivity or negative action taken by the subordinate may stifle the supervisor's leadership attempts and discourage the supervisor from exercising leadership.

From this analysis we can derive three degrees of leadership: (1) attempted, (2) successful, and (3) effective. *Attempted leadership* is when a supervisor has the intent, and is observed attempting, to influence the subordinate. *Successful leadership* is when the subordinate actually makes a change as a result of the supervisor's attempt to influence. *Effective leadership* is when the changes made by the subordinate result in attaining the goal, receiving some reward, or receiving some form of satisfaction from the change. Supervisors should generally be striving for effective leadership with all three consequences: goal attainment, reward, and satisfaction.

COMMUNICATION AND LEADERSHIP

Leadership and communication are intimately intertwined. As we are using the term, leadership consists of interpersonal influence achieved through communication. This concept excludes the use of direct physical force, since communication employs symbols to bring about influence; nevertheless, it does include directives, threats, and other verbal and symbolic forms of coercion conveyed through communication. Communication is therefore the only process by which a leader can exercise influence.

Individuals may have communication objectives other than influence. In fact, effective communication may be defined as sending a message that the receiver interprets consistently with what the communicator intended, without distortion. A leader, however, is interested in more than communicating without distortion. Moreover, a leader is usually interested in more than just producing attitude change. A leader wants action. A supervisor may communicate effectively—have a message interpreted without distortion—without being an effective leader. A supervisor may want to have a subordinate move some barrels from one location to another. The subordinate may say, "I understand that you want me to move those barrels from here to the other side of the yard," but take no action to move them. The subordinate and supervisor may have understood one another perfectly well, resulting in effective communication; however, the subordinate did not behave as the supervisor wanted, resulting in ineffective leadership.

ASSUMPTIONS ABOUT PEOPLE THAT UNDERLIE STYLES OF LEADERSHIP

A manager or leader's style of influencing subordinates or followers is grounded in some assumptions about people and what motivates them. McGregor (1960) identified two bipolar sets of assumptions or beliefs that managers and leaders have a tendency to hold. He called them *Theory X* and *Theory Y*. Most leaders probably do not embrace either of McGregor's theories in any pure sense, but the characterizations help us to visualize the mental set of an ideal type so that we can get a clear image of the thinking of a person who leans strongly in one direction or another.

Theory X

Theory X assumptions appear to be derived from a view of people as machines who require a great deal of external control. Theory X assumptions may be summarized as follows:

1. Most people think work is distasteful and try to avoid it.
2. Most people prefer to be directed and must often be forced to do their work.
3. Most people are not ambitious, do not want to get ahead, and do not want responsibility.
4. Most people are motivated primarily by their desire for basic necessities and security-safety needs.
5. Most people must be closely controlled and are incapable of solving problems in the organization.

It is probably fair to say that leaders who hold Theory X assumptions about people think of employees as tools of production, motivated by fear of punishment or by a desire for money and security. Managers who view workers in this way probably tend to watch them closely, make and enforce strict rules, and use the threat of punishment as a means of motivating them.

Theory Y

Theory Y assumptions tend to be derived from a view of people as biological organisms who grow, develop, and exercise control over themselves. Theory Y assumptions may be summarized as follows:

1. Most people think that work is as natural as play. If work is unpleasant, it is probably because of the way it is done in the organization.
2. Most people feel that self-control is indispensable in getting work done properly.
3. Most people are motivated primarily by their desire for social acceptance, recognition, and a sense of achievement, as well as their need for money to provide basic necessities and security.
4. Most people will accept and even seek responsibility if given proper supervision, management, and leadership.
5. Most people have the ability to solve problems creatively in the organization.

Managers who base their styles on Theory Y see employees as having a variety of needs. They believe their job is to organize and manage work so that both the organization and the employees can satisfy their needs. Theory Y managers assume that personal and organizational goals may be compatible. There is some evidence, however, to suggest that both cannot be achieved within the organizational context. Some personal and some organizational goals may be quite contradictory. Nevertheless, the manager who accepts Theory Y assumptions works with employees to set goals for the organization, encourages them to share in the decision-making process, and seeks to set high standards.

MANAGERIAL AND LEADERSHIP STYLES

From among a multitude of models, theories, and analyses, we have chosen to examine the following six popular systems for classifying and describing managerial and leadership styles:

1. Managerial Grid® Theory (Blake & Mouton)
2. 3-D Theory (Reddin)
3. Situational Theory (Hersey & Blanchard)
4. Four-Systems Theory (Likert)
5. Continuum Theory (Tannenbaum & Schmidt)
6. Contingency Theory (Fiedler)

Each of these ways of looking at leadership and managerial styles is associated with the researcher, writer, or theorist who popularized the point of view.

Managerial Grid®

One of the most widely discussed theories of managerial and leadership styles is that advanced by Blake and Mouton (1964), called the *Managerial Grid.*® The Grid is derived from the basic concerns of managers: concern for the task or that which the organization is designed to accomplish and concern for the people and elements of the organization that affect people. The Grid portrays the ways in which a manager's concern for the task and the people overlap and intertwine to produce styles of managing and leading. Figure 11.1 diagrams how these concerns are related to one another. The five extreme styles suggested by the Grid model are presented in summary form.

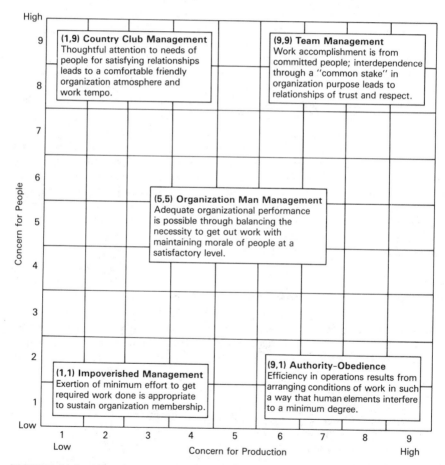

FIGURE 11.1   Managerial Grid Styles of Leadership (Source: From Robert R. Blake and Jane S. Mouton, *The Managerial Grid III: The Key to Leadership Excellence.* Houston: Gulf Publishing Company, 1985, p. 12. Reproduced by permission.)

1,1 Impoverished style. This style is characterized by very low concern for both the task and the people. The impoverished leader tends to accept the decisions of others; to go along with opinions, attitudes, and ideas of others; and to avoid taking sides. When conflict arises the impoverished leader remains neutral and stays out of it. By remaining neutral the impoverished leader rarely gets stirred up. The impoverished leader just puts out enough effort to get by. On a good day the impoverished leader may be intolerant and somewhat unfriendly, and on a bad day he or she tends to be obstinate and disagreeable.

5,5 Middle-of-the-road style. This style is characterized by moderate concern for both the task and the people. The middle-road leader searches for workable, although usually not perfect, solutions to problems. When ideas, opinions, and attitudes different' from those of the middle-road leader develop, the middle-road leader initiates a compromise position. When conflict arises the middle-road leader tries to be fair but firm and to evolve an equitable solution. Under pressure the middle-road leader may be unsure about which way to turn to avoid tension. The middle-road leader seeks to maintain a good steady pace.

9,9 Team style. This style is characterized by high concern for both the task and the people. The team leader places a high value on arriving at sound, creative decisions that result in understanding and agreement of organization members. The team leader listens for and seeks out ideas, opinions, and attitudes that are different from his or her own. The team leader has clear convictions about what needs to be done but responds to sound ideas from others by changing his or her mind. When conflict arises the team leader tries to identify reasons for the differences and to resolve the underlying causes. When aroused the team leader maintains self-control, although some impatience may be visible. The team leader has a sense of humor even under pressure and exerts vigorous effort and enlists others to join in. The team leader is able to show a need for mutual trust and respect among team members as well as respect for the job.

1,9 Country club style. This style is characterized by low concern for the task but high concern for people. The country club leader places a high value on maintaining good relationships with others. The country club leader prefers to accept opinions, attitudes, and ideas of others rather than to push his or her own. The country club leader avoids creating conflict, but when it does appear, tries to soothe feelings and to keep people working together. The country club leader reacts to events in a consistently warm and friendly way so as to reduce tensions that disturbances create. Rather than lead, a country club leader extends help.

9,1 Task style. This style is characterized by a high concern for accomplishing tasks but a low concern for people. The task leader places a high value on making decisions that hold. The task leader is a person whose main concern is with efficiency of operations and getting the job done. The task leader tends to stand up for his or her ideas, opinions, and attitudes even though they may sometimes result in stepping on the toes of others. When conflict arises the task leader tries to cut it off or to win his or her position by defending, resisting, or coming back with counterarguments. When things are not going just right, the task leader drives himself or herself and others.

According to Blake and Mouton, the 9,9 team style is the most desirable. A team style of leadership is based on an effective integration of both task and people concerns. In general the 9,9 leadership style assumes that people produce best when they have the opportunity to do meaningful work. Behind the 9,9 style is a commitment to involve organization members in decision making in order to use their abilities to achieve the highest possible results.

3-D Theory

Reddin (1967) builds upon the task-person grid of Blake and Mouton by adding a third dimension called *effectiveness*. The three dimensions are defined as follows:

Task Orientation—the extent to which a manager directs subordinates' efforts toward attaining a goal.

Relationship Orientation—the extent to which a manager has personal job relationships with subordinates characterized by mutual trust, respect for their ideas, and consideration of their feelings.

Effectiveness—the extent to which a manager achieves the production requirements for his or her position.

The 3-D grid results in eight managerial or leadership styles. Figure 11.2 shows the three aspects of the model and the resulting styles. Four of the styles are

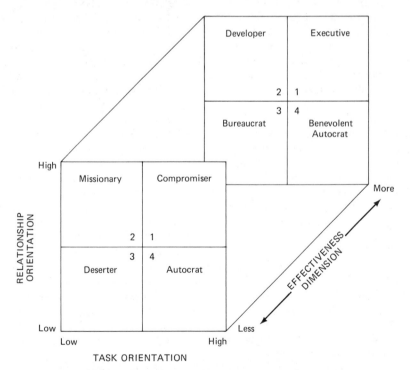

FIGURE 11.2   3-D Model of Leadership Styles (Source: From William J. Reddin, "The 3-D Management Style Theory." Copyright 1967, *Training and Development Journal,* American Society for Training and Development. Reprinted with permission. All rights reserved.)

less effective, and four of the styles are considered more effective. This implies that a low relationship orientation and a low task orientation, considered by Blake and Mouton (1,1 grid style) to be generally undesirable, may be effective when the person is viewed as being primarily conscientious about following rules and procedures in order to get the job done. A brief description of each of the eight styles follows:

MORE EFFECTIVE

Executive
High task, high relationships; seen as a good motivator who sets high standards, who treats everyone somewhat differently and who prefers to allow team management.

Benevolent Autocrat
High task, low relationships; seen as knowing what he or she wants and knowing how to get it without creating resentment.

Developer
Low task, high relationships; seen as having implicit trust in people and as being primarily concerned with developing them as harmony.

Bureaucrat
Low task, low relationships; seen as being primarily interested in rules and procedures for their own sake and as wanting to maintain and control the situation by their use; often seen as conscientious.

LESS EFFECTIVE

Compromiser
High task, high relationships where only one or neither is appropriate; seen as a poor decision maker and one who allows pressure to influence him or her too much; seen as minimizing pressures and problems rather than maximizing long-term production.

Autocrat
High task, low relationships where such behavior is inappropriate; seen as having no confidence in others, as being interested only in the immediate job.

Missionary
Low task, high relationships where such behavior is inappropriate; seen as being primarily interested in individuals.

Deserter
Low task, low relationships where such behavior is inappropriate; seen as uninvolved and passive.

Reddin (1967) explains that the four more effective styles may be equally effective, depending on the situation in which they are used. On the other hand, some managerial jobs require all four styles to be used at one time or another, whereas other jobs tend to demand only one or two styles consistently.

Situational Leadership

Hersey and Blanchard (1974, 1977) developed the concept of situational leadership from studies of leadership completed at Ohio State University (Stogdill & Coons, 1957) that showed, much as in Blake and Mouton's theory, two dimensions of leadership style: consideration and initiating structure, resulting in a grid like Blake and Mouton's. In addition Hersey and Blanchard identified a third variable—maturity—which functions in a way similar to Reddin's effectiveness dimension. Hence Hersey and Blanchard's model of situational leadership has an appearance like Reddin's. In fact, their interpretation of "effective" leadership is also quite similar: "The difference between the effective and ineffective styles is often not the actual behavior of leader, but the appropriateness of this behavior to the situation in which it is used" (1974, p. 6). The factor that determines effectiveness is described by Hersey and Blanchard as "the follower's level of maturity." *Maturity* is defined by a person's achievement-motivation, willingness and ability to take responsibility, and task-relevant education and experience. In other words, if the followers of a leader are highly mature—that is, motivated by high achievement, have high willingness and ability to take responsibility, and are experienced with the task at hand—a particular leadership style will be more effective than if the followers are less mature.

As the level of maturity of one's followers increases, the leader reduces the amount of supportive or relationship behavior accordingly. Figure 11.3 shows the patterns of leadership styles as they follow a bell-shaped curve going through the four leadership quadrants. For purposes of making quick diagnostic judgments, four styles of situational leadership are identified:

Style 1—Telling. High task, low relationship. This style is characterized by one-way communication in which the leader defines the roles of followers and tells them what, how, when, and where to do various tasks.

Style 2—Selling. High task, high relationship. This style is characterized by some effort at two-way communication, although most of the direction is provided by the leader. The leader also provides socioemotional support to get the followers to accept some responsibility for the decisions to be made.

Style 3—Participating. High relationship, low task. This style is characterized by having the leader and followers share in decision making through authentic two-way communication. The leader engages in much facilitating behavior since the followers have the ability and knowledge to do the task.

Style 4—Delegating. Low relationship, low task. This style is characterized by the leader letting the followers take responsibility for their own decisions. The leader delegates decisions to the followers since they are high in maturity, being both willing and able to take responsibility for directing their own behavior.

In contrast to both Blake and Mouton's and Reddin's theories, Hersey and Blanchard seem to regard low task, low relationship orientations as highly desirable when the followers are high in maturity. They argue that with people of high task-relevant maturity, Style 4 has the highest probability of success.

Four-Systems Theory

One of the most frequently discussed theories of managerial and leadership styles is that of Likert (1967). He devised four managerial styles or systems based on an analysis of eight managerial variables: (1) leadership, (2) motivation, (3) communication, (4) interaction, (5) decision making, (6) goal setting, (7) control, and (8) performance. Likert refers to the styles as

1. Exploitive-Authoritative
2. Benevolent-Authoritative

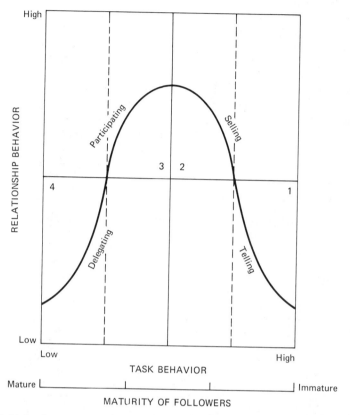

FIGURE 11.3 Situational Leadership Model (Source: From Paul Hersey and Kenneth H. Blanchard, "So You Want to Know Your Leadership Style?" *Training and Development Journal* 28 (February 1974), 22–37.)

3. Consultative
4. Participative

We shall briefly characterize each of the four systems.

System 1—Exploitive-Authoritative. This style is based on the assumptions of McGregor's Theory X in which the manager-leader provides strong guidance and control on the premise that employees are motivated best by fear, threats, and punishments. Superior-subordinate interaction is minimal, with all decisions coming from the top and with downward communication consisting primarily of directives and orders.

System 2—Benevolent-Authoritative. This style is basically authoritarian but encourages upward communication to voice the opinions and complaints of subordinates; however, interaction between levels in the organization is through formal channels. Communication is rarely frank and candid.

System 3—Consultative. This style involves fairly frequent interaction at moderately personal levels between superiors and subordinates in the organization. Information flows both upward and downward but with slightly more emphasis on ideas that originate from the top. The manager has substantial, but not complete, trust and confidence in employees.

System 4—Participative. This style is highly supportive, with goals for the organization being set through true employee participation. Information flows in all directions, and control is exercised at all levels. People communicate freely, openly, and candidly with little fear of punishment. The participative style is similar to Blake and Mouton's 9.9 team style. Generally the informal and formal communication systems are identical, ensuring authentic integration of personal and organizational goals.

The central issue in Likert's systems theory is decision making. System 4 (participative), with the highest level of employee participation, results in the highest level of productivity also. Likert's research indicated that most organizations prefer System 4 but, regretfully, actually use System 1.

Continuum Theory

Tannenbaum and Schmidt (1957) make control over decision making the key concept in their continuum of leadership behavior. They describe seven behavior points on a continuum from boss-centered leadership to subordinate-centered leadership. The seven points characterize leader-managers ranging from those who maintain a high degree of control to those who release control to subordinates. The continuum may be diagramed as in Figure 11.4.

Although the possible range of leadership styles may exist along a continuum as suggested, Tannenbaum and Schmidt characterize the successful leader as neither strongly control-oriented nor highly permissive. Rather, the most effective leader is one who adopts a style consistent with the demands of the situation. If direction seems appropriate, the leader gives direction; if participation in decisions is required, the leader releases control and allows the group to function in making decisions. The question generally left unanswered concerns what kinds of demands within a leadership situation call for each of the different styles. Some ideas for how to decide when to use a particular leadership style are suggested by *contingency theory.*

Contingency Theory

Many of the theories examined here implicitly, if not explicitly, acknowledge that effective leadership may be a function of or contingent upon the situation in which leadership is being exercised. Fiedler (1967) was instrumental in developing a theory of leadership styles based on the concept of contingencies. According to contingency theory the leader's effectiveness depends on the relationships within his or her style, as well as certain features of the situation. A leader's style is described in terms of variables already familiar to us: task and relationship; hence leaders are considered to be task-motivated or relationship-motivated.

The characteristics of a given leadership situation that seem most important are (1) leader-member relations, (2) task structure, and (3) leader's position power. Good *leader-member relations* exist when members like, trust, and respect the

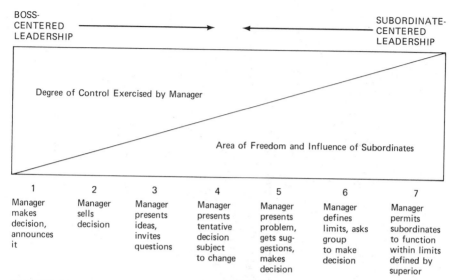

1	2	3	4	5	6	7
Manager makes decision, announces it	Manager sells decision	Manager presents ideas, invites questions	Manager presents tentative decision subject to change	Manager presents problem, gets suggestions, makes decision	Manager defines limits, asks group to make decision	Manager permits subordinates to function within limits defined by superior

FIGURE 11.4 Leadership Styles Continuum (Source: Reprinted by permission of the *Harvard Business Review*. An exhibit from "How to Choose a Leadership Pattern," by Robert Tannenbaum and Warren H. Schmidt (May–June 1973). Copyright © 1973 by the President and Fellows of Harvard College. All rights reserved.)

leader; this is regarded as the single most important condition for effective leadership. *Task structure* refers to the degree to which the way a job is to be done is explained in step-by-step detail; the more structured the task, the more influence the leader has over the group. *Position power* is defined in terms of the degree to which a leader can punish, reward, promote, discipline, or reprimand members; leaders have more position power when they can reward and punish.

Leader effectiveness is determined by the match between the style of leadership (task or relationship) and the favorableness of the situation. The most favorable situation exists when leader-member relations are good, the task is highly structured, and the leader has strong position power. The least favorable situation exists when leader-member relations are poor, the task is unstructured, and leader position power is weak. Of course, any situation may have varying levels of favorableness, which would include aspects of both better and poorer characteristics.

Table 11.1 portrays various combinations of style, characteristics, and favorableness. Eight basic contingencies result from the combinations. Research on the contingency model has shown that (1) Task-motivated leaders are more effective in highly favorable *and* highly unfavorable situations; (2) Relationship-motivated leaders are more effective in moderately favorable situations. Thus, task-motivated leaders tend to be more effective in situations in which they have either very much or very little influence. Relationship-motivated leaders tend to be more effective in situations in which they have moderate levels of influence.

Why certain leadership styles seem to be more effective in different situations is explained by looking at the requirements of favorable and unfavorable situations. In favorable situations you, as a leader, are well liked, have a clear task, and have

TABLE 11.1 Leadership Effectiveness (Based on a Leader Style, Situational Favorableness, and Contingencies)

Most Effective Leader	Task-Motivated			Relationship-Motivated			Task-Motivated	
Situation Favorableness	Highly Favorable			Moderately Favorable			Unfavorable	
Leader-member relations	Good	Good	Good	Good	Poor	Poor	Poor	Poor
Task structure	Highly structured	Structured	Unstructured	Unstructured	Structured	Structured	Unstructured	Highly structured
Leader position power	Strong	Weak	Strong	Weak	Strong	Weak	Strong	Weak
Contingency	1	2	3	4	5	6	7	8

high position power; under those conditions you obviously have everything going for you and should be able to exert influence over the group. The group should be willing to go along with your efforts to direct them; the strongest style for this situation is the task-motivated one. On the other hand, if you are disliked, have a vague assignment, and have little position power, then you are unlikely to have much influence over the group. In that case you should focus on the task and direct the group, relying on whatever influence you might have through the authority derived from the position. In either case—highly favorable and highly unfavorable—the task-motivated leader has the greatest likelihood of success.

Relationship-motivated leaders tend to perform most effectively in moderately favorable situations. When the situation is favorable, members do not require strong control. Tasks can be accomplished by subordinates with little task direction, but they need encouragement, support, and interpersonal trust, all of which are provided by the relationship-motivated leader.

SUMMARY

Leadership was defined as interpersonal influence, exercised in a situation and directed through communication processes, toward the attainment of a specified goal or goals. Three degrees of leadership were identified: attempted, successful, and effective. Theory X and Theory Y were reviewed to assist us in visualizing the mental set underlying many of the major theories of leadership style. Six popular systems of classifying leadership and managerial styles were discussed: Managerial Grid® (Blake & Mouton), 3-D theory (Reddin), situational theory (Hersey & Blanchard), four-systems theory (Likert), continuum theory (Tannenbaum & Schmidt), and contingency theory (Fiedler).

Most managerial and leadership theories suggest that different combinations of style and circumstances produce different levels of effectiveness. Certainly all of the theorists represented here would agree that no single style of leadership will guarantee that just the right type and amount of interpersonal influence is exercised in all situations. Interpersonal influence that results in goal attainment, rewards, and satisfaction may be communicated in a variety of ways, depending generally on the conditions identified by Fiedler—task structure, interpersonal relations, and leader power. Task-oriented leaders probably have a greater chance of being effective if the conditions are right; relationship-oriented leaders probably have an equally great opportunity of being effective if conditions are right for them.

A SUBJECTIVIST'S NOTATION

Leadership has meaning only as constructed and defined by organizational members. The same management styles in different contexts are likely to be perceived in different ways. But what about all the literature on management and communication that gives advice about the leadership styles that should be used? As Calder (1977) contends:

> Leadership cannot be taught as a skill. Skills may certainly help a person to perform more effectively, but leadership depends on how this performance and its effects are

perceived by others. To teach leadership is to sensitize people to the perceptions of others—that is, to sensitize them to the everyday, common-sense thinking of a group of people. The transfer of leadership from one group of actors to another thus becomes highly problematic. The would-be-leader must respond to attributions based on the meaning of leadership for each group with which he interacts. (p. 202)

Managers can become sensitive and responsive to organizational demands by understanding the interactions of members. Each organizational culture makes different demands in terms of what a manager can do and what the response of the manager ought to be in a particular context.

A provocative study is provided by Pettegrew (1982). After a review of leadership literature, he concludes:

> Conceptualizations of management style hold in common the notion that organizational leadership exerts strong stylistic pressure on other members of the organization. Depending upon certain needs and assets of its members, particular styles will have predictable outcomes for their attitudes and behaviors, the productivity of the organization as a whole, and the kind of communication which takes place laterally, vertically, and horizontally. (p. 181)

The traditional functionalist literature, then, suggests that managerial and leadership styles are strong determinants of the behavior of subordinates, and that different styles produce different outcomes.

Pettegrew examines the effects of leadership styles in his study of academic medical centers. In essence, the findings indicate that in the particular organization studied, employees perceived leadership as being the same in spite of the divergent leadership styles employed by managers. This conclusion gives rise to a different kind of framework for understanding the effects of leadership behavior on the organization. Pettegrew states:

> This alternative is termed "The S.O.B. Theory of Management." Its basic tenet holds that in nonprofit health and human service organizations . . . it doesn't matter what kind of management style one uses (from delegative to directive). The force of being a decision-maker within this particular organizational context makes one an S.O.B. to the majority of interest groups in such organizations. (pp. 178–180)

This statement generalizes more than interpretive researchers may like, but the important point is that the context, or culture, is a dominant factor in determining what behaviors mean. Pettegrew maintains that "there are frequently both situational and contextual factors which render received theories important. The scholar must be willing to abandon the received view and search for other, perhaps more rhetorical, interpretive frameworks for understanding the organization and the communication which takes place therein" (p. 191).

We would suggest that managers could benefit from an understanding of the ways organizational members interpret different management styles. Although the S.O.B. label seems harsh, it may not only be realistic but quite functional. Some cultures (organizations) may operate better with S.O.B.'s.

REFERENCES

Bass, Bernard M., *Leadership, Psychology and Organizational Behavior*. New York: Harper & Row, Pub., 1960.

Blake, Robert R., and Jane S. Mouton, *The Managerial Grid*. Houston: Gulf Publishing Company, 1964.

Blake, Robert R., and Jane S. Mouton, *The Managerial Grid III: The Key to Leadership Excellence*. Houston: Gulf Publishing Company, 1985.

Calder, Bobby J., "An Attribution Theory of Leadership," in *New Directions in Organizational Behavior*, Barry M. Staw and Gerald R. Salancik, eds. Chicago: St. Clair Press, 1977.

Fiedler, Fred, *A Theory of Leadership Effectiveness*. New York: McGraw-Hill, 1967.

Hersey, Paul, and Kenneth H. Blanchard, "So You Want to Know Your Leadership Style?" *Training and Development Journal*, 28 (February 1974), 22–37.

Hersey, Paul, and Kenneth H. Blanchard, *Management of Organizational Behavior: Utilizing Human Resources*, 3rd ed. Englewood Cliffs, N.J.: Prentice-Hall, 1977.

Likert, Rensis, *The Human Organization*. New York: McGraw-Hill, 1967.

McGregor, Douglas, *The Human Side of Enterprise*. New York: McGraw-Hill, 1960.

Pettegrew, Loyd S., "Organizational Communication and The S.O.B. Theory of Management," *Western Journal of Speech Communication*, 46 (Spring 1982), 179–191.

Reddin, William J., "The 3-D Management Style Theory," *Training and Development Journal*, 21 (April 1967), 8–17.

Stogdill, Ralph M., and Alvin E. Coons, eds., *Leader Behavior: Its Description and Measurement*, Research Monograph No. 88. Columbus, Ohio: Bureau of Business Research, Ohio State University, 1957.

Tannenbaum, Robert, and Warren H. Schmidt, "How to Choose a Leadership Pattern," *Harvard Business Review*, 36 (March–April 1957), 95–101. Reprinted in May–June 1973.

Tannenbaum, Robert, Irving R. Weschler, and Fred Massarik, *Leadership and Organizations: A Behavior Science Approach*. New York: McGraw-Hill, 1961.

12

Motivation and Communication

Of all the issues in the fields of communication, management, and leadership, probably the most popular is that of motivation. When we talk about motivation, we are talking about reasons why people devote energy to a task. For example, we hired Sue to serve as a staff assistant to a team of six employees. Her responsibilities included answering the telephone, scheduling appointments, maintaining files, typing correspondence and reports, arranging meetings, keeping the office neat, and handling the budget, including recording receipts and expenditures. When she came to the job, she had to begin filing, typing, recording, and scheduling immediately. The previous staff assistant had taken another job on very short notice and had left the office with numerous stacks of untyped reports, correspondence, and assorted clutter. The telephone rang constantly, and team members asked for schedules and assistance in locating supplies and materials.

At the end of the third day on the job, Sue remained after office hours to assess how she might deal with the demands of everything that needed to be done. She spent an hour sorting through rough drafts of letters and reports, arranging them in a tentative order for typing. She looked through the appointment book and thought about the hours it would take to schedule the interviews and meetings. She stood by the filing cabinets and ran her fingers across the tabs in some drawers, reflecting on how the materials could be sorted and inserted so as to be found at some later time. After two hours of sorting and looking and thinking, she slumped into a chair and stared at the floor.

The next morning she arrived at work before 7:00 A.M. and typed several

short items before other employees began to stop at her ᴄ
morning she typed, answered the telephone, and filled reqυ
hour, between bites of a sandwich and sipping a soda, Sue sᵗ
After lunch she completed a report and several pieces of cᴄ
ing time she had made good progress on the pile of tyᵖ
everyone else had left the building, Sue sorted and filed papᴇᵣₛ. ᴄᴄ
office at about 7:00 A.M. the next day.

A CONCEPT OF MOTIVATION

Sue was motivated. She was willing to devote large amounts of both physical and
mental energy into performing the job. Of course, individuals differ in the amounts
of energy, enthusiasm, and persistence they are willing to invest in their work.
Nevertheless, the more energy a person puts into a job, the more we say that person
is motivated. The question that has puzzled managers for a long time is, "Why do
some people work hard whereas others do as little as possible?" The answer lies in
the degree to which people are willing to direct their behaviors toward some goal.
Sue was willing to direct her behaviors toward a goal; she was motivated. Motivation was inside her. No one motivated Sue; she motivated herself.

FOUR THEORIES OF MOTIVATION

The most common theories of motivation refer to needs and goals as the driving
forces of human behavior. We shall review four explanations of how needs and
goals function to motivate people:

Hierarchy theory
ERG theory
Motivator-Hygiene theory
Expectancy theory

A *need* is something that is essential, indispensable, or inevitable to fill a
condition. The term *need* is also used to refer to the lack of something. Thus the
concept of a need is something that is lacking and must be filled. We are told that all
behaviors are responses to satisfy needs. What kinds of needs do we try to satisfy?

Hierarchy Theory

Maslow (1943, 1954) proposed that our needs fall into five categories: physiological, safety or security, belongingness or social, esteem, and self-actualization,
as portrayed in Figure 12.1. These needs, according to Maslow, develop in a
hierarchical order, with physiological needs being the most prepotent until satisfied.
A prepotent need has great influence over other needs as long as it is unsatisfied.
For example, it is difficult, although not impossible, to give full attention to saving
for the future when you feel strong hunger pains. As someone observed, it is tough

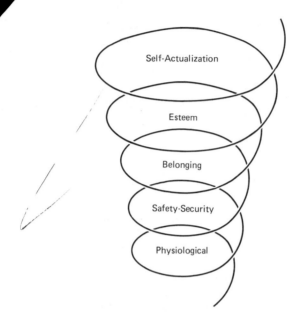

FIGURE 12.1 Maslow's Needs Hierarchy

to be concerned about mosquitoes when you are standing up to your waist in alligators. Thus physiological needs urge to be satisfied before all others. Nevertheless, a lower-order need might not have to be completely satisfied before the next higher one becomes active, as suggested by the overlapping lines of the spiral. You might very easily be concerned about your safety even if you seem fatigued. However, it is quite likely that a major portion of the prepotent need will have to be satisfied before the next order becomes a strong motivator. The concept of prepotency postulates also that a satisfied need is no longer a motivator. Only unsatisfied needs impel people to action and direct their behaviors toward a goal.

The five sets of needs are arranged in a hierarchical order, with physiological being the lower order, safety and security next, belonging in the middle, esteem needs higher, and self-actualization needs being the highest order. Once bodily needs are satisfied, a person seeks satisfaction for safety and security needs; then when a person feels secure, he or she is motivated by the next level of needs— esteem. When a worker is able to satisfy all of the lower needs, what he or she considers most important or satisfying is to be able to feel that he or she is doing something of value and is being fulfilled as a person.

On the job we tend to be motivated at the lowest level of need for which we have little satisfaction. When our need for security has been satisfied by a decent income or our need for esteem has been satisfied by good working conditions, improvements in those areas do not increase motivation. Since most people working in organizations have basic satisfaction of lower-level needs, the most appropriate means of motivation is through satisfaction of higher-level needs. The overlapping of needs orders is expressed by Ralph Waldo Emerson's observation that "our chief want in life is somebody who shall make us do what we can. This is the service of a friend. With him we are easily great.''

Research on Maslow's hierarchy of needs has *not* supported the five orders of needs particularly well. Wahba and Bridwell (1976) reviewed the literature on Maslow's model and concluded that a two-level hierarchy of lower-level and higher-level needs may exist but that the specific categories identified by Maslow were not verified. The idea of prepotency has also failed to be strongly supported by empirical research reviewed by Wahba and Bridwell. The evidence suggests that a person may very well have strong belonging, esteem, and self-actualization needs at the same time. It may be that the research was just unable to make fine distinctions between orders of needs and prepotencies.

ERG Theory

Alderfer (1972) identified three categories of needs, in comparison to Maslow's five levels of needs. The three types of needs are *existence* (E), *relatedness* (R), and *growth* (G). Existence includes physiological needs such as hunger, thirst, and sex, as well as material needs such as compensation and a desirable work environment. Relatedness needs involve relationships with those who are important to us, such as family members, friends, and work supervisors. Growth needs concern our desires to be productive and creative so as to achieve our potential. These three needs areas are similar to Maslow's and, in fact, span the entire range of needs as suggested by Maslow. In general the ERG needs concept is a refinement of Maslow's needs system, but they differ in two respects. First, although the order of the needs is similar, the idea of hierarchy is not included. Alderfer argues that if the existence needs are not satisfied, their influence may be strong, but the other need categories may still be important in directing behaviors toward goals. Second, he also claims that even though a need may be satisfied, it may continue as a dominant influence in decisions. You may, for example, have a reasonably good salary and a secure job but continue to seek raises, even though existence needs seem fairly well satisfied. In that case a satisfied need may continue to be a motivator. On the other hand, relatedness and growth needs may increase in intensity as they are satisfied. The more you discover ways to be productive and creative, the more you want to be increasingly productive and creative.

Motivator-Hygiene Theory

Herzberg (1966) attempted to determine what factors influence worker motivation in organizations. He discovered two sets of activities that satisfy a person's needs: (1) those related to job satisfaction and (2) those related to job dissatisfaction. The factors affecting job satisfaction are called *motivators*. These include achievement, recognition, responsibility, advancement or promotion, the work itself, and the potential for personal growth. All of these are related to the job itself. When these factors are responded to positively, employees tend to experience satisfaction and seem motivated. However, if these factors are not present in the work, employees will lack motivation but will not be dissatisfied with their work.

Those factors related to dissatisfaction are called *maintenance* or *hygiene* factors. Maintenance or hygiene factors include pay, supervision, job security, working conditions, administration, organizational policies, and interpersonal rela-

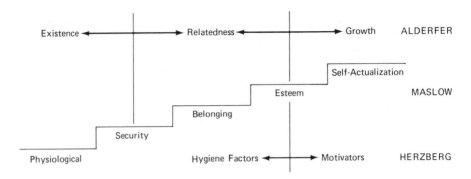

FIGURE 12.2   Three Categories of Needs

tionships with peers, superiors, and subordinates on the job. These factors are related to the environment or context of the job rather than the job itself. This is why programs to motivate employees using Herzberg's system refer to it as "motivation through the work itself." When these factors are responded to positively, employees do not experience satisfaction or seem motivated; however, if they are not present, employees will be dissatisfied.

Motivators are related to job satisfaction but not to dissatisfaction. Hygiene factors are related to job dissatisfaction but not to satisfaction. Thus to retain or maintain employees, managers should focus on the hygiene factors; however, to get employees to devote more energy to their jobs, managers should focus on the motivators. Managers adjust the job itself to motivate employees and adjust environmental factors to prevent dissatisfaction. For example, a supervisor who does a good job of creating positive relationships with employees will be disappointed if he or she thinks that those employees will be motivated to work harder as a result. Since supervisory relations is a hygiene factor, employees will most likely not be dissatisfied. To motivate employees, the supervisor will need to find ways to give employees greater freedom and more responsibility in doing their work, or at least give them more recognition for work done well. If employees do not get recognition, they will not necessarily be dissatisfied with their jobs, but they will not be motivated to work harder.

Comparison of Maslow's, Alderfer's, and Herzberg's Needs Categories

There is a great deal of similarity among these three ways of talking about motivation. Each system describes self-actualization, growth, and motivators in similar terms. Maintenance or hygiene factors tend to satisfy needs at the physiological and security levels as well as to satisfy the existence needs. Interpersonal relations and supervision might be considered ways to satisfy relatedness, belonging needs, and esteem needs. Figure 12.2 portrays relationships among the three approaches.

DIFFERENCES BETWEEN SUPERVISORS AND EMPLOYEES ON WHAT MOTIVATES WORKERS

Although a great deal has been written on the topic of motivation, managers often base their decisions about employee motivation on erroneous information about what actually motivates employees. The sad truth is that supervisors frequently are out of touch with what employees want from their jobs. Kovach (1980) argues that employee attitudes and actual factors that motivate employees change more rapidly than does a supervisor's knowledge about what motivates workers. He claims that most theories of motivation are outdated by the time they are implemented. To support his claim, Kovach replicated the 1946 study completed by the Labor Relations Institute of New York in which first-line supervisors and employees who worked directly for them ranked ten items that provide motivation on the job. The results indicated that a gap existed between what employees wanted from their jobs and what supervisors thought employees wanted. Kovach administered the 1946 questionnaire to a group of over 200 employees and their immediate supervisors to see if the results were similar. The findings of the 1946 study and Kovach's 1979 study are shown in Table 12.1. An analysis of the results indicates that with the exception of the ranking of "sympathetic help with personal problems," the gap between supervisors and their employees has not narrowed. For example, the items *security* and *wages* were ranked by employees in 1946 as having intermediate importance for them and were ranked by supervisors as having high importance for employees, whereas *appreciation of work* and *feeling in on things* were ranked as having high importance for employees, yet supervisors perceived those items as being of low importance to employees. The same discrepancies were discovered by the 1979 study. Differences in perceptions between supervisors and employees on what motivates employees still appear to exist.

Some of the differences between what employees feel motivates them and

TABLE 12.1   What Motivates Employees*

	1946		1979	
	Employee	Supervisor	Employee	Supervisor
Full appreciation of work done	1	8	2	8
Feeling of being in on things	2	9	3	10
Sympathetic help with personal problems	3	10	9	9
Job security	4	2	4	2
Good wages	5	1	5	1
Interesting work	6	5	1	5
Promotion and growth in the organization	7	3	6	3
Personal loyalty to employees	8	6	8	7
Good working conditions	9	4	7	4
Tactful discipline	10	7	10	6

Source: From Kenneth A. Kovach, "Why Motivational Theories Don't Work," *S.A.M. Advanced Management Journal* (Spring 1980), 54–59.

*Rankings range from 1 to 10: 1, most important; 10, least important.

what supervisors feel motivates employees may be found in changing attitudes and values. However, most people have choices to make between different ways of satisfying needs and between degrees of effort they will exert toward accomplishing a particular goal. A person's actual motivation (effort directed toward a goal) may be a function of his or her expectations that a certain investment of energy will result in the accomplishment of a particular goal. Vroom's expectancy theory of motivation helps to explain how what a person values and what a person expects can have an effect on motivation.

Expectancy Theory

Vroom (1964) has developed a theory of motivation based on the kinds of choices a person makes in seeking to achieve a goal, rather than on internal needs. Expectancy theory has three key assumptions:

1. Every individual believes that if he or she behaves in a particular way, he or she will get certain things. This is called an *outcome expectancy*. For example, you may believe (or have an expectancy) that if you score at least an 85 on the next test, you will receive a passing grade in the course. Also, you may have the expectancy or belief that if you receive at least a B grade in a class, members of your family will approve of what you are doing. Thus we may define an outcome expectancy as *a person's subjective assessment of the probability that a particular outcome will result from that person's actions*.

2. Every outcome has a value, worth, or attractiveness for a specific person. This is called a *valence*. For example, you may value a title or the opportunity for advancement, whereas someone else may value a retirement program or nice working conditions. The valence or value of some aspect of the job usually results from internal needs, but the actual motivation is a more complex process. Thus we may define a valence as *the value a person places on an expected outcome*.

3. Every outcome has associated with it a perception of how hard it will be to achieve the outcome. This is called an *effort expectancy*. For example, you may have the perception that if you study the textbook very hard, you will be able to score an 85 on the next test, but that you will have to devote an exhausting amount of effort to this course in order to score a 90. Thus we may define an effort expectancy as *the probability that a person's effort will lead to accomplishing a particular goal*.

Motivation is explained by combining these three principles. A person will be motivated when he or she believes that (1) a particular behavior will lead to a particular outcome, (2) the outcome has a positive value to him or her, and (3) the outcome can be achieved by the effort he or she is willing to exert. Thus a person will choose, when he or she sees alternatives, that level of performance that has the highest motivational force associated with it. When faced with one or more choices about how to behave, you will ask yourself a series of questions such as, "Can I perform at the expected level if I try?" "If I perform at the expected level, what will happen?" "Do I value those things that will happen?" You will then decide to do those things that seem to have the best chance of producing a positive, desired outcome. In other words, you will be motivated. You will be willing to devote the energy to accomplishing the tasks that you feel will lead to a positive outcome with the amount of effort you are willing to exert. A person's ability to perform a particular task plus the effort that a person is willing to exert to perform the task determines the level of performance. If you do not feel that you have the ability, it may not be worth the effort to try to accomplish the task. Motivation, in expectancy theory, is the decision to expend effort.

Nadler and Lawler's (1976) analysis of expectancy theory suggests some specific ways in which managers and organizations ought to handle their affairs in order to achieve the maximum motivation from employees:

1. *Determine what kinds of outcomes or rewards have value for employees.* It is easier to find out what people want than it is to change people to want what you have to offer. Thus the skillful manager emphasizes needs analysis rather than changing individual employees.

2. *Define precisely, in observable and measurable behaviors, what is desired from employees.* For example, tell them to "write three term papers" rather than "be a good student."

3. *Make certain that the outcomes are attainable by the employees.* If a person feels that the expected level of performance is higher than he or she can reasonably achieve, the motivation to perform will be low.

4. *Link desired outcomes to desired levels of performance.* For example, if an employee values external rewards, then you should emphasize promotion, financial gain, and recognition. Thus in expectancy theory, environmental factors such as salary may in fact be motivation. If the employee values internal rewards, then increased responsibility, challenge, and achievement should be stressed. We should not forget, however, that people's perceptions, not reality, determine their motivation. Motivation occurs only if an employee sees a relationship between rewards and expectations.

5. *Make sure that rewards are large enough to motivate significant behavior.* Trivial rewards, it is said, result in trivial effort.

6. *High performers should receive more of the desired rewards than do low performers.* Seek an equitable system of rewards, not an equal one. People and organizations usually get what they reward, not what they would like.

In Chapter 11 we looked at specific managerial and leadership styles that affect the decisions that employees make about devoting their energies to accomplishing tasks. Motivation may be the single most important goal of managing and leading in an organization.

SUMMARY

In this chapter we have briefly outlined the features of four theories of motivation. Maslow's hierarchy of needs theory postulates five internal needs which are arranged according to an order of prepotency. Thus physiological needs must be satisfied before safety-security needs motivate a person, and belonging and esteem needs must be satisfied before self-actualization needs become effective. Alderfer's existence-relatedness-growth theory appears to encompass a range of needs similar to those of Maslow, but it discounts the idea of hierarchy and argues that a satisfied need may continue to be a motivator. Herzberg's motivator-hygiene theory postulates two sets of needs, those concerning job satisfaction and those concerning job dissatisfaction. Satisfiers or motivators are primarily related to the job itself, whereas dissatisfiers or hygiene factors are related primarily to the environment. Vroom's expectancy theory of motivation suggests that a person will devote the energy to accomplishing a task if he or she believes that actions will lead to an outcome, that the outcome has a positive value for him or her, and that the effort he or she is willing to exert will achieve the outcome. All four of these theories contribute to our understanding of why people make the decision to expend energy to accomplish a task.

A SUBJECTIVIST'S NOTATION

Organizational members are best understood by observing their actions and how *they* make sense out of them. People make sense out of what they do before, during, and after their actions. Conscious decision making does not precede all human actions; people act and interact with others to make sense of what they have already done. The literature of symbolic interactionism conceptualizes *motives* as statements that people make about their conduct or the conduct of others (Hewitt, 1976). Viewed in this way, motives do not cause behaviors; they are socially acceptable verbalizations that help people justify their actions. Motives can be determined before, during, or after action.

How are motives selected? A member may select motives because they are acceptable in the organization. In addition, members choose motives on the basis of their understanding or conception of who they are. Foote (1951) suggests that this understanding is decided through interaction and mutual identification. Conceiving of motives as linguistic devices rather than inner drives or psychic forces allows one to see what justifications (accounts, motives) organization members *think* are operative. These justifications require discovery; they provide action linkages; they are contextual; they can be created; and it may be possible to manage them.

Managers should know their people well so that they might "manage meanings." A significant part of knowing them involves an awareness of the accounts given by individuals. Traditional theories of motivation conceptualize people as passive objects who contain forces (motives) that can be energized and directed. "Motivating" someone is just a matter of discovering what those forces are and then communicating in order to link the motives with expected behaviors. However, the level of predictability of behavior based on motive schemes has been disappointing at best. This in itself should indicate the potency of subjective processes. Staw (1977) suggests a move away from traditional concepts of motivation by emphasizing action rather than reaction. He concludes:

> The synthesis of motivation presented here is one in which the individual is an active constructor of his social reality. The individual is viewed not merely as an information processor confronting a number of possible behavioral paths—each with their attendant rewards and costs—but as an actor who can attempt to change the parameters or

"givens" of traditional motivation models. The individual can bargain, cajole, and ingratiate in order to change the contingencies between behavior and outcomes. . . . What we are facing, therefore, in describing a theory of individual motivation in organizations, is a highly complex system in which individuals have constructed a social and physical niche for themselves within the larger environment. This niche is built upon relationships developed over time with supervisors, subordinates, and peers in the organization and rests, in part, upon a role negotiation process. . . . This niche is also built upon the individual's idiosyncratic construction of his social reality. (p. 89)

Individuals cope with organizational demands and have the capacity to generate their own job satisfaction and motivation.

Determining how individuals have constructed their niche means looking at their unique behaviors and being sensitive to what they are saying. Motives might be provided for people in the sense that individuals can be given *rationalizations* that fulfill their predispositions. But the reasons (accounts, justifications, motives) are not the same for all individuals. Schrank (1978) makes this point when he contends that

Engineers, managers, or behavioral scientists, with their compulsive, competitive preoccupation with "making it," tend to see this as a paradigm for all workers. But many workers are not interested in "making it" in a career of power and responsibility, or even in increasing their autonomy and creativity. Some blue-collar workers prefer to make bowling the center of their lives. That may be a greater demonstration of autonomy and creativity than building a better high-speed box. (p. 144)

Rather than trying to generalize "psychic unseen forces," it will be more productive for both the researcher and the practitioner to discover *processes* of enactment and adaptation.

REFERENCES

Alderfer, C. P., *Existence, Relatedness, and Growth: Human Needs in Organizational Settings*. New York: The Free Press, 1972.

Foote, Nelson N., "Identification as the Basis for a Theory of Motivation," *American Sociological Review*, 16 (February 1951), 14–21.

Herzberg, Frederick, *Work and the Nature of Man*. New York: Collins Publishers, 1966.

Hewitt, John P., *Self and Society: A Symbolic Interactionist Social Psychology*. Boston: Allyn and Bacon, 1976.

Kovach, Kenneth A., "Why Motivational Theories Don't Work," *S.A.M. Advanced Management Journal* (Spring 1980), 54–59.

Maslow, Abraham H., "A Theory of Human Motivation," *Psychology Review*, 50 (1943), 370–396.

Maslow, Abraham H., *Motivation and Personality*. New York: Harper & Row, Pub., 1954.

Nadler, David A., and Edward E. Lawler III, "Motivation: A Diagnostic Approach," *Harvard Business Review* (February 1976), 26–38.

Schrank, Robert, *Ten Thousand Working Days*. Cambridge, Mass.: MIT Press, 1978.

Staw, Barry M., "Motivation in Organizations: Toward Synthesis and Redirection," in *New Directions In Organizational Behavior*, Barry M. Staw and Gerald R. Salancik, eds. Chicago: St. Clair Press, 1977.

Vroom, Victor H., *Work and Motivation*. New York: John Wiley, 1964.

Wahba, M. A., and L. G. Bridwell, "Maslow Reconsidered: A Review of the Research on the Need Hierarchy Theory," *Organizational Behavior and Human Performance*, 15 (1976), 212–240.

13

Relationships

One of the most distinctive features of organizational communication is the concept of relationship. Goldhaber (1979) defines an organization as a "network of interdependent relationships" (p. 14). When things are interdependent, this means that they both affect and are affected by each other. Organizations consist of people in positions who have a variety of interdependent connections between and among them. The relationships are affected by the people in the organization, and the people in the organization are affected by the relationship. Like the relations people have generally, organizational relations can be divided into two classes: (1) the person in relation to the physical environment and (2) the person in relation to other people; that is, person-to-thing and person-to-person relationships. This chapter focuses on the person-to-person aspects of organizational life.

DEFINITION OF RELATIONSHIP

A *relationship* is some type of emotional connection. Emotions arise when people care for one another. *Caring* means placing some value on people. Thus a relationship is a connection between individuals in which they value one another and care for each other (Pace & Boren, 1973). Only a cold, unfeeling person can look at another human being and be unconcerned about what happens. Relationships may exist between people and things—some people love their cars and have an emotional connection with them—or between people and people; individuals may work together and have only a relation, a connection, without the emotional dimension, without caring. D'Aprix, speaking of the importance of showing employees and coworkers that they have dignity and value to you, said: "You don't have to like them, but you do have to show them you care for them" (Goldhaber, 1979, p. 198).

We have identified three types of relationships that usually exist in organizations: interpersonal, positional, and serial. Let us study the characteristics of each of them for a moment.

INTERPERSONAL RELATIONSHIPS

The most intimate relationships we have with other people on a personal, friend-to-friend, peer-to-peer level are usually referred to as *interpersonal*. Our closest friends in an organization, on the job, in church, or at the club tend to care for us more than others. It is with them that we have our most satisfying interpersonal relationships. With them we *resonate, vibrate,* and *jibe,* indicating that we care for them. Hoopes (1969) has observed that "the alienated are those people who have been excluded or who have excluded themselves" (p. xii). In authentic interpersonal relationships no one is excluded, nor does anyone want to exclude others.

What are some characteristics of effective interpersonal relationships? My own analysis (Pace & Boren, 1973) of interpersonal relationships suggests that you will be successful if you do the following:

1. Maintain close personal contact without having feelings of hostility develop.
2. Define and assert your own identity in relation to others without having disagreements develop.
3. Pass information on to others without having confusion, misunderstanding, distortion, or other unintended changes occur.
4. Engage in open problem solving without provoking defensiveness or breaking off the process.
5. Help others to develop their own effective personal and interpersonal styles.
6. Participate in informal social interaction without engaging in tricks or ploys or devices that put a damper on pleasant communication.

Although you may think of other general goals to be achieved through effective interpersonal relationships, these will suffice to illustrate the direction of our thinking on this issue. Much of the content of later chapters will address the question that usually looms large at this point: How does one achieve those goals? I have suggested elsewhere (Pace, Boren, & Peterson, 1975) that interpersonal relationships tend to improve when both parties do the following:

1. Communicate feelings directly and in a warm, expressive manner.
2. Communicate what is happening in their private worlds through self-disclosure.
3. Communicate a warm, positive understanding of each other by giving relevant, understanding responses.
4. Communicate a genuineness toward each other by expressing acceptance both verbally and nonverbally.

5. Communicate an ongoing and unconditional positive regard for each other through nonevaluative, friendly responses.
6. Communicate why it may be difficult or even impossible to agree with each other in nonevaluative, accurate, honest, constructive confrontation.

Clearly interpersonal relationships exert a powerful and pervasive influence over organizational affairs. Where the conditions for good interpersonal relationships exist, we also tend to find positive responses to supervisors, responsiveness to personal and organizational needs, sensitivity to employee feelings, and a willingness to share information, all prerequisites for effective upward and downward communication. Sometimes increased productivity is also found. *Quality circles* represent a way of utilizing improved interpersonal relationships to facilitate increased productivity, but their success is contingent upon an organizational climate that may be very difficult to produce generally (see Zemke, 1980). To better understand the important but fragile nature of interpersonal relationships in organizations, we shall look at the second type of relationship: positional.

POSITIONAL RELATIONSHIPS

Positional relationships are defined by the authority structure and functional duties of members of the organization. The rationale for creating an organization based on positional relationships was presented in an earlier chapter on classical theories of organization. However, nearly all theories of organization place the concept of positional relationships at their center. Koontz and O'Donnell (1968) highlight these relationships in a chapter called "Making Organizing Effective." They cite a dozen common mistakes that thwart the effective and efficient performance of individuals in the organization. We shall refer to a few of the mistakes they develop at some length. For example, the first mistake is the failure to plan properly. Part of failing to plan properly is "organizing around people" (p. 407) rather than positions. Organizing around people leads to several problems that positional relationships avoid. In the first place, they suggest, you can never be sure that "all the necessary tasks will be undertaken" (p. 407). In the second place, a danger arises that "different people will desire to do the same things, resulting in conflict or multiple command" (p. 407). In the third place, through retirement, resignation, promotion, or death, "people have a way of coming and going in an enterprise . . . which makes organizing around them risky" (p. 407) and makes their duties hard to recognize and to fill easily. Koontz and O'Donnell cite "failure to clarify relationships" as the second mistake in organizing. They explain that failure to clarify organization relationships accounts for jealousy, friction, insecurity, inefficiencies, and buck-passing more than any other mistake in organizing. Jackson (1959) in discussing the communication problems of organizations, makes a similar observation: "I can think of nothing which would facilitate more the free and accurate flow of communication in an organization than consensus about questions of work, authority, prestige, and status relationships" (p. 20). Those elements are, of course, intimately tied in with positional relationships. For effective and efficient organizational functioning, positional relationships are probably the most critical to specify and clarify.

Superior-Subordinate Relationships

The most common positional relationship, and probably the most crucial to efficient and effective organizational functioning, is that of superior to subordinate. Positions in an organization are arranged in hierarchical order, creating a series of superior-subordinate relationships throughout the organization. In fact, except for the very top and the very bottom of the organization, all positions, and the people in them, have a subordinate relationship to some positions and a superior relationship to other positions. Thus regularities and patterns in superior-subordinate communication have implications for almost the entire organization. Where superior-subordinate relationships can be strengthened, the human resources of the entire organization can be strengthened.

The concept of superior-subordinate relationships rests firmly on differences in authority, which are translated into differences in status, privilege, and control. The superior is perceived, at least, as having higher status, more privileges, and certain areas of control over a subordinate. The subordinate has a lower status, fewer privileges, and is dependent on the superior. Although the subordinate is dependent on the superior and frequently defers to the superior, the superior is also dependent on the subordinate. The supervisor must depend on the subordinate to go along with the directives and suggestions, to complete the work, to accept instructions, to inform the superior of problems, and to relay information to others. The way in which a subordinate responds to a superior, according to research and observation (Sanford, Hunt, & Bracey, 1976), is contingent upon such factors as how much the subordinate trusts the superior, much as we suggested in our discussion of interpersonal relationships, and how badly the subordinate wants to move up in the organization—or upward mobility aspirations. Jackson (1959) suggested, for example, that employees are "always communicating as if they were trying to improve their position" and that they communicate with people "who will help them achieve their aims." That suggests, of course, that the quality of communication between a superior and a subordinate may very well be a function of the interpersonal relationship established between them and how the relationship satisfies the subordinate's needs.

Jablin's (1979) synthesis of superior-subordinate communication identified nine categories of issues: (1) interaction patterns, (2) openness, (3) upward distortion, (4) upward influence, (5) semantic-information distance, (6) effective versus ineffective superiors, (7) personal characteristics of dyads, (8) feedback, and (9) effects of systemic organizational variables on the quality of superior-subordinate communication. Figure 13.1 summarizes a few of the major findings on each of the nine issues of superior-subordinate communication.

The research on subordinate-to-superior communication indicates that subordinates tend to tell superiors what they think the superior wants to hear, or what the subordinate wants the superior to hear, and to send superiors information that reflects favorably on the subordinate or, at least, does not reflect badly on the subordinate (Krivonos, 1976; Maier, Hoffman, & Read, 1963; Mellinger, 1956; Pelz, 1952; Read, 1962). These consequences appear to be related to the nature of positional relationships in organizations and especially to the inherent hierarchical, superior-subordinate relationship that comes from the structure of organizations. On the other hand, the hierarchy may be essential and inevitable in handling large

Interaction Patterns

1. Between one-third and two-thirds of a supervisor's time is spent communicating with subordinates.
2. The dominant mode of interaction is face-to-face discussion.
3. The majority of interactions are about task issues.
4. Superiors are more likely than subordinates to initiate interaction.
5. Superiors are less positive toward and less satisfied with interactions with subordinates than with their superiors.
6. A subordinate's job satisfaction is positively correlated with estimates of communication contact with superiors.
7. Superiors think they communicate more with subordinates than subordinates think they do.
8. Subordinates feel they send more messages to their supervisors than the supervisors think they do.
9. Superiors who lack self-confidence are less willing to hold face-to-face discussions with subordinates.
10. Role conflict and role ambiguity on the part of superiors are correlated with direct interactions with subordinates.
11. Subordinates seek informal help in their work setting more from their superiors than from peers or subordinates.
12. Superiors are more likely to serve as liaisons about production rather than maintenance or innovation issues.

Openness in Communication

13. Subordinates are more satisfied with their jobs when openness of communication exists between superiors and subordinates.
14. Openness of communication appears to be related to organizational performance.
15. The willingness of superiors and subordinates to talk as well as the actual talk on a topic is a function of the perception of the other's willingness to listen.
16. Superiors and subordinates prefer supervisor responses that are accepting and reciprocating rather than neutral-negative (unfeeling, cold, or nonaccepting).
17. Subordinates dislike disconfirming responses from a superior and prefer those that provide positive relational feedback.

Upward Distortion of Communication

18. In superior-subordinate relationships when one person does not trust the other, the non-trusting person will conceal his or her feelings and engage in evasive, compliant, or aggressive communicative behavior and under- or over-estimate agreement on issues.
19. Subordinates will tend to omit critical comments in their interaction with superiors who have power over them.
20. Mobility aspirations and low trust tend to have a negative influence on the accuracy of communication between subordinates and superiors; however, even if the subordinate trusts his or her superior, high mobility aspirations reduce the likelihood of communicating potentially threatening information.
21. Subordinates seem to feel less free to communicate with superiors who have held the subordinate's position.

(continued)

FIGURE 13.1   A Summary of Some Findings on Superior-Subordinate Communication (Source: Extracted from the main points from Frederic M. Jablin, "Superior-Subordinate Communication: The State of the Art," *Psychological Bulletin*, 86 (1979), 1201–1222. Copyright 1979 American Psychological Association. Reprinted by permission of the publisher and author.)

22. Subordinates tend to see greater appropriateness, expect fewer harmful consequences, and have a greater willingness to disclose important, yet personally threatening, information to superiors in organic as compared with mechanistic organizational climates.
23. Subordinate tendencies to distort upward communication can be reduced by increasing the superior's consideration or by increasing the accuracy with which the superior transmits downward information.
24. Intrinsically motivated subordinates tend to distort messages less than do extrinsically motivated subordinates.

Upward Influence of a Subordinate's Superior, or the Pelz Effect

25. Supervisors who exercise influence upward with their own superiors are more likely to have subordinates with high levels of satisfaction, although extremely high influence may separate subordinates from superiors.
26. Subordinates who see their superior as having high upward influence also have a high desire for interaction with, high trust in, and a high estimation of accuracy of information received from the superior.
27. Subordinate confidence and trust in a superior are positively related to the superior's success in interactions with higher levels of management.

Semantic-Information Distance

28. The larger the semantic distance between superior and subordinate, the lower the subordinate's morale.
29. Superiors tend to overestimate the amount of knowledge subordinates possess on given topics.
30. Significant semantic distances exist between union and management personnel and between union leadership and their members.
31. Serious semantic distances are frequent between superiors and subordinates.

Effective versus Ineffective Superiors

32. More effective superiors tend to enjoy talking and speaking up in meetings, are able to explain instructions and policies, and enjoy conversing with subordinates.
33. More effective superiors tend to be empathic listeners, responding understandingly to silly questions; they are approachable and listen to suggestions and complaints.
34. More effective superiors tend to ask or persuade rather than tell or demand.
35. More effective superiors tend to be sensitive to the feelings and ego needs of subordinates.
36. More effective superiors tend to be more open in passing information along by giving advance notice of changes and explaining the reasons for policies and regulations.
37. Supervisory effectiveness tends to be contingent on such factors as task structure, superior-subordinate relations, and superior-position power.

Superior-Subordinate Personal Characteristics

38. Subordinates who have tendencies toward an internal locus of control see their superiors as more considerate than do external-control subordinates and are more satisfied with participative superiors.
39. Superiors who have tendencies toward internal locus of control tend to use persuasion to obtain subordinate cooperation, whereas externals tend to use coercive power more.
40. Superiors tend to rate subordinates as competent when they have values similar to those of the superior.
41. Superiors who are apprehensive communicators are not particularly well liked by subordinates.
42. Authoritarian subordinates seem most satisfied when they work for directive superiors.

FIGURE 13.1 *continued*

43. Subordinate satisfaction with his or her immediate superior is related to the subordinate's perception of the superior's credibility.

Feedback from Superiors and Subordinates

44. Subordinate feedback responsiveness is greater when subordinates are told what needs to be done with completed assignments, when the superior makes the assignment to the subordinate, and when the subordinate feels that he or she can secure clarification about assignments from the immediate superior.
45. Positive feedback to a superior tends to make the superior more task-oriented.
46. The performance of superiors tends to improve after feedback from a subordinate.
47. Feedback from a superior that shows a lack of trust results in subordinate dissatisfaction and aggressive feelings.

The Effects of Systemic Organizational Variables on Superior-Subordinate Communication

48. The technology of an organization tends to affect superior-subordinate communication.
49. Upper-level superiors tend to involve their subordinates more in decision making than do lower-level superiors.
50. Organizations with flat structures tend to reward superiors who favor sharing information and objectives with more rapid advancement than do organizations with tall structures.

FIGURE 13.1 *continued*

numbers of people, in controlling interaction, and, in fact, in getting the work done. In spite of this seeming anomaly, the hierarchy and superiors and subordinates tend to create workable relationships and occasionally to engage in effective communication. One explanation for these positive experiences may lie in an understanding of communication rules and how they affect superior-subordinate relationships.

COMMUNICATION RULES

The behavior of people in organizations, you will recall from our discussion of the characteristics of organizations, is governed by general but definite rules. Rules do lots of things in organizations: protect and restrict; facilitate effort and block it; encourage excellence and provide sanctuary for the inept; maintain stability and retard change; permit diversity and create conformity. Rules constitute both the organizational memory and the means for changing the organization (Perrow, 1972). We need to answer the questions: What are rules? How do they influence relationships? How does one function effectively by using the rules? Since we are concerned directly with rules that affect relationships, and especially positional relationships, we shall concentrate on what are popularly known as *communication rules* (see Farace, Monge, & Russell, 1977).

Definition of Rules

A *rule* is a principle designed to govern conduct, action, procedure, or arrangements of some sort. In the same sense a rule is the statement of some expectation or norm or a description of some appropriate form of behavior. Often we regard the customary or normal practice of something to be the rule—that is, because something is done regularly, we assume that there is some principle governing the way in which it is done. Thus we say that a person's behavior is rule governed when it occurs regularly and seems consistent with some principle that can be stated.

Some organizational rules are stated explicitly, such as when a person is to come to work and go home. Such rules are generally regarded as official and are usually written down in policy manuals or handbooks. We call them *formal* rules. Other organizational rules are not stated formally. We learn about them by living in the organization, by watching and violating the rules. We call them *informal* rules. The formal rules may be consistent or they may be inconsistent with the informal rules. Part of every employee's time is devoted to learning the rules and in deciding which rules take priority. In any case the rules tell us what to do and how to do it.

Communication rules indicate to us what we should communicate and how it should be communicated. Rules that indicate expectations of what should be communicated are called content rules; rules that indicate how the content should be communicated are called procedural rules (Cushman & Whiting, 1972). In the analysis of superior-subordinate relationships in organizations, the rules must be applied to clearly identifiable positional relationships—that is, the rules are assumed to govern the communicative behavior of a pair of organizational members who have a specific positional relationship. The content rules govern what the superior-subordinate pair will talk about, and the procedural rules govern how the interaction will take place.

For a particular superior-subordinate pair, content rules might indicate that they can talk freely about problems of getting the work done, that they can talk about some topics, such as employee benefits, company products, and their functions in relation to other departments, but that they may not discuss such topics as salary raises, promotion opportunities, company earnings, and union relations. On the other hand, content rules may indicate that some topics may be discussed at appropriate times, such as union relations right after collective bargaining sessions have ended or company earnings right before a stockholders' meeting. Content rules also apply to whether the personal problems of the employee are discussed with the supervisor and to what degree of openness, and whether mistakes, criticism, bad news, or other sensitive topics can be introduced into conversations.

Procedural rules indicate such actions as who starts a conversation—can the subordinate initiate interaction or must the subordinate wait for the supervisor to contact him or her—how delays are treated, how long a conversation will last, how frequently they will meet, who will terminate the meeting, how the conversation will be stopped, how interruptions will be handled, where the conversation will take place, who establishes the mood of the meeting, and who will decide what topics will be discussed. Procedural rules tend to govern how the parties in a conversation will be addressed. Slobin, Miller, and Porter (1968) studied the forms of address used in an organization. Their results showed that subjects always reported using first names (FN) in addressing subordinates (S), subordinates' subordinates (SS), and fellow workers (FW). There was a decrease in the use of first names when referring to the boss (B), but there was a large decrease in using first names when referring to the boss's boss (BB). In the case of upper management they all reported using first names within the firm. Persons of higher status reported being referred to by title and last name (TLN), whereas they used first-name references when communicating downward. The general manager and strangers from other departments were called by title and last name by persons of relatively lower status, such as those in the steno pool. The rule appeared to be *use title and last name in addressing persons of higher status or less intimacy, and use first name when addressing those of lower or equal status.* If you want to test the strength of this rule in an organization of which you are a member, just violate the rule. Address people differently from what the rule dictates. You'll see.

Satisfaction with Rules

A relationship represents a connection with some form of emotional dimension. When you seek to understand a relationship, knowing the rules and expectations that govern a person's behavior is often helpful. Most of the time, however, you need to know how satisfied the individuals in the relationship are with the rules. In a superior-subordinate relationship it is helpful to know that the superior operates by the rule that lets the superior interrupt the subordinate. An answer to the question of whether the subordinate, or the superior for that matter, is satisfied with that arrangement may tell us a great deal about the quality of the relationship. For almost any rule you can learn much by knowing how satisfied the parties are with it.

Co-orientation on Rules

Often the most important information about rules comes from determining the *co-orientation* on the rules of those involved in the relationship. Co-orientation involves whether the superior and the subordinate see things the same way. That is, on a rule about who interrupts whom, do the subordinate and the superior see the superior as the one who does the interrupting? If so, we say they have *agreement* on that rule. That is one part of co-orientation. Both parties react in the same way to how the rule is violated. Another part of co-orientation involves empathy, or how well one person can predict how the other person feels. If the subordinate is able to predict what the superior says about a particular rule, we say that the subordinate has an *accurate* perception of the rule in operation. In a relationship we are looking for both parties to have accurate perceptions of how each other responds to communication rules. If there is a high level of agreement and a high level of accuracy, we say there is *consensus* on those rules, or a high level of co-orientation. In instances where each party disagrees with the other but understands why they disagree, we say that there is *dissensus.* This represents the attitude of agreeing to disagree. Occasionally a superior and subordinate do not really agree on a rule, but they are equally unable to predict that they do not agree. This leaves them in a situation of disagreeing and not knowing it. This is called *false consensus,* because what they thought was agreement turned out not to be the case. Sometimes the superior and subordinate agree on a rule but have low accuracy—that is, the superior and subordinate agree, but they do not know that they agree. This is called *ignorance.* They agree but don't know it. One can diagram these four possible combinations of agreement and accuracy in a two-by-two table like Figure 13.2 (Scheff, 1967).

Looking at superior-subordinate, positional relationships in terms of co-orientation on communication rules can lead to what Wilmot (1975) calls a dyadic unit— when two people are aware that the other person understands them—"Each person sees the other seeing them" (p. 8). In other words, the superior and the subordinate

Accuracy

		Low	High
	High	Ignorance	Consensus
Agreement			
	Low	False consensus	Dissensus

FIGURE 13.2   Four Possible Combinations of Agreement and Accuracy (Source: From T. Scheff, "Toward a Sociological Model of Consensus," *American Sociological Review* (1967), 32–46.)

say of one another, "I see that you see me behaving consistent with the rules," or "I see that you see me violating a rule." Under those conditions the superior is aware that the subordinate is aware of him or her, and the subordinate is aware that the superior is aware of him or her. When both persons can say that, a dyad is created. When this occurs between a superior and a subordinate, we have a positional relationship.

Communication Competence

Knowledge and understanding of communication rules is often necessary for survival in many modern organizations; however, competence in using rules is a necessity for advancement in the organizational world. Several different levels of competence in dealing with rules have been described by Harris and Cronen (1970):

1. *Minimally competent.* This person has a knowledge of the rules necessary for day-to-day interaction in doing a job. The minimally competent person, however, does not know what to do to impress superiors in order to move up in the organization.

2. *Satisfactorily competent.* This person seeks out the rules of the organization and internalizes them as his or her own; however, this person is unable to initiate actions beyond those consistent with the organization's current operations. This makes the person an ideal employee, equipped for accomplishing short-term goals but inadequate for organizational leadership. This type of competence has been called *satisficing.* A satisficer meets a set of requirements rather than exceeds the standard by seeking to understand the complexity of a decision. Satisficers are not skilled at seeking and using information necessary for obtaining long-term benefits for the organization or for the individual.

3. *Optimally competent.* This person has the ability to know the rules of the organization, to see alternatives to the rules, and to recognize the likely consequences of each. The optimally competent person is able to detect contradictions and ambiguities in rules and is sensitive to multiple meanings stemming from differences in content and procedural rules.

Organization members, of course, vary in their communication competence. One may know what is wrong with a rule but may not be able to make any changes. Another may know the rules for participating in a staff meeting but may not know the rules for getting a contract signed.

SERIAL RELATIONSHIPS

People have interpersonal and positional relationships in organizations, as we have seen. In addition they have serial relationships. Information is transmitted throughout formal organizations by a process in which the person at the top of the hierarchy sends a message to a second person who, in turn, reproduces the message for a third person. The reproduction of the first person's message becomes the message of the second person, and the reproduction of the reproduction becomes the message of the third person (Haney, 1962). Situations in which information is disseminated by means of this person-to-person-to-person format are referred to as *serial*. Three individuals are involved: the person who originates the message, the person who relays the message, and the person who terminates the sequence (Pace, 1976). The key figure in this system is the *relayor* (Pace & Hegstrom, 1977).

Relayor Functions

Smith (1973) points out that some communicators are senders, some are receivers, and some are in between. The people in the middle are messengers; they are relayors. The relay person, he says, is a "very common figure in communication processes" (p. 313). John Alden, for example, was a relayor for Miles Standish who wanted to ask Priscilla Mullens to marry him. A librarian, a concert pianist, an actor, a reporter, a professor, a manager, and a supervisor are all relay persons at one time or another. The relayor receives a message and carries it part of the way toward some terminal point in much the same way as a "relay of fresh horses carries the riders along the route, and a relay man carries the baton onward in a track meet" (p. 314). In organizations, messages are carried forward by means of these serial relationships in which a relay passes the word from a superior to a subordinate downward or from a subordinate to a superior upward. The relayors carry the message along and thereby hold the organization together.

Smith (1973) identified four basic functions served by relay persons: to link, to store, to stretch, and to control. We shall summarize and briefly characterize each of these functions in order to better understand the serial or relayor relationship in organizations.

Linking

A supervisor tries to link an operative with a manager; the union steward connects union members with management; a line on an organization chart links one organization member to another. Although they may look simple, the links are more complicated than they appear.

Linking processes have at least three troublesome characteristics: they connect and disconnect; they make adjustments for the parties being linked; and they vary along several dimensions, including the distance, physically and psychologically, from the people they link.

Supervisors are links between management and workers. They can connect those parts of the organizational system, or they can disconnect them. They can send information forward, or they can hold it. Relayors, as communicators in the middle, can bring the ends together or they can untie the connections. A human relay functions much like a transmission system in a car. The relay connects two independent moving parts. Like a transmission, the relayor adjusts the inertias of one part to that of the other. Such adjustments avoid lurching, burning rubber, and breaking the system apart. A mediator, for example, adjusts labor and management to one another, using gears and clutches to speed up or slow down, to ease into a situation, or to shift into high gear on the open road. Finally, relayors vary in terms of the physical and psychological distance they maintain between those they link. Most professors, for instance, are closer to their books than to their students; some supervisors are closer to the workers than to management. This linking function, Smith argues, creates an ethic in which relayors value adjustment and assimilation of points of view above all else. Since the relayor must work with powerful forces on both sides of him or her, the task is one of bringing the forces together, of linking them so as to use the power of both. However, the linker cannot be assimilated by either of the sides and still be a person in the middle. The relayor must remain in the middle and not conform wholly to either side.

Storing

Storing is the second function of the relayor. When a section head receives a message from a manager to send on to an operator, he or she must store the message. If the section head forgets the message on the way, he or she would be unable to deliver it and would not be a relayor. Storing accomplishes a number of purposes beyond that of just holding the message. For about the same reason that a farmer stores hay in a barn, the relayor stores messages—to adapt to the needs of sender and receiver, to buffer against fluctuations in what the receiver wants to hear and what the sender wants said. Storing spans the tie space between the producer of a message and the consumer of a message. Storing implies a conservative ethic, because the relayor who stores preserves the system. As a storer, the relayor values the status quo.

Stretching

The process of adapting the parts of a system to one another involves making some changes. Stretching is a form of change involving the enlargement or amplification of the message. In this sense Paul Revere's ride stretched the light from his lamp from the belfry of a Boston church to Lexington. Reporters stretch the words of a speaker in New York all the way to Los Angeles. This is a matter of distance. Relayors also stretch, up to a point, the meanings associated with a message. They amplify the meaning of a message. At a political convention in 1980, reporters stretched and amplified the meaning of a statement about whether former President Ford would be the vice presidential candidate. In fact the meaning may have been stretched and amplified to such a point that it was mutilated. The relayor has to stretch, or amplify, meanings without mutilating, or distorting, them. Former President Ford was not the person selected to run as the vice presidential candidate; television reporters stretched and overinterpreted to the extent that they may have created a new message of their own. Some relayors underinterpret and lose some of the message. The ethic of the relayor is between the under- and the overinterpretation of a message. The relayor analyzes meaning, makes meanings apparent that seem obscure, internalizes meaning, which results in some changes; however, the analysis, the revelations, and the internalizing are all part of preparing the message for relaying.

Controlling

Linking, storing, and stretching are the foundations of the relayor's fourth function—controlling. The first thing that a relayor controls is the means by which links are made. A teacher, as a relayor, has control over the means by which the lesson will be presented in order to link the student with the source of the lesson. The reporter controls how the message will be presented. The travel agent controls information about airline routes. The manager controls how official information will be transmitted to workers. The relayor controls channels and media as well as information itself.

Relayors are the in-between people; they are in between senders and receivers. They link the units of a system together by adjusting them to one another. In adjusting and adapting to the units, the relayors change messages. Change is often necessary to produce harmony between units in the system, yet change is opposed to the ethic of preserving and conserving the system. Nevertheless, by regulating the transmission, the storage, and the interpretation of messages, the relayor has control over the communication system. In the end the relayor may no longer be the intermediary; the relayor may become master of the system. In the end, you remember, it was John Alden who married Priscilla.

Likert (1961) recognized the central role of the relayor in organizations when he described the linking-pin structure of organizations. In his model, almost every organization member is a relayor, serving as the link between the upper unit and the lower unit.

SUMMARY

Three types of relationships tend to occur in organizations: interpersonal, positional, and serial. Interpersonal relationships are based on caring, concern, kindness, and responsiveness. Positional relationships are based on authority, work, prestige, and status. The most common form of positional relationships is that of superior and subordinate. Communication rules describe expected and acceptable behaviors in organizations. Serial relationships are based on the need for people to serve as relayors of information in organizations.

A SUBJECTIVIST'S NOTATION

Organizational communication relationships are acted out within a cultural framework that guides the behavior of the participants. An important part of this framework is the power structure. A great deal of the literature on interpersonal communication tends to ignore this factor. Organizational communication relationships are also power relationships. The different degrees of power held by people in different positions are usually overt and rather obvious. However, the nature of power has prompted theorists to distinguish between *surface* and *deep* structures of power (Clegg, 1979; Conrad, 1983). Conrad (1987) explains that

> deep structures are pre-conscious guidelines and constraints whose appropriateness as ways of interpreting and responding to organizational situations is taken-for-granted by members of an organization. . . . In a sense, deep structures tell employees who they are—what their role in their organization is and where they "fit" in the formal and informal hierarchies that make up the organization. . . . Employees choose to act in certain ways, not because of overt threats or promises, but because doing so is consistent with their taken-for-granted assumptions about their identities and organizational roles and about what actions constitute natural, appropriate adaptations to the actions of others. (p. 14)

Deep structures of power tacitly guide and restrict the actions of organizational members. Conrad (1983) maintains that "deep structures of power are the limits that define and solidify a society or an organization. They *are* the power-related reality of an organization. . . . In normal times deep structures of power are the power relationships in organizations" (p. 187).

An interpretive approach suggests that examining organizational relationships means getting beyond a surface view. The deep structure must be brought to light so that organizations can see how they "organize." It is important to look at not only what is said, but also at what is *not* said. For example, Conrad (1983) points out that there are several *faces* of power. Power can be exerted in overt and covert ways. He contends that "Members of organizations may reinforce those norms, values, rules, or practices that ensure that only relatively innocuous issues are ever raised in public" (p. 177). Organization members may also operate under certain parameters that constrain decision making. Organizational relationships involve more than individual feelings and choice.

Consider the following dialogue. We have asked our students to look at the "talk" and describe what is happening.

At the Hospital

Jill: Hello, Dr. Johnson. How is Mrs. Andersen doing?

Johnson: She is looking better. I'm going to remove her stitches today.

Jill: *(Enthusiastically)* Great! Do you have everything you need?

Johnson: I need a Kelly clamp. Where are they?

Jill: We only have one on the entire floor and we keep it hidden. You'll have to sign in blood for it.

Johnson: *(Laughing)* Where do I sign? *(He turns away from Jill to get a patient's chart.)*

Jill: *(Reaches into a drawer and removes a clamp.)* We'll let it go without a signature this time. *(Gives clamp to the doctor who is now facing her.)*

Johnson: Thanks. I'll bring it right back.

(Mrs. South, the nursing supervisor, has come down the hall and overhears the rest of the conversation.)

Jill: When you're through, put it right back in this drawer. *(She taps on the desk drawer.)*
Johnson: The top one?
Jill: Yes. The top one.

(Dr. Johnson goes into the patient's room, and is out of hearing range.)

South: *(With a slight chuckle)* You're treating him like a little boy who has to put his own toys away.
Jill: *(Looks confused)* What?

(Mrs. South laughs and walks on.)

Student reactions vary widely. Some remark that the participants are passing the time of day and the hospital seems like a pleasant place to work. Others suggest that the talk reveals that Jill and Johnson are flirting with each other much as the characters do in hospital soaps on TV. Some criticize Mrs. South and point out that she's a busybody. Some look below the surface and ask why Jill is using this particular approach with the doctor. Of course, we have our favorite answers. There is a power structure in the classroom! We contend that a great deal is going on in this short conversation. Rather than provide those answers, we will suggest some questions that will point you toward the cultural structure that we feel is influencing this exchange. What are the characteristics of the interaction between Jill and Johnson? What is there about the organizational culture that might generate the language used? How aware is Jill of her interpersonal style? Are there factors in this type of organization that promote the strategies used? There are several plausible answers to these questions. The important point is that organizational culture has much to do with how communication relationships are executed and interpreted.

REFERENCES

Clegg, S., *The Theory of Power and Organization*. London: Routledge and Kegan Paul, 1979.

Conrad, Charles, "Organizational Power: Faces and Symbolic Forms," in *Communication and Organizations: An Interpretive Approach*, Linda L. Putnam and Michael E. Pacanowsky, eds. Beverly Hills, Calif.: Sage, 1983.

Conrad, Charles, "Power, Praxis and Self in Organizational Communication," Paper in preparation for *Advances in Organizational Communication Theory and Research*. Beverly Hills, Calif.: Sage, 1987.

Cushman, Donald, and Gordon C. Whiting, "An Approach to Communication Theory: Toward Consensus on Rules," *The Journal of Communication*, 22 (September 1972), 217–238.

Farace, Richard V., Peter R. Monge, and Hamish M. Russell, *Communicating and Organizing*. Reading, Mass.: Addison-Wesley, 1977.

Goldhaber, Gerald M., *Organizational Communication*, 2nd ed. Dubuque, Iowa: Wm. C. Brown, 1979.

Haney, William V., "Serial Communication of Information in Organizations," in *Concepts and Issues in Administrative Behavior*, S. Malick and E. H. Van Ness, eds. Englewood Cliffs, N.J.: Prentice-Hall, 1962.

Harris, Linda, and Vernon E. Cronen, "A Rules-Based Model for the Analysis and Evaluation of Organizational Communication," *Communication Quarterly* (Winter 1979), 12–28.

Hoopes, Ned E., ed., *Who Am I?: Essays on the Alienated*. New York: Dell Pub. Co., Inc., 1969.

Jablin, Frederic M., "Superior-Subordinate Communication: the State of the Art," *Psychological Bulletin*, 86 (1979), 1201–1222.

Jackson, Jay M., "The Organization and Its Communication Problem," *Advanced Management* (February 1959), 17–20.

Koontz, Harold, and Cyril O'Donnell, *Principles of Management*, 4th ed. New York: McGraw-Hill, 1968.

Krivonos, Paul, "Distortion of Subordinate to Superior Communication," unpublished paper presented at a meeting of the International Communication Association, Portland, Oregon, 1976.

Likert, Rensis, *New Patterns of Management*. New York: McGraw-Hill, 1961.

Maier, Norman, L. Hoffman, and W. Read, "Superior-Subordinate Communication: The Relative Effectiveness of Managers Who Held Their Subordinates' Positions," *Personnel Psychology*, 16 (1963), 1–11.

Mellinger, Glen D., "Interpersonal Trust as a Factor in Communication," *Journal of Abnormal and Social Psychology*, 52 (1956), 304–309.

Pace, R. Wayne, "A Model of Serial Communication," unpublished paper presented at the fall meeting of the New Mexico Communication Association, Las Cruces, New Mexico, November 1976.

Pace, R. Wayne, and Robert R. Boren, *The Human Transaction*. Glenview, Ill.: Scott, Foresman, 1973.

Pace, R. Wayne, Robert R. Boren, and Brent D. Peterson, *Communication Behavior and Experiments: A Scientific Approach*. Belmont, Calif.: Wadsworth, 1975.

Pace, R. Wayne, and Timothy G. Hegstrom, "Seriality in Human Communication Systems," unpublished paper presented at the annual conference of the International Communication Association, Berlin, 1977, 1–54.

Pelz, Donald C., "Influence: A Key to Effective Leadership in the First-Line Supervisor," *Personnel*, 29 (1952), 209–217.

Perrow, Charles, *Complex Organizations: A Critical Essay*. Glenview, Ill.: Scott, Foresman, 1972.

Read, William, "Upward Communication in Industrial Hierarchies," *Human Relations*, 15 (1962), 3–15.

Sanford, Audrey C., Gary T. Hunt, and Hyler J. Bracey, *Communication Behavior in Organizations*. Columbus, Ohio: Chas. E. Merrill, 1976.

Scheff, T., "Toward a Sociological Model of Consensus," *American Sociological Review* (1967), 32–46.

Slobin, D. I., S. H. Miller, and L. W. Porter, "Forms of Address and Social Relations in a Business Organization," *Journal of Personality and Social Psychology*, 8 (1968), 289–293.

Smith, Alfred G., "The Ethic of the Relay Men," *Communication: Ethical and Moral Issues*, Lee Thayer, ed. London: Gordon and Breach Science Publishers, 1973.

Wilmot, William W., *Dyadic Communication: A Transactional Perspective*. Reading, Mass.: Addison-Wesley, 1975.

Zemke, Ron, "Honeywell Imports Quality Circles as Long-Term Management Strategy," *Training* (August 1980), 91–95.

14

Group Processes and Conflict

Network analysis has shown us that organizations consist of individuals who communicate more or less exclusively with one another; we call these _cliques_ (Middlemist & Hitt, 1981, p. 186; Rogers & Rogers, 1976, p. 113). In the popular literature of our time, cliques are often referred to as _groups_. Cliques may meet the requirements of face-to-face groups, but some cliques are simply a number of individuals who communicate with one another. In both cases—cliques or groups—forces are at work that affect how members participate in the organization and contribute to their own well-being and the welfare of the organization. We call those forces _group processes._ This chapter is about group processes in organizations.

THE CONCEPT OF CLIQUE AS GROUP

The term _clique_ refers to different collections of people, but all cliques have the following common elements:

1. A number of individuals (more than two, which we call a _dyad_ rather than a clique);
2. who interact with one another (as opposed to interacting with those who are not members of the clique); and
3. who perceive themselves as sharing some common interests, likes or dislikes, attitudes, or goals as members of a group.

This definition does not preclude individuals who interact with one another over the telephone or by computer printout from being members of a clique. Nevertheless, it does distinguish between a collection of people watching a baseball game who do not interact with one another from being called a clique, even though they appear to share some common interests. Just because someone is employed by an organization does not make him or her a member of a clique or a group. In fact, some employees feel that they are isolates in a large organization because they have little regular interaction with a manageable number of other employees and do not perceive themselves to share many likes or dislikes with a small number of their colleagues. When a person begins to identify with the likes or dislikes of a few other individuals, that person feels as if he or she is a member of a clique. That is the beginning of group membership.

GROUP FORMATION AND DEVELOPMENT

If you are to affect groups and work to help them achieve social and organizational goals, it is desirable to understand the reasons that led to their creation. You may be able to influence the groups to become a positive value to the organization, thereby avoiding potential problems. Some of the work of professionals in human resource development is directed toward building productive groups and teams of employees.

Group Formation

People appear to have a natural proclivity for joining with others as a means of satisfying some of their interpersonal needs.

FORMING GROUPS THROUGH NEED SATISFACTION

The idea of interpersonal needs is based on the assumption that people want to have associations with other people. All of us must satisfy to some degree certain interpersonal needs. Schutz (1958) described three needs that constitute his theory of interpersonal relations called *FIRO* (fundamental interpersonal relations orientation): (1) the need for inclusion; (2) the need for control; and (3) the need for affection.

INTERPERSONAL NEEDS

Inclusion is the need to interact with other people. Some people like a lot of contact, whereas others prefer to work alone and maintain their privacy. Each person, to some degree, is trying to interact with others while attempting to maintain a certain amount of solitude. We seek to have other people initiate contact with us, but we also want to be left alone.

Control is the need to have power and influence. We all vary in terms of the degree to which we want to be controlled by others versus the degree to which we wish to control them. You may know someone who wants to be controlled completely by a friend or spouse. On the other hand, you may know, or be, a person who has strong feelings about being independent and in control of your own decisions.

Affection is the need to have warm, close, personal relationships with others. At the other extreme is the situation in which a person prefers impersonal and distant rather than close relationships with other people. Each of us has our preferences. One person may want others to show warmth and affection toward him or her but find it difficult to express affection toward them.

The description of each interpersonal need has suggested that there are two parts to each one: *the expressed behaviors,* or the behaviors a person initiates toward other people, and *the wanted behaviors,* or the behaviors a person prefers that others express toward him or her. Your fundamental interpersonal relations orientation (FIRO) is your usual approach to interpersonal relations in terms of the three needs (inclusion, control, and affection) and the degree to which you want and express behaviors relevant to each need. Schutz (1958) developed a questionnaire called FIRO-B (for "behavior") that allows individuals to be located in a matrix on the basis of scores in each need area. Table 14.1 shows the matrix.

FORMING GROUPS THROUGH ASSIGNMENT

There is little doubt that groups are created through voluntary association in response to the impelling motivation of interpersonal needs. In fact, most of us will join a number of groups over the years as a subtle way of satisfying those interpersonal needs. Nevertheless, we ought to recognize that in organizations, group membership is often brought about by the assignment of individuals to positions, committees, or teams. A considerably larger amount of interaction occurs as a consequence of assignment to some task in an organization rather than as a result of fulfilling some interpersonal need to belong. Assignment to a team helps to satisfy our need to be part of a group, but the team is formed through assignment. However, the very assignment to a team or formal group or promotion to a supervisory or managerial position allows for the development of group ties that strengthen and satisfy our interpersonal needs.   ·

Assignment to a work group in the organization provides for opportunities to participate in group problem solving, information sharing, and informal interaction. People who are in close proximity to one another tend to interact more, and interaction tends to help develop feelings of attraction. Assignment to a committee or work team gives you a chance to experience emotional reactions that aid in unifying a group. People are usually attracted to others who share common emotional experiences. The accomplishment of a particular task often leads to positive emotional experiences and strengthens group cohesiveness.

TABLE 14.1   Matrix of Scores on the FIRO-B Inventory

	Inclusion I	Control C	Affection A
Express (E)			
Want (W)			

Source: From William Schutz, *FIRO: A Three-Dimensional Theory of Interpersonal Behavior,* New York: Holt, Rinehart and Winston, 1958.

Group Development

An important theoretical and practical discovery about group processes is that every group, regardless of its purpose or composition, proceeds through four phases of development if given adequate time. For a group to progress from one phase to another, it must arrive at a general understanding or consensus of both interpersonal relationships and task aspects of group processes. If consensus has not been reached at one stage prior to proceeding to another, a regression often occurs later. What is particularly important to remember is that groups need to go through each of the stages. If they do not, the group is frequently stymied right when it should be accomplishing its objectives.

Several systems for describing stages have been created over the years (Bales & Strodtbeck, 1951; Bennis & Shepard, 1956; Fisher, 1970), but we shall use Tuckman's (1965) general system. It reflects the major stages identified in the research and represents a systematic way of thinking about stages in group development. The four stages and the interpersonal relation and task function issues associated with each stage in the model are summarized in Table 14.2.

Stage 1: Forming. At Stage 1 the task function is to make sure that individual group members are oriented to the work to be done—why they are there, what they are supposed to do, and how they are going to do it. Group members may be instructed on these points, or they may evolve the goals and orientation through interaction. On the interpersonal relations side, members must resolve a number of dependence-independence issues, such as the extent to which the designated leader will provide direction, the ground rules on which the group will operate, and the agenda that will be followed. At this stage group members are getting oriented to one another and the task to be accomplished.

Stage 2: Storming. Different feelings about authority, rules, the agenda, and leadership surface in the form of interpersonal conflict. Resolving those differences is critical to movement to the next stage. Unresolved conflict tends to deter the group from becoming a smoothly functioning team. In task functions the group is seeking to answer questions about who is going to be responsible for what tasks, what the work rules are going to be, and what the rewards will be. The creation of assignments and rules to govern work and interaction imposes organization and structure on the group.

Stage 3: Norming. As the differences are resolved and the group acquires structure, individuals begin to experience a sense of cohesion and a feeling of catharsis at having resolved interpersonal conflicts and survived the main interper-

TABLE 14.2 Stages in Group Development

Stage	Interpersonal Relations Issues	Task Function Issues
1. Forming	Dependence/independence	Orientation
2. Storming	Interpersonal conflict	Organization/structure
3. Norming	Cohesion	Information sharing
4. Performing	Interdependence	Problem solving

sonal issue. They begin to share ideas and feelings, give feedback to one another, solicit feedback, explore actions related to completing the task, and share information, the primary task function. Group members begin to feel good about what is going on. There is an emerging openness with regard to the task, and some playfulness even occurs. Groups that get stuck at this stage experience high levels of pleasantness about interacting with other members and evolve into what has been called a happy circle or a group with high morale and intense levels of interaction. Unfortunately the feelings of cohesiveness often stall the group and keep it from moving to the performing stage.

Stage 4: Performing.   At this stage members are both highly task- and highly person-oriented. They work singly, in subgroups, and as a total unit. Group members both cooperate and compete; there is support for experimenting with alternative ways of making decisions and solving problems. In interpersonal relations group members feel highly interdependent, but neither dependent nor independent. The task function is one of problem solving. Harmony for its own sake is replaced by individual freedom and a strong emphasis on productivity.

In real-life working groups, of course, the interpersonal relations issues and the task issues are dealt with jointly and simultaneously. Although we separated them at times for convenience, organizational groups cope with interpersonal problems and task problems as if they were pretty much the same. The ability to recognize some differences, however, may allow you to catch thorny issues that may be stalling the group, to separate interpersonal relations issues from the task issues, and to effectively aid the group in being productive.

All too often the major emphasis of the group is on trying to solve a specific problem without considering how group processes might be improved to solve problems more efficiently in the long run. Some attention should be paid to how the group itself functions, to what behaviors help the group accomplish its work. Groups, especially work groups, seldom examine how they operate. Except for the expletives uttered when something goes wrong later on, the group members focus almost exclusively on difficulties with the task. It may be that the group has interpersonal problems that interfere with the way in which it works. If a little time were devoted to trying to discover why the team functioned so badly, it might be making a solid investment with great dividends in the future.

GROUP DYNAMICS

A group usually serves three functions for its members: (1) it satisfies interpersonal needs, (2) it provides support for individual self-concepts, and (3) it protects individuals from their own mistakes (Hampton, Summer, & Webber, 1973). Besides helping individual members in those three areas, the group takes on an identity, or self-concept, of its own. The group acquires some goals of its own. Occasionally individual goals conflict with group goals; sometimes group goals differ from those of the organization, but sometimes they are all very similar. The way in which the group progresses through the four stages from getting organized to being productive is related to how the group copes with three important aspects of group life: (1) the roles or activities performed by group members, (2) the norms and differences in status that develop as members interact, and (3) the conflict that evolves from pressures to behave competitively rather than cooperatively (Huse & Bowditch, 1973). The interaction among individual needs, group goals, and the roles, norms, and conflict of group functioning is what we shall call the *dynamics* of a group. Let us now look at the three aspects of group life and how they contribute or detract from the way in which groups accomplish their goals.

Individual Group Roles

The types of behaviors, activities, and roles that take place in a group may be analyzed in terms of three goals: (1) what it takes to get the job done, (2) what it takes to keep the group together, and (3) what it takes to satisfy irrelevant personal needs (Benne & Sheats, 1948). The first type is usually called *task roles,* and the second type is referred to as *maintenance roles,* which are both considered to be contributors to the effectiveness of a group. The third type is called *self-serving roles,* which more often than not actually hinder effective group functioning. Self-serving roles represent ineffective behavior in groups and become the observable manifestations of interpersonal conflict.

Task Roles. Behaviors such as offering ideas, suggesting methods and plans, asking for information and opinions, prodding people along, and handling procedural activities, such as distributing papers and recording ideas, all contribute to the smooth functioning of a group. These types of behaviors help to get the job done.

Maintenance Roles. Behaviors such as providing praise, expressing warmth and support, mediating differences, listening to others, accepting group decisions, introducing some humor to relax the group, and bringing in group members who might not otherwise speak also contribute to the smooth functioning of a group. These types of behaviors keep the group together.

Self-Serving Roles. Behaviors such as attacking the status of others, opposing group ideas stubbornly and for personal reasons, asserting superiority to control and interrupt others, using flattery to patronize group members, clowning and engaging in horseplay and ridicule, and staying off the subject under discussion to avoid making a commitment represent ways to thwart the progress of the group. These types of behaviors prevent the group from getting the job done and discourage them from staying together.

Table 14.3 lists and defines some typical functional and nonfunctional roles which you might review in order to recognize desirable behaviors that are not being enacted in a group and undesirable behaviors that occur too frequently and deter the group from accomplishing its goals.

Group Norms and Status

As a group progresses through the stages in group development, it begins to acquire a life of its own, a history and culture, that is revealed through the expression of similar feelings, beliefs, and values among group members. A com-

TABLE 14.3 Typical Functional and Nonfunctional Individual Roles in Groups

Functional or Effective Behavior in Groups		Nonfunctional or Ineffective Behavior in Groups
Task Roles	Maintenance Roles	Self-Serving Roles
1. *Initiating:* suggests goals, methods, and procedures; starts the group moving.	1. *Energizing:* prods group to action, stimulates more activity.	1. *Blocking:* constantly raises unreasonable objections, insists that nothing can be done.
2. *Information seeking:* asks for data, factual statements, reports, and experiences.	2. *Supporting:* praises others, expresses solidarity and togetherness.	2. *Attacking:* expresses disapproval and ill will, deflates status of others, uses barbed jokes.
3. *Information giving:* gives estimates, personal experiences, reports, ideas, and facts.	3. *Gatekeeping:* brings in nonparticipators, prevents dominance by one or two, helps everyone interact.	3. *Dominating:* interrupts and orders people around, gives directions in a superior tone, controls through flattery and other patronizing behaviors.
4. *Opinion seeking:* asks for beliefs, values and expressions of feelings.	4. *Harmonizing:* conciliates feelings of others, mediates disagreements between others.	4. *Recognition seeking:* boasts, calls attention to own accomplishments, seeks sympathy or pity, claims credit for ideas of others.
5. *Opinion giving:* offers own beliefs, attitudes, values, and feelings.	5. *Tension relieving:* diverts attention of others from tense situations, relaxes others, introduces relevant humor.	5. *Clowning:* engages in horseplay and ridicule, disrupts with cynical remarks, diverts attention of group to tangents.
6. *Clarifying:* interprets issues, elaborates on ideas, gives examples and illustrations.	6. *Following:* listens to others, goes along with group decisions.	6. *Playboying:* shows lack of involvement, abandons group while being there physically.
7. *Summarizing:* pulls together related ideas, restates suggestions, demonstrates relationships among ideas.	7. *Compromising:* offers alternative ideas that improve member status, admits errors, and modifies position to aid progress.	7. *Confessing:* engages in personal catharsis, uses group as audience for talking about mistakes.
8. *Procedure facilitating:* passes out papers, arranges seating, runs projector, records ideas on paper, chart, or chalkboard.	8. *Consensus testing:* checks to see if the group is close to a decision or tries a trial idea.	8. *Special-interest pleading:* supports personal projects and interests and presses others for support, advocates interests not related to task.

monality of feelings and beliefs is often referred to as a *norm,* or standard of appropriate and acceptable behavior. The tendency to associate with people who share your feelings, beliefs, and values; to listen to and accept their ideas; and to defend their points of view also strengthens group solidarity and exerts pressure on group members not to deviate from group decisions.

If you happen to belong to a group whose values are different from yours or those of other groups of which you are a member—such as family, church, or consciousness-raising association—you will probably find yourself in a position in which you must decide whether (1) to accept the new values, (2) to try to bring about a change in the values of the group, or (3) to leave the group. Employment may bring you into an organization in which the values of the business are different from yours. You will have to decide how to cope with the norms of acceptable behavior in that organization.

Although norms in a group are strong influences toward conformity or similarity in behavior, they also reveal differences among members. Once you have established yourself in a group and demonstrate that you are able to behave according to group norms, a conflicting need often emerges: the need for status or prestige. Even within small work groups some subtle differences in status are usually apparent. The norms that indicate how we should behave in your presence define your status: the ''respect or disrespect, familiarity or unfamiliarity, reserve or frankness'' we are to show in your presence indicates how you are different from the rest of the group (Hampton, Summer, & Webber, 1973). If you fail to treat people with the appropriate degree of respect or disrespect, you may be subject to punishment for violating group norms.

The factors that accord individuals status in any particular group vary from group to group. A person's family background, name, or relatives may provide status in some organizations. In some jobs education, seniority, age, sex, or ethnic background may contribute to higher status. Such personal characteristics as physical size, dress and general appearance, sociability, friendliness, self-confidence, and status in another group (such as an athletic club) may all influence perceptions of status. On the job a person's title, job description, compensation, privileges, freedom from direct supervision, office location, furnishings, and potential for upward mobility may be considered when others assign status. Regardless of what elements determine status in your group, you can be pretty certain that the best positions will be occupied by high-status individuals.

Competition and Conflict within the Group

Individual group roles and group norms and status affect the way in which group members communicate with one another. In addition most group members have occasion to cooperate and to compete with each other. A situation in which rewards are limited so that when one group member gets the rewards other group members lose them is usually called one of *competition.* If group members believe, on the other hand, that no one will be rewarded unless they all contribute to the task, the situation will usually be called one of *cooperation.*

In a work group some external authority determines how the rewards are to be distributed among group members. The boss creates or works within a system in which pay, recognition, promotions, and other rewards are given according to conditions established by the organization. Thus whether the group members are to function in a competitive or a cooperative atmosphere is decided by the organization. For example, the organization could have a policy that the lowest producer on the team each month is to be fired, regardless of how well the team does. The consequence would most likely be a fairly competitive climate. A single member of a team might create a competitive atmosphere even if the organization was attempting to have groups work cooperatively. By monopolizing the time, using more space than others, consuming a large number of supplies, or traveling more than other group members, one individual can be viewed as taking something that is scarce but of value to all group members. If the resource is considered limited, the one member can make competition an inevitable consequence of being a group member just by getting more than his or her share.

Most groups, of course, have some cooperative activities and some competitive ones. In order to accomplish a task, they may be required to cooperate. Nevertheless, the group members may still compete for personal rewards such as admiration, approval, affection, and power. Few rewards, whether personal or material, are distributed equally. Differences in roles and status lead to perceptions that rewards will be distributed competitively.

EFFECTS OF COMPETITION

When group members view their roles as highly competitive, they tend to listen less to what other members say, to understand less well what was actually said, become less interested in high achievement, help one another less, have more difficulty coordinating their group's efforts, are more likely to duplicate the efforts of others in order to do the work themselves, tend to be less efficient, and tend to do lower-quality work. In addition they may not like what they have accomplished, the group with whom they worked, or each other as individuals as much.

EFFECTS OF COOPERATION

When group members view their roles as highly cooperative, they tend to show more coordination of their efforts. There is greater diversity of contributions per group member, with more subdivision of activities. Group members tend to be more attentive, have higher mutual comprehension of information, and make more common appraisals of information. Cooperative groups tend to exhibit a clearer orientation and orderliness with more pressures toward achievement. The interaction seems more friendly, and the group and its products are evaluated more favorably.

Not all jobs demand the same degree of competition and cooperation. Some kinds of work require creative performances that may receive strong stimulation from competition; other work requires the careful and complete cooperation of every team member in order to be successful. The ideal balance between competition and cooperation is a continuing issue and relates directly to the type of work that is being done. Regardless, competition and cooperation have different effects on team work. Competition is more likely to lead to conflicts within the group.

CONFLICT

It is possible to analyze conflict from a number of different communicative levels, such as the intrapersonal, interpersonal, intergroup, or interorganizational. We have chosen to look at conflict in a group setting since conflicts at both the intrapersonal and the interpersonal levels may be demonstrated in the group. Later in this chapter we shall briefly analyze intergroup processes and intergroup conflict.

Conflict has been defined as an "expressed struggle between at least two interdependent parties, who perceive incompatible goals, scarce rewards, and interference from the other party in achieving their goals" (Frost & Wilmot, 1978, p. 9). In this view the "struggle" represents differences between the parties that are expressed, recognized, and experienced. For conflict to occur, the difference must be communicated. Conflicts may be expressed in different ways; from very subtle nonverbal movements to all-out physical brawling, from subtle sarcasm to all-out verbal attack.

The concept of struggle is related to efforts designed to achieve goals, to secure resources, and to get rewards that are also being sought after by the other party. The implication is that people want to do different things and they also want to have the same things. These are the concepts of incompatible goals and scarce rewards. Early signs of conflict may be identified by an increase in the rate of disagreements among group members. Previously neutral comments take on an unfriendly tone. As the tension continues, more explicit signs of disagreement surface. The conflict is expressed through sighs, uneasy twitches in facial muscles, faltering silences, lapses in attention, slouching, doodling, turning away, and curt verbal utterances.

If members of a group have common goals, the likelihood of conflict developing is lowered. Goals involve a wide variety of desires that people would like to achieve, some of which are real and tangible and others of which are imagined and intangible. The goal of a company to reduce costs may in fact be quite incompatible with the goal of an employee to increase his or her income. However, some superordinate goal may encompass both of the incompatible goals to allow conflict to be managed to the advantage of both the company and the employee.

Rewards are of different kinds. Most of us are familiar with salaries, bonuses, promotions, corner offices, and vacations, but more personal reactions such as respect, time together, warmth, pride, listening and love are also rewards. Frost and Wilmot (1978) argue that in interpersonal conflict, "regardless of the content issue involved, the parties usually perceive a shortage of power and/or self-esteem reward" (p. 12). Thus conflicts may often be averted by showing that those rewards are less scarce than supposed.

Personal Conflict Styles

There seems to be general agreement that people have preferred ways of handling conflict, or at least habitual ways of dealing with conflict (Filley, 1975; Frost & Wilmot, 1978). A habitual way of behaving is one that is somewhat fixed and resistant to change because it is comfortable and natural. When two people come together expecting to claim their share of scarce resources, they somewhat habitually think about themselves and the other person. Thus conflict styles appear to be some combination of the amount of concern you have about accomplishing your own goals and the amount of concern you have about the other person accomplishing his or her goals. These concerns can be portrayed by two axes running from low concern to high concern. The resulting cells with mixtures of concern for accomplishing personal goals and concern for allowing or even helping the other person accomplish his or her goals represent styles that people have for dealing with conflict. Figure 14.1 identifies <u>five personal conflict styles which we shall briefly characterize.</u> The terms used to label the styles are derived from the writings of Hall (1969), Blake and Mouton (1970), and Kilmann and Thomas (1975).

1. *Competitor or tough battler.* The person who employs this style pursues his or her own concerns somewhat ruthlessly and generally at the expense of other members of the group. The tough battler views losing as an indication of weakness, reduced status, and a crumbling self-image. Winning is the only worthwhile goal and results in accomplishment and exhilaration.

2. *Collaborator or problem solver.* The person who employs this style seeks to create a situation in which the goals of all parties involved can be accomplished. The problem solver works at finding mutually acceptable solutions. Winning and losing are not part of his or her way of looking at conflict.

3. *Compromiser or maneuvering conciliator.* The person who employs this style assumes that everyone involved in a disagreement stands to lose, and he or she works to help find a workable position. A pattern of "giving in" often develops.

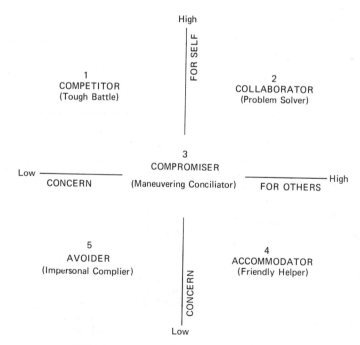

FIGURE 14.1 Personal Conflict Styles

4. *Accommodator or friendly helper.* The person who employs this style is somewhat nonassertive and quite cooperative, neglecting his or her own concerns in favor of those of others. The friendly helper feels that harmony should prevail and that anger and confrontation are bad. When a decision is reached, the accommodator may go along and wish later that he or she had expressed some reservations.

5. *Avoider or impersonal complier.* The person who employs this style tends to view conflict as unproductive and somewhat punishing. Thus the avoider gets away from an uncomfortable situation by refusing to be concerned. The result is usually an impersonal reaction to the decision and little commitment to future actions.

Unfortunately when conflict occurs we have tendencies to do and say things that perpetuate the conflict rather than reduce or eliminate it. Although frequently very difficult to do, there are usually a few actions that can be taken to start the deescalation of conflict. Disagreements seldom resolve themselves. In small groups conflict is usually handled best through the process of *integration*—the combination of each person's ideas into a group idea (Barnlund & Haiman, 1960).

Integration

The goal of integrative decision making is to achieve consensus. The philosophical basis underlying consensus is that differences in thinking, feeling, and behaving are best resolved by incorporating the points of view of all parties into the decisions or plans. Cooperative effort is achieved by finding, isolating, and clarifying areas of agreement and disagreement, thus systematically narrowing the area of difference and enlarging the area of acceptability (Pace, Peterson, & Burnett, 1979). Two areas of difference need to be managed: differences in understanding and differences in feelings.

Differences in understanding may be determined in three ways: (1) By discovering what the other person or party means. Many times a simple statement of what a person means prevents disagreements from escalating. (2) By checking the validity of evidence and reasoning. Disagreements and conflicts often develop because it is possible for two people to reason from the same data and arrive at totally different conclusions. You might want to locate the source of evidence in order to determine how accurate it is. (3) By identifying a more basic value or goal, sometimes called a *superordinate goal.* When a disagreement is based on differences in preferences or values, understanding may be increased by identifying a more basic value that is acceptable to all parties.

Differences based on feelings may be determined in five ways: (1) By increasing the self-esteem of those with whom you have the disagreement. A basic source of emotional resistance is loss of face. No one wants to appear foolish, illogical, or misdirected. Reduce disagreements based on feelings by providing ego support and ways of strengthening self-esteem. (2) By creating an atmosphere of inquiry. Get group members to probe into the issue by asking open-ended questions. Resistance often occurs because all alternatives have not been explored. (3) By involving each member of the group in the discussion. Emotional barriers and negative feelings flare up when we feel uninvited or discouraged from making contributions. Avoid squelching anyone, regardless of what they have said. (4) By using summaries to show the group where it has been and where it is going. Summaries can help objectify comments and reduce excessive generalizing and overstatement. Group members are allowed to respond to a more objective summary rather than the original emotional comments. (5) By providing for the release of feelings. Participants should have the opportunity to make highly emotional statements without argument or refutation. Many disagreements can be resolved simply by letting the other person dissipate the underlying feelings (Pace, Peterson, & Burnett, 1979).

The use of integrative decision making to reduce disagreements capitalizes on a merger of information, logic, and feelings to achieve the best collective judgment of the entire group. Conflict is used creatively and constructively.

CONFLICT AND INTERGROUP PROCESSES

So far in this chapter we have examined the processes involved in the formation, development, and maintenance of groups. In this final section we shall extend the discussion to issues surrounding communication between groups and the processes and factors that produce conflict between groups in the organization. Most large organizations consist of many small groups that can be distinguished on the basis of who belongs to them, the goals they have to achieve, the space they occupy, and their leadership. These groups ought to cooperate to achieve the goals of the parent organization, but they often end up fighting or at least competing vigorously among themselves for resources, power, status, and other rewards, in the same way that individuals compete against one another. Groups, like individuals, tend to protect, maintain, and enhance their own positions within the organization. They resist others whom they perceive as threats to what they value and possess. The result is often intergroup conflict (Coffey, Athos, & Raynolds, 1975).

One of the most important aspects of organizational life concerns relations among groups within the organization (Schein, 1969). The symptoms of bad relations are often somewhat easy to recognize. A breakdown in the flow of work or lack of coordination between groups usually stands out. Poor communication or a failure to exchange information adequately may be a symptom that accompanies lack of coordination. Delays and mistakes often lead to tensions and negative feeling. If groups must rely on one another to get their work done, the symptoms are often more dramatic. Conflict between groups is expressed in much the same way that interpersonal conflict is. "Criticisms, bickering, snide remarks, and intentional ignoring of others are clear indicators of difficult relations, just as the opposites indicate satisfying ones" (Coffey et al., 1975).

Intergroup Conflict

When one or more groups feel frustrated because they are being kept from accomplishing their goals, intergroup conflict occurs. Some groups look for the source of frustration inside their group—their own skills, methods, equipment, and procedures. Other groups look for the source of their frustrations outside their group. When they think they have found the source of their frustrations in some other group, a downward spiral of conflict develops. Seven stages seem to characterize the cycle:

1. Beginnings of doubt and distrust appear, and the climate between the groups deteriorates.
2. Perceptions of the outside group become distorted or stereotyped and polarized, with verbal comments dividing the "good" groups from the "bad" ones.
3. Cohesiveness and related feelings such as friendliness, attractiveness, closeness, and importance within each group increase.
4. Adherence to group norms and conformity also increase in each group.
5. Groups ready themselves for more authoritarian leadership and direction.
6. Hostile behaviors, reduced communicative contacts, and other signs of negative intergroup relations become apparent.
7. Complete separation is mutually desired, and any form of positive collaborative effort ceases (Coffey et al., 1975).

What happens to the competing groups when a decision is made and one is the winner and the other is the loser? Schein (1969) indicates that the winning group retains its cohesiveness and may even increase in that area. It also experiences a letdown and becomes complacent and casual. Along with the loss of its fighting spirit, the winning group experiences higher intragroup cooperation and concern for its members with an accompanying decrease in concern for task accomplishment. The winning group tends to feel that its positive image and the negative stereotype of the other group have been confirmed.

The losing group looks for an explanation for its loss in some external source such as the decision makers or dumb luck. When the group accepts its loss, it begins to splinter, internal fights break out, and unresolved internal conflicts surface. The losing group becomes more tense, gets ready to work harder, and appears desperate to find something to blame for the loss. The losing group places a high concern on recouping its losses by working harder, with less concern for member needs. The losing group tends to learn something about itself because its positive image was upset by the loss, forcing a reevaluation of the group's perceptions. Once the loss has been accepted realistically, the losing group tends to become more cohesive and more effective.

Reducing Intergroup Conflict

Huse and Bowditch (1973) suggest five ways for minimizing conflict within the existing organizational framework:

1. Make certain that information for solving problems is discovered and held in common by the groups involved. Representatives of different groups might meet regularly to study problem areas and to develop joint recommendations.
2. Rotate people among different groups. This suggestion implies the Buck Roger's era of organization theory with temporary work groups and project management. Some groups are too specialized to use this method of reducing conflict, but some work areas are well suited for rotating members.
3. Bring groups into close contact with one another. Bring the opposing groups together to clear the air and allow them to share perceptions.
4. Locate a common enemy. A competing company, the government, or some

other group may allow the groups in conflict to join forces and cooperate to repel the invader. This may bring the groups into closer contact and dissipate the conflict.

5. Identify or develop a common set of goals. This is the idea of locating a superordinate objective that both groups have in common.

SUMMARY

In this chapter we have discussed group processes in the organization. Both intra-group and intergroup activities and conflicts have been examined. A group, or clique, was defined as a number of individuals who interact with one another and who perceive themselves as sharing some common interests. This definition allows individuals who interact over the telephone or by computer printout to be members of a clique. Group formation was analyzed in terms of Schutz's three-needs theory of interpersonal relations: inclusion, control, and affection. Schutz's instrument, called FIRO-B, was mentioned as a way to locate individual need levels and determine their compatibility. A short discussion of the effects of forming groups through assignment rather than through satisfaction of interpersonal needs indicated that such a procedure simply accelerated the need to understand stages in group development. Four stages in the development of effectively functioning groups were discussed: forming, storming, norming, and performing. Four interpersonal relations issues and four task function issues were also analyzed.

The dynamics of group processes were discussed in terms of individual group roles or activities, group norms and status, and competition and conflict within groups. Eight task roles, eight maintenance roles, and eight self-serving roles were listed and defined. Cooperation and competition were characterized. Five personal conflict styles were discussed: the competitor, the collaborator, the accommodator, the compromiser, and the avoider. Ways of resolving conflict through the process of integration were also analyzed. Finally, intergroup processes and conflict were examined. A seven-stage cycle of frustration leading to intergroup conflict was explained. The effects on groups of winning and losing in competition and five ways of reducing intergroup conflict were discussed.

A SUBJECTIVIST'S NOTATION

Any number of factors can create groups that have subcultural possibilities within an organization. Specialization places the people who do the same kind of work together. Professionalization puts people together who share occupational identities. Automation groups people together who work with specific machines. Each group develops its own language, practices, and ideas about organizational goals. Subcultures are also created by acquisitions, mergers, and technological innovation. As interactional opportunities are altered, contrasting interpretive systems are constructed (Van Maanen & Barley, 1985).

The management of groups involves more than the consideration of individual personalities. Groups that have evolved into subcultures share organizational views that are constructed and reinforced by symbolic behavior. Van Maanen and Barley

(1985) point out that although members of subcultures may be aware of each other as persons, they may not recognize subcultural differences unless some unexpected event occurs. Although culture can be portrayed as a force for organizational solidarity, cultures are just as likely to provoke disintegration of organizational unity. Van Maanen and Barley contend, "whereas proponents of organizational culture sometimes argue that modern corporations suffer from a lack of culture, we submit that organizations often get more culture than they bargained for. . . . The study of cultural organization is therefore closely bound to the study of organizational conflict" (p. 48). Group processes, then, become a significant issue in the study and practice of organizational communication.

Groups that have continuity develop cultures and thereby share similar feelings, beliefs, and values. It is rather obvious that when groups compete for resources or a greater voice in organizational operations, differing perspectives produce conflict. It is less apparent that conflict itself is an organizational practice. Organizations differ on how they "do" conflict. Conflict may be carried out in active or passive ways. Denying conflict or pretending that it does not exist is a way of "doing" conflict. The purpose here is not to discuss the merits of various conflict behaviors. Different modes of conflict may be functional for different subcultures. After conflict behaviors have been negotiated and become routine in groups, they operate at a low level of the members' awareness. When groups confront each other, they must not only deal with the matter of conflicting goals and attitudes, but also with the conflict that results from the differing practices of conflict.

Both authors of this text have been involved in the mergers of university departments, and both can attest to what cultural clashes are all about. Mergers of academic departments produce the anxiety that comes from perceived loss of turf and the uncertainty of change. The conflict style of the groups comes into play. These conflict behaviors are easier to analyze in retrospect but are difficult to see objectively during the actual interactions. The following account of one experience during a merger illustrates the impact of different conflict styles on an organizational activity.

It was clear that the university administration wanted the merger of two departments. The college dean decided to bring the two departments together to start preliminary talks. The first step was the creation of a committee made up of representatives from each department. The committee was asked to discover areas where resources might be shared between the two departments. All of the committee members knew that the committee was the first step toward a merger and all were wary. All had investments in programs of study and research. The two groups sat on opposite sides of the table. One group engaged in behaviors that were interpreted as hostile by the other group. The other's behaviors were thought to be devious because they were not openly combative. It was as if two families had been thrown together. One family had been accustomed to shouting and taking extreme positions during negotiation while the other group had worked out a system of more moderate exchange. One group felt bullied while the other felt it was being "sweet talked" into a loss of identity. In one meeting I became so angry that I had to leave the room. I did return after cooling down. I had felt insulted by what I considered an inflammatory speech. The person who made the speech felt insulted because I wasn't willing to "face the issues." In retrospect all of this seems strange. The merger was accomplished some time ago and a culture has been created that has incorporated all behaviors. Those behaviors have had a moderating influence on one another. The greatest change has come about through the understanding and acceptance of the way conflict is done. Conflict is healthy for the organization; it keeps significant issues in full view.

REFERENCES

Bales, Robert F., and F. L. Strodtbeck, "Phases in Group Problem Solving," *Journal of Abnormal and Social Psychology,* 46 (1951), 485–495.

Barnlund, Dean C., and Franklyn S. Haiman, *The Dynamics of Discussion.* Boston: Houghton Mifflin, 1960.

Benne, Kenneth, and P. Sheats, "Functional Roles of Group Members," *Journal of Social Issues,* 4 (1948), 41–49.

Bennis, Warren G., and H. A. Shepard, "A Theory of Group Development," *Human Relations,* 9 (1956), 415–437.

Blake, Robert R., and Jane S. Mouton, "The Fifth Achievement," *Journal of Applied Behavior Science,* 6 (1970), 413–426.

Coffey, Robert E., Anthony G. Athos, and Peter A. Raynolds, *Behavior in Organizations: A Multidimensional View,* 2nd ed. Englewood Cliffs, N.J.: Prentice-Hall, 1975.

Filley, Alan C., *Interpersonal Conflict Resolution.* Glenview, Ill.: Scott, Foresman, 1975.

Fisher, B. Aubrey, "Decision Emergence: Phases in Group Decision-Making," *Speech Monographs,* 37 (1970), 53–66.

Frost, Joyce Hocker, and William W. Wilmot, *Interpersonal Conflict.* Dubuque, Iowa: Wm. C. Brown, 1978.

Hall, Jay, *Conflict Management Survey.* Austin, Tex.: Teleometrics, Inc., 1969.

Hampton, David R., Charles E. Summer, and Ross E. Webber, *Organizational Behavior and the Practice of Management* (revised). Glenview, Ill.: Scott, Foresman, 1973.

Huse, Edgar F., and James L. Bowditch, *Behavior in Organizations: A Systems Approach to Managing.* Reading, Mass.: Addison-Wesley, 1973.

Kilmann, Ralph, and Kenneth Thomas, "Interpersonal Conflict-Handling Behavior as Reflections of Jungian Personality Dimensions," *Psychological Reports,* 37 (1975), 971–980.

Middlemist, R. Dennis, and Michael A. Hitt, *Organizational Behavior: Applied Concepts.* Chicago: Science Research Associates, Inc., 1981.

Pace, R. Wayne, Brent D. Peterson, and M. Dallas Burnett, *Techniques for Effective Communication.* Reading, Mass.: Addison-Wesley, 1979.

Rogers, Everett M., and Rekha Agarwala-Rogers, *Communication in Organizations.* New York: The Free Press, 1976.

Schein, Edgar H., *Process Consultation: Its Role in Organization Development.* Reading, Mass.: Addison-Wesley, 1969.

Schutz, William, *FIRO: A Three Dimensional Theory of Interpersonal Behavior.* New York: Holt, Rinehart and Winston, 1958.

Tuckman, B. W., "Developmental Sequence in Small Groups," *Psychological Bulletin,* 63 (1965), 384–399.

Van Maanen, John, and Stephen R. Barley, "Cultural Organization: Fragments of a Theory," in *Organizational Culture,* Peter J. Frost et al., eds. Beverly Hills, Calif.: Sage, 1985.

15

Human Resource Analysis

Human resource analysis is used extensively in organizations to identify differences between what is happening and what ought to be happening. Like a medical diagnosis or an automotive diagnosis, human resource analysis provides a picture of what is happening. From the measurements and descriptions derived from the analysis, it is possible to recognize strengths and weaknesses and establish corrective actions.

DEFINITION OF ANALYSIS

Analysis is the process of studying the nature of something through determining its constituent elements and essential features and exploring the relationships between those elements. An organizational communication analyst discovers information about the communication of members of an organization as well as their other activities.

Analysis is grounded in the philosophy of problem solving. Before a decision is made, a problem should be clearly identified. A *problem* is defined as the difference between what *is* and what *ought* to be. The nature and location of the differences between what is happening and what we would like to have happen usually determine the strategies for making changes.

Analysis may be approached from two different perspectives: (1) from a *reactive* stance, after the act has occurred, or (2) from a *proactive* stance, or before the act has occurred. A reactive approach looks at how the organization is currently functioning and defines a problem as anything that deviates from the usual way of doing things. If things seem to be going smoothly, no problem exists; as soon as the organization shows signs of functioning differently from what has been the case, that is a clue that a problem may be developing.

A proactive approach defines a problem in the same way as a reactive approach—as the difference between what is happening and what ought to be happening—but recognizes a problem before some deviation in current functioning occurs. A proactive person may think that what is happening now may not be adequate, even though it meets minimal requirements. To discover "what ought to be happening" involves an effort to project into the future and picture something better than what we have now. Analysis, from a proactive perspective, is an effort to visualize better ways of doing things. A problem is the difference between the better way and the way it is being done now.

A reactive approach to analysis leads a person to wait until a deviation from the usual way of operating occurs before a problem can be defined. A proactive approach to analysis leads a person to create a picture of the future that is better than what is happening and define a problem as the difference between what the vision of the future could mean and what is happening now.

Figure 15.1 pictures the idea of a problem from the reactive and the proactive points of view. The baseline (what is happening now) is the point from which we view deviations in both cases. The proactive perspective projects a line into the future and suggests that we have a problem if we are not already accomplishing what is possible. The reactive perspective takes the baseline as satisfactory or even desirable and looks for deviations that dip below the baseline.

Creative analysis attempts to locate problems that involve projections of the future and determine how the resolution of those problems could lead employees and the company to do better. Nevertheless, reactive problem analysis often provides information of great value to the development of human resources and the organization. Both approaches to analysis may have benefits.

A human resource problem (proactive or reactive) involves a person who is

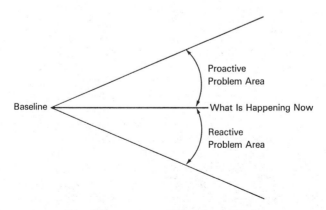

FIGURE 15.1 Diagram of a Problem

not performing as well as someone feels the person should be. That is, the person may lack information necessary to do the job well, or exhibit counter-productive attitudes, or lack the skills to do a job as well as it should be done. Through the process of analysis, difficulties can be recognized and classified so as to make them amenable to improvement. Human resource analysis can provide important information about knowledge, attitude, and skill deficiencies that affect both the organization and the human beings themselves.

THE PROCESS OF ANALYSIS

Before dealing with specific issues of analysis, we shall discuss a general model of the process of analysis that involves a five-stage process:

1. Point of concern
2. Point of Documentation
3. Point of Preference
4. Point of Comparison
5. Point of Classification

Stage 1: Point of Concern

Most organizational performance has some history. A drop in productivity is a move from one level of production to a lower one. The need to make an analysis is usually provoked by one of those changes that hurt. A *hurt* is some consequence that indicates that a person or the organization is beginning to suffer; it is one of those points of concern that impel us to take some type of analytical action.

Points of concern are usually of two types: (1) symptoms of a more basic problem, or (2) consequences of the basic problem. The difference between a *symptom* and a *consequence* lies primarily in the relationship between the problem and the manifestation of the problem. A symptom is a sign that the problem exists, but it is not the result of the problem. For example, absenteeism could be a symptom of some other condition, such as an undesirable organization climate. Lower sales figures are not usually considered to be the consequence of problems in the sales department, but they are symptoms of a problem. A consequence, on the other hand, is the result of some undesirable condition in the organization. A consequence results from the problem, whereas a symptom merely signals that the problem is present. For example, complaints and grumbling are usually symptoms of a problem such as poor working conditions or undesirable supervision; ineffective supervision, however, is more likely to be the consequence of inadequate selection and training programs.

In either case, symptoms and consequences both provoke a sense that something seems wrong; what has been done in the past is now producing symptoms and consequences that appear different and undesirable. If the organization is producing only positive results, it is unlikely that it will move to the next stage in the process of analysis. Some point of concern usually triggers interest in analysis. Most of the time, the point of concern is subtle; things just feel a bit different from how they felt in the past. The more someone in the organization hurts from the consequence or symptom, the more likely it is that someone will suggest moving to the next stage.

Stage 2: Point of Documentation

Once a concern has been recognized, the next stage is to provide some documentation for the hurt or concern. The example of a medical diagnosis reveals the process that most of us go through when moving from Stage 1 to Stage 2. Suppose you hurt your foot and it is quite painful. Most likely you will go home and lie down to see if the pain will go away. Isn't that the way most organizations function, also? Even with a hurt and some pain, we usually choose to see if it will just go away.

Now, suppose it doesn't go away. Your choices may be to just endure the pain or to go to a doctor to see if you can find out what the problem is. You decide to go to a doctor. You limp over to the office and sit for a while in the waiting room, holding your hurting foot. When your time comes, you hobble into the examining room.

The doctor comes in and asks you "What seems to be wrong?" You explain the problem. You remove your slipper and sock for the doctor to look at your foot. The doctor squeezes your foot and wiggles it a bit and you flinch with pain. The doctor says, "Hmm" and explains that it seems like you've hurt your foot. You think, "Of course, that's why I'm here."

Before we go further with this case, think some more. What do you want the doctor to do? One thing could be to make your foot better. But in most cases, the body has to make itself better. Another thing could be to determine for you what might be some of the causes of the pain in your foot. You choose the latter.

The doctor then volunteers that you could check into the hospital (at a daily cost of $165), have an X-ray ($50), and rest, but it seems likely that you just have a sprain, that the X-ray would not show much, and you can rest at home. Which plan do you choose? If you were the manager of a department, and the pain was a little absenteeism, the manager may choose to just go ahead and endure the pain. The doctor presented you with a plan for documenting the concern. In your case, let's assume that you select the hospital and X-ray route.

Although the doctor indicates that her analysis suggests a simple sprain, you want to have further documentation; thus, you opt for the X-ray and some wiggling of your foot in the hospital. You're paying for some documentation just as an organization would pay for some evidence to support the feeling of organizational hurt.

The real objective of the second stage in analysis is to discover *why* the individual or organization is hurting. The point of concern indicates that something is apparently wrong, and the task at the second stage is to provide information that reveals what the cause could be.

A *cause* is the source of the hurt or concern; it is the reason why you—or the organization—are hurting. In the case of your foot, the cause could be either a sprained ligament or a broken bone. The documentation procedures should provide information that reveals the cause. Likewise, an analysis of organizational processes should provide information that reveals the cause of undesirable consequences and symptoms in the organization.

A case for "cause analysis" is effectively presented by Plunkett and Hale (1982). They suggest that locating the cause of some consequence is a function of "isolating some unique differences" between or among two or more people, machines, work groups, or organizations. They cite the case of four machines in which one is malfunctioning. The malfunction is likely to be something unique to that one machine.

One of the key objectives of the documentation phase of analysis is to discover what is different or unique about the people or organization being analyzed in comparison to some other set of data, principles, or circumstances. The methods, instruments, and procedures of documentation involve measuring and recording characteristics of the people or the organization being analyzed in an effort to provide a basis for comparison.

In human resource analysis, we have found that it is possible to document differences from three points of view: (1) from the view of the task to be performed, (2) from the view of the person performing the task, and (3) from the view of the supervisor (or other third party) of the person performing the task. These types of documentation are referred to, respectively, as *task analysis, needs analysis,* and *performance analysis.* The methods, instruments, and procedures involved in task, needs, and performance analyses will be presented later in this chapter.

Stage 3: Point of Preference

The third stage in analysis, as suggested earlier, involves the development of a set of data, principles, or circumstances that could serve as guidelines or preferences against which to compare the documentations secured in Stage 2. The purpose of the guidelines is to help identify the differences between a situation in which there are no problems and the situation being analyzed.

The set of data, principles, or circumstances should help direct the analyst's thinking about what kind of performance, behavior, attitude, skill, or practice would be preferred in the situation being analyzed. These preferences are usually found in five different places: job and position descriptions; performance standards statements; organization policies; excellent practices and performances in other organizations; and organization, communication, and other theories.

Job and position descriptions indicate what employees are supposed to do in the organization. They define the authority, responsibility, and accountability of each person and position in the organization. They describe the requirements for occupying a position and for coordinating the activities of the position.

Performance standards statements indicate the level of proficiency at which employees should work. They reflect the expectations of the organization about how seriously each employee is to take his or her duties.

Organization policies are more general statements that reveal how employees should think about the decisions they make while carrying out the work of their positions. Policies state what ought to be done in order to have an efficiently functioning organization. Behaviors that are inconsistent with policies, performance standards, and job descriptions should be suspect, if not taken as clear symptoms that the organization has problems.

Excellent practices in other companies often serve as standards against which to compare practices of the organization being analyzed. If you compare your performance against someone who is doing something similar without problems, you may find some key differences that are the source or cause of your problems.

Theories more often than not describe ideal situations. If your personal and organizational practices differ significantly from what theories suggest, you may find that the differences provide some excellent clues about the source or cause of your problems.

Analysis requires a clear set of guidelines or preferred models to determine where potential causes of problems exist. The next stage in the process of analysis involves the actual comparison and the decision about whether and where a problem exists.

Stage 4: Point of Comparison

Patton and Giffin (1973) state that "in its simplest terms, the process of analysis consists of determining the difference between what you have and what you would like to have" (p. 141). The point of comparison is an attempt to determine whether the documented concerns represent activities in the organization that deviate from the preferences and guidelines. The point of comparison attempts to answer two key questions: (1) Are there differences between what is happening and what ought to be happening? and (2) Are the differences important enough to do something about? If the documentation and the guidelines and preferences are clear, the differences may be easy to recognize as definitely detrimental to the organization. In other instances, the differences may be more subtle and difficult to relate to objective data.

Many efforts in analysis are stymied at this point. Managers may recognize and accept the documentation of concerns and the preferences and guidelines, but they may disagree about the extent to which the differences actually represent important deviations from the guidelines. If key people fail to recognize or accept the fact that the differences cause problems for the organization, little support will be given to proposals to remove the deficiencies. Thus, the point of comparison may need to be developed very carefully, with the best data available and the clearest possible demonstration that the differences are the causes of the negative consequences in the organization.

Stage 5: Point of Classification

The fifth and final stage in the analytical process is to determine what kinds of problems exist in the organization. The basic types of problems tend to correlate with the types of documentation used. Three types of problems can exist:

1. Those having to do with deficiencies in employee knowledge, attitudes, and skills.
2. Those having to do with deficiencies in the ways in which supervisors and managers plan, organize, staff, direct, and control the physical and human resources in the organization.
3. Those having to do with deficiencies in the conceptualization and design of the mission, positions, duties, responsibilities, and authority of the organization.

Deficiencies in knowledge, attitude, and skill that interfere with the competent performance of an employee's job are called *training problems*. Deficiencies in knowledge, attitude, and skill that keep an employee from moving into higher-level jobs, positions, and careers are called *development problems*. These two deficiencies can be removed through human resource training and development strategies.

Deficiencies in the way in which supervisors and managers carry out their duties and responsibilities are called *performance problems*. Performance problems can be resolved through changes in management practices.

Deficiencies in the way in which an organization is conceived and designed are called *organization problems*. Deficiencies in organizational design can be alleviated through organization development procedures.

Stage 5 is devoted primarily to clearly classifying the types of deficiencies that exist in the organization. This stage is particularly critical because so many of the resources of an organization can be frittered away by attempting to remove deficiencies in knowledge, attitude, and skill by using organization development procedures; by attempting to remove deficiencies in supervisory and employee performance by using training and development procedures; or by attempting to remove deficiencies in organization design by using procedures to change management practices. The careful classification of problems confronting the organization can lead to more appropriate and powerful methods and strategies for solving problems.

APPROACHES TO DOCUMENTING HUMAN RESOURCE CONCERNS

We shall now turn our attention to the ways in which concerns can be documented. Several general approaches may be used to document a concern. Deficiencies in individual employee task performance may be documented through task analysis, performance analysis, and needs analysis.

Task Analysis

Task analysis is a method for determining the specific performance requirements of a job in order to identify what an employee must know and do to complete a job. "Task analysis is a method for specifying in precise detail and in measurable terms the human performance required to achieve specific management objectives, the tools and conditions needed to perform the job, and the skills and knowledge required of the employee" (Michalak & Yager, 1979, p. 43). A task analysis includes approximately ten steps to complete:

1. *Make a list of all major tasks and subtasks necessary to perform the job.* The idea is to identify what is to be done and what the steps are to get the job done. The tasks are usually listed in chronological order or in the time sequence in which they are done. Jobs that require quite a bit of physical activity usually have the steps in the job listed chronologically. For example, a good practice exercise involves listing the steps required to change a flat tire. Assume that you are driving down the freeway and hear air escaping from a rear tire. List the tasks you need to do in order to stop, change the tire, and get back on the road. List them in the order that they should be done.

Jobs that involve less systematic tasks may be analyzed more efficiently by completing a highly detailed job description. Some jobs have tasks to do but not in any particular order. For example, an executive secretary may answer the telephone, make appointments, schedule travel arrangements, brief the boss, supervise typists and clerks, and maintain surveillance over certain budget items. A task analysis of the executive secretary's job might be accomplished by preparing a list of the different types of tasks that are done from time to time, although not necessarily in any particular order. Of course, each of the tasks, such as answering the telephone, could be analyzed by listing the steps chronologically.

2. *Record when and how often each task is to be done.* The frequency with which tasks are completed should be noted. If a task is done each Tuesday, it may be treated differently from one that is done only every six months. The kinds of problems that may develop and the discrepancies that surface may imply quite different approaches for making changes, designing training sessions, and reinforcing learning.

3. *State the levels of acceptable performance associated with each major task.* Whenever possible, a specific quantifiable measure of acceptable performance should be noted. The best standards refer to such measures as time, distance, and number of errors. Scores of 90 percent may be acceptable, within three seconds, with a tolerance of .005 of an inch, or with a maximum of three typing errors. Some jobs are less amenable to objective measures and require a consensus of judgments. "With the concurrence of three of the five team members" might be an acceptable level of performance. "Written consistent with the guidelines provided by the manual" might also be an acceptable standard of performance.

4. *Note the perceived importance of each task to accomplishing the overall objectives of the job.* In performing the job of a student, there may be a difference in the importance assigned to attending class every period and completing the final examination. Missing the final exam may have considerably greater consequences on a positive evaluation of the student's performance than missing a day of discussion in class. The importance of the task may reveal quite a bit about the kinds of problems that may develop if the task is not done well.

5. *List the skills and knowledge required to do the job.* At this stage in the task analysis, we are interested in what the employee needs to know and what skills the employee needs to have in order to complete the tasks. In order to construct a sidewalk, knowing what cement to use and how to mix it might be helpful.

6. *Note the type of learning activity involved.* Some tasks require the employee to tell the difference between two or more items, others require remembering names for tools, a third may require determining whether something is correct, a fourth may require executing some physical movements, whereas a fifth may require special uses of speech.

7. *Record the conditions under which the task is to be performed.* Some tasks must be performed under a great deal of pressure with people watching whereas others are done in relative solitude where corrections can be made in private. Some tasks are done with other people whereas others are done alone.

8. *Make an estimate of how difficult it seems to learn to perform the task.* On a scale from one to ten, some tasks are ones and others are nines in terms of figuring out how to do them. More time and effort may have to be expended in alleviating problems with difficult-to-learn tasks.

9. *Itemize the equipment, tools, and materials needed to do the task.* Difficulties in the performance of some tasks may be related to the number and quality of tools

and other equipment to be used. Complicated pieces of equipment may create more problems than they solve.

10. *Note where the skills seem to be acquired best.* Some skills, such as operating a terminal on a sales floor, may be introduced in a simulated situation, but the actual learning and skill acquisition may take place more effectively on the floor.

Task analysis is frequently the basis for identifying and solving problems in industrial settings. The development of an industrial or technical training program, for example, is usually grounded in a task analysis of each task and piece of equipment. A training manual, leader's guide, and tests are all part of a technical training package. They nearly always evolve from a sound task analysis (Dowling & Drolet, 1979).

Once the task analysis has been completed, it must be validated or compared to the way in which the task is performed in the actual work location. Observation and on-site interviews with those who do the work is essential.

Performance Analysis

The way in which the task is done is clearly an important component in documenting a concern about what is happening in the organization. The ability of employees to do tasks and the motivation with which they do the tasks are important considerations in achieving high productivity. Documentation that employees are unable to do particular tasks or are unable to do them with peak efficiency would clearly reveal evidence that something is wrong in the organization.

How well employees are doing their jobs is frequently determined by a performance appraisal. Appraisals are performed not only to help maintain control over the organization's resources but also, especially, to measure the efficiency with which the human resources are being utilized and to identify places where improvement needs to take place (Cummings & Schwab, 1973). Appraisals can be an important factor in increasing both employee performance and satisfaction. Areas of deficiency in employee abilities can be identified and relationships between performance and on-the-job goals and rewards can be clarified, thus leading to increased motivation. With the ability to perform tasks efficiently and with high-intensity motivation, employees have the potential for increased productivity.

Cummings and Schwab (1973) describe four major appraisal methods: (1) comparative procedures, (2) absolute standards, (3) management by objectives, and (4) direct indexes. *Comparative procedures* focus on employee-to-employee evaluations; *absolute standards* focus on employee-to-common-standards assessments; *management by objectives* focuses on employee-to-specific-objective appraisals; and *direct indexes* focus on objective measures of behavior.

COMPARATIVE PROCEDURES

These procedures usually involve comparing one employee with another on one or more global or general criteria that attempt to assess the employee's overall effectiveness in the organization. The question to be answered is something like, "Which one of the employees is the most successful, competent, effective, and valuable?" Two general types of comparative procedures are used: ranking and forced distribution.

Ranking.   Three types of ranking procedures are the most common: straight ranking, alternative ranking, and paired comparisons.

Straight Ranking.   This procedure involves arranging the employees being appraised in the order of excellence on the criterion being used, assigning the very best performer a ranking of one, the next best a ranking of two, and so on through all employees being evaluated.

Alternative Ranking.   This procedure is a little more complex and begins with an alphabetical list of employees being appraised. The evaluator is asked to identify the very best employee and the very weakest employee from the list. The best employee is ranked number one, and the weakest employee is ranked last. Their names are removed from the list, and the best employee and the weakest employee are again identified from among the remaining employees on the list. Each time the best and weakest employees are removed from the list and added to the separate rankings. In this way the evaluation alternates between selecting the best and the poorest employee from an ever-reducing list.

Paired Comparison.   This procedure has each evaluator compare each employee being appraised with every other employee, one at a time. A matrix listing every employee along both the X and Y axes, as illustrated in Table 15.1, is used. The evaluator simply picks the one employee from the pair who ranks highest. The employee's final evaluation and ranking is determined by how many times he or she is chosen.

Forced Distribution.   This system requires the evaluator to assign a percentage of the employees being appraised to each of several categories based on several performance factors. Typically a forced distribution assigns 10 percent of the employees to a superior category, 20 percent to an excellent category, 40 percent to an average category, 20 percent to a below-average category, and 10 percent to a poorest category. Table 15.2 illustrates the forced distribution system of appraising employees. The forced distribution system minimizes leniency in ratings, but the employees as a group may not fit the distribution all that well in terms of actual performance.

TABLE 15.1 Paired Comparison Matrix for Five Employees

	Sara	Don	Jim	Jo	Mel	Times Chosen	Rank
Sara		Sara	Jim	Jo	Mel	1	4
Don	Sara		Jim	Jo	Mel	0	5
Jim	Jim	Jim		Jo	Mel	2	3
Jo	Jo	Jo	Jo		Mel	3	2
Mel	Mel	Mel	Mel	Mel		4	1

TABLE 15.2   Forced Distribution System for Appraising Employees

Employees Being Evaluated	Poorest	Below Average	Average	Above Average	Superior
20	2	4	8	4	2
9	1	2	3	2	1

ABSOLUTE STANDARDS

Systems that evaluate employees using absolute standards compare individuals with an authoritative model or measure rather than with other employees. A *standard* is a statement that describes what is expected in terms of behavior, value, suitability, and other characteristics. There are two basic ways of applying absolute standards: qualitative and quantitative.

Qualitative Methods.   We shall comment on three qualitative methods, all of which ask the evaluator to determine whether a particular standard applies to a specific employee. In general the appraiser makes an either-or judgment—the employee does what is asked or the employee does not do what is asked.

The Critical-Incident Method.   The steps involved in using critical incidents begin with the collection of examples of when any employee is considered very effective or very ineffective—the middle ground is usually not included—from supervisors and others who are familiar with employees who do a particular job. The examples, illustrations, or incidents are analyzed for similarities and grouped under a number of general categories. In the International Communication Association (ICA) Organizational Communication Audit Project, researchers collected hundreds of critical incidents reflecting highly effective and highly ineffective communication in organizations. Eight general categories of issues emerged from the analysis of incidents: (1) clarity of role, (2) adequacy of information, (3) syntactic disparity, (4) adequacy of feedback, (5) channel usage, (6) participation in decision making, (7) perception of interpersonal relationships, and (8) personal communication competencies.

After the categories are identified and defined, each evaluator is given a list to use in recording positive and negative incidents involving the employee being appraised. The incidents secured are used as the basis for determining whether the employee does what is expected of effective employees.

Weighted Checklists.   Checklists are developed by collecting a comprehensive list of statements about employee performance when they are doing the job to be rated. Each statement is evaluated by a group of supervisors or people familiar with the job in terms of how favorable or unfavorable the statement is for successful performance on the job. On a seven-point scale, unfavorable values have low scores, and favorable values have high scores. Statements on which the judges cannot agree are eliminated from the list. The items retained are weighted by the average score obtained from the group of evaluators.

Each evaluator is given a copy of the checklist, without the weightings, and indicates whether the employee performs the behavior mentioned in each item in the checklist. The final evaluation is determined by summing the scores of the items that have been checked.

The Forced-Choice Method. This method involves gathering statements about the performance of a job from individuals familiar with the job. Judges evaluate very effective and very ineffective employees using the statements. Items that distinguish between the best and the worst employees are given weights. Judges also classify each statement according to whether it is favorable or unfavorable to job effectiveness. Items are then clustered so that several are capable of discriminating between effective and ineffective employees and at the same time determining favorability or unfavorability.

A forced-choice instrument, for example, might have four items. The evaluator would choose between A and B and between C and D. Items A and B would both be favorable to the job, but only B would discriminate between effective and ineffective employees. Items C and D would both be unfavorable to the job, but only C would discriminate between effective and ineffective employees. The person doing the appraisal would have the items without knowing which ones were favorable or unfavorable or which ones distinguish between effective and ineffective employees. The evaluator would check the item among the four that was most descriptive of the employee and the item least descriptive of the employee. The employee's score consists of the sum of the indexes for the items checked. High scores represent more desirable performance; low scores indicate less desirable performance.

Quantitative Methods. Two general types of quantitative methods are used: conventional rating scales and behaviorally anchored rating scales. Unfortunately conventional rating scales permit a *halo effect* to occur which may consistently bias evaluations for or against an employee. They also tend to focus on personality characteristics rather than on performance. Nevertheless, conventional rating scales are widely used. Behaviorally anchored rating scales are designed to reduce bias and error while providing useful information for employees during a development program.

Conventional Rating Scales. This method generally consists of a series of statements about employee characteristics. A scale is established for each characteristic, usually ranging from unsatisfactory to outstanding on a five-point scale. The evaluator places a check along the scale to represent his or her evaluation of the employee. From 5 to 25 characteristics may be evaluated. Figure 15.2 illustrates a typical conventional rating form for appraising employee performance.

Behaviorally Anchored Rating Scales. These scales are developed by using critical-incident procedures. Supervisors and others familiar with the persons being evaluated describe incidents in which the employees have been highly effective or highly ineffective. The incidents are grouped under a small number of categories based on similarities in behaviors. Judges, supervisors, and others then rate each incident on the basis of how well it represents extremely good performance or

RATING SCALE

PERFORMANCE CATEGORIES	Unsatisfactory	Satisfactory			
		Meets minimum	Average	Above average	Outstanding
1. Accuracy, thoroughness, and completeness of work					
2. Presentability of work					
3. Care and maintenance of property and space					
4. Judgment					
5. Communication (oral and written expression)					
6. Leadership					
7. Public relations					
8. Safety of self and others					
9. Productiveness					

FIGURE 15.2 Conventional Rating Scale Form

extremely poor performance. The incidents are ordered according to the average value assigned by the judges, and the incidents are placed along a scale from extremely poor performance to extremely good performance. The evaluator is given the scale with the critical incidents describing specific behaviors at each point on the scale. The employee is evaluated on each general category; the sum of the assigned scores across all categories is the employee's rating. A specific development program can be devised on the basis of weaknesses as revealed by the ratings.

MANAGEMENT BY OBJECTIVES

In addition to the use of comparative procedures and absolute standards, a third type of appraisal method is that of management by objectives. MBO, as it is called, is based on the assumptions that goals can be accomplished better if a person knows what is to be accomplished and progress toward a goal should be measured in terms of the goal to be accomplished. These seem like simple-minded premises, but they call our attention to the fact that clearly understood goals are easier to accomplish than are unclear ones.

Another assumption of MBO is that both the subordinate and the supervisor are to be involved in defining and clarifying the goals to be accomplished. A well-stated goal, also, is one that is as quantitative as possible, with specific figures and dates. The process of involvement continues through the period of MBO, with the employee doing what is necessary to accomplish the goals. Finally, periodically the supervisor and the employee compare the employee's performance against the goals that were set. During the meeting the level of goal accomplishment is discussed, and the reasons why shortcomings occurred and how performance can be improved are reviewed. MBO is clearly a human resource development procedure that can be used to upgrade below-standard performance, to maintain acceptable levels of performance, and to strengthen high levels of performance that may lead to advancement, unique contributions to personal growth, and organization accomplishment.

The four basic phases in MBO may be summarized as follows (Cummings & Schwab, 1973):

1. Planning the objectives.
   a. The manager and employee meet and discuss the goals to be accomplished during the next review period—4, 6, or 12 months.
   b. The goals, stated in written form, identify (1) the specific tasks to be accomplished and (2) the measures of satisfactory performance.
   c. During the meeting the manager and the employee discuss and resolve any differences between their perceptions of the size of the goals to be accomplished and where accomplishment of the goals will lead.
   d. The meeting to establish objectives should also include the identification of specific operational and measurable targets against which a performance program can be compared.
2. Working toward accomplishment of objectives.
   a. The employee implements a plan leading to the accomplishment of the objectives.
   b. The observable checkpoints are used to measure progress.
3. The manager and the employee meet later at some specific time to review jointly what has happened during the performance period. This usually begins with a self-appraisal by the employee which is submitted to the manager in writing. The self-appraisal is reviewed jointly by the manager and the employee. An analysis of why some goals were not met and others were and the successes experienced is made.
4. New objectives are set and continuing objectives reinforced.

Both the strength and weakness of the MBO system lies in its ability to provide unique objectives and standards for each employee. Individual differences and personal contributions can be considered. Regretfully the identification and allocation of rewards on an equitable basis is much more difficult to achieve. Because the employee plays a fairly direct role in identifying, setting, and evaluating goal accomplishment, employee performances may vary considerably, or the entire system may be subverted to the interests of employees.

DIRECT INDEXES OF PERFORMANCE

Cummings and Schwab (1973) refer to two direct indicators of performance: (1) units of output and (2) turnover and absenteeism. Number of items made, number of items sold, number of students taught, number of majors in a program, number of clients interviewed, and number of cartons shipped are all units of production. The frequency of absences and tardiness and the number of permanent terminations and resignations are special measures of employee productivity, especially the performance of supervisors. Complaints, grievances, and reprimands may also be indicators of supervisory performance.

So far we have discussed methods associated with two forms of documenting individual employee task performance: task analysis and employee performance appraisal. Straight ranking, alternative ranking, paired comparison, forced distribution, critical incident, weighted checklists, forced choice, conventional rating scales, behaviorally anchored rating scales, and management by objective have been discussed as measures of individual employee task performance. We shall continue our discussion of methods for documenting the concern by examining needs analysis procedures.

Needs Analysis

A needs analysis looks at those things that are keeping employees from making their strongest contribution to the organization. Procedures for conducting a needs analysis consist mainly of talking to employees about their work and having employees respond to feelings about their work in writing. Two other basic approaches also provide information about what is keeping employees from making the best of their resources: files analysis and clinical observation. We shall discuss the methods of conducting a needs analysis by looking at files analysis, clinical observations, interviewing, and the use of questionnaires.

FILES ANALYSIS

Files analysis consists of a study of (1) organization policies, plans, organization charts, and position descriptions; (2) employee grievance, turnover, absenteeism, and accident reports; (3) records of meetings and program evaluation studies; (4) past performance appraisals and attitude surveys; and (5) audits and budget reports. The files and documents are examined for indications of deficiencies and circumstances that appear to interfere with optimal performance of employees.

CLINICAL OBSERVATIONS

Clinical observation refers to making a set of observations that are extremely objective and realistic, in contrast to highly subjective observations in artificial settings. Objectivity is achieved by observing behaviors that can be counted and verified. Realism is achieved by observing employees working at their jobs. The purpose of clinical observations is to identify and record the frequency with which critical behaviors occur. Clinical observations represent a system for discriminating between very high and very low performing individuals or groups. Clinical observations are most useful when differences between employees concern frequency or quantity of performance rather than quality of performance.

Clinical observations help to verify critical incidents and represent an application of Vilfredo Pareto's principle of the unequal distribution of wealth. Pareto discovered that about 80 percent of the wealth of Italy was controlled by 20 percent of the population. This principle has been demonstrated in other ways, such as 20 percent of a company's sales force makes 80 percent of its sales; that 20 percent of the sales generates 80 percent of the profits; and 20 percent of a person's effort results in 80 percent of his or her productivity. Clinical observations seek to identify those behaviors in the 20 percent category that differentiate between high and low producers and result in 80 percent of the organization's effectiveness.

Three general steps are involved in making clinical observations: (1) Determine the behaviors to be observed. Tentative decisions about specific behaviors to be observed could be derived from interviews and, possibly, experience. Eventually a clearly stated description of some clusters of behaviors to be observed should be used. Four types of behaviors might be observed in public contact situations: rude behaviors that are curt, short, and argumentative; indifferent behaviors, such as speaking to a customer only when addressed, making few eye contacts, speaking in an impersonal tone; pleasant behaviors, such as smiling and greeting the customer warmly, making definite eye contact, and ending the contact with a personal comment; and value-added behaviors, such as smiling at, greeting, and chatting with customers during the transaction, offering information, and making statements that are adapted to the customer, with a personal salutation at the end. (2) Observe some highly effective employees and some highly ineffective ones and keep the observations on separate record forms. (3) Make observations of each group of employees for a specified period of time, such as thirty minutes at a time in the morning and in the afternoon for five days.

Portray the data in Pareto-type diagrams. The procedures for creating a Pareto diagram include summarizing the data from the record form to show the number of times (frequency) each employee observed engaged in the types of behaviors described. Arrange the data in order from the largest to the smallest numbers and total them. Compute the percentage of behaviors exhibited by each person observed. Plot the percentages on a graph. Construct a bar chart putting the longest bar (highest frequency) on the far left. The vertical scale (up the left-hand side) shows the percentage, usually in multiples of 10 percent, and the horizontal scale (along the bottom) shows the type of behaviors. Separate charts should be constructed for high performers and for low performers. Figure 15.3 illustrates a Pareto diagram. The

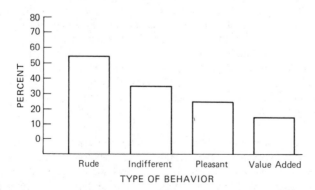

FIGURE 15.3   Pareto Diagram of Behaviors of Ineffective Public-Contact Employees

arrangement of the bar graphs from highest frequencies on the left to lowest frequencies on the right provides a quick visual picture of where the problems are occurring. By developing a behavioral frequency Pareto-type diagram before and after training and development, the effectiveness of certain strategies can be determined.

INTERVIEWING

Interviewing or talking to people about their work is one of the most commonly used methods for conducting a needs analysis. Interviews are also a basic method for gathering information for task analyses, performance appraisals, and organizational communication systems analysis. Interviews in needs analysis are often referred to as *gap interviews* and are designed to gather information about opinions and attitudes, values, thoughts and ideas, and expectations. Interviewing allows employees to talk about their perceptions of a problem or need and their proposed solutions.

Interviews are frequently used at different stages of documenting a concern, but they are especially helpful early in a needs analysis to get an idea of the general feelings of select organization members. An early interview is usually called *exploratory* since it seeks to get a sense of what is happening in order to select other procedures and develop instruments.

Interviews may be conducted with one person or with a group, often employing brainstorming or nominal group processes, and can be either face to face or over the telephone. Interviews can be formal or casual, structured or unstructured, lengthy or brief. Interviews are probably most effective in revealing employee feelings, causes of problems, and expectations and anticipated difficulties. Because they are usually personal and involve predominantly oral communication, they help establish and strengthen relationships between parties involved in the needs analysis.

Interviews have their disadvantages also. They may be somewhat costly when one interviewer works with one employee. They may seem quite slow when only four or five individuals are interviewed in a day. Employee responses are almost entirely qualitative, making them difficult to analyze and interpret. The quality of an interview may depend heavily upon the interpersonal skills of the interviewer, particularly in face-to-face interviews. Employees can feel very uneasy and self-conscious with an unskilled interviewer. If employees doubt that their comments will be held in confidence, they may be reluctant to answer questions openly, fully, and candidly. Interviewers must have the sensitivity to nonverbal behaviors to tell when the employee wants to say more, to talk in greater confidence, or to discuss something controversial.

Individual Interviews.   One-on-one interviews are conducted near the employee's place of work and cover certain basic questions while allowing the employee to comment on what topics he or she prefers. Procedures for conducting a needs analysis interview follow closely its use in other types of analyses and involve arranging for a private location in which to conduct the interview, such as an office or secluded work area.

Put the interviewee at ease and assure him or her that what is being discussed will be handled so as to maintain confidences and the anonymity of information and the interviewee. Ask each question in the order presented on the interview schedule. Record the interviewee's answers to the questions as accurately as possible. The responsibility of the interviewer is to secure and record precise and accurate answers to each question asked. If possible, note the exact, verbatim wording of answers, especially when the answers respond directly to questions. You may find, however, that interviewees provide information relevant to some other question; record answers as unobtrusively as possible, but under the question for which they are the answers, then guide the interview back to the original question and continue with the sequence. When you arrive at the later question and discover that you have already recorded answers, simply pose the question to verify that the responses are accurate and to allow the interviewee to elaborate on answers. Record the answers to each question on a separate sheet of paper. This will facilitate the analysis later.

The interview schedule for a supervisory needs analysis might include the following questions (Kirkpatrick, 1971):

1. What problems exist in your department?
2. What problems do you expect to develop in the future?
3. What ought to be included in a training program to resolve the problems?
4. What information would help you to do your job better?
5. When would be a good time to hold a training session?
6. What is the best time for you to attend a training session?

The interview should be opened with some comments to establish rapport and goodwill with the interviewee, then reveal the purpose of the interview. Give some assurances that the confidences will be maintained and that no names or personal identification will be associated with any response. Mention that only general needs and group concerns will be included in any reports. Request permission to take notes. Make a transition to the first question.

Analysis of Interview Responses. Interview responses are analyzed in an eight-step procedure:

1. Assign a code number to each interview schedule; put the code on all pages.
2. Place the answers to Question One from all schedules together.
3. Sort the answers to Question One according to some prearranged category system—position, years in service, level of authority.
4. Bring all answers to a single question together on one or more pages—cut, paste, and Xerox or type the answers.
5. Identify themes occurring in the answers of the respondents to each question.
6. State each theme and excerpt some typical responses from the lists, appropriately disguised to protect the anonymity of interviewees, to illustrate how you arrived at the theme.
7. After all responses to all questions of all interviewees have been reviewed for themes, look for similarities and differences among and between the themes and compare and contrast individual and group responses of different categories of employees.
8. Write an analysis of the interview response to indicate what the needs are.

Group Interviews. Group interviews are often held to get the ideas and needs of a work group or team. In addition to following the procedures for personal interviews, including having a set of clear questions in the form of an interview schedule that is adapted to the group, two techniques can be used to get the maximum benefit from group interaction and to reduce the pressures toward conformity implicit in face-to-face interaction. Brainstorming, force-field analysis, and nominal group process are three techniques that can be used effectively to identify needs in groups (Pace, Peterson, & Burnett, 1979).

Brainstorming. This is a group session in which members think up ideas without being critical or giving judgmental reactions. A question such as "What do we need to do our jobs better?" could be used in brainstorming. A brainstorming session is most effective when some simple guidelines and rules are adhered to; the leader should call the meeting to order and review the following:

1. No questions should be asked during the brainstorming period; all questions should be answered before the start of the session.
2. To maintain order, the leader recognizes each person, as quickly as possible, who has an idea; if you are not called upon immediately, jot down your idea for use later.
3. Avoid elaborating on, defending, or editorializing on any suggestion; merely state the idea without personal reservations, as quickly and concisely as possible.
4. Suggest even the obvious, since some apparent need may trigger some ideas in others; don't be guilty of self-criticism.
5. Don't be afraid to restate an idea in a different way.
6. Strive for the workable but allow the ridiculous to occur.
7. Follow all brainstorming rules faithfully. Four rules must not be violated; the leader may ring a bell or slam a gong if even one is:
   a. Criticism is not allowed.
   b. Freewheeling is encouraged.
   c. Quantity is wanted.
   d. Combination and improvement are sought.

The person doing the needs analysis is usually the leader. After the session is over, the ideas and needs are processed and grouped in much the same way that ideas from an interview are handled.

Force-Field Analysis. This is the special application of group interviews and brainstorming (Michalak & Yager, 1979). Its basic objective is to provide a way of systematically identifying factors that produce and deter action in the organization. The idea of a force-field is one of balance. In an organization, the current way of doing things is a result of counterbalancing factors, some producing and some deterring. As shown in Figure 15.4, the technique is relatively simple and involves a flip chart with newsprint, a felt pen, and a brainstorming group. The leader/interviewer draws a force-field diagram on the flip chart, with the issue stated at the top of the page. A vertical line running down the page represents the

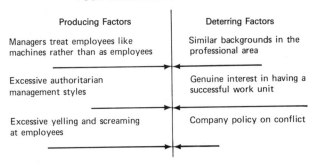

FIGURE 15.4 Sample Force-Field Analysis (Source: From Donald F. Michalak and Edwin G. Yager, *Making the Training Process Work,* New York: Harper and Row, Pub., 1979.)

way things are being done now. The arrows represent the producing and deterring factors.

As group members call out forces that produce or deter the current status, the leader/interviewer should record each item as close to verbatim as possible in order to avoid interrupting the group with questions of interpretation and meaning. Along with each force, the leader/interviewer draws a horizontal line toward the vertical line to represent the strength of the producing or deterring force. Each line will be a different length depending upon the strength of the force. The current circumstances are a balance between the forces. To make a change, a force-field analysis suggests, remove or strengthen the forces that produce or deter the kind of action that you want.

Nominal Group Process.   This is a structured group meeting in which participants alternate ideas silently, listing ideas in serial order orally for posting on a flip chart, offering pro and con and clarifying comments, and voting on ideas.

Nominal group process balances the influence of high-status, highly expressive, strong personalities, allowing equality of participation and consideration of ideas. NGP facilitates more open discussion and the contribution of unusual and controversial ideas while applying simple mathematics to reduce errors when individual judgments are combined into group decisions.

Nominal group process involves a number of stages plus some preparation. Since NGP relies heavily on the posting of ideas in front of the group, it is essential to have a flip chart and newsprint to be mounted on an easel or attached to the wall. A roll of masking tape, 3 × 5 cards, felt pen, and paper and pencil for each participant are important also. The NGP develops as follows:

1. Welcome participants, and explain the process. Place the question before the group: "What kinds of problems are you experiencing in your work?"
2. Each member writes ideas in response to the question, working silently and independently.

3. The leader-recorder asks for one idea from each group member, going around the table one at a time; the recorder writes the ideas on the flip chart without comment about the ideas until all are posted.
4. Each idea in the list is taken in the order listed, and comments of clarification are made about each one; the purpose of this period is to clarify, not to argue, the merits of any idea.
5. From the list of ideas on the flip chart, the group selects a specific number that seem to be the most important—from five to ten items. Each group member writes the priority items on separate 3 × 5 cards and rank-orders the items from one to ten. The cards are collected, shuffled, and recorded on newsprint in front of the group. The sum of the rankings across all group members is the final order of items. Group members may discuss the final rankings and rate the importance to them of each need. The results represent the needs analysis.

Consensus Ranking.   This is a two-stage group activity in which employees (1) individually rank a list of potential needs and (2) as a group arrive at consensus on a ranking of the same items. A sample ranking form is illustrated in Figure 15.5. Instructions for the group consensus step should read something like those in Figure 15.6.

Card Sort.   Another approach to interviewing employees about needs is to use a card-sort activity (Bellman, 1975). Use of the card-sort technique involves (1) preparing the cards and (2) conducting the survey interview. Pick a target population, such as supervisors, and develop a long list of responsibilities. Translate the responsibilities into questions. Group the questions into common areas, such as motivation, delegation, training, planning, time use, teamwork, or communication.

INDIVIDUAL TRAINING NEEDS RANKING FORM

Instructions: Below are listed 15 training needs identified by typical employees. Your task is to rank-order them in terms of their importance to your personal needs. Place a 1 in front of the type of training that you feel to be your greatest need, and so on, to 15, your lowest training need.

_____ Coping with stress
_____ Fulfilling management functions
_____ Maintaining interpersonal communication
_____ Writing memos and reports
_____ Inducting new employees
_____ Appraising employee performance
_____ Listening
_____ Planning
_____ Interviewing
_____ Training new employees
_____ Problem solving and decision making
_____ Developing self
_____ Supervising ethnic minorities
_____ Motivating employees
_____ Handling complaints and grievances

FIGURE 15.5   Sample Consensus Ranking Form for Needs Analysis

GROUP RANKING FOR TRAINING NEEDS

Instructions: This phase of the needs analysis is designed to discover the most important *group* needs. Your group is to reach consensus on rankings for the 15 employee needs. This means that the final rankings for each of the needs must be agreed upon by each group member before it becomes part of the group decision. Consensus may be difficult to achieve; therefore, not every item will meet with everyone's complete approval. Try, as a group, to make each ranking one with which all group members can at least partially agree. Here are some guidelines in reaching consensus:

1. Avoid arguing for your own individual judgments; approach the task on the basis of logic.
2. Avoid changing your mind only in order to reach agreement and avoid conflict; support only needs with which you are able to agree somewhat, at least.
3. View differences of opinion as helpful rather than as a hindrance to reaching agreement.

FIGURE 15.6 Sample Instructions for Group Consensus Exercise

Transfer the questions to cards. Put only one question per card. Number each card on the reverse side so that each group of questions is represented by a sequence of numbers, such as 1, 2, 3, 4. With the questions on cards, a supervisor can quickly compare one question with another and physically separate the cards into stacks and sequences. You are now prepared to conduct the survey interview.

Begin the interview by explaining the purpose of the interview, how the employee can help, and the card deck. Give the cards to the employee while asking, "If you could have the answers to ten of these questions, which ten would be most helpful to you in doing your job?" Ask the employee to select the ten most important questions and to place them in order from most important to least important. Explain that after the cards have been selected and ordered, you will return and discuss them. Leave the room until the employee has finished, about ten to fifteen minutes.

When you return, have the employee read the number of each question (on the reverse side) while you record the rank order of the ten questions for later analysis. Assign the most important question ten points, the second most important nine points, down to the least important question, which is given one point. Review the sheet on which you recorded the rankings and the weightings, answering questions for the employee. Ask the employee to respond to the question, "What is happening in your job that caused you to select this question?" Ask the question in a variety of ways for each of the ten questions selected. Elicit specific job performance comments. Record the employee's comments on index cards, putting one to a card for easier sorting later. Code the index cards and the cards with questions in the same way so they can be sorted according to location, work group, position, and demographic characteristics such as experience or age, depending on what might be important.

At the end of the interview, review the cards with the employee to make certain they are accurate. Assure the employee that the comments are for your use only and no identities will be revealed. Conclude by explaining when the analysis is to be finished, how the employees will learn about the results, and how the data will be used to determine needs.

Analyze the card sorts by portraying the results in a matrix like that illustrated in Figure 15.7, with the horizontal axis reading from 1 to 10 and the vertical axis running from 1 to the number of times any question was selected most frequently. Using the matrix, the more important questions are located in the upper-right-hand quadrant.

Telephone Interview.   A final interviewing procedure is to use telephone interviews. Interviewing over the telephone is a common market-research technique (Downs, Smeyak, & Martin, 1980). Calls are usually made to a random sample of individuals using an interview guide or schedule. The schedule must be developed carefully. Downs et al. suggest that the schedule should be as simple as possible in order to reduce fatigue, that respondents should not be asked questions they cannot answer, that the questions should be restricted to essential information, and that the smallest sample size consistent with the objectives of the study should be used.

The telephone interviewer should ask questions exactly as they are worded in order to have comparable information from all respondents. Interviewers should probe answers when necessary to avoid incomplete or unclear responses. The interviewer should not be drawn into giving answers. Finally, some answer should be recorded for every question. Avoid leaving blank spaces, either by probing or writing in "don't know." Telephone interviewing requires a great deal of skill and patience, but few survey techniques are as quick and economical.

QUESTIONNAIRES

Questionnaires and other written instruments and procedures are probably the most widely used methods for conducting a needs analysis. Questionnaires can provide fairly precise information from large and small groups of employees. A

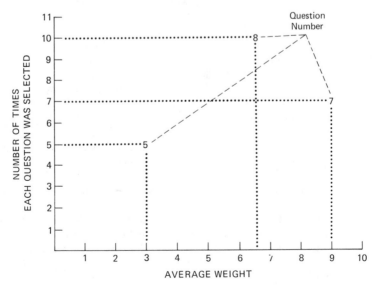

FIGURE 15.7   Sample Matrix for Displaying Card-Sort Data

variety of questions can be used and combined with other written instruments, such as rating scales, rankings, and free-response questions. Questionnaires can be administered individually or in groups or can be mailed to employees. They are relatively inexpensive to use and can reach a large group of people in a fairly short time. The responses to a questionnaire are about as easy to summarize, analyze, and report as any needs analysis procedure. Questionnaires can be simple or complex. The major problem associated with questionnaires is that they may require a great deal of time and expertise to develop effective instruments.

An effective questionnaire for use in needs analysis should be as simple as possible to achieve the purpose of the survey (Zemke & Walonick, 1980). Questionnaires of two or three pages may appear unnecessarily complex and may intimidate employees. Longer questionnaires can be used, of course, but they require special expertise to construct. Wilson (1980) argues that needs analysis can profitably use "demonstrably valid surveys" developed by professionals. Although well-constructed questionnaires are important to getting accurate information, some simple instruments can be very effective.

Figure 15.8 illustrates a needs assessment questionnaire that covers four general areas and includes twenty-four items about specific abilities. The items are fairly specific and the response categories ask for indications of importance to the job as well as the need for training or organizational changes.

From an analysis of the differences between what is required and what the employee possesses in areas of importance, some critical needs can be identified.

SUMMARY

This chapter has discussed the process of analysis in human resource development and organizational communication. A point of concern is the first stage in the process of analysis and involves recognizing that something seems wrong. The second stage is documentation of the concern by answering the question, "What is happening now?" The third stage, point of preference, involves the development of guidelines in response to the inquiry, "What ought to be happening tomorrow?" The fourth stage is a point of comparison that involves identifying a problem or problems by answering the questions, "Are there differences between what is happening and what ought to be happening?" and "Are the differences important enough to do something?" The final and fifth stage is the point of classification where the problem is classified as a training, development, performance, or organization problem.

Three general approaches to documenting a concern were explained and illustrated: (1) task analysis, (2) performance analysis, and (3) needs analysis. Specific techniques and methods explained were chronological listing of tasks and job description; comparative procedures such as straight ranking, alternative ranking, paired comparison, and forced distribution; absolute standard methods such as critical incidents, weighted checklists, and forced choice, as well as conventional rating scales and behaviorally anchored rating scales; management by objectives; direct indexes of performance; file analysis; clinical observation; interviewing, including individual and group interviewing methods such as brainstorming, force-field analysis, nominal group process, consensus ranking groups, a card-sort technique, and telephone interviews; and questionnaires.

SURVEY OF TRAINING AND DEVELOPMENT NEEDS

	This Ability Is Important to My Job					I Could Do My Job Better If	
	Not Important		Very Important			I Had More Training	Some Conditions Were Changed in the Organization
	(circle a number)						
Planning Abilities							
1. Set objectives or develop projects	1	2	3	4	5	_____	_____
2. Develop plans	1	2	3	4	5	_____	_____
3. Set priorities for work	1	2	3	4	5	_____	_____
4. Use program budgeting procedures	1	2	3	4	5	_____	_____
5. Use special budgeting systems	1	2	3	4	5	_____	_____
6. Use time effectively	1	2	3	4	5	_____	_____
Managing Abilities							
7. Assign work to people	1	2	3	4	5	_____	_____
8. Delegate	1	2	3	4	5	_____	_____
9. Motivate people	1	2	3	4	5	_____	_____
10. Understand people of different ages, races, backgrounds	1	2	3	4	5	_____	_____
Problem-Solving Abilities							
11. Recognize and analyze the problems	1	2	3	4	5	_____	_____
12. Identify solutions to problems	1	2	3	4	5	_____	_____
13. Decide which solution is best	1	2	3	4	5	_____	_____
14. Make decisions in emergencies	1	2	3	4	5	_____	_____
Communication							
15. Inform supervisor	1	2	3	4	5	_____	_____
16. Inform subordinates	1	2	3	4	5	_____	_____
17. Answer questions about programs	1	2	3	4	5	_____	_____
18. Answer questions about merit, production, EEO, and classification	1	2	3	4	5	_____	_____
19. Conduct formal briefings	1	2	3	4	5	_____	_____
20. Lead meetings	1	2	3	4	5	_____	_____
21. Listen and accept views of others	1	2	3	4	5	_____	_____
22. Provide negative information	1	2	3	4	5	_____	_____
23. Complete reports and forms	1	2	3	4	5	_____	_____
24. Write formal letters	1	2	3	4	5	_____	_____

FIGURE 15.8 Sample Needs Analysis Questionnaire

REFERENCES

Bellman, Geoffrey, ''Surveying Your Supervisory Training Needs,'' *Training and Development Journal* (February 1975), 25–33.

Cummings, L. L., and Donald P. Schwab, *Performance in Organizations: Determinants and Appraisal.* Glenview, Ill.: Scott, Foresman, 1973.

Dowling, John R., and Robert P. Drolet, *Developing and Administering an Industrial Training Program.* Boston: CBI Publishing Company, Inc., 1979.

Downs, Cal W., G. Paul Smeyak, and Ernest Martin, *Professional Interviewing.* New York: Harper & Row, Pub., 1980.

Kirkpatrick, Donald L., *A Practical Guide for Supervisory Training and Development.* Reading, Mass.: Addison-Wesley, 1971.

Michalak, Donald F., and Edwin G. Yager, *Making the Training Process Work.* New York: Harper & Row, Pub., 1979.

Pace, R. Wayne, Brent D. Peterson, and M. Dallas Burnett, *Techniques for Effective Communication.* Reading, Mass.: Addison-Wesley, 1979.

Patton, Bobby R., and Kim Giffin, *Problem-Solving Group Interaction.* New York: Harper & Row, Pub., 1973.

Plunkett, Lorne C., and Guy A. Hale, *The Proactive Manager.* New York: John Wiley & Sons, 1982, 11–30.

Wilson, Clark, "Identifying Needs with Costs in Mind," *Training and Development Journal,* 34 (July 1980).

Zemke, Ron, and Dave Walonick, "The Non-Statistician's Approach to Conducting and Analyzing Surveys," *Training/HRD* (September 1980), 89–99.

16

Organizational Systems Analysis

In the preceding chapter, we reviewed the methods, instruments, and procedures for conducting analyses that reveal training and development and performance problems. In this chapter, we will examine analytical techniques for discovering and identifying organization problems. Because performance deficiencies are often associated with the structure of the organizational system, this chapter will also include methods that reveal performance problems from a systems perspective.

Systems analysis, in this context, refers to organizational processes, in contrast to human resource analysis, which examines individual skills, attitudes, and knowledge. We assume that both functional and interpretive methods can be used to analyze organizational processes and identify problems.

The two major analytical traditions evident in the field of organizational communication—the functional and the interpretive—were described in Chapters 1 and 2, and throughout other chapters the major directions implied by the theories have been identified and inculcated into discussions of organizational issues. We will now introduce the methods of analysis associated with each of the traditions.

INTERPRETIVE METHODS OF ANALYSIS

This section will explore basic interpretive methods, such as participant observation, account analysis, story analysis, metaphor analysis, and in-depth interviews. The definitions and methods of interpretive research vary considerably. Strine and

Pacanowsky (1985) remark, "Some pieces of interpretive research strongly resemble traditional 'org. comm.' studies complete with numbers. But others look like critical analyses of plays, filled with indented dialogue. Still others resemble new Journalism or fiction" (p. 284). It is obvious that each interpretive method requires a different level of sophistication. Although this section may not prepare you to write a novel or engage in rhetorical criticism, it should provide the basic concepts that will enable you to do some useful analysis. We will discuss some of the basic insights and procedures that must be mastered before one can move to an intermediate level of sophistication. The analytic concepts we discuss are selected for illustrative purposes and should not be thought of as *the* concepts to use.

General Considerations

Traditional studies rely mainly on instruments such as inventories, attitude questionnaires, and structured interviews. The interpretive method of analysis relies more heavily on the researcher as the instrument; hence, it is up to interpretive researchers to present a strong case for their findings. The investigator cannot rely on such statements as "My findings are valid because my questionnaire is valid and reliable." An interpretive study must persuade the readers that they are gaining knowledge through the discoveries made by a careful and insightful researcher. The critical question is, "Can the researcher 'discover' and 'interpret' significant organizational behaviors?"

What does the researcher look for? The search is for symbolic behavior that has organizational significance. What do the symbols allow organization members to see and do? How might they enable or constrain organizational activity? To repeat Smircich (1985), "What are the words, ideas, and constructs that impel, legitimate, coordinate, and realize organized activity in specific settings? How do they accomplish the task? Whose interests are they serving?" (p. 67). We suggested earlier that a culture can be "imaged" by considering its indicators and displayers. These indicators and displayers appear in a variety of cultural schemes. Lundberg (1985) discusses four levels of organizational culture: artifacts, perspectives, values, and assumptions. *Artifacts* can be verbal, behavioral, or physical. A verbal artifact could be a story, for instance. Behavioral artifacts include rituals and ceremonies. The visual images (pictures, plaques, prints, clippings, and cartoons) and actual objects, such as golf clubs, sculptures, or vases exhibited by members of an organization are examples of physical artifacts. *Perspectives* refer to the shared rules and norms of an organization. *Values* represent those ideas that organizational members use for judging situations, acts, and goals. They are the standards and ideals of the organization. *Assumptions* are the tacit beliefs that organizational members hold. They are often implicit and so taken for granted that members do not consciously think about them. In that way, assumptions are the underpinning of the first three levels. Deal and Kennedy (1982) posit four key attributes of organizational cultures: values, heroes, rites and rituals, and cultural-communication networks.

Although Lundberg's and Deal and Kennedy's categories are helpful, it is important at this point to issue a caution. In our view the best cultural analyses focus on *discovering* the symbolic behavior that *drives* organized activity. The idea is not to select the best system of cultural categories and then apply them. Finding indicators and displayers of organizational culture and cataloging them does not tell much about the significance of such factors. Each list of cultural components should be regarded as some potential categories that may emerge as important anchors of meaning. In one organization a particular component of culture may guide behavior while in another it has little significance. Because culture is constructed by its members, it is unique; the researcher must discover that uniqueness. The researcher observes and records specific behaviors, develops themes out of those behaviors, and then assigns the theme to a category. A new category may have to be developed.

Interpretive research requires that the investigator be able to *see* taken-for-granted behavior and its significance. Taken-for-granted behavior is embedded in everyday talk and routines. Sometimes when organizational members have agreed to be observed, they say, "Well, you can observe us, but you will be disappointed because nothing ever happens here." However, to an outsider who is trying to understand an organization, a great deal is going on and much of it is unclear. If you have seen the television show *The Waltons,* then the following example will make sense. One family member, upon discovering that John Boy plans to become a writer and that he plans to write about the family, says, "I don't see how he can write about the family; we never do anything!" All of us are so accustomed to certain behaviors that we do not see them or how they have structured our world. When the behaviors are made visible and interpreted, one might be fascinated, amused, and even prepared for change. Comedians (Bill Cosby and George Carlin, for example) have a special talent for taking the everyday language and routines that people take for granted and making them not only quite visible but also problematic. It is the capacity to make people conscious of their unconscious behaviors that must be developed by the interpretive researcher.

Gathering data presents another challenge. Pacanowsky and O'Donnell-Trujillo (1982) stress that interpretive researchers must become very "familiar" with the organizational behavior that is being studied, but at the same time they must remain in a position to experience the behavior as "unfamiliar" so that it can be questioned and understood. As the researcher becomes more familiar with organizational routines, it becomes more difficult to see or question them. Students who are assigned a cultural analysis project often ask if they can do an interpretive study of an organization that employs them. The good news is that they are familiar with the organization, but it is also bad news that they are familiar with the organization. When individuals examine their own workplace cultures, particular care must be taken to make organizational behaviors "strange." We will elaborate on this notion in the discussion of procedures.

What may appear to be mundane language or interaction can embody significant organizational processes and beliefs. For example, Roy (1960) describes and analyzes the interaction that takes place within a group of factory machine operators. His account of the "first awareness" of what was happening around him is important to the interpretive researcher. He states, "What I heard at first, before I started to listen, was a stream of disconnected bits of communication which did not make sense. . . . What I saw at first, before I began to observe, was occasional flurries of horseplay so simple and unvarying in pattern and so childish in quality that they made no strong bid for attention" (p. 161). As he developed familiarity with the communication system, the interaction started to reveal structure. He discovered that there were "times" and themes that emerged out of the communication. The breaks during the day were labeled: There was coffee-time, peach-time, banana-time, fish-time, coke-time, and lunch-time. The themes were those of verbal interplay and included such items as "kidding themes." His interpretation contends that the times and themes were used as a source of job satisfaction and as a way of coping with monotony. There are certainly more implications, but the important point for the researcher is that what appears to be mundane has meaning, pattern, and significance.

If a researcher intends to make some sense of an organizational culture, it is difficult, if not impossible, to specify what is being looked for except in a general way. There is a search for the *sense patterns* of the organizational membership that drive, legitimate, coordinate, and make possible their activity. Although there is value in understanding the available methods of analysis and the cultural components to which the methods are applied (Bantz, 1981, 1983, 1987), these represent *potential* methods and components. The researcher must discover the sense making that is taking place and then describe its significance.

Procedures

What culture is examined? We suggested earlier that an organization is likely to have several subcultures. In view of this a researcher will have to set some boundaries at the outset, even if they are arbitrary ones. The size of the organization may dictate those boundaries. Cultural analysis requires time, and in this regard it is not an inexpensive process. The boundaries selected at the outset may be altered as the study progresses. Even small organizations may contain several subcultures that become apparent in the course of study.

What is the focus of study? Our discussion of culture indicated that studies of workplace culture can focus on different issues, such as the origins, manifestations, outcomes, and management of cultures. Our focus has been on obtaining an "understanding" of organizational culture. This approach has the advantage of presenting a more comprehensive picture of the organization and focuses on significance that is generated by members of the organization. The language of the other foci of study treats culture as a given—an end product that is made up of certain elements that have an impact on other elements. In that sense it represents functional research more closely than interpretive research.

What constitutes data? *Talk* is the primary data of cultural analysis. It is in the talk that cultures are brought to life and acted out or, as Pacanowsky and O'Donnell-Trujillo (1983) would suggest, organizational reality is brought into being. In traditional studies data usually consist of numbers, whereas the data in interpretive studies are organizational *messages*. These messages may be selected from communicative interactions, organizational documents, organizational outputs, and physical artifacts. Language is the dominant subject in analyzing interaction, but nonverbal aspects should not be discounted. Ideally, interactions should be videotaped so that nonverbal cues can be included in the analysis. However, even a description of the nonverbal behavior can help the reader understand the interaction. The analysis of documents can give insight into the official version of an organization, and the congruence or divergence between document statements and actual behavior may add an interesting dimension to cultural analysis. Bantz (1983) suggests that organizational messages that are actual products of the organization as well as those that serve an image-building function for the organization can be analyzed by (1) examining how they are discussed and reconstructed by organizational members, and (2) studying the way in which the output (report) is used by the members to construct meanings and expectations of the organization. Physical artifacts of the organization also send messages about the culture of that organization. Furniture, art, space, and design are artifacts that convey meaning and feeling in an organization. They are a type of data.

How are the data gathered? The two major means of gathering data are participant observation and interviewing. Participant observation means that the researcher observes, then interviews organizational members about the observations and what they might mean. The observer gets involved with the meanings of organization members who are observed. Interviews are used to clarify observations. Pacanowsky and O'Donnell-Trujillo (1982) point out that "what is required then are details—detailed observations of organizational members 'in action' and detailed interviews (formal or informal) of organizational members accounting for their actions" (p. 127). Detailed data are necessary for a rich description and plausible presentation of an organizational culture. Enough time must be spent to become very familiar with the organization. Depending on the situation, the researcher takes notes, makes tape recordings, takes pictures, and collects documents and other outputs. Field notes are extremely important for illustrating communicative exchanges. Writing down or recording exactly what was said is a real challenge. If the researcher is going to capture the nuances of organizational communication, however, precise and accurate records are important.

How are data generated? The discovery of sense-making processes necessitates techniques that illuminate taken-for-granted behavior. In this regard, data are generated or "brought to light." People engage in everyday routines without thinking about them, and they hold tacit knowledge or understanding that they never verbalize. How are taken-for-granted behavior and tacit knowledge revealed so that the investigator can see how people are making sense of their behaviors? Pacanowsky and O'Donnell-Trujillo (1982) suggest that researchers should constantly ask organizational members "Why?" when referring to particular behaviors or statements. This sort of digging can produce accounts that reveal sense making. It must be remembered that "why" questions are used to determine *how* organizational members are making sense. Nevertheless, *why* people are *really* doing or saying something is *not* the issue. Louis (1985) suggests that the researcher can get at tacit knowledge by looking for (or provoking) conditions under which such knowledge becomes accessible. Conditions that allow for getting at tacit knowledge include disruptions or crises, because what is normal is disturbed and brought to light. Individuals who experience *contrast* (multiple roles) can often provide descriptions or tacit knowledge held by various groups. The investigator might probe (or provoke) by asking a group to produce an image of itself or discuss what epitomizes that group. Another technique is to focus on a *critical incident,* and then ask the group to reflect on its meaning.

How are data interpreted? The researcher must have sufficient data, be able to see what organizational members are experiencing, discover patterns of sense making, and finally, interpret the significance of the sense making. In the final analysis the researcher is responsible for the interpretation. However, the thorough researcher will seek out supplemental inputs and perspectives. This step enables greater scrutiny of data and permits an investigator to state the type of bias that may be in a final report. Louis (1981, 1985) discusses levels of interpretation in a research process. She suggests that they include (1) the member's interpretations, (2) negotiated interpretations between member and researcher, (3) the researcher's interpretations, (4) negotiated interpretations between two researchers, (5) validation of a researcher's interpretations between two researchers, (6) validation of a researcher's interpretations by an organizational member, and (7) critical interpretations of the researcher. The appropriateness of these levels depends on the particular study and researcher. What is important is the notion of various perspectives so that different nuances of the organizational culture do not elude the investigator.

Up to this point we have stressed the basic considerations and procedures for analyzing organizational culture from an *emergent* perspective. That is, the researcher discovers the culture as it is being performed, accomplished, or enacted. After the researcher determines what is important to the culture in terms of what drives it, labels may be attached to or created for particular constructs.

Although we favor the emergent approach, there are other ways to conduct interpretive analyses. One such approach, a *preconceptualized* one (Bantz, 1987), lays out what is important in advance on the assumption that the items examined will give significant insights into organizational culture. Bantz states that

> the Organizational Communication Culture [OCC] approach entails a methodology that (1) gathers messages; (2) analyzes the messages for four major elements—vocabulary, themes, architecture, and temporality; (3) analyzes the symbolic forms in the messages—metaphors, fantasy themes, and stories; (4) infers patterns of organizational meanings from the elements, symbolic forms, and the messages themselves; (5) infers patterns of expectations from the elements, symbolic forms, meanings, and the messages themselves; and (6) weaves these patterns of meanings and expectations into a tapestry of the Organizational Communication Culture. (p. 6)

Researchers who adopt a preconceived approach tend to analyze messages in terms of symbolic forms. Three such symbolic forms that have been found useful in organizational study include *account analysis, story analysis,* and *metaphor analysis.* These forms tell about organizational cultures, although it must be stressed that they do not tell all.

Account analysis involves asking people to provide explanations for their behavior. *Accounts* are the kinds of statements people use whenever their actions are challenged (Scott & Lyman, 1968). In other words, people usually give accounts when they are asked to justify their actions; givers of accounts provide explanations that they perceive as socially acceptable. For example, if you were asked why your term paper was late, you would no doubt try to present verbal justifications that you thought were socially (culturally) acceptable. This account would tell how you make sense of the culture and what you think is important. Getting at *legitimate* behavior in the organization tells us a great deal about organizational constraints. When an individual accounts for a particular behavior, more is involved than giving reasons. The verbalization is an act that has a number of implications. Account analysis has been used to illustrate (1) organizational identification (Cheney, 1983), (2) the link between organizational decision making and identification (Tompkins & Cheney, 1983), (3) the reconstruction of an event's context (Buttny, 1985), (4) account acceptability in the organizational setting (Buckholdt & Gubrium, 1983), and (5) identification of organizational culture (Faules & Drecksel, 1986). Accounts can be obtained by observing naturally occurring interaction, by interviewing, and by administering a questionnaire. Account analysis can help the *change agent* discover what justifications members *think* are operative in the organization. Knowledge of accounts may also help managers realize that different cultural contexts require different managerial strategies.

Story analysis examines organizational narrations or stories. The *story* is a form of organizational symbolism that "members use to reveal or make comprehendible the unconscious feelings, images, and values that are inherent in that organization" (Dandridge, Mitroff, & Joyce, 1980, p. 77). Stories are used to give meaning to critical events. There are different types of stories and story analysis, including *myths* (Sykes, 1970), *legends* (Brunvand, 1980), *sagas* (Borman, 1972, 1983), and *master symbols* (Smith). Stories are used for sense making. Members use stories to determine what organizational events and activities mean. You have probably been involved in an organization where stories have been used to socialize new members (Brown, 1985), convey policy, make a particular point, epitomize what the organization is "all about," or illustrate what really counts "around here."

Stories are potent anchors of meaning. Martin (1982) suggests that the story is an effective tool for communicating a policy in that it is more memorable and believable than other symbolic forms. Wilkins (1978) found that the number and type of stories told may be related to the level of employee commitment. The content of stories, who tells them, and how they are told can give insight into significant organizational behaviors. How does the researcher obtain stories? Mitroff and Kilmann (1975) suggest that "stories are like dreams. Most of us have to be trained not only to recognize them, but also to appreciate their significance. For this reason, it is almost impossible to get at the stories that govern organizations directly. Like dreams they have to be gotten at indirectly" (pp. 19–20). Of course, it would be ideal to observe stories as they are told in everyday interaction. However, this method may require an excessive amount of time. Observation may provide data, but the researcher must rely primarily on the interview. Faules (1982) used story analysis to examine performance appraisal.

> The interview strategy was to (1) get respondents to talk about what organizational members talk about in reference to performance appraisal, (2) get respondents to focus on stories about performance appraisal, and (3) get respondents to develop those stories with as much detail as possible. A typical sequence of questions would include: What do people talk about when they are discussing performance appraisal? What are the major concerns? What are the favorable and unfavorable factors in the appraisal system? Can you give me an incident that would illustrate that factor? Describe the incident in as much detail as you can. How often are such incidents discussed? Are there other incidents that you have seen or heard about? Describe those for me. (pp. 153–154)

Stories should be looked upon as creations. In the creating and re-creating process, organizational members reveal the sense making of that organization. Members can be asked to create stories that embody the practices, aspirations, and climate of an organization. Stories can be analyzed by looking for dominant themes and patterns of thought.

We have already discussed the *metaphor* as a potent device in the construction of reality. The metaphor is certainly a way of thinking that is used so often that it operates at a low level of awareness. What is important is how metaphors shape thinking. As the reader has already discovered, the metaphors used to describe an organization can limit and direct what is possible to think about in regard to the organization. For example, if organizations are thought of as "garbage cans" or places where problems, people, situations of choice, and solutions are dumped (Cohen, March, & Olsen, 1972) rather than as "machines," a variety of behaviors can be considered. In addition, it must be remembered that from a subjective position, "rather than a person perceiving a world and then giving it an interpretation or meaning, perception is of an already meaningful (interpreted) world" (Koch & Deetz, 1981, p. 2). Metaphors, then, reflect the organizational world and operate as an inherent part of the thinking and behavior of members.

Metaphors are gathered by observing and recording members' talk. In addition to naturally occurring exchanges, the researcher can interview, set up group sessions, or ask members to write on topics that might generate metaphors. Organizational documents may also provide useful data. To analyze metaphors, the researcher should look for patterns and dominant themes.

Some Final Comments

In an earlier discussion of cultural analysis we pointed out that this type of study may tell *too much*. It is highly descriptive, and individuals may be identified by the specific language they use. This raises the issue of how cultural analysis should be conducted and presented. Even when presented in nonevaluative terms, such research can be threatening. Should an organization's culture be put on public display? This question raises more arguments than we can possibly deal with here. However, we would like to specify some of the conditions that lead to responsible research. The confidentiality of participants should be protected. Participants should be informed that they have the right to refuse observation or questioning. Final reports should be available to participants. The participant-observer process depends on trust, and the researcher should think very carefully about the impact of what is finally written. If someone is gracious enough to allow the researcher to enter a private world, the researcher has a responsibility to avoid destroying that world for the sake of a "good story."

Cultural analysis reports should take advantage of the nature of this type of research. Write for effect! If the interpretive analysis includes the dimension of "feeling," then the writer should not be tied to the format of a technical report. Much of the style of the report depends on the audience and its expectations. However, such reports ought to contain *thick description*. This means dialogue and description that provokes imagery. The *display* might take the form of dialogue, debate, a diary, novel, or short story. There are different ways of knowing, and these ways can be portrayed in a variety of formats.

FUNCTIONAL METHODS OF ANALYSIS

Methods of conducting a functional analysis of organizational communication are tied closely to what can be analyzed in an organization. Instruments and tools are currently available for analyzing many dimensions of organizational communication, and each year brings a new array of sensitive ways of identifying deficiencies in communication.

Figure 16.1 itemizes and describes some of the instruments and procedures used in making an analysis. We shall briefly define the features and explain some of the primary approaches.

Feature 1: Authority Structure

The first task in a functional systems analysis is to describe and portray the authority structure, duties, and responsibilities of the *communication units* in the

---

Step 1: Portray and describe the authority structure, duties, and responsibilities of *communication units*—people in positions.
a. Locate or create an organization chart, position descriptions, and operating procedures with accompanying manuals, directives, and instructions.
b. Complete an equipment and documents inventory.
c. Complete a linear responsibility chart for the unit under analysis.

Step 2: Describe the flow of information and the technology to facilitate it.
a. Make a diagram of the location of communication equipment and technology.
b. Create a flow chart of paper production.
c. Complete a log of mail procedures and processing.
d. Complete a personal contact record form for selected personnel.
e. Conduct a network analysis.

Step 3: Measure message fidelity and distortion in information flow.
a. Conduct a modified ECCO analysis focusing on the fidelity of messages using tests, unit analysis, or theme analysis.
b. Look at communication load scores and locate sources of overload and underload in the system.

Step 4: Measure information adequacy as related to downward communication.
a. Identify areas of key information and prepare an information adequacy test and administer to employees.
b. Prepare and administer a Bateman-type information adequacy inventory.

Step 5: Measure communication satisfaction.
a. Administer Downs and Hazen's Communication Satisfaction Questionnaire.
b. Interview employees about their satisfaction with communication.

Step 6: Measure communication climate.
a. Administer the Peterson-Pace Communication Climate Inventory.
b. Administer Siegel and Turney's Survey of Organizational Climate.
c. Complete a communication rules analysis.
d. Gather and analyze critical communication incidents.
e. Interview employees about the communication climate in the organization.

As an alternative to the use of individual instruments and procedures, consider administering the Organizational Communication Profile instrument to secure data on eight key features of communication in organizations.

FIGURE 16.1   Designing a Functional Organizational Communication Systems Analysis

organization. A communication unit is a person in a position. Some of the methods of analysis are described below.

Organization charts help portray how positions are classified and distributed to create the organization. *Position descriptions* describe how the functions are divided and delegated to individual units as duties, authority, and responsibilities. *Operating procedures* structure the individual duties into work flow patterns. *Directives, instructions, and manuals* represent how the communication system is designed to guide individuals in carrying out their duties.

Taken together, organization charts, position descriptions, operating procedures, and manuals of directives describe the structure and activity of an organization. They represent, however, a static picture of the organization as embodied in massive written statements. Nevertheless, the basic authority structure, the duties, and the responsibilities assigned to people in positions may be described in these written documents, and this is where a functional analysis of organizational communication begins.

A *linear responsibility chart* (LRC) is another way of creating a picture of the authority structure of an organization (Larke, 1954). *Factory* (March 1963) reported that the LRC is "being used in dozens of organizations to cut overhead costs, break bottlenecks, find training needs, spot responsibility gaps, even out work loads, uncover overlap and empire-building, clear up misunderstandings, weed out paper work not related to particular jobs, simplify control, and speed up decisions" ("Linear Responsibility Charting," 1963). In view of the vast array of potential problems revealed by the LRC, it can be a powerful tool for functional organizational communication analysis.

A linear responsibility chart is created by developing a matrix or grid with two axes. The horizontal axis (across the top) lists the positions in the unit being analyzed. The vertical axis (down the left-hand side) lists the functional responsibilities or work to be done. A system of symbols spells out who does what work, under whose supervision, and what kinds of relationships are involved. Figure 16.2 shows a completed LRC to illustrate the use of symbols for designating work procedures.

Number 1 means that the activity or function described is actually performed by the designated individual.

Number 2 means that the important aspects of planning, delegation, and control of the function described are handled daily, with the hour-by-hour direction of the designated individual.

Number 3 means that the individual has specific responsibility over the subordinate who carries out the work.

Number 4 means that the individual coordinates two or more individuals or groups who must work cooperatively on the same or similar activity and bring about a unified approach to the function.

Number 5 means that the individual is a specialist who must be approached for technical decisions affecting part of the overall problem; or delegation is extensive and questions are referred to the individual only occasionally. The decision of the individual marked number 5 must be followed.

Number 6 means that before a decision is made or an action taken, the individual indicated must be consulted. The individual's opinion must be heard, although his or her advice need not be followed.

Number 7 means that when someone makes a decision or takes an action, the

POSITIONS

DUTIES	Administrator	Assistant Administrator	Sales Training Specialist	Manufacturing Training Specialist	Clerical/Secretarial Training Specialist	Management Development Specialist	Program Design Specialist	Materials, Equipment, and Facilities Coordinator
Prepares T&D philosophy and policies	1	6						
Prepares department budget	2	1	6	6	6	6	8	8
Develops programs for secretarial/clerical personnel	2	3			3	3	5	6
Arranges for materials, equipment, and facilities		3						1
Edits written materials			4	4	4		1	
Conducts training	2			1	1	1		
Counsels employees on personal goals	1	4				1		
Produces audiovisual and video			2	2	2		4	
Schedules training programs	2	3	1	1	1	7		
Keeps records of financial transactions		2						
Develops course outlines, handouts, and exercises			6	6	6		1	
Evaluates training courses			2	2	2			

FIGURE 16.2   Linear Responsibility Chart

individual indicated must be informed. The assumption is that knowledge of the action or decision will assist the individual in carrying out his or her own responsibilities.

Number 8 means that there is no need to consult this person and that the person has no right of consultation, but it is normally done, likely to be done, or pertinent to do.

The LRC is begun by naming the function, program, set of relationships, particular group, unit, or organization to be analyzed. In the spaces across the top of the grid, the positions in the unit to be analyzed are entered, arranged from high to low levels or from broad to narrow authority. Down the left side of the grid, the types of work are listed, preferably in some logical sequence. The grid is completed by assigning a number to each block to indicate who does what, under whose supervision, and in what kinds of relationship to others. The LRC should graphically portray the entire unit being analyzed, including complex work flows, involved procedures, and potentially confusing responsibilities. The LRC will be a factual source of information about organization structure, job descriptions, and procedures when completed accurately.

Feature 2: Information Flow and Associated Technology

Information flow has to do with how information is distributed throughout an organization; it is the process of making information available to organization members and securing information from them. Specific patterns of information flow evolve out of regular contacts and routine ways of sending and receiving messages. Formal organizations exert control over the information flow process by designating authority and work relations, assignment of offices, and the creation of special communication functions. We will now describe the methods of analyzing the flow of information.

Documents and Equipment Inventory.   This method seems like a reasonable place to begin because it represents one of the most visible and conscious elements involved in information dissemination. In fact, an inventory of documents and equipment might even precede the graphic portrayal of the authority structure, because the documents inventoried may serve as sources of information for constructing the structure.

Paper Flow Diagram.   The flow of information often begins with the preparation of written materials. Figure 16.3 shows some typical trouble spots identified by a prominent manufacturer of duplicating equipment about how the flow of paperwork is handled in an office. A similar analysis of any office might identify problems in the flow of information.

Mail Log.   One frequent source of difficulty in the flow of information involves the processing of mail. A mail log form describes both incoming and outgoing mail, listing the sender and the receiver of a piece of mail, the general content of the correspondence, the disposition and type of reply, and the time lapse between receipt and reply. The mail log is usually maintained by an individual assigned to sort and distribute the mail. Each item is logged in a central location as it is delivered to the organization or just prior to being picked up by the mail service.

Personal Contact Record Form.   Much of the information flow in an organization is accomplished through personal contacts. Two methods of recording contacts are used: (1) Diary completed by the person who engages in the contact, and (2) A *shadow* who is a person who follows an employee at a short distance and maintains the record but who checks periodically with the employee on the accuracy

How many paperflow troublespots can you spot?

No, this isn't a game for time-study men. It's an exercise for top management. A walk around the office like you've never taken before.

Start where the mail comes in. Ever wonder why it's late to your desk? Or ripped? Or minus a return address? Is your mail opened by hand?①

Ever get a copy of a report that has two page 2's? Or, worse yet, none? Peek into the conference room. Chances are, you'll see hands gathering sheets of paper into sets.②

Walk by your office. Secretary missing again?③ She's probably been "volunteered" for another folding and inserting session.④

Stop by the mailroom on your way home. Can your mailing equipment handle the billing that's got to get out tonight?⑤ Do your hand-typed invoices look businesslike? Is every name and address correct?⑥

Why take this walk? Simply this. Since paper represents the written record of your business, your business can travel only as fast as the paper can flow in, through and out of your office.

FIGURE 16.3   Paper Flow Diagram (Reprinted with permission of Pitney Bowes.)

of the record. The shadow should be as unobtrusive as possible, but close enough to make an accurate record.

A simple personal contact record form is divided into five parts: direction of contact, form of contact, authority relationship of those involved in the contact, content of the information, and length of contact. This form records only personal contacts; a separate record may be kept of formal written materials handled by the mails.

ICA-Type Network Analysis Record Form.   This form is used to gather data to show relationships among organization members in terms of who gives information to whom. Figure 16.4 shows a sample form. It consists of spaces for subjects to recall and record the names of the individuals they contact for each category of information and the general way in which the contact is made (telephone, face-to-face, written). The form and procedures allow the names and work locations of all organization members to be preprinted on the form. Each organization member simply scans the list of employees, checks off the names of people with whom he or she makes contact, and completes the form. The recall method may result in fewer names being identified than may the roster method, but in large organizations the roster is impractical and employees may not complete them because of the time it would require.

In this case, the instructions for completing the network analysis form ask each person to recall the names of those persons contacted during a specific period for each type of information. Each subject is asked to write the number of contacts that took place with each person identified for each form or medium of communication.

ECCO-Type Survey of Information Flow.   ECCO is an acronym for Episodic Communication Channels in Organizations (Davis, 1953). This method gathers information about the flow of messages by means of a questionnaire given to employees at each level in the organization; preferably, all employees should receive questionnaires.

As employees arrive at work, they are handed a set of four or five envelopes containing questionnaires. Each envelope has a time-of-day record on the outside indicating when the employee should open it and complete the questionnaire. Upon

During the Past Week (June 16–June 20)

Personnel	Work Location	I received information directly related to doing my job from the following people:			I talked about matters not directly related to doing my job with the following people:		
		Face-to-Face	Telephone	Written	Face-to-Face	Telephone	Written

FIGURE 16.4   Sample ICA-Type Network Analysis Record Form

completion, which should take no longer than three to four minutes, the question-naires are returned to the envelopes and placed where they can be picked up by the analyst.

Flow Diagram.   The flow of information can be portrayed by a sociometric diagram consisting of circles representing employees with lines connecting em-ployees who receive information from and tell information to one another. Em-ployees are coded for anonymity by using the first letter of the person's last name (C) and the last four digits of the person's telephone number (8723). Figure 16.5 illustrates an information flow diagram.

Feature 3: Message Fidelity and Distortion

As information is disseminated in an organization, the content is often trans-formed by omissions, additions, and other changes (Guetzkow, 1965) that result in the distortion of information. Part of the analysis of organizational communication involves determining whether information is being distorted and, if so, what kinds of distortions may be occurring during the information dissemination process. The methods of analysis include the following.

Listing Bits of Information.   Employees can be asked to list the information they know about a message. The list can then be compared against a previously prepared list of the information actually contained in the message.

Administer True-False Test.   A short true-false test over bits of information in the original message can be constructed and administered to employees.

Administer Multiple Choice Test.   Experts estimate that a good test writer, thoroughly familiar with the subject, ought to be able to write ten multiple-choice test items in an eight-hour day, but that possibly two of the ten items will end up being good measures. The other eight items will be good ideas, but they will be too difficult, too easy, or will not discriminate among test takers.

A good test will *not* try to trick the test taker into selecting a wrong answer; neither will the choices make it easy to guess the correct answer. Thus, all possible clues, tricky wording, and unnecessary information should be removed from the test items.

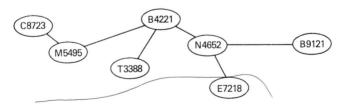

FIGURE 16.5 Hypothetical Information Flow Diagram

Conduct an Information Unit Analysis.   An IUA consists of comparing each word or series of words in a reproduced message with comparable words or phrases in the original message. Give one point for each information unit, even if it is slightly altered in tense or by substitution of synonyms. Score one-half point for each information unit that is significantly altered yet retains the sense of the original. Give zero points for errors, distortions, and units of information with no correspondence to the original message. Sum the scores for each reproduction, and determine the amount of information reproduced accurately.

Conduct a Theme Analysis.   Theme analysis consists of making a list of themes in the original message, phrasing each theme as a question, and scoring one point for each theme present in a reproduction of the original message, regardless of the accuracy of the details (Pace, Peterson, & Boren, 1975). An example of a theme question might be: ''Was anything about complaints of slow or overcrowded serving lines mentioned?''

Feature 4: Information Adequacy

The adequacy of information that an employee receives from higher levels in the organization may be analyzed in two ways: (1) through an employee's estimate of the adequacy of the information, or (2) through a test of what an employee actually knows about certain topics (Bateman, 1979). Perceptual measurements or estimates may be standardized, at least somewhat; however, tests must be developed individually for each organization (Stead, 1983). Excerpts from Bateman's survey are included in Figure 16.6.

ICA Survey.   The survey instrument developed for the International Communication Association (ICA) Audit Project measures perceptions of information adequacy by responses to two basic assertions: (1) ''This is the amount of information I receive now,'' and (2) ''This is the amount of information I want to receive.'' If organization members indicate that the amount of information they receive about pay and benefits, for example, is about the same as the amount they want to receive,

Among the following fringe benefits, policies and practices, please indicate your understanding of the item by circling the appropriate number:

1 = no understanding
2 = slight understanding
3 = average understanding
4 = good understanding
5 = excellent understanding

a. My health (hospital) insurance   1 2 3 4 5

b. My life insurance coverage   1 2 3 4 5

FIGURE 16.6   Bateman's Information Adequacy Survey (Source: From David A. Bateman, ''Measuring Communication Effectiveness,'' Paper presented at the annual convention of the American Business Communication Association, Seattle, Washington, December 1979.)

we can conclude that information is adequate, regardless of what organization members actually know about pay and benefits.

LTT Questionnaire.   The questionnaire developed by Wiio (1976) to audit organizational communication also measures information adequacy. Organization members are asked to indicate answers to three questions: (1) "How much information do you get about the organization from . . . ?" (2) "How much information do you get about your own work from . . . ?" and (3) "What kinds of information do you get enough of?"

Feature 5: Communication Satisfaction

In contrast to information adequacy, communication satisfaction is concerned with how employees feel about the information they get and from whom they get it, regardless of the amount of information received.

Communication Satisfaction Questionnaire.   Downs and Hazen (1977) developed the most extensive measure of organizational communication satisfaction available. The four parts of the CS Questionnaire ask about employee satisfaction with (1) the amount or quality of information, (2) sources of information, (3) communication activities, and (4) estimates of productivity patterns. Figure 16.7 includes an excerpt from Downs and Hazen's questionnaire.

Feature 6: Organizational Communication Climate

The communication climate of an organization consists of perceptions, attitudes, and expectations of organization members that indicate to them that levels of trust, supportiveness, openness, candor, participative decision making, and concern for high performance goals exist in the organization.

Organizational Communication Climate Inventory.   One of the most direct measures of organizational communication climate is Peterson and Pace's Communication Climate Inventory (Pace & Peterson, 1979). The inventory consists of twelve items that measure six aspects of communication climate. Figure 16.8 contains the CCI.

A. Listed below are several kinds of information often associated with a person's job. Please indicate how satisfied you are with the *amount* and/or *quality* of each kind of information by circling the appropriate number at the right.

4. Information about my progress in my job.   1 2 3 4 5 6 7

5. Personnel news.   1 2 3 4 5 6 7

6. Information about company policies and goals.   1 2 3 4 5 6 7

FIGURE 16.7 Excerpt from Downs and Hazen's Communication Satisfaction Questionnaire (Source: From Cal W. Downs and Michael D. Hazen, "A Factor Analytic Study of Communication Satisfaction," *The Journal of Business Communication,* 14 (1977), 63–73. Used by permission of C. W. Downs and M. D. Hazen.)

COMMUNICATION CLIMATE INVENTORY

Brent D. Peterson and R. Wayne Pace

Please respond to *all questions* as honestly and frankly as you possibly can.

In *no way* will your identity be associated with your responses nor will your responses be used in such a manner as to jeopardize you or your job.

Unless the working of a particular item specifically indicates otherwise, respond in terms of your own impressions of the entire organization in which you work.

Indicate your response to each item by *circling just one of the five numbers* in the right-hand column. *Please do not omit any item!* Use the following code to interpret the meaning of the numerical symbols:

5—Circle this number if, in your honest judgment, the item is a true description of conditions in the organization.

4—Circle if the item is more true than false as a description of conditions in the organization.

3—Circle if the item is about half true and half false as a description of conditions in the organization.

2—Circle if the item is more false than true as a description of conditions in the organization.

1—Circle if the item is a false description of conditions in the organization.

Please, do not attempt an intensive "word analysis" of the questions. And—of course—your responses should reflect your own judgments, not those of other people. There are no right or wrong answers.

Answer all questions in terms of your impressions concerning your own organization!

1. Personnel at all levels in the organization have a commitment to high performance goals (high productivity, high quality, low cost).   5 4 3 2 1 (1)

2. Superiors seem to have a great deal of confidence and trust in their subordinates.   5 4 3 2 1 (2)

3. Personnel at all levels in the organization are communicated to and consulted with concerning organizational policy relevant to their positions.   5 4 3 2 1 (3)

4. Subordinates seem to have a great deal of confidence and trust in their superiors   5 4 3 2 1 (4)

5. Information received from subordinates is perceived by superiors as important enough to be acted upon until demonstrated otherwise.   5 4 3 2 1 (5)

6. All personnel receive information that enhances their abilities to coordinate their work with that of other personnel or departments and that deals broadly with the company, its organization, leaders, and plans.   5 4 3 2 1 (6)

7. A general atmosphere of candor and frankness seems to pervade relationships between personnel throughout all levels of the organization.   5 4 3 2 1 (7)

(continued)

FIGURE 16.8 Communication Climate Inventory (Reprinted with permission of Organizational Associates.)

8. There are avenues of communication available for all personnel to consult with management levels above their own in decision-making and goal-setting processes.   5 4 3 2 1 (8)

9. All personnel are able to say "what's on their minds" regardless of whether they are talking to subordinates or superiors.   5 4 3 2 1 (9)

10. Except for necessary security information, all personnel have relatively easy access to information that relates directly to their immediate jobs.   5 4 3 2 1 (10)

11. A high concern for the well-being of all personnel is as important to management as high performance goals.   5 4 3 2 1 (11)

12. Superiors at all levels in the organization listen continuously and with open minds to suggestions or reports of problems made by personnel at all subordinate levels in the organization.   5 4 3 2 1 (12)

Scoring and Analysis

1. *Trust Climate Score*—Sum numbers 2 and 4 on each inventory and divide by two. This is an individual score. To get a composite Trust Climate Score sum all the inventories and divide by the total number of respondents.

2. *Participative Decision Making Climate Score*—Sum numbers 3 and 8 on each inventory and divide by two. This is an individual score. To get a composite Participative Decision Making Climate Score, add all the inventories and divide by the total number of respondents.

3. *Supportiveness Climate Score*—Sum numbers 7 and 9 and divide by two. This is an individual score. To get a composite Supportiveness Climate Score sum all the inventories and divide by the total number of respondents.

4. *Openness in Downward Communication Climate Score*—Sum numbers 6 and 10 on each inventory and divide by two. This is an individual score. To get a composite Openness in Downward Communication Climate Score sum all the inventories and divide by the number of respondents.

5. *Listening in Upward Communication Climate Score*—Sum numbers 5 and 12 on each inventory and divide by two. This is an individual score. To get a composite Listening in Upward Communication Climate Score sum all the inventories and divide by the number of respondents.

6. *Concern for High Performance Goals Climate Score*—Sum numbers 1 and 11 on each inventory and divide by two. This is an individual score. To get a composite Concern for High Performance Goals Climate Score sum all the inventories and divide by the number of respondents.

7. *Composite Climate Score*—Sum the individual responses to all twelve items and divide by twelve. This general average gives an Individual Composite Climate Score (ICCS) for each respondent. For the Organization Composite Climate Score (OCCS) sum all ICCCs and divide by the total number of respondents.

FIGURE 16.8 *continued*

Survey of Organizational Climate. The SOC was developed in the U.S. Office of Personnel Management as a "general diagnostic perception and attitude questionnaire for use in organizations with diverse functions and organizational structures" (p. 1). It measures six broad categories of characteristics, including organizational communications (authority, trust, conflict, and change orientation), and supervisory, group, individual, job, and work outcomes.

Consistent with our concept of analysis and its use, Siegel and Turney (1980) explain in the *Manager's Guide* that the survey is "best viewed as a tool to be used by managers . . . to confirm his/her suspicions that 'something is wrong'; to add substance to those undefined perceptions" (p. 12).

Communication Rules Analysis. Communication rules are the expectations of organization members that influence how they interact in superior-subordinate dyads. Farace, Monge, and Russell (1977) indicate that the first step in a rules analysis is to identify each person's immediate supervisor and the supervisor's subordinates; hence, the "initial task is to generate a hierarchical list . . . of manager-subordinate relationships in which each person is clearly and unambiguously placed in the overall hierarchy" (p. 215).

The next step in the analysis is to define the topics covered by communication rules. Although the rules may differ from situation to situation, questions covering thirteen different topics are typical (Johnson, 1977, pp. 388–389). An excerpt from a usual rules questionnaire is included in Figure 16.9.

A rules questionnaire often asks employees to indicate their level of satisfaction with the manner in which certain relationships are managed. The questionnaire asks for how the employee perceives the way in which communication rules are used, and it also asks how the employee thinks the superior (or subordinate) perceives those same rules.

With information from both parties about their own perceptions and how they think the other person feels about each of the rules, a measure of agreement and

---

Indicate your impressions of how you conduct "talk" with your supervisor. In the space on the right side, indicate your guess about how your supervisor would answer the question.

My perception: Supervisor would probably say:

_____   3.   When two people get together, one of them   3. _____
has to decide what they'll talk about.
Generally, when you and your immediate
supervisor talk, who usually decides on the
topics to be discussed?
A. He usually decides.
B. I usually decide.
C. It's split about evenly between us.

_____   3a. How satisfied are you with this arrangement?   3a. _____
A. I'd like more to say about what we talk
about.
B. I'm satisfied.

FIGURE 16.9   Analysis of Communication Rules

Step 1. *Feasibility Visit:* Analysts make organization on-site feasibility visit to determine whether doing the analysis is possible.

Step 2. *Initial Meeting:* Meet with all unit personnel to preview philosophy, assumptions, expectations, and procedures associated with the analysis.

Step 3. *Administer Profile:* Administer the Organizational Communication Profile (Peterson-Pace) instrument to all personnel in the unit being studied to secure data on key features and variables.

Step 4. *In-depth Data on Variables:* Explore key features and variables on OCP using interviews, observations, and other procedures and instruments.

Step 5. *Complementary Units Data:* Gather data from complementary units, the public or community, and related groups concerning perceptions of organizational effectiveness and communication practices of organization members. Structured interviews and simple measuring instruments are used where appropriate.

Step 6. *Comparison of Data:* Compare organization profile data (Step 3), in-depth data (Step 4), and complementary units data (Step 5) to locate points of similarity and difference.

Step 7. *Data Sharing Meeting:* Meet with all unit personnel and selected invited guests to review preliminary data on item-by-item basis to identify, examine, elaborate, and delete problem areas.

Step 8. *Interim Report:* Write preliminary report and distribute it to all unit personnel and, if desired, to invited participants.

Step 9. *Form Task Groups:* Create and organize task groups consisting of unit personnel and, if desired, invited participants, for purpose of evaluating preliminary report.

Step 10. *Task Group Evaluations:* Task groups meet and review preliminary report in terms of personal meaning for them. Groups identify and enumerate problems and provide tentative alternative ways for taking corrective action. Task groups prepare their own reports.

Step 11. *General Meeting:* All task groups meet to share their reports with one another. Selected task members, usually elected by groups, are assigned to merge group reports and prepare a single, unified document.

Step 12. *Analyst's Final Report:* Using their own preliminary report, the final report of task groups, and other data, analysts prepare final report and list of specific recommendations.

Step 13. *Final Report Meeting:* All unit personnel, invited guests, and analysts meet for purpose of having unit administrators and managers respond to reports of task groups and analysts and to discuss how to proceed after report.

Step 14. *Turnover Meeting:* Analysts meet with administrative staff to review procedures for organization members to assume full responsibility for continuing analysis and implementation of recommendations on long-range basis.

FIGURE 16.10 Pace-Peterson Organizational Communication Systems Analysis. (Reprinted with permission of Organizational Associates.)

similarity of perception is secured. Questionnaire responses also indicate how well one member of the dyad knows the other. The degree to which the superior predicts what the subordinate will say measures the accuracy of the superior's views of the overall communication relationship.

Critical Incidents. A critical incident report describes an event that illustrates behaviors that are critical to the success or failure of a particular task. Critical incidents represent either very effective or very ineffective ways of doing things.

The critical communication incident approach involves having employees describe specific experiences involving communication with others in the organization that have been very effective or very ineffective in getting information across. An incident is acceptable if, in the employee's opinion, it relates to an important aspect of the job and describes behavior that is very effective or ineffective communication.

Each incident should be presented as a miniature case and report the specific behaviors and actions involved; should be recent enough to be remembered easily; should be reported by a person in a position to observe what happened; and should be consistent, clear, and reasonably complete or self-contained.

The incidents are analyzed by identifying and underlining the statements that describe the critical behaviors. The critical elements are recorded in a list and studied for categories of problems and strengths. Descriptive titles are assigned to the categories. The procedures are similar to the theme analysis method mentioned earlier.

Six features of organizational communication have been identified along with selected instruments, tools, and procedures for analyzing the features. Procedures for conducting an organizational communication systems analysis have been described in some detail over the years (see Goldhaber, 1976). However, R. Wayne Pace and Brent D. Peterson, doing business as Organizational Associates, outlined specific procedures in the early 1970s for analyzing organizational communication that have been used extensively (Goldhaber et al., 1979, p. 325; Goldhaber, 1986, p. 382). Figure 16.10 summarizes the steps in the Pace-Peterson process and shows where instruments described above might be used to advantage.

SUMMARY

This chapter has examined ways to analyze an organizational communication system from two perspectives: an interpretive approach using naturalistic methods and a functional approach using empirical methods. Specific techniques, instruments, and procedures were discussed.

REFERENCES

Bantz, Charles R., "Interpreting Organizational Cultures: A Proposed Procedure, Criteria for Evaluation, and Consideration of Research Methods," Paper presented at the SCA/ICA Summer Conference on Interpretive Approaches to the Study of Organizational Communication, Alta, Utah, 1981.

Bantz, Charles R., "Naturalistic Research Traditions," in *Communication and Organizations: An Interpretive Approach,* Linda L. Putnam and Michael E. Pacanowsky, eds. Beverly Hills, Calif.: Sage, 1983.

Bantz, Charles R., "Understanding Organizations: Analyzing Organizational Communication Cultures," Paper presented at the University of Utah Summer Conference on Interpretive Approaches to the Study of Organizational Communication, Alta, Utah, 1987.

Bateman, David A., "Measuring Communication Effectiveness," Paper presented at the annual convention of the American Business Communication Association, Seattle, Washington, December 1979.

Bormann, Ernest G., "Fantasy and Rhetorical Vision: The Rhetorical Criticism of Social Reality," *Quarterly Journal of Speech,* 58 (1972), 396–407.

Bormann, Ernest G., "Symbolic Convergence: Organizational Communication and Culture," in *Communication and Organizations: An Interpretive Approach,* Linda L. Putnam and Michael E. Pacanowsky, eds. Beverly Hills, Calif.: Sage, 1983.

Brown, Mary Helen, "That Reminds Me of a Story: Speech Action in Organizational Socialization," *Western Journal of Speech Communication,* 49 (Winter 1985), 27–42.

Brunvard, Jan H., "Heard About the Solid Cement Cadillac or the Nude in the Camper?" *Psychology Today,* 14 (1980), 50–62.

Buckholdt, D. R., and J. F. Gubrium, "Practicing Accountability in Human Service Institutions," *Urban Life,* 12 (1983), 249–268.

Buttny, Richard, "Accounts as a Reconstruction of an Event's Context," *Communication Monographs,* 52 (March 1985), 57–75.

Cheney, George, "On the Various and Changing Meanings of Organizational Membership: A Field Study of Organizational Identification," *Communication Monographs,* 50 (December 1983), 342–362.

Cohen, M. D., J. G. March, and J. P. Olsen, "A Garbage Can Model of Organizational Choice," *Administrative Science Quarterly,* 17 (1972), 1–25.

Dandridge, Thomas, Ian Mitroff, and William Joyce, "Organizational Symbolism: A Topic to Expand Organizational Analysis," *Academy of Management Review,* 5 (1980), 77–82.

Davis, Keith, "A Method of Studying Communication Patterns in Organizations," *Personnel Psychology* 6, (1953), 301–312.

Deal, Terrence E., and Allan A. Kennedy, *Corporate Cultures: The Rites and Rituals of Corporate Life.* Reading, Mass.: Addison-Wesley, 1982.

Downs, Cal W., and Michael D. Hazen, "A Factor Analytic Study of Communication Satisfaction," *The Journal of Business Communication,* 14 (1977), 63–73.

Farace, Richard V., Peter R. Monge, and Hamish N. Russell, *Communicating and Organizing.* Reading, Mass.: Addison-Wesley 1977.

Faules, Don F., and G. Lloyd Drecksel, "Organizational Cultures Reflected in a Comparison of Work Justifications Across Work Groups," Paper presented at the University of Utah Summer Conference on Interpretive Approaches to the Study of Organizational Communication, Alta, Utah, 1986.

Faules, Don, "The Use of Multi-Methods in the Organizational Setting," *Western Journal of Speech Communication,* 46 (Spring 1982), 150–161.

Goldhaber, Gerald M., "The ICA Communication Audit: Rationale and Development," Paper presented at the Academy of Management Convention, Kansas City, August 1976.

Goldhaber, Gerald M., Harry S. Dennis, III, Gary M. Richetto, and Osmo A. Wiio, *Information Strategies.* Englewood Cliffs, N.J.: Prentice-Hall, Inc., 1979.

Goldhaber, Gerald M., *Organizational Communication,* 4th ed. Dubuque, Iowa: Wm. C. Brown, 1986.

Guetzkow, Harold, "Communication in Organizations," in *Handbook of Organizations,* J. G. March, ed. Chicago: Rand McNally, 1965, 534–573.

Johnson, Bonnie McDaniel, *Communication: The Process of Organizing.* Boston: Allyn and Bacon, Inc., 1977.

Koch, Susan, and Stanley Deetz, "Metaphor Analysis of Social Reality in Organizations," Paper presented at the SCA/ICA Summer Conference on Interpretive Approaches to the Study of Organizational Communication, Alta, Utah, 1981.

Larke, Alfred G., "Linear Responsibility Chart—New Tool for Executive Control," *Dun's Review and Modern Industry* (September 1954).

"Linear Responsibility Charting: Fast Way to Clear up Confusion," *Factory* (March 1963).

Louis, Meryl Reis, "A Cultural Perspective on Organizations: The Need For and Consequences of Viewing Organizations as Culture-Bearing Milieux," *Human Systems Management,* 2 (1981), 246–258.

Louis, Meryl Reis, "An Investigator's Guide to Workplace Culture," in *Organizational Culture,* Peter J. Frost et al., eds. Beverly Hills, Calif.: Sage, 1985.

Lundberg, Craig C., "On the Feasibility of Cultural Intervention in Organizations," in *Organizational Culture,* Peter J. Frost et al., eds. Beverly Hills, Calif.: Sage, 1985.

Martin, Joanne, "Stories and Scripts in Organizational Settings," in *Cognitive Social Psychology,* A. Hastorf and I. Isen, eds. New York: Elsevier-North Holland, 1982.

Mitroff, Ivan I., and Ralph H. Kilmann, "Stories Managers Tell: A New Tool for Organizational Problem Solving," *Management Review,* 64 (1975), 19–20.

Pacanowsky, Michael E., and Nick O'Donnell-Trujillo, "Communication and Organizational Cultures," *Western Journal of Speech Communication,* 46 (Spring 1982), 115–130.

Pacanowsky, Michael E., and Nick O'Donnell-Trujillo, "Organizational Communication as Cultural Performance," *Communication Monographs,* 50 (June 1983), 126–147.

Pace, R. Wayne, and Brent D. Peterson, "Measuring Organizational Communication Climate," Unpublished paper, Brigham Young University, 1979.

Pace, R. Wayne, Brent D. Peterson, and Robert R. Boren, *Communication Experiments: A Manual for Conducting Experiments.* Belmont, Calif.: Wadsworth Publishing Company, 1975, 171–188.

Roy, Donald, "Banana Time: Job Satisfaction and Informal Interaction," *Human Organization,* 18 (1960), 158–168.

Scott, M. B., and S. M. Lyman, "Accounts," *American Sociological Review,* 33 (1968), 46–62.

Siegel, Alan L., and John R. Turney, *Manager's Guide to Using the Survey of Organizational Climate* (Washington, D.C.: Superintendent of Documents, November 1980).

Smircich, Linda, "Is the Concept of Culture a Paradigm For Understanding Organizations and Ourselves?" in *Organizational Culture,* Peter J. Frost et al., eds. Beverly Hills, Calif.: Sage, 1985.

Smith, David H., "The Master Symbol as a Key to Understanding Organizational Communication," Unpublished and undated paper.

Stead, James A., "The Relationship of Information Adequacy/Confidence to Job Satisfaction Among Credit Union Employees," Master's thesis, Brigham Young University, 1983.

Strine, Mary S., and Michael E. Pacanowsky, "How to Read Interpretive Accounts of Organizational Life: Narrative Bosses of Textural Authority," *The Southern Speech Communication Journal,* 50 (Spring 1985), 283–297.

Sykes, A. J., "Myths in Communication," *Journal of Communication,* 20 (1970), 17–31.

Tompkins, Phillip K., and George Cheney, "Account Analysis of Organizations: Decision Making and Identification," in *Communication and Organizations: An Interpretive*

Approach, Linda C. Putnam and Michael Pacanowsky, eds. Beverly Hills, Calif.: Sage, 1983.

Wiio, Osmo A., "Organizational Communication: Interfacing Systems in Different Contingencies," Paper presented at the Annual Conference of the International Communication Association, Portland, Oregon, April 1976.

Wilkins, Alan, "Organizational Stories as an Expression of Management Philosophy: Implications for Social Control in Organizations," Unpublished doctoral dissertation, Stanford University, Stanford, Calif., 1978.

17

Five Theories of Change

A strategy is a method, plan, or activity used to accomplish a specific goal. In the field of organizational communication, strategies are usually selected after an analysis of the human resources and organizational processes has been completed. Strategies are usually more effective if they are based on solid analyses.

Each strategy for improving human resources and organizational systems is grounded in some philosophical, ideological, or theoretical approach to change. Some authors refer to these approaches as theories of behavior modification (Bandura, 1969), but we prefer to call them *theories of change*. We shall briefly review five theories of change and describe some of the methods and procedures associated with each one.

RATIONAL THEORY

An approach to change based on rational theory begins with the assumption that *what we believe determines how we behave*. Beliefs are those statements we make to ourselves and others that represent what we accept as true. Rational theory suggests that what we accept as true determines the strategies we select and use to perform tasks and to deal with others. For example, if you believe, as a supervisor, that you can influence an employee to work harder if you are direct, you will tend to speak more directly to employees and act in more direct ways toward employees. As a supervisor, you will communicate more directly if you believe that directness is more effective.

From the perspective of rational theory, a program to change the behavior of an employee should focus on changing beliefs. The change in beliefs would then affect how the employee behaves. The old adage ''a person convinced against his will is of the same opinion still'' reflects the philosophy of rational training. Without a change in beliefs, a person will continue to follow old patterns of behavior or revert back to them at the earliest opportunity.

In discussing the training of professional workers, Combs, Avila, and Purkey (1971) argue that they should be provided with ''opportunities for discovering personal meanings'' (p. 9), which are the guides for day-to-day behaviors they will use in carrying out their professional duties. *Personal meanings* are the images that one holds about people, events, and objects. Personal meanings are expressed in the ways we talk about things.

Craighead, Kazdin, and Mahoney (1976) note that ''individuals respond to language in the form of instructions, commands, and rules that govern behavior. However, there are more subtle means, such as in self-verbalizations, through which language influences behavior'' (p. 145). A rational approach to change builds on the powerful impact that beliefs, personal meanings, language, and self-verbalizations have on behavior.

The foundational premise of rational-emotive training (RET), one rational approach, is expressed by Ellis and Harper (1975) as follows:

> Unlike lower animals, people tell themselves various sane and crazy things. Their beliefs, attitudes, opinions, and philosophies largely . . . take the form of internalized sentences of self-talk. Consequently, one of the most powerful and elegant modalities they can use to change themselves . . . consists of their clearly seeing, understanding, disputing, altering, and acting against their internal verbalizations.'' (p. x)

Rational theory assumes that problems result from irrational thinking and verbalizing; thus, the emphasis is on the cultivation of rationality. In this context, rational thinking means that our beliefs and verbalizations accurately represent reality and that our actions are consistent with our beliefs and verbalizations. Irrationality, in contrast, occurs when our beliefs and verbalizations do not match reality and our actions are inconsistent with our beliefs.

Rational theory argues that individual change is facilitated by presenting problems in which one's perceptions, beliefs, and personal meanings of reality are tested for accuracy by comparing them with external sources. Rationality is cultivated by confronting so-called irrational concerns and by implementing specific ways of thinking and talking about them.

Rational-emotive training has been called a form of *semantic therapy*. Ellis and Harper (1975) acknowledge that they may have developed a way of applying the teachings of general semantics, which Bois (1978) says ''deals with the meaning we find or put in whatever we do and whatever happens to us'' (pp. 43–44). Rational theory deals directly with the verbal communicative aspects of behavior and is belief-oriented. Even our desires and emotions have deep biological and social foundations that are directly related to our thinking processes and are, consequently, also largely under our control when approached as personal meanings and beliefs.

The work of Spice (1982) on *thought selection* is typical of those attempting to apply rational theory. She observes that "thought selection, self-suggestion, belief development, affirmation, self-talk, internal dialogue, and possibility thinking are all phrases alluding to the notion that what we say to ourselves about ourselves at a conscious or subconscious level affects our results." The formula, she says, is a simple: "knowledge + congruent beliefs = action . . . knowledge + negating beliefs = 'good intentions' (and often guilt)" (p. 58).

Chamberlain's book (1978) on self-defeating behaviors (SDB's) illustrates how to develop a program for change based on rational theory. He identifies seven steps through which a person moves to change behavior.

1. *Identify a behavior (a way of responding, reacting, or acting) that is keeping you from accomplishing some goal.* If you are not able to recognize a behavior that is a hindrance to a more complete and satisfying life, read down the following list and select one or more that seem to fit you:

Feelings of inferiority
Attitude of superiority
Lack of motivation
Procrastination
Compulsive lying
Uncontrollable temper
Excessive worry
Feelings of loneliness
Inability to say "no"
Wasting time
Forgetfulness
Fear of commitment
Extreme nervousness
Feeling inadequate

Choose only one behavior to focus on at a time. Choose a behavior that you would like to change and that causes problems not only for you but for others also. Write down the behavior you would like to change. Finally, describe *how you do the behavior you want to change.* For example, if you wrote, "withdrawing under pressure" as the behavior, you should describe what you do to withdraw under pressure, how you withdraw, etc.

2. *Accept responsibility for the behavior.* Part of the process of eliminating behaviors that hinder you is to accept responsibility for them. We often disown our behavior by *labeling ourselves,* which shifts responsibility for the behavior to our heredity. Labels indicate that we *are* something. To be something indicates that we have an inherited condition. Identify a label that represents the behavior that is to be changed. It should be a negative label, such as "I am a withdrawer."

Change the label to give a more positive connotation by changing the label from a state of existence to some action. Thus, in the withdrawing example, the label might read, "I do withdrawing" rather than "I am a withdrawer." In some cases it is necessary to change the negative label to the exact opposite, such as "I stay involved," in order to give the positive connotation.

Another way to shift responsibility is to blame other people for the behaviors that hinder us. "My mother made me do it," "I can't control my feelings," and "My family hurt me" are statements that shift responsibility. Your task is to write about the behavior so as to accept responsibility for it. Thus, rewrite how you do the behaviors by inserting terms of personal responsibility such as "I choose to withdraw."

3. *Identify the short- and long-range prices paid for the hindering behavior.* Some prices we pay for behaviors include the following: not being fully happy, feelings of depression, poor relationships, lack of energy, shame, and loss of control. Make a list of all the prices you pay for the hindering behavior. Continue listing until the price is too high to accept. Now, list ways that you minimize the prices. For example, "I joke about the prices," "I conclude that I was destined to be that way," "I ignore that I am being hurt," "I feel that the bad behavior can't be helped," or "I keep busy and occupied so as to avoid the price."

4. *Recognize that you can make inner choices.* All of our outer choices are based on some inner, deeply felt values and priorities. To gain control over our behavior, we need to control the inner choices that lead to behaviors. The inner choices or beliefs are with you all the time. It may appear to you that behaviors are activated automatically, but the inner choices are often made in a split second and you may find it difficult to catch yourself making the choices or to recognize the choices you actually make. You need to realize that you do make inner choices based on values or beliefs in order to activate external behaviors. You decide to carry out the inner choices in a series of outer movements and behaviors. Work through these seven phases:

a. List some inner choices that help you maintain the behavior you want to eliminate.
b. Catch yourself making an inner choice and become aware of the behavior that follows from it.
c. Practice making other choices.
d. Monitor yourself and catch yourself making choices, then consciously make alternative self-enhancing choices.
e. Get ahead of your own game; lessen the time between making a choice and your recognition of having made the choice.
f. If you suffer a relapse, learn from it.
g. Experience alternative choices in advance by closing your eyes and visualizing or imagining yourself responding in your best, controlled self.

5. *Recognize the techniques that are used to activate hindering behaviors.* Techniques such as getting discouraged, comparing yourself with others, and behaving in an impatient manner are used to activate hindering behaviors.

6. *Face the fears you may have of being without the hindering behavior.* Fears

are a form of belief. "I will fail" represents a fear that encourages hindering behaviors. Recognize that you will have fears if you change your behavior. For example, you may fear that you will find out that "I am a person I don't like," or "I am dumb and incompetent after all." These are statements that most of us fear, even though they may be untrue.

7. *Face your fears by testing them against reality.* Let go of the hindering behavior and see what happens.

BEHAVIORAL THEORY

Behavioral theory is firmly rooted in the assumption that changes in the way people behave can be produced more efficiently by focusing on observable behaviors than by focusing on beliefs and ways of thinking, as rational theory suggests. In fact, both attitudes and internal thought processes are understood by observing and measuring overt behavior. This is not to say that behaviors are unaffected by internal processes and thinking; it simply means that *observable behaviors* are the focus of attention. The behavioral philosophy also assumes that changes in behaviors typically produce corresponding changes in thoughts and attitudes. Bartlett (1967) argued that "it is easier to change behavior than attitudes! Why launch a direct onslaught upon the latter when they will follow if the former is changed?" (p. 39).

The basic premise underlying the behavioral approach to training and development is that behavior occurs as a consequence of reinforcement—any event that rewards the behavior immediately preceding it. Williams and Long (1975) apply the principles of behaviorism in a program for developing self-management and argue that "effective self-management primarily involves the rearrangement of behavioral consequences so that desired behavior is *immediately* reinforced" (p. 22).

Three Behavioral Strategies

Three general strategies represent the applications of behaviorism in training and development: (1) structuring contingencies, (2) simulations, and (3) modeling.

STRUCTURING CONTINGENCIES

Contingencies are consequences that positively reinforce desirable behaviors or punish undesirable behaviors. Contingencies may be a natural part of the work environment, such as assignments to work shifts, use of old versus new equipment, reporting procedures, arrangements of offices, and communication contacts and channels. They may all involve positive or negative consequences that serve as contingencies. Organization development strategies frequently involve structural changes in the organization that serve to reduce negative consequences and increase positive consequences. Changes in behavior are often a direct result of structural changes in both task and nontask situations in organizations. Since most training and human resource development departments do not have the power to create structural changes in the organization, training and development programs tend to focus on making behavioral changes in organization members.

Communication behaviors are frequently the focus of training and development programs, especially when a behavioral approach is used. This is understandable if we accept Schein's (1969) observation that "one of the most important processes in organizations, and one of the easiest to observe, is how the members communicate with each other, particularly in face-to-face situations" (p. 15). Communicative behaviors can be changed by the external management of reinforcement contingencies, by self-directed efforts in which individuals regulate their own behavior by arranging appropriate contingencies for themselves, or by both methods.

Williams and Long (1975) describe an approach to self-management of a person's life that is based on behavioral principles. They suggest that "effective self management primarily involves the rearrangement of behavioral consequences so that desired behavior is *immediately* reinforced" (p. 22). The principle of immediate reinforcement of desired behaviors is fundamental to a behavioral approach. Frequently the unwanted behaviors are rewarded naturally; thus the program of self-management requires the individual to administer his or her own punishment for unwanted behaviors and to reward the desired behaviors more vigorously.

Five steps epitomize the implementation of a behavioral training program involving the structuring of contingencies.

1. *Select a goal.* Identify a single goal so that you work on one change at a time. There are four considerations involved in selecting an appropriate goal:

a. *Select a goal that is important to you.* If you experience some form of pain, such as embarrassment or anxiety, any positive improvement will be noticeable and reinforcing. You should be somewhat cautious in trying to change well-entrenched behaviors at the beginning. It may be better to take a goal that seems important but that involves behaviors that might be changed more easily.

b. *Define the goal in measurable behavioral terms.* In this context *behavioral* means some type of overt action that can be seen and recognized by others. Nodding, smiling, speaking up, stepping back, and holding hands are overt behaviors. Feeling better, being more confident, and doing what's right must be translated into some type of behavior before we understand what is actually happening. For example, being more confident is expressed in some overt behavior. What do you do? How about looking right into the eyes of a person who disagrees with you? At least you can tell when you are being more confident with that kind of goal. By identifying the overt behaviors clearly, you can carefully select contingencies that help strengthen new and desirable ones. By changing overt behaviors, the behavioral approach contends, you change the internal feelings associated with them.

c. *Set a goal that is readily attainable.* One mistake often made in behavioral modification programs is to set goals too high. It is important to set goals that are only a little bit higher than your present level of behaving. When you can regularly perform a new behavior, then raise your standards and set a higher goal. Behaviorally we change in small increments.

d. *State the goal positively.* The end result of the behavior-change program is to develop the presence of positive behaviors. You might eliminate a great many negative behaviors and still not produce much improvement in what you do. It is also easier and more motivating to recognize and experience the presence of positive behaviors than to notice the absence of negative ones.

2. *Record the quantity and the context of behaviors.* This step allows you to recognize the extent to which offending behaviors occur and the circumstances in which they take place. You might discover that you say, "Oh Yea!" more frequently when someone disagrees with you in a group than at any other time. Keeping a record of the behavior to be changed will sensitize you to the progress you are making. Three major types of records of behavior can be used in behavior modification.

a. *Frequency counting.* This involves tabulating the number of times a particular behavior occurs. To be counted, a behavior must be defined in terms of discrete cases. The behavior must occur over a short period of time and have an identifiable beginning and ending.

b. *Duration of behavior.* Staring, crying, dozing, and other types of behaviors do not occur in discrete instances all of the time and are best recorded in terms of the amount of time devoted to the behavior. The simplest approach to recording the duration of behavior is to indicate when it starts (with a stopwatch or by recording the time) and when it stops.

c. *Results of behavior.* Rather than recording the behavior directly, occasionally you can monitor the behaviors by keeping track of what happens as a result of the behavior. By recording the amount of waste in a manufacturing plant, it is often possible to tell a great deal about the behaviors occurring in the plant. Weighing yourself can give you information about your eating habits. Nevertheless, to make changes, you will need to identify the specific behaviors that lead to waste or to being overweight.

The very act of making a recording may lead to changes in behavior. When a person is able to see an objective report of a behavior, he or she may be motivated to change. Identifying the behavior and maintaining a record of how frequently it occurs may be all that some people need to do to implement a behavior modification program. Some, on the other hand, may need to proceed to the next step.

3. *Change the situation in which the behavior occurs.* Some behaviors are triggered by the situation in which they occur. One way to modify behavior is to change the situation that encourages it. This can be done in two different ways:

a. *Avoid the situation.* Although staying away from someone because he or she tends to provoke an angry response in you will not eliminate your undesirable behavior entirely, it will do much to limit the situations in which it does occur. Ultimately you will need to deal with the behavior directly; nevertheless, at the beginning, avoidance may help you get control of and start to modify the behavior.

b. *Alter the situation.* If you tend to get sleepy sitting in a lounge chair, modify the behavior by sitting in a chair that seems less conducive to sleeping. On the other hand, if you tend to eat snacks at your desk, you might put the snacks in a sealed container and place the container in a file drawer so that you have to think about what you are doing before engaging in the behavior. You might even put a mirror on the desk so that you have to watch yourself eating.

By altering the situation you are providing yourself with supportive settings in which to control behavior. These are ways of applying contingencies to modify behavior. The direct application of contingencies, however, is important in a behavioral approach to change.

4. *Arrange reinforcing or punishing consequences.* A behavioral approach assumes that a person's behaviors are controlled by the consequences that result from them. If you unnecessarily argue with other people, but in the end you receive a lot of praise and encouraging comments, you will tend to be reinforced in your arguing. A difficulty in arranging consequences is that most of us have not thought about how things affect us. We are not sure how a particular event will affect our behavior. Thus we nearly always need to broaden the list of consequences that might be used as reinforcers or punishers.

    a. *Require yourself to exhibit the preferred behavior before participating in the reinforcing activity.* This means that you earn certain privileges by behaving in certain ways. If speaking in a negative manner to others is the behavior you wish to change, a highly satisfying or reinforcing privilege should be made contingent to or conditional upon speaking in a positive way to others. The reinforcers will be most effective if they are applied immediately after the desired behaviors are exhibited and if the new behaviors are not too hard to perform. Because it is not entirely feasible to give direct rewards immediately, a system of credits may be used. When you earn five or ten credits, they apply toward the direct reward, such as going to a movie or having some quiet time.

    b. *Use punishers as well as reinforcers.* Although the idea may not seem very appealing, the idea of flipping yourself with a rubber band or administering pain in some other way when you fail to carry out the new behavior is clearly a procedure consistent with a behavioral approach to changing behavior. Pain can be administered through social disapproval also. You can arrange a punishing contingency by telling those with whom you work about what you are trying to accomplish and asking them to administer the contingency or to simply remind you to administer the punishment.

5. *Focus on and verbalize the contingencies.* The strongest program for managing behavior change through contingencies keeps the person aware of and focusing on the consequences of his or her behavior. One of the main problems in behavior change is impulsive responses. We often react before we have had a chance to think about the consequences. Behavior modification seeks to heighten a person's awareness so he or she thinks about the consequences of his or her behavior before acting. One way to do this is to talk about the consequences to yourself before behaving. The verbalizations must be said aloud, at least in the beginning. It appears that the sound, as well as the statements, heighten awareness more than just the thought or silent verbalization of behavior.

Craighead et al. (1976) describe procedures for modifying marital problems by using contingencies. Couples are taught how to "pinpoint" the behaviors they wish to change, how to discriminate between positive and negative responses, how to improve their listening skills, how to share communication equally, how to reduce aversive behaviors, how to solve problems as a unit, and how to contract for the application of contingencies—consequences that positively reinforce compliance with agreed-upon changes and punish failures to comply. The entire process represents a training program based on a behavioral approach.

SIMULATIONS

A second strategy for applying the principles and philosophy of behaviorism to training and development is called *simulation*. The term *simulation* refers to some type of vicarious experience. The behaviors in which a person participates have the characteristics of or are similar to those that occur on the job. The term *simulator* is frequently used to refer to machines that have the appearance of the real thing but that are mounted in a laboratory rather than in the field. In a simulation the trainee gets to engage in the behavior that is desired back on the job without taking all of the risks associated with authentic work conditions.

Odiorne (1970) has referred to the use of simulations in training as *action training* and explains that "the specific forms of action training break down into different kinds of simulations. The common element is that all of them simulate the situation in which the trainee must operate in the real world and require him to behave in a way that he might behave back in that environment if he were to apply the new behavioral skills desired" (p. 264). In simulation the important requirement is to have a plausible resemblance to the main task.

Through a task analysis the specific behaviors to be acquired are identified and defined. Behavior is changed by having the trainee engage in the desired behaviors in a progression of small steps. At each step in the training the trainee obtains information on how well he or she is performing the behaviors.

Bartlett (1967) has suggested that simulation is "one unconventional method for changing behavior, strong enough to pierce the 'attitudinal' sound barriers" (p. 40). Consistent with the behavioral theory on which it is based, he notes that "this involves, under the guise of skill training, having subjects (Ss) practice doing differently (in a laboratory situation). As they are given rewards for doing differently, their attitudes will (absent pressure) tend to soften." Bartlett proposes that a training program to improve communication should be the primary vehicle to use when attempting to improve interpersonal competence on the job.

Communication training is a more or less neutral subject that focuses on processes and behaviors rather than on company policies and procedures. Skill training in communication provides employees with practice in listening and telling and lends itself naturally to broadening their perspectives with regard to perceptions of human behavior. Interpersonal competencies develop by doing things differently, by behaving as a communicatively competent person. To bring about changes in a person's communication skills and to enhance the transference of the new patterns of behavior from classroom simulations to the real world of the job, Bartlett argues that the training should be conducted in a company conference room that is used exclusively for the program.

There are two basic strategies for conducting simulations: role playing and games. We shall look at each of these briefly to illustrate how a behavioral philosophy can be implemented through simulations.

Role Playing. As a simulation method role playing involves acting out a situation that parallels real-life experiences (Pace, Peterson, & Burnett, 1979). Role playing can be carried out in two different ways: structured and spontaneous (Wohlking & Weiner, 1981). Wohlking and Weiner compared structured and spontaneous role playing on four stages involved in the use of role playing: (1) objectives, (2) warmup, (3) enactment, and (4) post–role-playing techniques. We shall briefly review their analysis to highlight the training applications of role playing.

Structured role playing is accomplished by having a series of written role descriptions with guidelines for the facilitator that structures the situation and sets the scene. Spontaneous role playing evolves somewhat naturally from the discussion of a problem, during which a potential solution is identified and tested through role playing.

Objectives.   Structured role playing is designed to develop skills in areas such as problem solving, interpersonal communication, and interviewing; to teach procedures and instruct in how to do tasks; and to modify attitudes involved in superior-subordinate relationships. Spontaneous role playing, on the other hand, is designed to provide insight into a person's own behavior and the behavior of others, to modify attitudes and perceptions, and to develop ways of diagnosing problem situations.

Warm-up.   Regardless of how the role playing is conducted, time should be spent preparing participants to engage in the role playing activity. They should be ready to participate by understanding the relevance of the problem and by wanting to be involved physically in role playing. The warm-up for structured role playing can be accomplished by presenting a lecture on a principle related to some aspect of effective organizational communication, for example, or by showing a film on the topic, which includes principles that can be translated into skills in role playing. In addition the written case itself can be analyzed, or a general discussion conducted on a problem area, which can lead to the question, "How would you handle such a situation?" The warm-up period for spontaneous role playing often consists of identifying problems that the group would like to explore.

Enactment.   In structured role playing, separate roles are distributed to the participants prior to conducting the activity. The written statements give role descriptions and identify role behaviors and points of difference. The trainer avoids intervening during the enactment, allowing the entire scene to proceed uninterrupted until the situation reaches a climax. In contrast, during the enactment of a spontaneous role play, the trainer intervenes frequently in an effort to highlight feelings and focus on individual responses.

Post–Role-Playing Techniques.   All role playing should be followed by a period of discussion in which the insights developed during the enactment are articulated by participants and observers. A discussion led by the trainer should focus on how the methods used in the role playing facilitated or hindered communication between the roles, not on the individuals taking the parts. Observers could be asked to report what they noticed, which may lead to a discussion about the problems of translating principles into actual communication skills. In spontaneous role playing the trainer asks each role player to react to the feelings, emotions, and tensions that developed during the enactment. The group is then asked for its reactions to the role play.

Role playing is an effective way of helping people understand the behavior of others. Much can also be learned from the other major type of simulation—games.

Games. A game is "any simulated contest (play) among adversaries (players) operating under constraints (rules) for an objective (winning)" (Gordon, 1972, p. 8). In human resource development serious games are used. They tend to simulate real-life problems and include a complex combination of cooperation, competition, winning, and losing. Some players or even teams of players may be more successful than are others, and in some cases, if the problem is solved, all players may win. In some instances winning is not the most crucial part of the game; how the participants use their resources to attain the maximum benefit may be more important than accomplishing the objective.

In training and development, games tend to follow two basic approaches: board games and role-playing games (Gordon, 1972). Board games are designed to be played on a gameboard on which the action occurs. Role-play games usually have written materials that include a scene and profiles of the players. In most cases all the players receive the same background information, but each one receives a unique role description that describes his or her specific role and relationship to other players, and the player's objectives. The information is provided to give players some basis for responding during the action. Rules are the only other information required. In role playing the rules are generally quite broad and define in what activities and decisions the player may be involved. Olivas and Newstrom (1981) conclude that "games can change attitudes, develop interpersonal skills, and achieve ready acceptance by the trainees. Most critical, simulations generally incorporate active participation and practice opportunities, thereby increasing the probability of learning and ease the transfer to the work environment" (p. 66).

BEHAVIOR MODELING

The third and final strategy for implementing a behavioral approach to human resource development is called *behavior modeling*. Zenger (1980) refers to behavior modeling as "the most exciting new technology in training" (p. 45). Research suggests that nearly all learning that results from direct experience can be acquired vicariously through observation of another person's behavior and the results for the person being observed (Bandura, 1969). Bandura suggests that a person can "acquire intricate response patterns merely by observing the performances of appropriate models" (p. 118).

Behavior modeling is based, according to Zenger (1980), on the idea that people learn by "(A) seeing a good example, (B) being provided a cognitive framework to understand the important elements of the skill to be learned, then (C) practicing or rehearsing the skill, and finally (D) receiving positive feedback when one succeeds in doing it properly" (p. 45). Behavior modeling assumes that (1) specific skills are learned by practice and that (2) such activities as managing, leading, and problem solving involve a series of concrete behaviors that can be modeled, observed, practiced, reinforced, and integrated into the total behavioral repertoire of a manager.

Behavior modeling is implemented best through the preparation of a series of videotapes that participants can view, identify with the situations, rehearse the modeled behavior under the coaching of a trainer, and transfer the skills back to their jobs (Rosenbaum, 1979). In a typical videotape modeling how a supervisor should handle a corrective interview, the model supervisor is to do the following:

1. Define the problem in terms of lack of improvement since the previous discussion.
2. Ask for, and actively listen to, the employee's reason for the continued behavior.
3. If disciplinary action is called for, indicate what action you must take and why.
4. Agree on specific actions to be taken to solve the problem.
5. Assure the employee of your interest in helping him/her to succeed and express your continued confidence in the employee.
6. Set a follow-up date.
7. Positively reinforce any behavior change in the desired direction. (Rosenbaum, 1979, p. 42)

ACHIEVEMENT THEORY

Many popular behavior change programs are based in what some authors call *motivational* or *success theory* (Gorman, 1979, pp. 61–85). Our preference is to refer to this large body of literature as *achievement theory,* because much of the basic philosophy is derived from research and practice on personal achievement and persuasion processes.

Some superficial similarities may appear between rational theory and achievement theory, but they should not be confused because there are significant differences that distinguish between the two perspectives on change.

Achievement theory is based on the assumption that changes in behavior occur because an individual wants to be successful. Individuals who have a strong predisposition toward doing things better have the highest probability of making changes and achieving something. Another major assumption is that if a person spends most of his or her time thinking about doing things better, that person will exhibit drive, energy, and a desire to become successful and, most likely, will achieve more of their objectives.

According to McClelland (1953), a pioneer in achievement research, individuals with a high need for achievement can be differentiated from others by four characteristics:

1. *They like work that involves moderate challenges.* If the work is too easy they get little satisfaction; if it is too hard, they tend to fail.
2. *They like to have concrete feedback on whether they have succeeded or not.* If they cannot tell when they are achieving, they tend to dislike the task.
3. *They like to be personally responsible for working on the task.* If they need to work on a committee or take a big chance, they feel they are not in charge. They prefer to do it themselves because they can feel satisfied with the outcome.
4. *They are restless, tend to be innovative, and travel a lot.* When something gets routine, the probability of success goes up and they are sure they can do it. They start searching for more challenging tasks, leaving the old ones and finding new ones.

Achievement theory of change can be expressed by five principles that lead people to change their behavior in the direction of achievement.

1. *Change is a result of achieving psychological success.* Hill (1967), for example, argues that the act of psychologically foreseeing success as a reality is the beginning of success itself. Bandura and Cervone (1983) conclude from their empirical research on goal accomplishment that "by representing foreseeable outcomes symbolically, future consequences can be converted into current motivators and regulators of behavior" (p. 1017).

Achievement theory initiates the change process by inducing or at least facilitating psychological success. Techniques of visualization are often employed to create the success set. Teaching the martial artist to visualize his or her hand on the other side of the broken board, rather than visualizing his or her hand breaking the board, is an example of psychological achievement.

2. *Inadequate performance or achievement is a result of low aspirations.* This principle is essentially the contrary of Principle 1 because it argues that an individual who assumes that he or she cannot achieve is adopting a self-defeating, pessimistic attitude and will be unable to exceed the lower expectations. The factor affecting achievement and behavioral change is not skill and capability but low aspirations. As Maltz (1960) has suggested, "within you right now is the power to do things you never dreamed possible."

Deese (1967) concludes from his analysis that "clearly, our expectancies do determine our behavior, and they do so by not only telling us what we think is going to happen but by telling us how much we are going to like or dislike what is going to happen" (p. 128). A person with a history of not succeeding may be excessively cautious and set his or her level of aspiration much too low. Research has shown that the things we think about and *how* we think about them have an enormous influence upon both our levels of aspiration and the direction our energy takes us.

3. *Change occurs when our attention is persistently focused on a goal.* James Winans (1917), a pioneer in the field of persuasion, observed that "what holds attention governs action." Writing down and reviewing goals, for example, directs both our conscious and unconscious attention toward them. The persistent focusing of attention on what you want or need to accomplish, in and of itself, leads the mind and body to pursue that goal. If you give full, fair, and undivided attention to a goal, you are much more likely to achieve it.

The use of the technique of stating "positive affirmations" is one way to focus persistently on a goal. To have a person stand and say confidently, "I can say 'No'! I can say 'No'! I can say 'No,' " focuses the person's attention on that goal and blocks out distracting interferences.

4. *Achievement is enhanced through group support.* Research on crowd behavior, conformity, and contagion attest to the motivating force of group support (Davis, 1969; Gordon, 1971; King, 1975; McGuire, 1969). The old adage, "It is easier to do anything if someone else is doing it with you," implies that achievement will tend to increase when group support is given. The effect may be explained in various ways, but Birch and Veroff (1966) see an *affiliation incentive* as the prime stimulator. They suggest that a person feels reassured that he or she is accepted and subsequently devotes more energy to accomplishing the goal.

The *standing ovation* is a technique used in achievement training that provides spontaneous support from the group for the accomplishment of one of its members.

As the target person watches and hears his or her group stand and applaud, the feeling that achieving is important intensifies.

5. *With the realization that one is achieving, efforts intensify and more energy is devoted to accomplishing the goal.* As a person completes a task successfully, he or she tends to view himself or herself as more capable. This phenomenon is observed each year on Easter when children search for candy eggs hidden the night before. If a youngster cannot find a piece of candy before someone else finds one several times in a row, discouragement sets in; but the child who locates one right away immediately gets a surge of confidence and intensifies the search for a second piece. The adage "success breeds success" illustrates this principle.

Failure to succeed does not necessarily deter a person, however, especially if he or she feels that success is possible. For example, Bandura and Cervone (1983) concluded, following one of their studies, that "the higher the self-dissatisfaction with a substandard performance and the stronger the perceived self-efficacy for goal attainment, the greater the subsequent intensification of efforts" (p. 1017). Stated in simpler terms, their conclusion suggests that people tend to work harder if they are dissatisfied with their performance and think attaining the goal is important.

POSITIONAL THEORY

Positional theory is based on the premise that a person's behavior is largely determined by the role he or she occupies, although each person may have separate sets of expectations for different positions. A role is a repertoire of behaviors characteristic of a person in a position; it is a set of expectations, standards, norms, or concepts about how to behave in a social position.

Positional theory derives its concepts from role theory (Biddle & Thomas, 1966), and role analysts study *patterned forms* of real life behavior using concepts of role theory. Individual patterns of behavior, aggregates of individuals, and institutional behavior are examined with an emphasis on how one's past and present environment influence behaviors and produce predictable patterns.

The fundamental premise of positional theory is that the behavior of individuals is influenced and shaped by the demands, expectations, and rules of others, as well as by the individual's understanding of what behavior he or she should exhibit in situations. Although this view does not deny the facts of individual differences, it does focus attention on the conditions under which expectations, norms, rules, and sanctions are influential.

The corollary assumption is, of course, that changes in role expectations bring about changes in role behaviors. This assumption means that people learn and develop new behaviors by changing their attitudes toward their own roles and the roles that surround them. In order for an individual to exhibit behaviors appropriate to a particular role, he or she must understand the demands on the position and have the ability to respond with relevant behaviors.

Positional theory has been implemented with the technique called *role negotiation* described by Roger Harrison (Berger, 1972). He says role negotiation involves "changing by means of negotiation with other interested parties the *role* which an individual or group performs in the organisation" (p. 85). Role, in this context, means the work requirements; what duties a person performs; what decisions the person makes; to whom the role occupant reports and about what and how often; and who can give him or her orders and under what circumstances. It also includes the informal understandings and agreements with others that determine how the person or group fits in with others.

For the technique to work, one basic assumption must be met: that participants "must be open about what changes in behaviour, authority, responsibility, etc. they wish to obtain from others in the situation" (p. 86). Harrison notes that if those involved in role negotiation take the risk and specify concrete changes they would like to see on the part of others involved in the negotiation, then important changes in behavior and work effectiveness can be achieved.

Stubbs, Hill, and Carlton (1978) reported on the use of role negotiation in a behavior change program instituted at Diamond Shamrock, a multinational chemical and petroleum company. Hill (1983) has developed a training program based on positional theory and role negotiation that is patterned after Harrison's work. He writes that "the change process is essentially a give-and-take situation in which two or more members each agree to change behavior in exchange for some desired change on the part of the other. The emphasis is on behavior rather than upon feelings, thus making the process safer for the team members" (p. 7). Hill reports that there are seven basic steps in the process, all of which must be completed for the program to be effective. They all depend on clearly identifying the work group or team that will serve as the focus of change.

1. *Identification process.* For each member of the team, list three sets of activities: (1) things that each team member should do more or do better, (2) things that each team member should do less, and (3) things that each team member does that facilitate the effectiveness of the others and should not be changed.

2. *Clarification process.* Post the lists and review each item for each team member in order to make certain that all members of the team *understand* every item. This process does not mean that anyone either accepts or agrees to make any changes. The entire focus should be on understanding what the statements mean.

3. *Setting priorities.* Using only the *Do More and Do Less* lists, sort out the issues in terms of their importance. If a particular request holds some personal interest for an individual, that individual should initial the item, so that the target individual can engage in negotiation with those who initialed the particular item.

4. *Negotiating process.* The negotiation process takes place in two formats: one-on-one and group. Every attempt should be made by all team members to deal with all items and to meet with others to help them complete their negotiations.

Each person meets with every other person and negotiates changes in behaviors on a "something for something" basis. That is, each pair or group agrees to do something if the other party agrees to do something. Each member must stick with the procedure until all needs are met.

5. *Contracting.* When the negotiations between team members near resolution, a contract should be drafted to reduce agreements to a few written words. Contracts should specify the following:

With whom the agreement is made

What you agree to do

In exchange for doing what

Date on which agreement is to be reviewed and evaluated

Signatures of both parties to the agreement

6. *Group meeting.* Team members meet as a group, briefly summarize their agreements with others, and acquaint the team with the significant contract issues. This step should be done in a round-robin fashion, with each member in turn describing the agreements and the exchanges.

7. *Contract review.* After approximately three months, a contract review should be held on each agreement. The review should indicate information on four results:

Agreements that were achieved

Agreements that were overachieved

Agreements that were underachieved

Special circumstances that negated agreements

The review process should be very open, to the extent of posting a grid on newsprint on the wall so that all agreements may be viewed by all team members.

As Hill points out, role negotiation may expose which organization members have real power and influence and may threaten those who bluff and those who operate behind the scenes. Nevertheless, much is to be gained through open, honest communication and negotiation, possibly even more than through coercion, private competition, withholding of information, and other strategies.

EXPERIENTIAL THEORY

An experiential approach to behavior change is based on the premise that people are more likely to believe their own experiences than those of others. People change their behaviors, according to this view, by examining their current beliefs in light of their reactions to situations in which they feel some significant emotional arousal. By reflecting on what happened to them, they develop a personal explanation for their reactions and make a conscious effort to try alternative ways of behaving in another setting.

There seems to be fairly widespread agreement that learning that results from direct experience is significantly different from learning that results from more cognitive methods (Springer, 1981). Part of the reason for the stronger impact of experiential learning is the combination of physical activity and thinking activity that occurs when a person experiences something. In some ways, change through experiential learning is a natural extension of the rational approach to change, because experiential learning allows individuals to test reality in safe situations. Each experience is a form of reality testing in which a person senses how he or she reacts to a concrete activity.

Behavior change as a result of experiential learning may occur both inside and outside the training area. People have experiences, create meaning from them, and try new ways of behaving, regardless of where they are. Unfortunately, there is often little analysis of the experience outside the training room, and the discussion that does occur may be unguided or misdirected. Experiences in the training area should be structured so that trainees learn how to learn from their own experiences.

The major advantages of using an experiential learning approach can be summarized in five key points (Hall, Bowen, Lewicki, & Hall, 1975):

1. Experiential learning is more active than other approaches.
2. Experiential learning is problem centered but also incorporates theory for a solid base.
3. Experiential learning involves two-way communication to a greater extent than do other forms of learning.
4. Experiential learning shares control over and responsibility for the learning process with participants.
5. Experiential learning integrates thoughts, feelings, and actions into a more holistic approach to behavior change.

Experiential Learning Model

Contemporary concepts of experiential learning have evolved from the work of Kolb in the development of a *learning styles inventory* (Kolb, Rubin, & McIntyre, 1974). He describes a four-stage cycle through which a person proceeds to learn from experience:

1. An immediate, concrete experience is the basis for
2. observation and reflection; the observations are assimilated into an explanation consisting of
3. abstract concepts and generalizations, which serve as guidelines for testing
4. new behaviors in different situations.

In this view a person learns by participating in a concrete experience, reflecting on the experience, formulating generalizations from the reflections, and trying new behaviors that test the generalizations.

Michalak and Yager (1979) designed a six-stage experiential learning model that expands Kolb's sequence and creates a systematic design process. Their six stages include (1) experience, (2) content input, (3) analysis, (4) generalizations, (5) practice, and (6) transfer. In this model, each training sequence begins with an experience, followed by the presentation of content information and an analysis of the experience in terms of the information and principles. The trainees then formulate generalizations that may be tested in the practice stage. The final step is devoted to preparing trainees to use their new knowledge and skills back on the job.

Although all aspects of designing and conducting training for purposes of changing behavior—such as writing objectives and evaluating the process—are not represented in the preceding models, they suggest four types of activities that go into an experiential training sequence (see Figure 17.1).

1. The *experience,* which involves supervising an exercise that allows a trainee to encounter some aspect of reality to the extent that it evokes an emotional response in the trainee.
2. Explanatory *information,* which consists of presenting theory that helps ex-

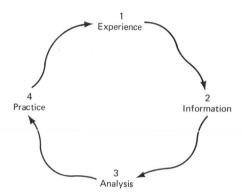

FIGURE 17.1   Experiential Training Model

plain what happened to the trainee or why the exercise was able to evoke the response.

3. An *analysis,* which involves assisting participants to make sense out of the experience by using the theory to explain what happened, to formulate principles for use later, and to identify and recognize specific skills involved in the reality.

4. A *practice* session, which consists of preparing and leading trainees through the recognition and rehearsal of the skills to provide for transfer of the skills to the workplace.

Experiential Training Methods

The steps in producing behavior change through an experiential approach may be described according to each of the four activities involved in the training model.

SUPERVISING EXPERIENCES

An experience is an encounter with some aspect of reality that evokes an emotional response. Examples of experiences that may evoke emotional responses include taking a field trip to a new and exotic site, participating in a "trust walk" in which a person is blindfolded and led through a maze of unpredictable events, or hiking in the mountains. All of those activities meet the conditions of an experience.

To bring about behavior change, experiential learning should involve a degree of structuring; a point of view imposed on the process allows participants to generalize and recognize patterns and skills. The term *structured experience* has been coined to refer to this special type of experience.

Middleman and Goldberg (1972) describe a structured experience as a closed system, deliberately constructed and set in motion by the facilitator. The experience might consist of simple or complex activities in which participants actually do something. It might take the form of role playing or making an object. It could involve completing a questionnaire or inventory. Some structured experiences have participants solve puzzles, analyze problems, create designs, or engage in activities like brainstorming and simulations.

Pace (1977) identified thirty-six different exercises for teaching concepts in organizational communication, all of which have been used in training sessions over the years. One of the most common sources of structured experiences is the Pfeiffer and Jones handbooks for human relations training and for group facilitators. The *Reference Guide* (1985) classifies the contents of twenty-four books of exercises. The structured experiences are classified according to six categories: (1) personal, including self-disclosure, feelings, values, life and career planning; (2) communication, including oral and nonverbal awareness, trust, listening, interviewing, and assertion; (3) group characteristics, including process, power, styles, motivation, leadership, and stereotyping; (4) task behavior, including problem solving, generating alternatives, feedback, competition, collaboration, conflict, and consensus; (5) organizations, including diagnosis, team building, decision making, and consultation skills; and (6) facilitating learning, including getting acquainted, forming subgroups, expectations, blocks to learning, building trust, openness, energizers, evaluating group process, facilitator skills, and closure.

Casse (1981) has prepared a unique manual for international/intercultural trainers that includes seventeen workshops with exercises and materials to prepare individuals for crossing cultures. The entire book illustrates the use of structured experiences in experiential learning.

Each structured experience should include a statement of the goals of the exercise, the materials necessary, the physical setting and group size for which it is best suited, step-by-step procedures and the estimated amount of time required to complete the exercise, and copies of worksheets, questionnaires, scales, or tests used in the exercise (Grove, 1976).

To set the stage for analysis of the experience and to get the most out of the process, participants should be encouraged to

1. Get involved in the exercise and participate with enthusiasm in the activities.
2. Consciously think about the relevance of the exercise to the theory and information presented for use in the analysis phase.
3. Think about and make notes on what kinds of generalizations might be developed from the exercise and what specific skills might be identified that could be practiced.

The following exercise illustrates how a structured experience is designed and supervised:

The Fractured Puzzle Exercise

Goal. To demonstrate that the critical act of communication is assigning meaning or significance to people, objects, and events.

Group size. Minimum of five individuals, with one to serve as communicator and the others to serve as communicatees.

Time required. About forty-five minutes.

Materials and equipment needed.

1. A master five-piece puzzle
2. Copies of puzzle for audience members

3. A 2 inch × 3 inch cardboard screen
4. Small table on which to put puzzle and screen
5. Chair for communicator
6. Student desks or tables and chairs for communicatees

Physical setting. Communicator is seated at table, behind screen, with completed puzzle in front of him or her; communicatees are seated at student desks or tables with scrambled pieces of puzzle in front of them.

Procedures or process. The following ten steps should be completed.

1. The facilitator explains to the group that he or she would like to conduct an exercise that demonstrates a major characteristic of communication.

2. The facilitator explains that to perform the demonstration, it will be necessary to select a person whom others consider to be a reasonably effective communicator.

3. The volunteer or person selected takes a seat at the front of the room at the table so that the small cardboard screen is between the volunteer and the group. The communicator and the group should be able to hear each other, but they should not be able to see one another.

4. The facilitator distributes pieces of the puzzle to communicatees, either singly or in groups, depending upon the number of puzzles available. If in groups, one person is assigned to work with the pieces while the others observe quietly. The five pieces of the puzzle should be gently tossed onto the table in front of the individual with instructions to remove the rubber band holding them together and wait for instructions.

5. The volunteer communicator is given the five pieces of the master set, identical in size and shape but having a different color combination. The communicator's set should be assembled behind the screen out of view of the group, in front of the communicator by the trainer.

6. The facilitator explains the nature of the problem to the communicator and communicatees: Communicatees are to play the role of machine operators who have been given the parts of a new machine, but with no instructions on how to assemble it. The communicator is to play the role of a manager who must explain to the operators how to assemble the machine. The manager has an assembled machine in front of him, made of pieces that are the same size and shape as those which the operators have.

7. The facilitator explains that the manager may say anything he or she wishes to the operators, but the operators may *not* talk back, ask questions, or make any audible sounds during the explanation.

8. As the manager gives instructions, the facilitator monitors the operators for violations of the no-talking rules and for examples of misinterpretations of what the manager says on the part of operators as they attempt to assemble machines.

9. The manager completes his or her instructions on how to assemble the machine, which may take fifteen minutes or less. As soon as the manager has completed giving instructions, the facilitator asks everyone to "freeze" (not to move puzzle pieces any further) while the manager walks around and observes the results of his or her instructions. The facilitator asks the manager to look for information (called *feedback*) about the results of his or her instructions and anything that might be useful in modifying them.

10. The facilitator interviews the manager for a few minutes about what he or she observed, attempting to draw out and highlight some of the sources of misinterpretation that occurred, such as assuming that all of the pieces were the same color, using unfamiliar or complex terminology, giving instructions too rapidly, or neglecting to explain the ultimate objective of his or her instructions—to assemble a figure that looks like the shape of his or her puzzle (a block T or F or H). Whenever possible, the reactions and behavior of the operators should be related to the main idea that assigning meaning is the key feature of communication.

This ends the exercise on structured experience. The next step in the experiential process would be the presentation of explanatory information or theory, which helps participants to understand *why* problems in communication occurred.

PRESENTING INFORMATION

Information can be presented in a variety of ways. Three basic categories of methods represent a convenient way of classifying them. Below is an outline of the most commonly used methods for presenting information:

ORAL METHODS

1. Presentational
   a. Lecture (one person)
   b. Dialogue (two persons)
   c. Colloquy (three to five persons)
2. Forum (presentation with audience participation)
   a. Interview (more formal two-person)
   b. Panel (more formal colloquy)
   c Symposium (formal speeches from panel members)

WRITTEN METHODS

1. Descriptive
   a. Essay—articles, books
   b. Programmed materials
   c. Incident
   d. Case history
2. Pictorial
   a. Diagrams
   b. Charts
   c. Pictures
   d. Slides
   e. Overhead transparencies

AUDIOVISUAL METHODS

1. Mediated
   a. Sound filmstrips
   b. Videotapes
   c. Motion pictures

2. Simulated
   a. Demonstration
   b. Role plays
   c. Dramatizations/Vignettes
   d. On-the-job coaching

FACILITATING ANALYSIS

This phase in the experiential learning process is designed to assist the participants in discovering the meaning to them of the exercise and to formulate some generalizations and principles that can serve as guidelines for behaving differently in the future. Participants must be encouraged to develop generalizations from the activities in which they participate. Talking about experiences, films, diagrams, role playing, and reading immediately after they are exposed to them is often more important than are the experiences themselves. When experiences are related to information presented as part of the content input, we refer to the discussions as *information processing.*

Analysis and information processing are facilitated by creating an atmosphere of inquiry among participants. Inquiry is accomplished by stimulating participants to probe into the meaning of the exercise and to explore alternative interpretations of what happened. As a facilitator, pose questions, then wait and listen; since during long silences almost everyone is thinking, it is important for you to allow sufficient time for participants to think through what they wish to say. Work to get participants to offer suggestions and analyses of the experience. Assist them in phrasing their ideas clearly, concisely, and completely. Strive to have every person contribute to the analysis and avoid allowing one member to monopolize the interaction. Keep the comments moving among all participants by frequently asking for more ideas. When discussion is slow, gently play the devil's advocate by introducing ideas that provide other ways of thinking about a situation. Throughout the analysis period, maintain and enhance the self-esteem of the participants by acknowledging any reactions, praising ideas, pointing out positive behaviors and their effects on others, and recording participants' ideas on a flip-chart.

Analysis can be facilitated by letting participants engage in small group discussions and by making reports.

Discussion Formats.   Analysis can be facilitated by using one or more of these formal group formats:

1. Buzz groups—Divide participants into groups of three and let them discuss the experience.
2. Phillips 66—Groups of six participants who discuss for six minutes.
3. Ring response—Start the discussion with a buzz group, then enlarge the discussion as others get involved.
4. Fishbowl—This consists of arranging the participants in a double circle—half inside and half outside; the inner group analyzes the experience while the outer group listens, then the groups change places.

Reporting Formats. Analysis frequently continues as participants prepare for and listen to reports presented in front of the groups; on other occasions private reports in the form of notes or journal entries are effective ways to facilitate the analysis of experiences. Four reporting formats are

1. Individual summaries of reactions given to small groups.
2. Team representative reports.
3. Consultative or listening group reports.
4. Private journal reports or diary entries.

Following small-group analysis and reports, the trainer should assemble the entire group and facilitate a large-group analysis designed to formulate workable generalizations. Specific suggestions should be stated and printed on newsprint for group members to study, analyze, and modify. The next step in the training process is to have participants engage in the practice of specific skills that might be used to do their jobs.

DIRECTING PRACTICE

The basic idea of practice is to apply the skills learned to the job. Although the practice session occurs in the training setting, the principles for effective practice are essentially the same as on-the-job instruction. Figure 17.2 summarizes the four standard steps in directing the practice of on-the-job skills (Dooher & Marquis, 1956).

Prepare the trainee for practice. Let the trainee know that the skill can be learned with some reasonable effort and that you are interested in helping him or her learn a skill that will make work more efficient. Create motivation to learn the skill by relating the skill to the trainee's ability to do his or her work more easily and more effectively and to make a better living.

Set the pattern or sequence. The steps to complete simple skills should be presented in some sequence. Explain and demonstrate the pattern or sequence for doing the skill one step at a time. Focus on the main steps and key points. Avoid giving too much information at one time. Use simple, direct language. Demonstrate how the skill is to be performed. Highlight those behaviors that are essential to executing the skill well. Set a high standard. As the trainee watches, you will be serving as a behavior model. The performance you give not only demonstrates how to do the skill but also represents how to do it well.

When the skills are more complex, mental traces or patterns must be established prior to learning meaningful motor skills. That is, mental rehearsal must precede the motor development of skills. With communication skills, especially, some well-established ways of behaving have already been formed. Learning, in those cases, is as much an *unlearning* process as it is a direct learning one. For individuals to effectively display key actions and overcome "old" behaviors, it is essential that the rehearsal of physical motor skills be preceded by visualization and mental rehearsal.

Begin to form a habit. Habits are formed by doing, so the trainee should actually perform the skill. In addition, through guided practice the trainee builds self-confidence and strengthens his or her willingness to try other skills. Start with

Steps	How to Do It
1. Prepare the trainee for practice.	A. Put the trainee at ease. B. Mention the name of the skill. C. Comment on the purpose of the skill. D. Relate the skill to the trainee's past experience.
2. Set the pattern or sequence of the skill in the trainee's mind.	A. Explain any materials needed to perform the skill. B. Demonstrate the skill, explaining each step slowly and clearly. C. Review the name, purpose, and steps in performing the skill.
3. Help the trainee perform the skill and begin to form a habit.	A. Listen and watch as the trainee performs the skill. B. Question the trainee on weak and key points. C. Have the trainee repeat the performance until the manual skills *and* the habits of thought have been acquired.
4. Check how well the trainee has acquired the skill.	A. Have the trainee perform the skill alone. B. Compare the performance against the standards of excellence. C. Review both areas of excellence and weakness for additional repetition.

FIGURE 17.2 Four Steps in Directing the Practice of a Skill (Source: Reprinted, by permission of the publisher, from Effective Communication on the Job, M. Joseph Dooher and Vivienne Marquis, eds. © 1956 American Management Association, New York. All rights reserved.)

simple behaviors and gradually work toward the more difficult ones. As the trainee practices, have him or her tell you how and why the skill is done that particular way. Correct errors and omissions as the trainee makes them. Rather than criticize the trainee, show him or her how the skill could be executed better; a correction becomes instruction and is usually accepted more eagerly. The best way to make corrections is to have the trainee make the adjustments. Thus a good procedure is to compliment the trainee on the practice effort and then ask the trainee if he or she can think of anything that could be done to make the performance better. If the trainee is unable to identify what needs to be corrected, then make the instructional suggestion. Avoid correcting too frequently. Exercise restraint in correcting during practice.

Check on how well the skill has been learned. Allow the trainee to perform the skill without your help. Encourage the trainee to ask questions about performing the skill. No matter how simple the question appears, respond with instructions that are serious and respectful. Check the trainee's performance as he or she does it alone but gradually taper off as his or her ability to perform the skill increases. Finally, if the trainee is doing well, tell him or her.

SUMMARY

In this chapter we have discussed the strategic role in human resource development. Strategies are methods, plans, and activities used to accomplish a specific goal. Five underlying philosophies and theories for producing change were discussed: rational, behavioral, achievement, positional, and experiential.

REFERENCES

Bandura, Albert, *Principles of Behavior Modification*. New York: Holt, Rinehart & Winston, 1969.

Bandura, Albert, and D. Cervone, "Self-Evaluative and Self-Efficacy Mechanisms Governing the Motivational Effects of Goal Systems," *Journal of Personality and Social Psychology*, 45 (1983), 1017–1028.

Bartlett, Alton C., "Changing Behavior through Simulation: An Alternative Design to T-Group Training," *Training and Development Journal*, 21 (August 1967), 38–52.

Biddle, Bruce J., and Edwin J. Thomas, eds., *Role Theory: Concepts and Research*. New York: John Wiley & Sons, 1966.

Birch, D., and J. Veroff, *Motivation: A Study of Action*. Belmont, Calif.: Wadsworth Publishing Co., 1966.

Bois, J. Samuel, *The Art of Awareness*, 3rd ed. Dubuque, Iowa: Wm. C. Brown, 1978.

Casse, Pierre, *Training for the Cross Cultural Mind*, 2nd ed. Washington, D.C.: The Society for Education, Training and Research, 1981.

Chamberlain, Jonathan M., *Eliminate Your SDBs*. Provo, Utah: Brigham Young University Press, 1978.

Combs, Arthur W., Donald L. Avila, and William W. Purkey, *Helping Relationships: Basic Concepts for the Helping Professions*. Boston: Allyn & Bacon, 1971.

Craighead, W. Edward, Alan E. Kazdin, and Michael J. Mahoney, *Behavior Modification: Principles, Issues, and Applications*. Boston: Houghton Mifflin, 1976.

Davis, James H., *Group Performance*. Reading, Mass.: Addison-Wesley, 1969.

Deese, James, *General Psychology*. Boston: Allyn & Bacon, 1967.

Dooher, M. Joseph, and Vivienne Marquis, eds., *Effective Communication on the Job*. New York: American Management Associations, 1956.

Ellis, Albert, and Robert A. Harper, *A New Guide to Rational Living*. North Hollywood, Calif.: Wilshire Book Company, 1975.

Gordon, Alice Kaplan, *Games for Growth*. Chicago: Science Research Associates, Inc., 1972.

Gordon, George N., *Persuasion: The Theory and Practice of Manipulative Communication*. New York: Hastings House, 1971.

Gorman, Walter, *Selling: Personality, Persuasion, Strategy*. New York: Random House, 1979.

Grove, Theodore G., *Experiences in Interpersonal Communication*. Englewood Cliffs, N.J.: Prentice-Hall, 1976.

Hall, Douglas T., Donald D. Bowen, Roy J. Lewicki, and Francine S. Hall, *Experiences in Management and Organizational Behavior*. Chicago: St. Clair Press, 1975.

Harrison, Roger, "Role Negotiation: A Tough-Minded Approach to Team Development," in *Group Training Techniques*, M. L. and P. J. Berger, eds., 83–97. New York: John Wiley & Sons, 1972.

Hill, Napolean, *Think and Grow Rich*. New York: Hawthorne Books, 1967.

Hill, Richard L., *Role Negotiation: Participant Workbook.* Plymouth, Mich.: Human Synergistics, 1983.

King, Stephen W., *Communication and Social Influence.* Reading, Mass.: Addison-Wesley, 1975.

Kolb, David A., Irwin M. Rubin, and James M. McIntyre, *Organizational Psychology: A Book of Readings,* 2nd ed., 27–42. Englewood Cliffs, N.J.: Prentice-Hall, 1974.

Maltz, Maxwell, *Psycho-Cybernetics.* Englewood Cliffs, N.J.: Prentice-Hall, 1960.

McClelland, David C., J. W. Atkinson, R. A. Clark, and E. L. Lowell, *The Achievement Motive.* New York: Appleton-Century-Crofts, 1953.

Michalak, Donald F., and Edwin G. Yager, *Making the Training Process Work.* New York: Harper & Row, Pub., 1979.

Middleman, Ruth R., and Gale Goldberg, "The Concept of Structure in Experiential Learning," *The 1972 Annual Handbook for Group Facilitators,* 203–210. Iowa City, Iowa: University Associates, 1972.

Odiorne, George S., *Training by Objectives.* New York: Macmillan, 1970.

Olivas, Louis, and John W. Newstrom, "Learning through the use of Simulation Games," *Training and Development Journal* (September 1981), 63–66.

Pace, R. Wayne, "An Experiential Approach to Teaching Organizational Communication," *The Journal of Business Communication,* 14 (Summer 1977), 37–47.

Pace, R. Wayne, Brent D. Peterson, and M. Dallas Burnett, *Techniques for Effective Communication.* Reading, Mass.: Addison-Wesley, 1979.

Pfeiffer, J. William, and John E. Jones, "Design Considerations in Laboratory Education," *Reference Guide to Handbooks and Annuals,* 13–31. San Diego: University Associates Publishers and Consultants, 1985.

Rosenbaum, Bernard L., "Common Misconceptions about Behavior Modeling and Supervisory Skill Training (SST)," *Training and Development Journal* (August 1979), 40–44.

Schein, Edgar H., *Process Consultation: Its Role in Organization Development.* Reading, Mass.: Addison-Wesley, 1969.

Spice, Martha B., "The Thought Selection Process: A Tool Worth Exploring," *Training and Development Journal* (May 1982), 54–59.

Springer, Judy, "Brain/Mind and Human Resource Development," *Training and Development Journal* (August 1981), 42–49.

Stubbs, Irving R., Richard L. Hill, and G. G. Carlton, "Training and Development of Internal Consultants at Diamond Shamrock," *The Personnel Administrator* (July 1978).

Williams, Robert L., and James D. Long, *Toward a Self-Managed Life Style.* Boston: Houghton Mifflin, 1975.

Winans, James A., *Public Speaking.* New York: The Century Co., 1917.

Wohlking, Wallace, "Attitude Change, Behavior Change: The Role of the Training Department," *California Management Review,* 13 (Winter 1970), 45–50.

Wohlking, Wallace, and Hannah Weiner, "Structured and Spontaneous Role-Playing," *Training and Development Journal* (June 1981), 111–121.

Zenger, Jack, "The Painful Turnabout in Training," *Training and Development Journal* (December 1980), 36–49.

18

The Design, Conduct, and Evaluation of Human Resource Training

General approaches to and methods for bringing about behavior change in an organization were outlined in the preceding chapter; the specifics of designing, conducting, and evaluating human resource training programs will be covered in Chapter 18. In the past, models of training design have been adopted from the literature on instructional design without adequate adjustments for the differences between learning technical skills and learning management skills.

In this chapter we will emphasize design of training for management skills, and Chapter 19 will focus more on design for the development of technical materials. As you will see, the individual stages in design models, whether for management development or technical development, have similarities, but the manner and order in which they are implemented are distinctly different.

TRAINING MODEL

Carnarius (1981) has provided a model for design that fits the realities of management training; thus, we shall structure this chapter around his design model, with some minor modifications to adapt it to our overall philosophy. As Figure 18.1 indicates, the model consists of seven steps: (1) Identify and outline content, (2) List possible activities, (3) Write objectives, (4) Consider methods and match with objectives, (5) Sequence session, (6) Check agenda, and (7) Prepare materials.

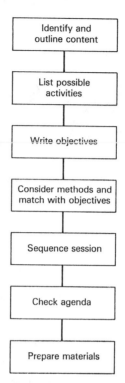

FIGURE 18.1 Training Design Model (From Stan Carnarius, "A New Approach to Designing Training Programs." Copyright 1981, *Training and Development Journal,* American Society for Training and Development. Reprinted with permission. All rights reserved.)

Step 1: Identify and Outline Content

The content of any given training session is usually identified jointly by the training staff and the line managers based on practical experience and the theory that evolves out of an analysis. We usually begin with the content in training design because this information often represents prerequisite concepts that the trainee needs to know in order to accomplish the objectives and perform the job up to standard. To outline the content, describe in a general way what trainees ought to know in order to perform the skills or do the work to be addressed in the training session, then make an outline of what information ought to go into the session. The result should be a two- or three-level outline of the topics as illustrated in Figure 18.2 for a seminar on supervision.

A typical outline on how to manage meetings more effectively is shown in Figure 18.3, and a training session designed to strengthen skills in managing employees who do not perform up to par might contain the content outlined in Figure 18.4.

Step 2: List Possible Activities

In the process of designing a training sequence, the identification and selection of possible activities—which include experiences, instruments, simulations,

Supervision

The supervisor's role and functions
    The basic functions of the supervisor
    The essentials of planning
    The requirements of good plans

Assigning work
    The role of organizational level in affecting work assignments
    The reasons why supervisors fail to assign work effectively
    Guidelines for making effective work assignments

Decision making
    Learning to make a decision
    Decision making and other supervisory functions
    Implementing the decision

Motivating employees
    The basics of motivation
    The overestimated role of money
    Current theories of motivation

Realities that shape managerial style
    The traditional leadership role
    Newer approaches to leadership
    The essence of effective leadership

Supervising for results
    Setting job objectives for employees
    Creating performance standards
    Scheduling
    Getting commitment

Managing supervisory time
    The pressures of time
    Guidelines for effective use of time
    Basic questions concerning time utilization

Training employees
    Instillation of good work habits
    Principles of effective training
    Follow-up with the learner

Communication: A Management Tool
    What makes effective communication
    What leads to good communication
    How to improve listening skills
    What body language can reveal

FIGURE 18.2 Topics Used in Supervisory Training

role plays, questionnaires and inventories, and puzzles—and all of the materials and instructions necessary to direct the activity, occurs early, usually before the clear statement of objectives.

On the other hand, after the objectives have been stated and refined, focus on the activities and make final decisions about which ones will actually be used during the session. Most people who design training programs have large files of activities and boxes of materials that they consult at this stage in the design process.

Conducting Meetings

Why meetings are important
    The role of effective meetings in increasing productivity
    The incredible costs of meetings

What goes wrong at meetings
    Confusion between process and content
    Hidden agendas, repetition, wheel-spinning

When to hold a meeting and when not to
    Hierarchical vs. horizontal meetings

How managers can increase group participation
    How to increase participation without losing control
    How to become a more effective participant

How to handle key meeting behaviors
    Facilitative methods and behaviors
    Things you can do to avoid problems
    Use of win/win decision methods

How to arrange meetings
    How to manage them
    How to build effective agendas
    How to set up a meeting room
    How to insure meeting follow-up

How to analyze your problem-solving style
    What is a model of human problem solving
    How to be a better problem solver

How to solve meeting problems
    How to reach consensus
    How to deal with difficult people
    How to remove organizational blocks
    How to get more people solving more problems
    How to use problem-solving training
    How to set up an internal problem-solving center

FIGURE 18.3 Topics for Training in Conducting Meetings

One of the most extensive and useful collections of activities is that of University Associates, a publishing company in San Diego, California. Since about 1972 they have published annual collections of structured experiences (including instruments, lecturettes, instructions, and other aids) for use in leadership and management training and development as well as personal growth.

In 1985 University Associates published a *Reference Guide to Handbooks and Annuals* (ten volumes including entries for the years 1972–1985) that classifies, describes, and indexes over 400 activities. The materials themselves are published in single 8½ × 11 format and distributed in a box for immediate and convenient use. They are divided into six categories:

1. Personal activities that focus on the expansion of personal insight, awareness, and development of interpersonal skills.

Unsatisfactory Employee

How to recognize unsatisfactory performance
    The marginal employee
    The unsatisfactory employee
    Definitions of poor employees

Causes of problem performance
    Managerial causes
    Organizational causes
    Individual problems
    Outside influences
    Abrasive employees

Laziness
    Reasons for apparent laziness
    Lack of motivation
    Unsatisfactory employee syndrome

Deciding who to salvage
    Moral and ethical considerations
    A matrix for making decisions

Managing the unsatisfactory employee
    Preventive approach
        Selection and screening
        Early detection of potential problems

    Therapeutic approach
        Coaching, counseling, training
        Getting commitment to improve

    Punitive approach
        Discipline
        Demotions, transfers, retirement

Problems with marginal employees
    Performance inadequacies
    Personal problems

How to handle people problems
    Age
    Sex
    Children

How to sever if you don't salvage
    How to handle fear of firing
    How to terminate

FIGURE 18.4 Topics for Training in How to Manage the Unsatisfactory Employee

2. Communication activities that emphasize verbal and nonverbal skills in interpersonal and intragroup relationships.
3. Group characteristics activities that examine how individuals affect group functioning.
4. Group task behavior activities that focus on how groups organize and function to accomplish objectives.

5. Organizations activities that help individuals and groups function within an organizational context.
6. Facilitating learning activities that create a climate of responsiveness and encourage skill development.

Ninety paper-and-pencil instruments are included and classified as personal, interpersonal, management/leadership, organization, and group behavior.

Although the activities published by University Associates constitute a valuable collection, activities are also published by many other groups. Consult your library and training and development professionals in your community for additional sources.

Pfeiffer and Jones (1985) explain that "each activity within the training experience should build from the previous sequence of activities and toward the next one" (p. 20). In addition, the activities should incorporate relevant content, especially in leadership and management development. The concerns and problems that participants face in their own work should be reflected in the activities.

Pfeiffer and Jones also argue that an "organic sequence of activities" exists in leadership development. They offer the following sequence as an "organic, logical, and effective flow of activities that need to take place in leadership development workshops" (p. 28).

1. *Getting acquainted.* These activities help create a climate in which participants have easy access to one another.
2. *Closing expectation gaps.* These activities help make the goals and objectives of the workshop explicit and correlate them with the goals and objectives of participants.
3. *Roles and shared leadership.* These activities introduce the concept of roles and functions of different group members and the notion of individuals as leaders in relation to others.
4. *Learning about feedback.* These activities provide instruction in the feedback process so that effective sharing can occur throughout the workshop.
5. *Developing an awareness of process.* These activities explore the dynamic processes emerging in the workshop and provide skills for occasionally stopping the interaction to examine the process that is occurring.
6. *Competition.* These activities examine the functional and dysfunctional effects of interpersonal competition.
7. *Collaboration.* These activities demonstrate that collaboration is possible within a culture that rewards the competitive spirit.
8. *Consensus.* These activities illustrate the concept of synergy and involve a number of people in arriving at collective judgments that are superior to individual judgments.
9. *Planning back-home application.* These activities help participants make definite plans for using particular behaviors in the work environment.

Although the identification of activities may start even before the precise statement of objectives, it may be very helpful to keep in mind this general sequence for the development of leadership as you tentatively select activities.

Step 3: Write Objectives

Two somewhat different philosophies govern the statement of objectives in training and development. The first philosophy argues that individual development is achieved most effectively when the skills and behaviors to be acquired are specified in advance. The statement of objectives to be reached describes what the person is to be like after the training and development experience. A well-stated objective successfully communicates to the trainees or participants what you want them to do; a poorly stated objective allows for more interpretations and fails to indicate directly the trainer's or developer's intentions (Mager, 1962). Barton (1973) argues, however, that stating objectives in advance is useful only when trainees are to acquire a "predetermined behavioral outcome" (p. vii).

Three conditions need to be met, however:

1. Trainee and trainer efforts need to be focused to develop specific behaviors in a minimum amount of time.
2. The results of training should be evaluated.
3. The behaviors to be mastered need to be precisely defined.

Thus if it is not desirable to concentrate on the development of specific, well-defined behaviors that can be clearly assessed, then the statement of performance objectives in advance may not be particularly useful. Those who advocate a performance or behavior objective approach to development also argue that it is possible, more often than not, to specify the kind of behavior that should be demonstrated by the trainee at the end of the training period. If the objectives cannot be stated, they contend, it is impossible to determine whether the program is meeting the objectives.

The second philosophy suggests that specific behaviors are not particularly important, that specific competencies or behaviors often do not tell the difference between effective and ineffective employees, especially in complex and not well-defined situations. When the task consists of problems for which there may be many appropriate solutions, training in specific competencies may be more limiting than helpful. Barton (1973) explains that when the major concern is the process of having a new experience, or where trainees are attempting to discover the value or meaning of something, or where the situation consists of problems with few common characteristics, the statement of predetermined behavior objectives is less useful than is the design of trainee-centered activities. Combs (1965) has argued effectively that in education, the effective teachers use "themselves as instruments" (p. 9) to accomplish their goals. Some tasks are immensely personal and cannot be translated into behavior competencies.

Dyer (1978) suggests that managers need to develop abilities to "move into any situation and then learn how to observe, gather feedback, and learn what is happening" (p. 55). He contends that "complex organizational training exercises are needed to give managers experience in the total cycle from the gathering of data to implementation of action and evaluation of the consequences of the action" (pp. 55–56). Although some specific behaviors may apply in many situations, the implication is that many problems call for different actions from different managers and that the ability to recognize those differences may be more important than are specific behaviors; hence training with behavior objectives may be counter-productive.

As you may recognize, these two philosophies tend to express the theories of change represented by the rational and the behavioral strategies discussed in the preceding chapter. The former stresses discovering the meaning to the individual of experiences, and the latter stresses the acquisition of specific behaviors that are measurable and identifiable in advance. The effort to meld the rational and behavioral philosophies into a single, unified approach that integrates belief and action was referred to earlier as an experiential approach. Regardless of whether the activity is individual training and development, which emphasizes both technical and interpersonal skills acquisition, or organization development, which emphasizes intergroup and systems analysis and change, the ultimate concern is with what the trainee can do at the end of the training period. This suggests that the objectives of a training and development program ought to be stated in terms of performances. At the same time the development process should be structured so as to allow individuals to examine their beliefs and assumptions and develop personal meanings and explanations to undergird the specific behaviors and competencies.

In general, objectives are used to identify the performances expected of participants during and after a training session. *Intermediate objectives* indicate the specific performances that are expected of trainees when they successfully complete a particular segment of a training session. *Terminal objectives* refer to the performance that is expected of trainees when the complete the entire session and prepare to return to their jobs. If trainees successfully complete each section of a training course, they should be able to demonstrate a group of behaviors (one or more for each segment of the course). If the trainees are able to demonstrate all of the specific behaviors at the end of the complete course, general skills can be used and maintained in the organizational setting to which they return. Figure 18.5 shows the relationship of intermediate objectives to terminal objectives. The design of any training and development program begins with the statement of terminal objectives. Each terminal objective can be classified according to the content or deficiency that it is designed to alleviate.

In most cases three factors account for training deficiencies: (1) lack of information, (2) lack of psychomotor skills, or (3) lack of appropriate attitudes (which include beliefs, feelings, values, and preferences). Figure 18.6 shows how these three factors interrelate to affect performance. For an employee to perform at a minimally acceptable level, he or she must *understand* (have accurate and accept-

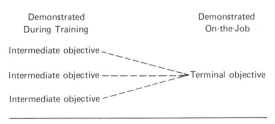

FIGURE 18.5 Types of Performance Objectives and Where They Are Demonstrated

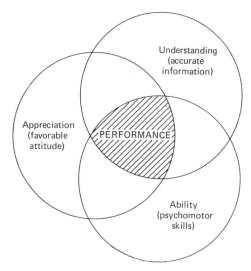

FIGURE 18.6   Three Factors That Account for Adequate Performance

able personal interpretations of the information), *appreciate* (have a favorable set of beliefs, feelings, values, and preferences), and have the *ability* (skill to physically and mentally execute the behaviors) to do the job.

Deficiencies in any or all of the three areas may lead to inadequate performance on the job. The statement of terminal objectives for any training program should be based upon the analysis completed and the concerns documented. If attitudinal concerns were identified, the training program should include terminal objectives designed to increase favorable attitudes; if informational concerns were identified, terminal objectives designed to increase understanding should be included; if inabilities to perform relevant psychomotor skills were identified, terminal objectives designed to improve psychomotor skills should be included.

Training objectives of any type require that individuals change their behavior. Training deficiencies cannot be alleviated by changing the system or by managing people more carefully. Hence objectives to be accomplished during the training session are usually stated in specific behavior terms. Intermediate objectives should be related directly to one of the terminal objectives and refer to trainee behaviors. The statement of the intermediate objectives will tell both the trainer and the trainee exactly what the trainee should be able to do at the end of a given segment of the training session. Since intermediate objectives influence the selection of training methods most directly, we shall discuss how to state those kinds of objectives next.

An *intermediate objective* can be defined as the statement of a specific performance or set of behaviors that will be expected of the trainee upon completion of a specified training segment. Acceptable statements of intermediate objectives must meet the following criteria:

1. *They must make direct reference to some observable behavior.* The verb in the statement must refer to some action, or product of some action, that can be observed by a person. Verbs that refer to observable behavior include the following:

define	diagram	rate
list	compare	choose
underline	categorize	revise
describe	distinguish	install
explain	compose	rearrange
identify	assemble	write
use	create	imitate
demonstrate	set up	role play
sketch	design	report
solve	fix	replace

2. *They must omit any reference to instructions, directions, and training activities.* The mastery of objectives by the trainees can be determined at any time, regardless of whether they are engaging in the training program. Learning activities should help trainees master the objectives, but engaging in the learning activities is not part of the measurement process. Such phrases as "after participating in . . . ," "following an analysis of . . . ," and "observe a dyad interacting . . ." are either training activities, directions, or instructions and are inappropriate for performance objectives.

3. *They must include reliable and easily understood qualitative and quantitative ways of measuring the performance.* Performance objectives should indicate quantitative and qualitative standards for determining whether trainees have achieved the objectives. A *quantitative* standard is expressed in terms of how many, how frequently, or with what percentage something occurs. A *qualitative* standard is expressed in terms of how well something is done or qualities of excellence.

4. *They must refer to the important conditions under which the performance is to occur.* Some examples of relevant and important conditions are "with the aid of an organization chart," "in a ten-minute interview," "on a timed-test," "working in a group of five individuals," "when verbally presented by the trainer," and "by interacting for five minutes with another person." The main physical and psychological circumstances and pressures associated with the task to be accomplished should be indicated.

5. *They must specify the tools and supplies or reference materials available to the trainee; if no references are mentioned, the trainee is to perform the task from memory.* Statements such as "by looking at a picture," "given the use of a list," "by using only newsprint on a flip-chart and a felt pen," and "with the aid of one person and a standard set of tinker toys" refer to supplies, references, and assistance available for demonstrating the skills.

Following are some sample statements of objectives for training in communication skills. Each statement includes the phrase, "At the end of the training period, trainees will be able to . . . ," which is a reminder that the objective describes what the trainee is to do, *not* what the trainer does. At the end of the training period:

1. When given a written communication incident, trainees will be able to underline examples of five elements of communication.
2. Using an official organization chart of the unit in which they work and

working in teams of five or six individuals, each team will be able to trace and explain how three different types of messages are disseminated into the organization along upward, downward, and horizontal channels.

3. Trainees will be able to identify in writing at least one different scene from the film *The Eye of the Beholder,* which illustrates each of the following principles:
   a. Desires, goals, and purposes influence how and to what a person responds in any given situation.
   b. People describe what they believe an event, person, or object to be rather than what it really is.

4. Trainees will be able to recognize self-disclosure statements that occur during five minutes of interaction with an individual who has been instructed to explicitly communicate one bit of information from each of five different headings on a list of self-disclosure items. After five minutes participants will prepare a written list of the five bits of information and compare them with those intended to be communicated by the other person. Four of the five items should appear on the presenter's list.

5. Trainees will be able to interact with a presenter who is role playing an emotionally agitated employee for five minutes during which they use each of the following techniques at least three times: reflection, paraphrase, open question, extending support. An observer should be able to identify each of the techniques by writing brief quotations of representative statements and/or describing behaviors exhibited by them in using each technique. During a ten-minute discussion period the presenter, the subject, and the observer should agree on the accuracy of the observer's identification on three out of four techniques.

6. Trainees will be able to demonstrate procedures for handling a complaint interview consistent with principles presented during the training session by interacting for ten minutes with a complainant in a role-playing interview. An observer should report that the procedures used are consistent with those described during the training session.

Objectives should be stated that indicate both terminal and intermediate performances desired of trainees. Clearly stated objectives should provide trainees with precise descriptions of the intentions of trainers. Well-stated objectives also provide specifications for the preparation of evaluation procedures and instruments. In fact, if objectives are carefully stated, actual evaluation procedures are suggested. Of course, objectives aid in focusing training methods in order to accomplish the goals established for the training session, to reduce irrelevancies, and to eliminate inadequacies.

Step 4: Consider Methods and Match with Objectives

Once the precise terminal and intermediate objectives are stated, you need to return to the possible activities and match them with the objectives. The match, of course, should be made on the basis of how well the activity achieves the objective. Your first task is simply to come up with as many relevant activities as you can. With a large number of activities for each objective, you can select those that are most appropriate. With few activities, you are limited in the choices you can make.

As Carnarius (1981) suggests, you are something like a chef, "with things cooking at various stages in your kitchen. What you need to do is serve it up in the right fashion so it will not only be nourishing, but pleasing as an experience" (p. 43). Matching objectives and considering methods is refined in the next stage, because sequencing requires putting things in the order that will achieve the greatest impact.

Step 5: Sequence the Session

A *training sequence* consists of those activities associated with the accomplishment of an intermediate objective. Training sequences combine to constitute a *training session,* which may run from one hour to two weeks in length. Training sessions combine to constitute a *training program,* which is made up of all of the training sessions available to a particular group of employees. A supervisory training program, for example, consists of all of the training sessions that a supervisor might take.

The arrangement of a training sequence is governed largely by the basic approach chosen. Five theoretical approaches were illustrated in the preceding chapter: rational, behavioral, achievement, positional, and experiential. However, the design of a training sequence within any basic approach may be strengthened by adhering to four principles of *activity alternation* (Lynton & Pareek, 1967):

Principle 1: Alternate stimulation with reflection. Training sequences are something like great dramas; they provide tension but allow for relaxation. Continuous activity should not be regarded as the primary method. Trainees need time to reflect on the activity and to make sense out of what is happening.

Principle 2: Alternate personal involvement with safe distance. Training sequences need to be balanced between intense personal experiences and opportunities to offer detached, analytical, and conceptual comments. Continuous intensity may produce stress rather than learning, so alternate intensity with detachment.

Principle 3: Alternate talking about something with practicing it. Training sequences need to provide practice opportunities until improvement in the skill tapers off. Then time needs to be devoted to thinking and talking about those things that still present problems in order to prepare for the next practice session.

Principle 4: Alternate individual tasks with group processes. Training sequences ought to have a balance of individual events and group events, in which the group activities provide stimulation and the individual activities allow participants to push themselves along as individuals.

AN EXPERIENTIAL TRAINING SEQUENCE

The experiential approach contains the elements of training that quite naturally provide for the alternation of stimulation and reflection, personal involvement and detachment, talking and practicing, and individual and group tasks. The model includes four distinct types of activities—experience, information, analysis, and

8:00- 8:10	Clearing the Agenda Activity	Experience
8:10- 8:20	Ice-Breaker Activity	
8:20- 8:30	Lecturette	Information
8:30- 8:45	Large-Group Discussion	Analysis
8:45- 9:00	Self-Analysis Instrument	Experience
9:00- 9:05	Lecturette/Summary	Information
9:05- 9:15	Small-Group Discussion	Analysis
9:15- 9:30	Break/Informal Conversation	
9:30-10:00	Assertiveness Exercise	Experience
10:00-10:15	Lecturette	Information
10:15-10:45	Small-Group Discussion to Identify Relevant Skills	Analysis
10:45-11:00	Break/Informal Conversation	
11:00-12:00	Role-Play Skills	Practice

FIGURE 18.7   Sample Training Sequence Illustrating the Application of Elements in the Experiential Training Approach

practice—as shown in Figure 17.1. The order of activities in the training sequence should follow the order in the model.

The process of ordering activities may be illustrated by arranging a half-day sequence. Figure 18.7 shows how the experiential activities combine to make a training sequence. The training sequence develops in approximately the same order as the elements in the experiential model, moving from experience to information to analysis; the sequence then returns to experience and moves to information and to analysis twice more before the culminating practice session. The number of preliminary rounds (from experience to information to analysis) that needs to be completed before a practice segment is introduced depends upon the complexity of the skills being developed and the amount of prerequisite information and analysis desirable for successful performance of the skills. The final stage in the design of a training session is the selection and refinement of exercises, instruments, discussion questions, and lecturettes so they fit the time periods and so they are consistent with the principles of alternation.

The completed design of a training session may consist of a large number of sequences, each involving several rounds of experience, information, analysis, and practice, plus detailed instructions for supervising experiences, presenting information, facilitating analysis, and directing practice. In addition a comprehensive daily training guide is usually prepared for use by the session leader in conducting the training. The entire package often extends to a hundred pages or more, since it contains copies of all materials to be used with exercises, including detailed instructions for conducting them, outlines of lecturettes, a list of equipment and material needs, evaluation forms, and the training room floor plan with indications for placement of equipment, tables, and chairs.

Step 6: Check the Agenda

A training session consists of a set of objectives, some division of labor between staff and participants, a temporal sequence of time periods, and some identifiable training activities (Havelock & Havelock, 1973). The combination of objectives, activities, labor, and time periods is called an *agenda*.

TIME BLOCKS

The amount of time to be devoted to any given training program is usually decided by a combination of organizational factors such as staff budgets available, number of employees who should be trained, physical facilities, costs, and workload. When those issues are settled, the length of the training program is usually determined by the specifications of different training methods. Frequently, however, a time block of three days is assigned to a particular training program. The task of the training staff is to design a program that will fit the amount of time available. Thus you start with a one-, three-, or five-day block of time and select the objectives, methods, and activities that can be handled during that period. Although some training programs run for as long as eighty hours, most training occurs in blocks of eight to forty hours.

DAILY SCHEDULE

When working with adult employees, the day often begins at 8:00 A.M. and ends at 5:00 P.M., although it can vary from 7:30 to 9:00 A.M. for starting times and from 3:30 to 6:00 P.M. for ending times. Most training programs should provide for segments long enough to conduct exercises and analyze them but short enough to keep participants from getting tired. In general the schedule for any given day should appear somewhat like that portrayed in Figure 18.8, ranging from 60- to 75-minute segments. As illustrated in the sample daily schedule, planning for detailed training events occurs within 75- and 60-minute blocks. Each period is usually planned so that it is self-contained and so that exercises, simulations, lecturettes, analysis, and practices will fit within the allotted time.

Each 75- and 60-minute block usually has one or more intermediate objectives associated with it. Each day or half-day culminates in the accomplishment of a terminal objective.

To check the agenda, it is a good idea to lay out the entire training session according to small time periods showing the discrete activities associated with each of the goals to be accomplished. The objectives to be achieved by the trainees will be associated with each time block and portrayed at the beginning of the 60- or 75-minute time block. The agenda is often checked best by looking at what the *trainer*

Daily Schedule

8:00 A.M. — 9:15 A.M.	Activities (75 min.)
9:15 A.M. — 9:30 A.M.	Break
9:30 A.M. —10:45 A.M.	Activities (75 min.)
10:45 A.M. —11:00 A.M.	Break
11:00 A.M. —12:00 A.M.	Activities (60 min.)
12:00 noon— 1:00 P.M.	Lunch
1:00 P.M. — 2:15 P.M.	Activities (75 min.)
2:15 P.M. — 2:30 P.M.	Break
2:30 P.M. — 3:45 P.M.	Activities (75 min.)
3:45 P.M. — 4:00 P.M.	Break
4:00 P.M. — 5:00 P.M.	Activities (60 min.)

FIGURE 18.8 Sample Daily Schedule

is to do within each of the 60- or 75-minute time blocks to accomplish the objective for that time block.

To illustrate this process, we have created a series of time periods for a training session on customer service with descriptions of the trainer goals and the instructions for what should be done during each time period to accomplish the goals. Even though some time periods may consist of only a few minutes, it is a good idea to put all of the information for each time period on a separate page; hence, as often as possible, each page in the trainer's manual is somewhat self-contained.

SAMPLE AGENDA

Time Block: 9:00–10:15 A.M.

Intermediate Objectives. At the end of this time block, each participant will (1) appreciate the importance of great customer service (affective objective) and (2) be able to explain the elements that constitute the *fast-action model* of customer service (cognitive objective). (These are abbreviated forms of the actual statement of intermediate objectives used to prepare the workshop.)

Time Period 1: 9:00–9:05 A.M.

Goals: To welcome participants, review housekeeping details, and create some structure.

Instructions:
1. Get the attention of participants.
2. Greet them warmly.
3. Explain smoking policy.
4. Point out restrooms and other facilities.
5. Review agenda and breaks.

Time Period 2: 9:05–9:15 A.M.

Goals: To introduce the trainer, show why the workshop is being presented, demonstrate that customer service is important to the company, describe how the session was designed, and present the objectives of the workshop.

Instructions:
1. State your name and position and give information such as education and experience that enhance your credibility as a trainer.
2. Explain that customer service is widely misunderstood because customers demand greater service than in the past and expect a different type of service than in the past.
3. Explain that this workshop is being presented to provide a new philosophy and tools that will build on a legacy of customer service.
4. Explain that great customer service has benefits that will make the employees big winners for themselves as well as the company.
5. Show poster-size quotations from company officials that illustrate their commitment to customer service.

6. Explain that the workshop consists of doing, reading, listening, discussing, and trying out and experiencing new ideas and values.
7. Present the objectives of the workshop in terms of what participants will get out of it:
   a. They will have a clearer idea of what modern customer service means.
   b. They will discover that great customer service is based on "fast action" and self-actualization values.
   c. They will see how visions lead to victories for themselves as well as the company.
   d. They will learn how to make customer service a positive difference in their own lives.

Time Period 3: 9:15–9:30 A.M.

Goals: To show the relationship between values and actions.

Instructions:
1. Explain that you would like each participant to stand at his or her seat and explain something he or she did recently that represented good customer service and then explain *why* he or she did it.
2. Give an example of what might be said, such as "I suggested that a customer going on a trip take travelers checks rather than cash." The reason: "I thought it would be dangerous to take cash."
3. As workshop leader, condense the "why" statement into the form of a value; in the above explanation, the value might be "concern for others" or "helpfulness."
4. After all participants have shared their experiences and explained why and have listed their values on a flip chart, point out that the values were the keys to what they did and how they acted.

Time Period 4: 9:30–10:15 A.M.

Goals: To show and describe the *fast-action model* of customer service.

Instructions:
1. Explain that customer service involves three general levels of employee activity: nonresponsive, reactive, and fast-action.
2. Divide participants into small groups of five individuals each. Ask each group to prepare three role-playing skits to illustrate the three types of employee reactions to customers.
3. Ask each group to assign members of their group to enact the three examples, then contrast the responses of the three customers, and relate them to what the employees said and did.
4. Explain the theory of fast-action customer service to the entire group.
5. Lead a discussion about how the role-playing skits illustrated the theory.
6. Divide into small groups again and have members make a list of the behaviors that seemed to make the greatest difference in customer satisfaction, both positive and negative.
7. Call up the groups and have each one select a specific behavior that makes a positive difference in customer satisfaction and prepare to practice the behavior.

Break for restroom and refreshments

With this outline, it is possible to check the agenda for consistency, flow, the relevance of the activities to the objectives, and the quality of the entire sequence.

Step 7: Prepare Materials

As soon as the agenda has been checked and the workshop schedule is ready, you now begin the task of preparing materials. You will need to develop the trainer's guide; lecturettes and other ways of presenting information; instruments and other items for supervising exercises; questions for discussion and ways of facilitating the analysis; handouts that go with lectures, discussions, exercises, and practice periods; and audiovisual materials.

Chapter 21 describes methods and procedures for designing and developing media products. The models and principles presented there underlie the preparation and creation of all forms of media. The final task is to make copies of both the trainer's manual and the participants' workbooks for use in the training session. At that point, you will want to review all of the other details associated with conducting a training session, including how to evaluate the effectiveness of the training.

HOW TO CONDUCT A TRAINING SESSION

The conduct of a training session involves considerably more than standing in front of a group. Although the design of the session and the preparation of a leader's guide should provide most of the basic information and directions for supervising, presenting, facilitating, and directing activities, other details must also be taken care of. The list that follows is a summary of most of the major issues that need attention (Davis & McCallon, 1974).

1. Dates (month, week, days) for the session must be established and scheduled.
2. Facilities (meeting rooms) must be secured and scheduled.
3. Equipment (projectors, screens, flip-charts) must be located and scheduled or rented.
4. Materials (prereadings, handouts, instructions, instruments, puzzles, and other items involved in the activities) must be prepared, reproduced, sorted, stacked, and ordered for use.
5. Aids (pencils, felt pens, paper and notebooks, newsprint, overhead projections, pictures, and other aids) must be purchased, located, and boxed.
6. Participants (trainees) must be identified, recruited, and prepared to attend.
7. Promotion (advertising, notices, clearances) must be prepared and distributed with adequate information to make it simple for people to attend.
8. Accommodations and travel (sleeping rooms, ground and air transportation) often need to be arranged.
9. Food and refreshments (special luncheons, banquets, regular meals, refreshments for breaks) must be arranged, menus studied, and guarantees made.
10. Meeting room setup (arrangements of tables, chairs, screens, microphones, and easels) must be negotiated or handled by the training staff.
11. Staff and consultants (those who will conduct and assist with the session and invited guests, including organization officials who may wish to or ought to extend greetings and openings, as well as award certificates of completion at the end) must be determined, contacted, and contracted with or invited.

12. Budget (itemized list of funds available and disbursed and projected costs) sheets must be prepared to account for and explain expenditures. Items for which there is usually a chargeable cost include materials, staff, consultants, aids, facilities, accommodations, travel, meals, refreshments, promotion, and participant salaries.

After taking care of the many issues that must be considered in preparing for a training session, the actual training activity may seem like a very small part of the entire process.

Getting a Training Session Started

When all of the participants are assembled, materials are in place, and the physical surroundings have been checked for comfort and workability, you are ready to open the training session. Sometimes a formal welcome and greeting is in order, but in any case you will need to create a warm and cordial atmosphere. Frequently participants need to get acquainted with and accustomed to each other. Ice-breaker and get-acquainted exercises are very helpful at the beginning. The ground rules for participating in the session should be reviewed and participant expectations acknowledged. A review of the schedule and the topics and skills to be developed often help establish anticipation and increase motivation. Check the seating arrangements, ventilation, temperature, acoustics, and lighting as you proceed so that adjustments can be made before starting the first training segment. When the schedule is right, move into the first exercise. Materials should be nearby and a system set up to distribute them quickly to participants. Follow the plan, supervising experiences, presenting information, facilitating discussions, and directing practice sessions. At the end of each day have a dramatic motivational closing to leave trainees on an exciting high.

EVALUATION OF TRAINING

Few people working in human resource development deny the claim that the evaluation of training is not only the most important aspect of the entire process but also the most difficult. Smith (1980) argues convincingly that failures to evaluate the training process may be explained by three reasons: (1) *No one sees a need for evaluation.* The sessions and the support activities seem to be going along fairly well, so the actual need to evaluate does not seem particularly important. (2) *Evaluators do not know how to evaluate.* The major deficiencies lie in not knowing how to state evaluation objectives in precise and measurable terms or how to analyze the data once it has been gathered. Many trainers just do not know how to summarize data so that it can be interpreted and understood. (3) *The complexity of the trainer's job leads to other tasks having higher priority.* Training courses are often without adequate instructional guides, and frequent changes occur in course content. In addition there may be a long time lag between the training activity and the trainee's opportunity to apply the skills to improve job performance. Finally, the trainers and trainees may feel that they, rather than the training, are the subjects of evaluation, and they may not cooperate with evaluators.

Four problems result from these causes:

1. No evaluation data are collected.
2. Evaluation data are unreliable and misleading.
3. Evaluation data fail to be presented in a timely fashion, often too late to be used effectively.
4. Evaluation data are incomplete, frequently lacking information about potential causes.

Planning an Evaluation

As with other aspects of training, to be effective, evaluation must be planned. The first step in the process is to identify what should be known about training. The second step is to decide what should be measured. The third step is to identify ways of getting the data.

Answers to five questions seem critical in evaluating a training program:

1. Are the trainees satisfied?
2. Did the trainees experience information gain?
3. Did the trainees acquire the skills being developed?
4. Do the trainees use the skills on the job?
5. Does using the skills have a positive effect on the organization?

Finding answers to those questions constitutes the evaluation process. Table 18.1 summarizes what should be measured to answer each question and what kinds of data might produce relevant answers.

In order to evaluate satisfaction with the training experience, some measurement of trainee perceptions both during the training session and after the session when trainees return to the job is important. Satisfaction with program content, instructor styles, learning experiences, facilities, and related accommodations may all affect the quality of the training session. Information gain is usually measured directly by administering some type of test, either objective or subjective; however,

TABLE 18.1 Summary of Evaluation Issues

What Should Be Investigated	What Should Be Measured		What Should Be Examined
	During the Session	After the Session	
Trainee satisfaction	Perceptions after training segments	Perceptions on the job	Oral and written comments and reactions to questionnaires
Trainee information gain	Knowledge of concepts	Explanations of concepts to others	Scores on objective tests, performance during exercises, observations of work
Trainee skills acquisition	Skills exhibited in practices	Skills used on the job	Performance review reports, observations of work, employee-reported problems
Effect of skills on the organization	Perceptions of others of value of changes to the organization	Actual value of changes to organization	Perceptions of supervisors, cost-effectiveness figures, problems reported by supervisors

much can be learned about what a person knows by listening to him or her explain ideas to others.

The evaluation of how well a trainee has developed the psychomotor skills needed to perform behaviors more effectively is a difficult task. Measures of performance are frequently based on observation and are quite subjective at times. How well a person performs a particular skill in practice sessions during training is often difficult to determine, and whether the skills are actually transferred and used on the job is generally not easy to determine either. Performance review reports, observations of work, and employee-reported problems may all give some indication of how well the trainee has acquired and uses the skills presented during the training session.

Whether the behaviors developed in the training session will have a positive effect on the functioning of the organization is something that can only be predicted, especially when evaluated during the training session. Instructions to select the two or three most important job-related objectives and to evaluate how well they have been accomplished during the training may give an indication of the value of the objectives to the organization. As supervisors observe the work of employees, they may recognize problems or may notice trainees using behaviors that are of value to the organization. Naturally production figures and other objective indicators of performance that can be related to employee behaviors are usually excellent indicators of the effect of training on the organization.

SUMMARY

This chapter has discussed the design, conduct, and evaluation of strategies of training and development. Two philosophies of specifying objectives were summarized: (1) performance objectives can be stated and are essential for determining the effectiveness of training programs; (2) specific behaviors and competencies often do not tell the difference between effective and noneffective employees, and trainee-centered activities develop more flexible employees. It was suggested that an experiential approach to training combines the major benefits of both philosophies. Terminal objectives describe what trainees should be able to do back on the job, whereas intermediate objectives indicate what trainees should be able to do following specific training sequences. Appreciation and understanding of and the ability to perform behaviors were identified as factors that account for a person's performance. Objectives designed to produce favorable attitudes, provide accurate information, and develop psychomotor skills should be included in training programs.

Five characteristics of acceptable performance objectives were discussed. They include reference to observable behaviors, omission of references to directions and training activities, reliable and easily understood qualitative and quantitative ways of measuring the performance, inclusion of important conditions under which the performance is to occur, and inclusion of the tools, supplies, and references available to the trainee. Six sample statements of performance objectives were given.

The content of a training program is usually determined by what the trainees need to know and is portrayed in a two-level outline of topics. Three examples of program content were presented.

A training program was described as consisting of a set of objectives, a division of labor, blocks of time, and identifiable training activities. The sequence of training events was described in terms of a weekly and a daily time schedule. It was explained that training sessions are developed around 60- and 75-minute self-contained blocks.

A training sequence was defined as those activities associated with the accomplishment of an intermediate objective. Four principles for alternating training activities were discussed. The experiential training sequence was analyzed as an approach that naturally provides for the alternation of the key principles. A daily schedule for implementing the elements in experiential training was described. Twelve major issues in preparation for conducting a training session were listed. How to get a session started was discussed.

Three reasons why evaluation of training fails to be done and the four problems resulting therefrom were explained. Five questions critical to evaluating a training program were analyzed. Finally, trainee satisfaction, trainee information gain, trainee skills acquisition, and the effect on organization function of using the skills were identified as the key variables to be evaluated.

REFERENCES

Barton, Grant E., *Performance Objectives.* Provo, Utah: Brigham Young University Press, 1973.

Carnarius, Stan, "A New Approach to Designing Training Programs," *Training and Development Journal,* 35 (February 1981), 40–44.

Combs, Arthur W., *The Professional Education of Teachers.* Boston: Allyn & Bacon, 1965.

Davis, Larry Nolan, and Earl McCallon, *Planning, Conducting, and Evaluating Workshops.* Austin, Tex.: Learning Concepts, 1974.

Dyer, William G., "What Makes Sense in Management Training?" *Management Review,* 67 (June 1978), 50–56.

Havelock, Ronald G., and Mary C. Havelock, *Training for Change Agents.* Ann Arbor: The University of Michigan, 1973.

Lynton, Rolf P., and Udai Pareek, *Training for Development.* Homewood, Ill.: Richard D. Irwin, 1967.

Mager, Robert F., *Preparing Instructional Objectives,* Belmont, Calif.: Fearon, 1962.

Pfeiffer, J. William, and John E. Jones, "Design Considerations in Laboratory Education," *Reference Guide to Handbooks and Annuals,* San Diego: University Associates Publishers and Consultants, 1985, 13–31.

Smith, Martin E., "Evaluating Training Operations and Programs," *Training and Development Journal* (October 1980), 70–78.

19

Design and Development of Media

Gordon E. Mills

Instructional design is a process used to develop media products and technical training materials. Design includes the analysis, planning, and decision making about who is going to be taught, what message will be presented, how the ideas or facts will be transmitted, what media will be used, and what performance level will be sought. Design is the planning and organization phase of training and is the key to producing quality, cost-effective training materials (Ingrisano, 1985).

DESIGN PROCESS

Costs for developing media products and technical materials are usually high, and design can help control these development expenses. Costs for production can take a large share of the budget for achieving a training objective; therefore, careful planning and painstaking analyses are necessary to extend and preserve the resources of the training budget. Figure 19.1 represents eight steps involved in the design process. The model provides a set of systematic guidelines for developing media and technical materials.

Although there are some similarities between this model and the one in the preceding chapter, the focus of instructional design is on the task itself and developing skills to perform a job more effectively. Thus, job-specific considerations such

Steps

1	Task Analysis
2	Sequencing and Grouping Activities
3	Establishing Objectives
4	Create Test Measures
5	Strategy Development and Media Selection
6	Preproduction Planning and Development
7	Production
8	Tryout and Revision

FIGURE 19.1   Design and Development of Media

as learning technical skills, rather than interpersonal and management development issues, are emphasized with this approach.

DESIGN MODEL

A number of models have been prepared to describe the design process for technical materials (Briggs, 1970; Davies, 1973; Merrill & Bunderson, 1981; O'Sullivan, 1976). While all the models differ, activities common to most of them are included in the eight steps of the instructional design model shown in Figure 19.1. We will present a definition and discussion of each step in the model and provide an example to demonstrate how the model guides the designer in preparing and testing instructional materials. We will use the example of training a person how to develop and do the preplanning to produce a two-camera videotape project.

Step One: Task Analysis

A task analysis involves listing both the skills and knowledge required for a person to perform a job (Davies, 1973; Edwards, 1977). Three common methods used to gather this information include (1) observing others performing the task, (2) interviewing them about their work, and (3) using surveys. These approaches were outlined in an earlier chapter. From these data, the specific requirements of what the employee must know and do are defined and built into the instructional design process.

To begin the task analysis, let's look at the example chosen to demonstrate this process and state the specific task: *Develop, create, and test the training materials necessary to enable a trainee to produce a two-camera videotape project.*

Step one is to list the skills and knowledge required to develop and plan the videotape project. Figure 19.2 shows how this step could be completed. Stating in detail all that must be learned and the skills that need to be acquired gives the trainer a description of what the training session should cover.

As you review Figure 19.2, note how the task analysis produced the list of skills and knowledge required to produce the video project. The task analysis sets down the key elements that must be included in the training process. At this point, you might note some omissions from the list, such as in the areas of writing, use of music and sound effects, and lighting. Each of these skills have additional subtasks that need to be detailed and systematically defined in order to produce a complete list.

Step Two: Sequencing and Grouping Activities

Although some of the skills may appear to be rather simple, this is usually not the case because most skills, when thoroughly analyzed, are a series of complex behaviors that usually occur in a specific sequence. Recognizing this sequence and planning the materials to be presented involves two tasks: (1) establishing the logical order for effective learning, and (2) grouping and sequencing these activities in a series.

ESTABLISHING THE LOGICAL ORDER FOR EFFECTIVE LEARNING

To determine the sequence, a consideration described by Bloom (1956) is used. Bloom indicates that learning occurs in a sequence where simple facts must be learned before more complex material can be mastered; basic math skills need to be learned prior to doing algebra, for example. Efficient learning at the lower levels must precede learning at the higher levels. In Bloom's taxonomy, the lowest level of learning is *knowledge* and represents information such as definitions of terms, recall of basic facts, and recognition of events that occur in a sequence. A task, such as repeating from memory the Pledge of Allegiance, would represent this level of learning. *Comprehension* is the second level of learning and includes the ability to interpret, paraphrase, or summarize information. Comprehension is a more complex activity and requires the basic knowledge learned at the first level of learning. Describing in your own words the meaning of the Pledge of Allegiance would represent comprehension. Succeeding at the second level requires a good foundation of the basic facts, terms, events, and names acquired earlier. Applying and using ideas and information in new situations, such as showing how the Pledge of Allegiance relates to patriotism, is representative of the *application* level of learning and builds on both knowledge and comprehension. At the fourth, or *analysis,* level, one is able to compare and contrast ideas, such as breaking down the Pledge of Allegiance into its basic components and comparing it to formal statements about the flag of other countries. This step also requires the foundation of the preceding levels of learning. Two additional levels, *synthesis,* where the trainee produces new learning such as writing a new pledge, and *evaluation,* where he or she assesses consistencies and determines quality and flaws or errors, complete Bloom's hierarchy. In summary, sequencing and ordering information to be learned is essential to efficient learning. Analyzing information, through considerations such as those reported by Bloom, will bring some precision to this evaluation. You can often achieve a similar result by asking the question, ''What must we really know before we can do this?'' With this question answered, sequence the information accordingly.

Note that during this process, knowledge should precede skill development. For example, consider the knowledge and skills list (Figure 19.2) while asking the question, ''What must we know to do this task (represented under skills)?'' In short, knowing how to define the how, what, when, where, and why of the plan is essential to actually using this skill to establish production schedules and set deadlines. In a similar manner, knowing what makes video scripts, graphics, or music effective is critical and mandatory in order for good scripts and visuals to be created. Knowledge must precede the act of doing. Therefore, with each skill, the sequence of learning information will be followed by skills development and practice.

GROUP AND SEQUENCE ACTIVITIES IN A SERIES

Two natural groupings, developing and planning, are present in the list. The skills under the heading Developing the Product are presented in a sequential order. Visualization or scripting need to occur prior to adding graphics, music, or sound effects. Building transitions and adding director cues follow. In contrast, the sequence of the second group of skills listed under the heading Planning Associated with Development is not as critical. Although there is a logical order to these activities, such as assigning and selecting crew and talent, establishing deadlines and schedules, and scheduling production and post-production facilities, these skills could be developed in any sequence without harm to the learning process.

In short, after you have determined where sequencing is critical for efficient learning, complete the sequencing phase for both the skills and knowledge, and then group the learning activities into the appropriate-sized modules and common mental or physical learning tasks. As you review Figure 19.2, note that grouping occurred in two areas, that of developing and planning. Therefore, two modules would be taught to develop the skills included in each of these areas.

Step Three: Establishing Objectives

With the detailed task analysis and the grouping and sequencing complete, objectives can be developed. The objectives formalize and detail the specifics for the media product by (1) defining the audience, (2) stating the observable behaviors to be developed, (3) listing the conditions under which the behavior will be performed, and (4) specifying the expected level of achievement (Davies, 1973; Mager, 1984).

As stated in the preceding chapter, objectives clarify what outcomes are expected through the training effort. The objectives directly influence all subsequent considerations of the design process and represent the reference point for all future decisions. Substantial effort should be made to assure that they meet the training need identified during the process of analysis.

Rather than providing the exhaustive list of all the objectives associated with the task represented in Figure 19.2, the example will be narrowed to include only number eight in the list of skills (listing the director's commands), and number six in the area of knowledge (assigning the director's commands).

As noted in step two, knowledge precedes the act of doing. Therefore, at least two types of objectives are necessary to prepare the trainee to accomplish this task. The first type of objective represents gaining the knowledge of the language used by the director to coordinate the production staff. Two basic commands are used: The first is a preparatory or warning directive that alerts the staff to prepare to do something. The word "ready," along with identifying the person, is stated, such as "Ready on camera one." After the warning or ready cue, the command of execution follows: "Take camera one." The second type of objective is applying that knowledge to showing, demonstrating, and displaying the use of that language. Thus, objectives might be stated as follows.

Skills and Tasks Needed to Produce Product

Developing the Product
1. List the idea to be developed.
2. List the steps that develop the idea and correctly sequence them.
3. Visualize the sequence of ideas on a storyboard.
4. Create the script to match the visualized elements.
5. Provide graphic reinforcement.
6. Enhance with sound effects and music.
7. Reconsider visual elements, script, graphics, sound effects, and music as a collective unit and monitor flow and transitions between these elements.
8. List the director's commands.
9. Determine lighting requirements.
10. Determine make-up and wardrobe needs.

Planning Associated with Development
11. Assign crew and select talent.
12. Establish production schedule and set deadlines.
13. Schedule production facilities.
14. Schedule postproduct editing.

Knowledge Required to Produce Project

Developing the Product
1. How to create and use a storyboard.
2. How to make a good video script.
   a. Writing for ear.
   b. Use of subject, verb, predicate construction and avoiding complex sentences.
   c. Knowing your audience.
3. How to make a good television graphic.
   a. Simplicity.
   b. Three/four aspect ratio.
   c. Font faces and point size.
4. Sources for music and sound effects.
   a. Omni and BBC collections (licensing agreement).
   b. Copyright issues.
5. Role of music and sound effects in video presentation.
   a. Create tones and mood.
   b. Reinforcement.
6. How to use the commands of a director and know what they mean.
   a. Preparatory commands.
   b. Execution commands.
   c. Visually represent different shots called for by the director.
7. How to use lighting to achieve desired results.
8. How to use make-up to achieve desired results.
9. How to acquire and use a wardrobe to achieve the desired results.

Planning Associated with Development
10. How to use who, what, when, where and why questions in making a plan.
11. Select personnel needed.
    a. Technical.
    b. Talent.
    c. What the roles of the technical people are.
    d. How to audition and select crew and talent.
12. List technical equipment needed in production facility.
    a. Video.
    b. Audio.
    c. Lighting.
13. List props and graphics needed.
14. How to schedule the production and postproduction facilities.
15. List postediting technical facilities and personnel needed.

FIGURE 19.2 Task Description and Analysis for Creating a Two-Camera Videotape Project

KNOWLEDGE OBJECTIVES

1. Given ten statements of a typical video director's commands, the trainee will correctly label each as either preparatory or execution.
2. Given a blank storyboard, a written description of ten shots used to produce video projects, and a visual demonstration with a video segment of those ten shots, the trainee, using stick-drawn figures, will correctly draw five of the ten shots on a storyboard.
3. Given a storyboard that represents twenty different visual shots for a theoretical video project and a list of eight terms to classify them, the trainee will correctly label eighteen out of twenty shots.
4. Using a two-minute visual segment, the trainee will correctly name eight of the ten types of video shots included.
5. In a second playing of the same two-minute visual segment, the trainee will correctly list five of the director's preparatory commands and five of the execution commands used to produce the videotape.

SKILLS OBJECTIVE

6. Given a prescripted storyboard that includes music and sound effects, the trainee will, with 80 percent accuracy, classify and label the shots and list both the director's preparatory and execution commands.

In each of the six objectives stated here, the word *trainee* defines the audience for the training. The trainer should really know more about the trainee than is suggested here. To effectively prepare training materials, it is essential to know the extent of the trainee's skills, knowledge, and attitudes about the subject and some demographic information such as age, educational background, and work experience. This knowledge will help you target the information to this audience so that it adequately meets their needs.

The second aspect of a good objective is that it defines the conditions under which the trainee will perform the desired behavior. Here, the condition includes the "givens" and restrictions placed upon the trainee. This is usually represented in the first part of each objective just before the words, "the trainee will." The third aspect, the behavior, is then defined with the expected level of achievement listed at the end.

The first five objectives must be mastered to enable the director's cues to be placed on the prescripted storyboard. Objective 1 differentiates between preparatory and execution commands; 2 is the first phase of defining terms used to classify shots; 3 is a classification activity of those terms; 4 is recognizing those shots in an actual video product; and 5 is the combination of all the preceding four objectives. This sequence enables the trainee to move to the demonstration of that skill as listed in objective 6. In short, with the five knowledge objectives achieved, the application or skill objective, number 6, could be displayed.

Step Four: Create Test Measures

Correctly stated objectives outline what types of tests should be developed to measure the expected performance of those who are trained. By using action verbs in the objective, the test measure becomes apparent. For example, with action verbs such as "list," "name," "label," and "select," test items are quite evident: "Correctly list four characteristics of a good behavioral objective." The verb "list" in the objective specifies the question to ask in order to measure the knowledge.

Objectives, then, are the key to measurement. Objectives that call for application should include terms like "demonstrate," "compute," "construct," or "show" (Davies, 1973). The test procedures here should evaluate how well the person can apply the skill. Measuring analytical and synthesizing skills is more complex. Verbs such as "compare," "contrast," "criticize," "judge," or "justify" require a different approach to measurement. A test item that asks, "Compare and contrast the differences between print and electronic media," would require an extended essay. The answer may include the definition of each medium's strengths and limitations, cite specific examples of how each medium is typically used today, look at production costs, etc. The responses to the test items will be different for each person, and the action verb used in the objective should reflect that expectation.

The six objectives listed above have various levels of mastery built into them. For example, in objective 1, a correct answer is 100 percent; objective 2, 5 of 10; objective 3, 18 of 20; objective 4, 8 of 10; objective 5, minimum of five for each command; and objective 6, 80 percent. The tests created, then, have a minimum performance level already assigned in the objective. The objective also includes the key to how the measurement will occur. The condition part of the objective identifies the test instrument, while the action verb describes how testing will occur. In objective 1, ten statements (the given) need to be labeled (the action verb) as either preparatory or execution. In objective 3, a storyboard with eight alternatives (given) is to be labeled (action verb). A video segment is used in objectives 4 and 5 as the cuing device, and the shots and commands (the given) are then labeled (action verb). These first five tests all measure the trainee's knowledge of how to classify both the visual elements and language used by the director to guide the production and help formalize and coordinate the effort of the production team.

In objective 6, the task or skill of assigning the director's commands is evaluated. The test is the display of the skill. With skills evaluation, the test becomes the performance to be transferred to the job. The skill is tested in the

---

Label each of the statements listed below as either a video director's preparatory command or command of execution. Put a "P" in front of those which are preparatory and an "E" for those that are execution.

_____   1. Quiet in the studio.
_____   2. Roll VCR.
_____   3. Ready to cue talent and bring up music.
_____   4. Take camera 1, bring up music, music under, cue talent, music out.
_____   5. Ready camera 2 on 2-shot.
_____   6. Pan right camera 2.
_____   7. Ready to roll credits.
_____   8. Dissolve to graphic.
_____   9. Fade to black.
_____ 10. Roll VCR 1, take 1.

FIGURE 19.3   Test for Objective 1

training environment, where coaching, reinforcement, and encouragement are given during practice activities.

The test to measure the first objective is shown in Figure 19.3. The performance expected on the test is 100 percent.

Essentially, the test performs two functions. First, it evaluates how well the person can perform the task. Not all learners are alike; there is a range in performance levels. Second, the test provides feedback on the value of the training. Basically, did the media product work as it was designed?

In review, the objective strongly influences the tests you create to measure the performance of those trained. The test items are described in the conditions of the objective; the action verb defines how to proceed to measure the desired behavior; and the objective lists what performance should be achieved.

Step Five: Strategy Development and Media Selection

The systematic strategy for selecting which medium to use is represented in Figure 19.4. The figure shows sixteen alternatives for media listed at the top of the figure, ranging from electronic to print format. Five major considerations, which include twenty-five factors, are stated at the right. The strategy for selecting a medium is based on the "if, then" principle. By eliminating all media that are unacceptable or partially acceptable, the choice of the medium becomes apparent. To see this more clearly, let's briefly review the twenty-five factors and then supply an example of the strategy selection process.

OBJECTIVES CHARACTERISTICS

Six different types of learning activities can be found in objectives (Goodman, 1971). In some cases, multiple learning activities may be found within an individual objective. Because the objective is so critical to the design process, we will define and provide an example for each of the characteristics of an objective.

Factual Information. Learning specific facts, terms, names or classifications are some of the types of information that are included in this learning activity. Example: Correctly state the name of a closed figure that has four equal sides and right angles.

Visual Identification. Recognizing shapes, differentiating or showing similarities between objects, or pointing out unique features is a second characteristic that could be found in an objective. Example: Given three small blocks, correctly name which is a triangle, a square, and a pentagon.

Principles, Concepts and Rules. When facts and/or visual identifications are organized into broad categories that have unique meaning, they form a concept or principle or become the foundation for a rule. For example, the concept of a four-sided, closed figure would include those visual identifications and facts associated with a trapezoid, polygon, square, rectangle, diamond, parallelogram, and rhombus. Example: Correctly list one common element in the following figures: polygon, square, rectangle, and rhombus.

Procedure. A systematic set of events that, when combined, achieve a specific result is called a procedure. Example: Given a formula to determine the area of a triangle, correctly determine the area of three triangles with the following dimensions: $3 \times 3 \times 3$ inches.

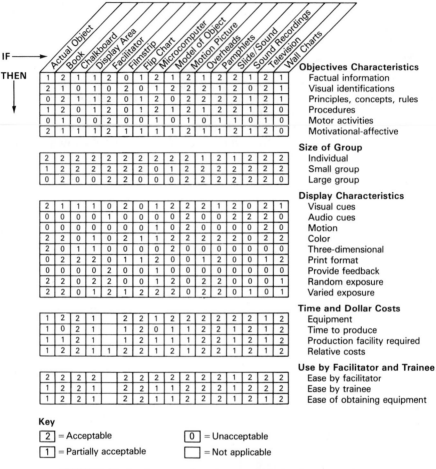

Key

$\boxed{2}$ = Acceptable $\boxed{0}$ = Unacceptable

$\boxed{1}$ = Partially acceptable $\boxed{}$ = Not applicable

FIGURE 19.4   Strategy Development Media Selection Guide

Motor Activities. The fifth learning activity is motor skill development such as tasks requiring eye-hand coordination. Example: Given the proper supplies and a set of measurements, the trainees will draw within one-sixteenth-inch tolerance a rhombus, trapezoid, and parallelogram.

Motivational-Affective. Influencing, motivating, or inspiring a group of trainees may be the learning outcome desired. Here, encouraging changes in performance is sought through the training function. Example: Given a before and after measurement to determine the trainees' interest in line drawings and basic figures used in design, the trainees will increase their scores by two points.

GROUP SIZE

Group size is a factor to consider when developing instructional material. Materials designed for an individual might well differ from those for a small group or large audience. As the audience size changes, the method of delivery needs to adapt in order to maximize the potential of the training.

Nine display characteristics of media have been identified (Briggs, 1970). Essentially, the characteristics describe the types of cues available to the trainee from each medium during the presentation. Two different types of cues, visual and aural, as well as possible feedback or exposure rates, are possible to select during strategy development.

Visual Cues. Line drawings, photographs or films, graphic displays, and actual objects represent different types of visual cues.

Aural Cues. Sound effects, music, narratives, and other aural stimuli have a rich potential to produce learning and are often overlooked. Aural information can become the theatre of the mind and can produce many results that a visual presentation is incapable of doing. The return of radio drama has made this more apparent. The mind, through aural cues, creates the visual detail and imagery that would take thousands, if not millions of dollars, to produce with a visual medium.

Motion. Motion is often necessary to show events occurring in a series, such as motor skill behavior.

Color. Color adds additional information and detail to a message and often embellishes the presentation. Preference for color over a monochrome picture has been shown, but greater learning does not always occur when it is used. Color should be added when the learning objective requires color discrimination (Dwyer, 1987).

Three-Dimensional Cues. The perspective of the third dimension is often required in learning. The mind, as described above with aural cues, can create the third dimension of an object. This abstracting ability varies with age and individuals. Thus, if the third dimension is required in the learning activity, analyze your audience carefully on this issue.

Print. This is the oldest medium and perhaps the most frequently used. Make sure that the trainee has adequate reading skills and that the material can be easily seen by the reader. Selecting the right typeface and size to present the material is important.

Feedback. Feedback enhances learning (Borg, 1987; Wexley & Latham, 1981) and should be included in technical training. In many cases, training materials are used with a facilitator present who provides the feedback and coaching necessary to develop the skill. Materials that are presented without the facilitator can be designed to approximate feedback by using rhetorical questions within the presentations. These questions are those that would typically be asked if a facilitator were present.

Random Exposure. Going from point to point in a book, such as flipping from page to page or front to back, is done with relative ease. A motion picture, in contrast, is linear and does not have a random exposure capability. Some objectives require this versatility in moving from point to point in the presentation with ease, but many do not.

Varied Exposure. This factor represents whether the trainee needs to be able to go at his or her own pace. If the training needs to proceed faster or slower than average, you should take this into account. Reading a book allows for self-pacing, whereas a motion picture has a fixed pace.

COSTS (TIME AND MONEY)

Budget matters always influence the strategy development process. As the budget decreases, options decrease also. Beyond the dollar cost is the issue of time. Given sufficient time, the options are expanded, but as deadlines impose significant time constraints, options decrease. When you are asked to have the project by tomorrow, limitations on the cost and time determine the type of medium that will be used.

EASE OF USE

Determining how easy it is for the facilitator and learner to use the medium is an important question to answer when determining the strategy. Material that is not easy to use will seldom be chosen. There is a built-in resistance to using things that appear difficult. For example, many people have chosen not to use a computer if it is not "user friendly." Media that require use of complex equipment are also seen as "unfriendly" and are not often used because of this fear. A second user consideration is how easy it is to obtain the equipment. As the equipment becomes more difficult to schedule or obtain, the amount of use decreases.

Let's now use the "if, then" principle within the strategy selection process by looking at objective 4 stated above: "Using a two-minute visual segment, the trainee will correctly name eight of the ten types of video shots included."

To begin the strategy selection process, begin with the factors at the right of Figure 19.4. Review the objective with these six factors in mind. Within objective 4, two *characteristics* are needed: visual identifications and factual information. Knowing both the name of a shot and its definition are involved in the task. All media qualify on factual information by scoring either 2 (acceptable) or 1 (partially acceptable), but the narrowing process begins when visual identification is included. Four of the media are disqualified because they score 0 (unacceptable). Move down Figure 19.4 to "Size of Group." The use of the microcomputer is eliminated at the group size consideration because the training group is small. Again, all other media not previously eliminated may be used here and are still in the running.

In the display characteristics category, visual cues and motion are necessary. At this point, only television and motion pictures are viable alternatives because they have not been eliminated by the factors listed above. Cost in terms of dollars and time again narrows the field. With facilities and equipment available, television might become the best alternative because of the shorter time required to produce the two-minute segment. Motion pictures might be excellent, but time to produce it may not be available. Because the topic is teaching television production, television is by far the best alternative. Again, this process may appear to be labored and unnecessary. However, it helps one question the preconditional bias for a specific medium and forces the instructional designer to look at all the alternatives to satisfactorily answer the what, why, and how of development. In this objective, television can effectively present the factual information, can display visual cues and motion, is cost sensitive, and is easy to use for the size of the group involved.

Step Six: Preproduction Planning and Development

The planning phase of preproduction includes listing the production tasks, setting schedules and deadlines to follow, and identifying the people who will be needed to complete the project. By using objective 3 as an example, Table 19.1 displays this planning process.

With the plan for the project completed, development begins. The development phases—although all media differ—represents the visualization, written, and graphic support processes. Begin the development phase by reviewing the sequencing and grouping activities reviewed earlier and noting the skills, knowledge, and sequence you will develop. Next, determine what visual material will develop the skills. A storyboard is usually produced to represent the visual elements of the production. Next, support the visual elements with text material. Either visualization or scripting can precede the other, but both are necessary. The text material,

TABLE 19.1   Planning Activities: Two-Camera Project for Objective 3

Begin Day	Finish Day	Production-Scheduling Tasks	Check When Finished
1	1	Task description/analysis	[ ]
1	1	Grouping and sequencing activities	[ ]
1	1	Establish objectives	[ ]
1	1	Create test measures	[ ]
1	1	Justify medium	[ ]
1	1	Establish if material already published	[ ]
2	2	Develop script	[ ]
2	2	Develop storyboard	[ ]
2	2	Determine graphic support	[ ]
2	2	Determine audio/music support	[ ]
2	2	Reconsider all elements	[ ]
2	2	List director's commands	[ ]
2	2	Make studio diagram	[ ]
2	2	Make equipment list and schedule	[ ]
2	2	Make prop and graphic list	[ ]
2	2	Make personnel list	[ ]
2	2	Schedule production facility	[ ]
3	3	Make graphics	[ ]
3	3	Audition talent	[ ]
3	3	Select crew	[ ]
3	4	Schedule talent rehearsal	[ ]
2	4	Schedule and meet with director	[ ]
2	4	Schedule and meet with crew	[ ]
3	5	Assign set up tasks	[ ]
5	5	Set up studio	[ ]
5	5	Create and transmit objectives to accomplish during run through/rehearsal	[ ]
5	5	Final shooting	[ ]
3	3	Schedule post-editing facility	[ ]
5	5	Post-editing	[ ]

script, or narrative is then matched to the visual elements. Graphic elements, although visual, are considered independently. Graphic material is used to reinforce the message and clarify points that are not clear.

At this point, ideas are formalized on paper. Steps 1 through 6 in the instructional design model are reviewed. Changes can be made at this point, and when all revisions have been made, the project is ready for production.

Essentially, development activities begin on the second day according to the planning chart shown in Table 19.1. The storyboard shown in Figure 19.5 represents the development activity for the two-minute video segment. As you can see, the storyboard becomes the worksheet for the visualization and scripting activity. To begin, fill in the boxes with the stick figures to represent the visual sequence. Place the audio or script material to the right of the picture, list the camera direc-

FIGURE 19.5

tions at the bottom of each box, and note the camera or video source. Add the graphic support and sound effects where needed. The storyboard is then studied to determine what graphics need to be made, what props must be obtained, what the wardrobe requirements will be, and what talent will be required.

Planning and development occur simultaneously. Planning guides development, and as development occurs, planning follows. For example, initially, once all the tasks to be accomplished are defined, some tentative deadlines are suggested and some of the personnel, such as a producer, are selected. At some point, control within those deadlines shifts to the producer or project director. Some phases of development are assigned and completed before the auditioning of talent or scheduling of facilities can occur. Although planning establishes deadlines, changes or delays may alter the schedule.

Step Seven: Production

With the development and planning activities completed, you are prepared to go to the studio and shoot and postedit the video segment. The real key to success here is the thoroughness of the planning and development that has already occurred. In the budget set aside for a video project, production constitutes as much as 90 percent of the costs. This cost will vary from project to project and from medium to medium. Video projects are costly because of the equipment needed and the number of people required for production. In the kind of project shown in Figure 19.5, eleven people could be required just to shoot the two-minute segment. The crew would include operators for cameras one and two, producer, director, technical director, floor manager, engineer, audio and video technicians, and the actor and actress. In some cases, an individual performs multiple roles, such as producer-director-technical director or engineer-video-audio technician; the floor manager may not be used. This plan limits the crew and talent to just six. Where unions are involved, the number could exceed fifteen. Costs for talent, crew, and equipment are usually based on an hourly rate, and as time mounts, costs follow. Equipment required to produce this product might exceed a million dollars. Again, the design function is cost-effective because it most often reduces the time needed within the studio and editing facilities.

Step Eight: Tryout and Revision

The real test of the products created through this design process is on-site training. In short, do the products work as planned? Through careful use of the steps for sequencing the session, checking the agenda, and preparing the materials, a fair test of the value of the product can be made. The procedure for testing the technical training is similar to the process described in Figure 18.1. An agenda is planned (step 6) and the training occurs as listed in the description of step 7 of that model. In each case, tests are given to measure the objectives shown in Figure 19.1 and to check the mastery of the material. A second test can determine how well the material prepared the trainee to perform the task or skills listed in the task analysis. If weaknesses are noted, the following questions should be asked. Is it a grouping and sequence issue that is preventing him or her from achieving the results we would desire? Are the objectives stated properly and do they measure what we intended? Does the test truly evaluate the key behaviors that we would like to see the trainee perform on the job? Would there be more effective ways to present this information and/or would a more appropriate strategy work?

Careful instructional design helps to avoid these timely and costly reviews. If these questions have been thoroughly reviewed during the design process, the training should have been sufficient to bring about the anticipated results. Minor reviews may need to occur and are acceptable, but the need for major reproduction should be eliminated by good planning.

SUMMARY

This chapter has discussed the instructional design process used to create media materials and technical training. Technical training deals with issues such as operating equipment and performing routine tasks. These routine tasks can be classified into a basic set of skills. These skills are a set of subtasks and duties that often occur in specified sequences. Proper task analysis will record both the knowledge and skills required to effectively perform these duties on the job. It was suggested that once the list of skills and knowledge has been defined, the grouping and sequencing of the skills and information necessary to perform them should occur so that effective learning will be possible. Objectives were then developed that would produce a change in existing behavior or establish new ones in order to achieve the desired results. The objectives were shown to be a direct force in the development of the testing measures and strategies. Five issues relating to strategy and media selection were discussed, including the learning requirements of the objective, group size, media display characteristics, costs, and ease of use. Considerations of these five factors provided a systematic process for selecting media that would complement the training objective.

The vital role of preproduction planning and development through the design process was shown as a cost and quality control measure. A small portion of the budget is allocated to this procedure, but it has a far-reaching impact on the end product and its effectiveness in the training setting.

Production is the culmination of the design process. The instructional design process guides you through a systematic set of considerations that makes the outcome more effective. The final test of the design process is the use of new skills in the workplace.

REFERENCES

Bloom, B., *Taxonomy of Educational Objectives, Handbook I: Cognitive Domain*. New York: David McKay Company, 1956.

Borg, Kirstin D., "The Implications of Practice and Feedback on Subjects Acquiring Five Listening Skills Using the Behavior Modeling Technique," Master's thesis, Brigham Young University, 1987.

Briggs, L., *Handbook of Procedures for Design of Instruction*. Pittsburgh, Penn.: American Institute of Research, 1970.

Davies, I., *Competency Based Learning: Technology, Management, Design*. New York: McGraw-Hill, 1973.

Dwyer, F., *Strategies for Improving Visual Learning*. State College, Penn.: Learning Services, 1987.

Edwards, C. H., *A Systematic Approach to Instructional Design*. Champaign, Ill.: Stipes Publishing Company, 1977.

Goodman, I., "Systematic Selection," *Audiovisual Instruction,* 16 (December 1971), 37–38.

Ingrisano, John R., "A Guide to Cost-Effective Video," *Training,* 22 (1985), 41–44.

Mager, R., *Preparing Instructional Objectives,* revised 2nd ed. Belmont, Calif.: David S. Lake, 1984.

Merrill, P., and Bunderson, V., "Preliminary Guidelines for Employing Graphics in Instruction," *Journal of Instructional Development,* 5 (1981), 7.

O'Sullivan, K., "Audiovisuals and the Training Process," R. Craig, ed. *Training and Development Handbook.* New York: McGraw-Hill. 1976.

Wexley, K. N., and Latham, G. P., *Developing and Training Human Resources in Organizations.* Glenview, Ill.: Scott, Foresman, 1981.

In addition to the sources listed on page iv, the following are gratefully acknowledged:

Pages 92–94: From Norman B. Sigband, "Needed: Corporate Policies on Communications," *S.A.M., Advanced Management Journal,* April 1969 (New York: Society for Advancement of Management, 1969), pp. 63 and 65. Reprinted by permission of the publisher.

Pages 109–110: Reprinted, by permission of the publisher, from "Upward Communications: A Project in Executive Development" (pages 304–318) by Earl Planty and William Machaver, *Personnel,* January 1952 © 1952 American Management Association, New York. All rights reserved.

Pages 115–116: From William L. Davis and J. Regis O'Connor, "Serial Transmission of Information: A Study of the Grapevine," *Journal of Applied Communication Research,* 5(1977), 61–72. Used by permission of William L. Davis and J. Regis O'Connor.

Pages 127–128: From David N. Bateman and Jeffrey L. Miller, "Measuring the Effectiveness of Employee Communications," Paper presented at the annual meeting of the American Business Communication Association, December 1979. Used by permission of the authors.

Pages 129–130: From Alan D. Meyer, "How Beliefs, Stories and Metaphors Uphold Ideologies that Supplant Structures and Guide Reactions," Paper presented at the SCA/ICA Jointly Sponsored Summer Conference on Interpretive Approaches to the Study of Organizational Communication, Alta, Utah, July 26, 1981. Used by permission of Alan D. Meyer.

Page 143: From Ronald F. Pace, "A Study of Opinion Leaders in Summit County and Their Attitudes toward Federal Aid Programs Affecting Local Education and Highway Systems," unpublished master's thesis, Institute of Government Service, Brigham Young University, May 1969. Used by permission of Ronald F. Pace.

Page 257: From Charles R. Bantz, "Understanding Organizations: Analyzing Organizational Communication Cultures," Paper presented at the University of Utah Summer Conference on Interpretive Approaches to the Study of Organizational Communication, Alta, Utah, 1987. Used by permission of Charles R. Bantz.

Page 259: From Susan Koch and Stanley Deetz, "Metaphor Analysis of Social Reality in Organizations," Paper presented at the SCA/ICA Summer Conference on Interpretive Approaches to the Study of Organizational Communication, Alta, Utah, 1981. Used by permission of Susan Koch and Stanley Deetz.

Pages 279–281: From Jonathan M. Chamberlain, *Eliminate Your SDBs* (Provo, Utah: Brigham Young University Press, 1978). Used by permission of Jonathan M. Chamberlain.

Pages 291–292: From Richard L. Hill, *Role Negotiation: Participant Workbook.* Plymouth, Mich.: Human Synergistics, 1983. Used by permission.

Name Index

Subject Index

12/6/09 "Damage Noted"
<u>UNDERLINING</u>